Africa in the New Millennium

ABOUT THIS SERIES

The books in this new series are an initiative by CODESRIA, the Council for the Development of Social Science Research in Africa, to encourage African scholarship relevant to the multiple intellectual, policy and practical problems and opportunities confronting the African continent in the twenty-first century.

CODESRIA in association with Zed Books

Titles in the series:

African Intellectuals: Rethinking Politics, Language, Gender and Development
Edited by Thandika Mkandawire (2005)

Africa and Development Challenges in the New Millennium: The NEPAD Debate
Edited by J. O. Adésìnà, A. Olukoshi and Yao Graham (2006)

Urban Africa: Changing Contours of Survival in the City
Edited by A. M. Simone and A. Abouhani (2005)

Liberal Democracy and Its Critics in Africa: Political Dysfunction and the Struggle for Social Progress
Edited by Tukumbi Lumumba-Kasongo (2005)

Negotiating Modernity: Africa's Ambivalent Experience
Edited by Elísio Salvado Macamo (2005)

Insiders and Outsiders: Citizenship and Xenophobia in Contemporary Southern Africa
Francis B. Nyamnjoh (2006)

African Anthropologies: History, Critique and Practice
Edited by Mwenda Ntarangwi, David Mills and Mustafa Babiker (2006)

Intellectuals and African Development: Pretension and Resistance in African Politics
Edited by Björn Beckman and Gbemisola Adeoti (2006)

Kenya: The Struggle for Democracy
Edited by Godwin R. Murunga and Shadrack W. Nasong'o (2007)

About CODESRIA

The Council for the Development of Social Science Research in Africa (CODESRIA) is an independent organization whose principal objectives are facilitating research, promoting research-based publishing and creating multiple forums geared towards the exchange of views and information among African researchers. It challenges the fragmentation of research through the creation of thematic research networks that cut across linguistic and regional boundaries.

CODESRIA publishes a quarterly journal, *Africa Development*, the longest-standing Africa-based social science journal; *Afrika Zamani*, a journal of history; the *African Sociological Review*, *African Journal of International Affairs* (AJIA), *Africa Review of Books* and *Identity, Culture and Politics: An Afro-Asian Dialogue*. It co-publishes the *Journal of Higher Education in Africa*, and *Africa Media Review*. Research results and other activities of the institution are disseminated through 'Working Papers', 'Monograph Series', 'CODESRIA Book Series', and the *CODESRIA Bulletin*.

KWAME BOAFO-ARTHUR | editor

Ghana

One decade of the liberal state

CODESRIA Books
DAKAR

in association with

Unisa Press
PRETORIA

EPP Book Services
ACCRA

Zed Books
LONDON | NEW YORK

Ghana: one decade of the liberal state was first published by Zed Books Ltd, 7 Cynthia Street, London N1 9JF, UK and Room 400, 175 Fifth Avenue, New York, NY 10010, USA in 2007

<www.zedbooks.co.uk>

in South Africa by Unisa Press, PO Box 392, UNISA 0003

<www.unisa.ac.za>

and in Ghana by EPP Books Services, LA Education Centre, PO Box TF490, Trade Fair, Accra

<www.eppbookservices.com>

in association with CODESRIA, Avenue Cheikh Anta Diop, X Canal IV, BP3304 Dakar, 18524 Senegal

<www.codesria.org>

CODESRIA would like to express its gratitude to the Swedish International Development Cooperation Agency (SIDA/SAREC), the International Development Research Centre (IDRC), Ford Foundation, MacArthur Foundation, Carnegie Corporation, the Norwegian Ministry of Foreign Affairs, the Danish Agency for International Development (DANIDA), the French Ministry of Cooperation, the United Nations Development Programme (UNDP), the Netherlands Ministry of Foreign Affairs, Rockefeller Foundation, FINIDA, NORAD, CIDA, IIEP/ADEA, OECD, IFS, OXFAM America, UN/UNICEF and the Government of Senegal for supporting its research, training and publication programmes.

Cover designed by Andrew Corbett
Set in Arnhem and Futura Bold by Ewan Smith, London
Index: ed.emery@britishlibrary.net

Distributed in the USA exclusively by Palgrave Macmillan, a division of St Martin's Press, LLC, 175 Fifth Avenue, New York, NY 10010.

A catalogue record for this book is available from the British Library.
US CIP data are available from the Library of Congress.

ISBN   978 1 84277 829 6 pb

Transferred to Digital Printing in 2008

Contents

Tables and figures

Tables

Figures

Acknowledgements

The collection of papers in this volume is the outcome of the work done by the CODESRIA National Working Group on Ghana. We acknowledge with gratitude the financial support granted to the Working Group by CODESRIA. Two workshops were organized for the National Working Group: the first workshop helped to reshape some of the topics; at the second, the final drafts of the papers were presented and benefited from the comments of an even larger audience. All papers in this volume benefited immensely from the informed comments of participants at both workshops. Comments by peer reviewers provided further insights and helped in reworking some of the chapters. We greatly appreciate their informed suggestions.

The Department of Political Science, University of Ghana, Legon, is grateful to CODESRIA for sponsoring the project and appreciative of the institutional support given to the Department. We would like to thank the hard-working Godfried K. Mantey who did the preliminary typesetting. The views expressed, however, are those of the individual authors.

K. Boafo-Arthur
Department of Political Science
University of Ghana, Legon

Abbreviations and acronyms

AFC	Alliance for Change
AFD	French Development Agency
AFRC	Armed Forces Revolutionary Council
AGC	Ashanti Goldfields Corporation
AGOA	African Growth and Opportunity Act
AICs	advanced industrialized countries
ALU	Association of Local Unions
AMA	Accra Metropolitan Assembly
APRM	African Peer Review Mechanism
ASB	Alcatel – Shanghai Bell
BOP	balance of payments
CA	Consultative Assembly
CBC	Catholic Bishops Conference
CBOs	community-based organizations
CDD	Centre for Democratic Development
CDR	Committee for the Defence of the Revolution
CHRAJ	Commission on Human Rights and Administrative Justice
CNTCI	Chinese National Trading Company International
CPP	Convention People's Party
CRC	Convention on the Rights of the Child
CSA	Civil Servants' Association
CSOs	civil society organizations
CSPIP	Civil Service Performance Improvement Programme
DACF	District Assembly Common Fund
DCE	district chief executive
DPP	Democratic People's Party
DWM	31 December Women's Movement
EC	Electoral Commission
ECOMOG	ECOWAS Monitoring Group
ECOWAS	Economic Community of West African States
EGLE	Every Ghanaian Living Everywhere
EPA	Environmental Protection Agency
ERP	economic recovery programme
FDI	foreign direct investment
fob	freight-on-board
GAF	Ghana Armed Forces

GAWU	Ghana Agricultural Workers' Union
GBA	Ghana Bar Association
GCL	Ghana Confederation of Labour
GCPP	Ghana Consolidated Popular Party
GDP	Gross Domestic Product
GES	Ghana Education Service
GFW	Ghana Federation of Women
GHABA	Ghana Hairdressers' and Beauticians' Association
GIHOC	Ghana Industrial Holding Corporation
GLSS	Ghana Living Standards Survey
GNA	Ghana News Agency
GPRS	Ghana Poverty Reduction Strategy
GPVOP	Ghana Association of Private Voluntary Organizations in Development
GWL	Ghana Women's League
HIPC	highly indebted poor countries
HPAEs	highly performing Asian economies
ICJ	International Commission of Jurists
ICOR	incremental capital–output ratio
ICT	information and communication technology
ICU	Industrial and Commercial Workers' Union
IFC	International Financial Consortium
IFI	international financial institutions
IMF	International Monetary Fund
INEC	Interim National Electoral Commission
IPAC	Inter-party Advisory Committee
JFM	June Fourth Movement
LDCs	least developed countries
LET	Labour Enterprise Trust
LRP	Labour Redeployment Programme
LSAIP	Legal Sector and Administrative Improvement Programme
MCE	Municipal Chief Executive
MFJ	Movement for Freedom and Justice
MoU	Memorandum of Understanding
MOWAC	Ministry of Women and Children Affairs
MPC	Monetary Policy Committee
NAM	Non-Aligned Movement
NCD	National Commission for Democracy
NCGW	National Council of Ghana Women
NCP	National Convention Party
NCWD	National Council on Women and Development

NDC	National Democratic Congress
NEDEO	Network of Democratic Election Observers
NEPAD	New Partnership for Africa's Development
NIC	newly industrializing countries
NIP	National Independence Party
NIRP	National Institutional Reform Programme
NLC	National Liberation Council
NPP	New Patriotic Party
NRC	National Reconciliation Commission
NRC	National Redemption Council
NRCD	National Redemption Council Degree
NRP	National Reform Party
NTEs	non-traditional exports
NUGs	National Union of Ghana Students
NWO	National Women's Organizer
OAU	Organization of African Unity
OECD	Organization for Economic Cooperation and Development
PAGA	Presidential Adviser on Governmental Affairs
PAMSCAD	Programme of Action to Mitigate the Social Costs of Adjustment
PCP	People's Convention Party
PHP	People's Heritage Party
PIB	Prices and Incomes Board
PM	Presiding Member
PNC	People's National Convention
PNDC	Provisional National Defence Council
PNP	People's National Party
PP	Progress Party
PPAEs	poorly performing African economies
PPDD	People's Party for Development and Democracy
PSIs	Presidential Special Initiatives
PUFMARP	Public Financial Management Reform Programme
PWD	Public Works Department
RCBs	rural and community banks
RUF	Revolutionary United Front
RWOD	Rural Workers' Organization Division
SAP	Structural Adjustment Programme
SDF	Social Democratic Front
SMC	Supreme Military Council
SOEs	state-owned enterprises
SSA	Sub-Saharan Africa

SSS	senior secondary school
TEWU	Teachers' and Education Workers' Union
TFP	total factor productivity
TUC	Trades Union Congress
UN	United Nations
UTAG	University Teachers' Association of Ghana
WAJU	Women and Juveniles Unit
4BN	Fourth Battalion of Infantry

1 | A decade of liberalism in perspective

KWAME BOAFO-ARTHUR

Since attaining political freedom in 1957, Ghana has tried varied modes of governance; some have been imposed with scant regard to the wishes of the generality of the people and others were the result of democratic elections. Liberal economic and social policies, and varying degrees of authoritarianism, command economics and redistributive policies, policies aimed at minimizing external dependence and so on have all been pursued at various junctures. These tendencies – a combination or succession of state control, freedom of the market and welfare politics – were evident even when the military was in control of the state, as it was for the greater part of the nation's independent existence.

In January 1993 Ghana embarked on a new democratic experiment after more than a decade of military rule. A new political liberalism was instituted alongside neoliberal economic management strategies that had been practised for some years with the unflinching support of the Bretton Woods institutions and other donor or development partners. Thus, the key motivation for this book is to put the liberal democratic-cum-neoliberal processes over the past decade in clear perspective. Admittedly, a decade is too short to expect significant results from the rather long and tortuous journey into democracy that the country has embarked on; but it is long enough for the liberal state to have yielded some signposts as guides for this journey into the future, as well as providing reasonable grounds for interrogating its record so far. This task is carried out in the following chapters by academics whose areas of teaching and research include Political Science, Economics and Law.

Before 1993, different modes of economic management practices had led over the years to the evolution of a hybrid political economy which engendered various forms of developmental crises. These crises, with economic, political and general developmental implications, became distinctive features of the nation. Each constellation of class forces that dominated the state produced a crisis specific to the policies that it pursued. By the close of the 1970s, the politics and economy of the country had been plunged into severe crises that required immediate and apparently radical measures to prevent the total collapse of the economy. Paradoxically, the challenges involved in restoring the stagnant economy fell on the revolutionary military government of the Provisional National Defence Council (PNDC). However, contrary to its initial Marxist-Leninist agenda, the government of the PNDC that usurped political power in the early 1980s was compelled by the magnitude of the economic problems confronting the state to pursue a neoliberal or free market agenda after its initial socialist posturing, while at the same time supporting internal social democratic forces with an antithetical economic and political agenda. The contradiction produced by that unnatural equation was resolved in favour of a liberal democratic state that would guarantee the growth of a neoliberal economy. January 1993 marked the beginning of yet another democratic journey by the state. The key question to ask is, how does the process of re-democratization get started? This is important because the mode of societal change invariably affects the manner through which the society and economy are managed. For instance, violent left-wing societal changes tend to result in a semblance of a welfare state or administration.

The road to democracy: a brief overview

Various writers have pointed to the fact that the Rawlings-led PNDC was not overly interested in Ghana's democratization process (Yeebo 1991; Shillington 1992; Folson 1993). That was to be expected, because no dictatorial regime gives up without a struggle. In the case of the PNDC, Ghana's return to democracy could be attributed to unanticipated changes in the international system as well as to internal agitation by civil society groups. The weak economic base of the nation made the PNDC government extremely vulnerable to external pressures, especially in the late 1980s when leading donors and development partners imposed political conditions on aid recipients in undemocratic regimes. This imposition emboldened civil society organizations whose struggles for political openings had previously been largely uncoordinated and inconsistent. Confronted with both external and internal pressures for democratization, the PNDC adopted several measures to end its dictatorial rule. The main measures were:

1. The holding of district-level elections in 1988 and 1989.
2. The collation of views on the democratic future of the country by the National Commission for Democracy (NCD) set up by the PNDC.
3. The promulgation of a law on 17 May 1991 setting up a nine-member Committee of Experts (Constitution). The mandate of the committee was to prepare a draft proposal (constitution) taking into account previous constitutions of Ghana since independence and any other relevant constitution(s) as well as matters referred to it by the PNDC.
4. Inauguration on 26 August 1991 of a 260-member Consultative

Assembly to draw up a draft constitution (based on the work of the Committee of Experts) for the country.

5. Submission to the PNDC on 31 March 1992 of a draft constitution by the Consultative Assembly. Consequently an Interim Electoral Commission (INEC) was set up.
6. A referendum on the draft constitution was held on 28 April 1992 with 92.6 per cent of eligible voters voting in favour of the draft constitution.
7. Lifting of the ban on political party activities on 15 May 1992. Flight Lieutenant Jerry Rawlings, chairman of the PNDC, founded the National Democratic Congress (NDC) to contest the presidential and parliamentary elections.
8. Holding of presidential election on 3 November 1992 and the parliamentary election on 28 December 1992.
9. The inauguration of the Fourth Republic on 7 January 1993 with Rawlings as the President.

The neoliberal mode of economic management had already taken root before the inauguration of the Fourth Republic on 7 January 1993, since the PNDC had dutifully implemented several IMF- and World Bank-inspired and sponsored structural adjustment programmes (Rothchild 1991). The problem was that whereas, under the PNDC, IMF and World Bank programmes had been implemented by executive fiat, it was imperative for the new democratic NDC government led by Jerry Rawlings to involve the people in economic decision-making. There was therefore another seeming contradiction between the democratization process and the demands of structural adjustment programmes. Could the two be pursued together? What were the likely problems of such a mode of economic management? Experiences under the PNDC had proven that the less consultation there was on the modalities of the programme, the more easily it was implemented. Would the new democratic dispensation sound the death-knell of structural adjustment programmes?

Liberal triumphalism

The impetus for the resolution of this apparent contradiction was the liberal triumphalism (Fukuyama 1992) of the late 1980s that more or less made the pursuit of liberal politics and free market policies indispensable for the majority of developing countries, including Ghana. This was the period of hard-nosed Reaganomics and Thatcherism that not only glorified political liberalism and neoliberal economic pursuits but also perceived them invariably as the alpha and omega of political and economic management practices. The international discourse on governance

3

had also affirmed the liberal option as the ultimate and the most sensible choice (Dunn 1992). Francis Fukuyama noted: 'what we are witnessing is not just the end of the Cold War, but the universalization of Western liberal democracy as the final form of human government' (cited in Starr 2004). Western liberal democracy moved in tandem with neoliberalism. The neo-liberal creed, as pointed out by Jeremy Clift, emphasizes macro-economic, particularly fiscal, discipline, a market economy and openness to the world economy (at least with respect to trade and foreign direct investment) (Clift 2003). More importantly, development policies pursued by international financial institutions during the 1980s and 1990s came to be labelled the 'Washington consensus' or neoliberalism and entailed a more circumscribed role for the state, with economic activities unduly influenced by market forces. In the minds of most people, the Washington consensus, according to Stiglitz, 'has come to refer to development strategies focusing around privatization, liberalization, and macro-stability (meaning mostly price stability); a set of policies predicated upon a strong faith – stronger than warranted – in unfettered markets and aimed at reducing, or even minimizing, the role of government' (Stiglitz 1998: 6). It is precisely the way in which the term has been applied since it was coined by John Williamson in 1989, in connection with the adoption of economic management practices in Latin America, that has compelled Williamson to attempt a further definition. According to him, the Washington consensus has been invested with a meaning that is a clear departure from what he originally intended and he has summarized his original version into ten propositions:

- fiscal discipline
- a redirection of public expenditure priorities towards fields offering both high economic returns and the potential to improve income distribution, such as primary healthcare, primary education and infrastructure
- tax reform (to lower marginal rates and broaden the tax base)
- interest rate liberalization
- competitive exchange rate
- trade liberalization
- liberalization of inflows of foreign direct investment
- privatization
- deregulation (to abolish barriers to entry and exit)
- secure property rights (Williamson 2000: 252–3)

He conceived his propositions as an attempt to summarize policies widely viewed as supportive of development at a time when economists had become convinced that 'the key to rapid economic development lay not in a country's natural resources or even in its physical or human capital but, rather, in the set of economic policies that it pursued' (ibid.: 254). Even though Williamson has been at pains to explain the misapplication of the term and his propositions, it is hard to believe that his propositions, when examined alongside the ongoing neoliberal postulates of development policies the Bank applied to Latin America, Africa and Asia, do not conform in principle to his position. Originally, the policy prescription was applied to Latin America, but Williamson agrees that there would have been no marked difference if he had been asked to apply it to Africa or Asia (ibid.: 255). And as pointed out by Jeremy Clift (2003), the policy measures were quickly seen as a model for the wider developing world.

The sweeping political changes that followed the capitalist triumphalism and the end of the Cold War had both economic and political repercussions in Africa and the communist stronghold of China. Though many African countries, including Ghana, had no choice but to open up the political space, what was perceived as bourgeois liberalism was brutally repressed by China in Tiananmen Square. The fact remains, however, that neoliberal economic management practices and the accompanying liberal democracy have gained unprecedented adherents since the collapse of the Eastern bloc. It was argued that liberal democracy would be the most appropriate political arrangement to allow room for the implementation of neoliberal economic policies. What, then, is the nature of liberalism and what are the benefits? What is the relationship between liberalism or political openness and neoliberalism?

Features of liberalism and its assumed benefits

The liberal state, its exponents argue, guarantees a congenial environment for the growth of capitalist civilization. That is, the capitalist economy and society thrive on a stable and secure environment provided by the liberal state through its laws and other regulations. The liberal state protects private property, guarantees appropriate conditions for its growth, and ensures the creation of material wealth that will be for the good of the whole society. Above all, it guarantees political stability; liberal democracy is the best form of social interaction to strive for if the dignity of individuals is to be assured. Liberal democracy is based on the will of the majority. Its distinguishing features include free institutions, representative government, free elections, and guarantees of individual liberty, freedom of speech and religion, and freedom from political oppression. It is incontrovertible that liberalism is also committed to protecting the freedom to choose, question and revise one's own conception of the good life. This explains why 'liberalism defends (among many other things) freedom of conscience, expression and association, as well as mandatory, universal education' (Lowry 2000). Liberalism sees the main function of the state as to provide sufficient protection to allow individuals the greatest possible freedom to exercise their basic human rights and fulfil their potential. This is in contrast to systems that rely on terror and oppression, a controlled press and radio and the suppression of personal freedoms (Spiegel 1995). Stanley Hoffman (1995) points out that 'liberalism was and is, in large part, an expression of revulsion against illegitimate violence: that of tyrants at home and of aggressors abroad'. Put simply, liberal democracy affords humankind the only political arrangement that lays exclusive claim to set the standard for legitimate political authority.

C. B. Macpherson points out that liberalism is generally taken to mean 'the democracy of a capitalist market society' or 'a society striving to ensure that all its members are equally free to realize their capabilities' (Macpherson 1977: 1). He contends, therefore, that 'the central ethical principle of liberalism' is 'the freedom of the individual to realize his or her human capacities' (ibid.: 2). In other words, liberalism creates avenues for the full realization of the potential of individuals in the state. Modern liberalism, as John Kane-Berman (2004) argues, 'has drawn strength from the fact that the most contented and prosperous people are those living in open societies which are both economically and politically free and in which the rule of law prevails'. The laws have a persuasive and salutary role to play in this process because it is the effective application of the law that gives the individual the freedom to enjoy civil and other liberties. The intellectual vibrancy and deep political involvement of citizens are influenced by the state's adherence to the rule of law. On this, Peter Biro points out that 'liberalism depends, for its sustainability, on the notion that the individual members of society will remain continually engaged in the never-ending process of balancing personal aspirations with community objectives and, wherever possible, actualizing one in the pursuit of the other ... Participatory democracy in the liberal state requires a constant critical ... compliance with the laws' (Biro 2000: 14) by both the rulers and the governed. In its various philosophical guises, liberalism, as noted by Hoffman (1995), 'was and is a ram against authoritarian regimes. It tries to free individuals from tyranny by providing them with the right to consent to their political institutions and to the policies pursued in the framework of these institutions, as well as with a set of freedoms protected from governmental intrusions and curtailments'. The key question is, does the current liberal Ghanaian state exhibit all the features of liberalism as enunciated above? What constrains the adherence to the principles of the rule of law and respect for the fundamental rights of the people, for instance?

The liberal Ghanaian state in perspective

Ghana has been on this liberal path before: the First Republic from 1957 to 1966, the Second Republic from 1969 to 1972, and the Third Republic from 1979 to 1981. Ironically, the liberal democratic experiment during the First Republic was replaced with a one-party state that extolled state planning and democratic centralism and never allowed the finer features of liberalism such as freedom of expression and association to be enjoyed by the citizenry. Those liberal regimes that could, to a large extent, lay some modicum of claim to adherence to the liberal creed were overthrown by the military. The PNDC that overthrew the Limann administration on 31 December 1981 turned out to be not only the longest-lasting military government but also the only one that succeeded itself as a civilian government with the ushering in of the Fourth Republic in January 1993. Thus, the carving of the National Democratic Congress (NDC) out of the PNDC to contest general elections in 1992 could equally be construed as an unprecedented and significant event in the political history of the country. The PNDC successfully converted its pseudo-military structures into effective party wings. A confluence of factors explains the transition from the autocratic military regime of the PNDC to the liberal state of the Fourth Republic (Ninsin 1998; Nugent 1995). As noted, the NDC had been formed by the erstwhile military regime, the PNDC led by Rawlings, to ensure self-succession and indirectly perpetuate its rule under the guise of a democratic constitution. The defeat of the NDC in the 2000 general elections, after being in power for two successive terms of eight years, was therefore a significant landmark that vindicated the virtues of liberal democracy as the only political form for stabilizing and legitimizing the exercise of state power. More importantly, the PNDC demonstrated unprecedented and relentless pursuit of liberal economic policies after its initial socialist posturing had been abandoned. These were done in a draconian political environment that had successfully suppressed the fundamental liberties of the people. This state of affairs also raises the question as to whether, given its background, the NDC was able during its two terms of democratic rule to cultivate the finer grains of the liberal state within the context of the 1992 Constitution of the Fourth Republic. This is important given the fact that the key national players during the two terms of the NDC government were also the leading players during the era of the authoritarian PNDC. The liberal state thrives basically on respect for the rights of the people and it would be interesting to know how the state has conformed to its liberal

7

constitutional underpinnings. Has there been any significant change with regard to the sustenance of the core strands of liberalism in the wake of the defeat of the NDC at the polls and the emergence of the New Patriotic Party (NPP) as the ruling party? The answers are provided, to a large extent, by Kofi Quashigah in Chapter 2 of this volume, dealing with the promotion and protection of human rights under the 1992 Constitution. He rightly perceives human rights as a key aspect of governance and this is why several parts of the 1992 Constitution are concerned with this concept. Quashigah provides a brief overview of human rights prior to the 1992 Constitution and he delineates the various rights it protects, especially in Chapters 5, 6 and 12 that guarantee fundamental human rights, the Directive Principles of State Policy, and freedom and independence of the media respectively. The unambiguous liberal underpinnings of the Constitution are inhered in Article 33(5) which accepts the existence of other rights 'considered to be inherent in a democracy and intended to secure the freedom and dignity of man' apart from those expressly noted in the Constitution. As the author rightly points out, this Article links the 1992 Constitution to the ever-growing number of rights on the global plane. With appropriate legal cases to back his position, he delves through aspects of the rights of the individual and how they are either being promoted and protected or undermined by political leaders.

Chapter 2 further delves into constitutionally guaranteed institutions whose functions strengthen governmental observance of individual rights, such as the Commission on Human Rights and Administrative Justice (CHRAJ). In addition he discusses legislative initiatives that equally enhance the observance of various rights such as the Children's Act and the Criminal Code (Repeal of Criminal Libel and Seditious Laws) (Amendment) Act. He concludes that the 1992 Constitution has enthroned the liberal state and relatively enhanced the enjoyment of fundamental rights.

Prior to Ghana's political liberalization, the PNDC had resolutely pursued economic liberalization, and this, as in all developing countries, led to renewed interest in the relationship between economic and political reforms. Mark Robinson clearly points out that a distinction can be made between three broad types of relationship: (i) sustained economic reform followed by political liberalization; (ii) political liberalization followed by economic reform; and (iii) simultaneous reform (Robinson 1996: 70). Ghana, like most African countries, was characterized by the first type in that the PNDC, as noted, carried out a comprehensive economic reform programme before the collapse of the Eastern bloc and the end of the Cold War. These were key international events which had broad ramifications for the nurturing of liberalism in both economic and political terms, especially in developing countries. The insistence of development partners and the Bretton Woods institutions on political liberalization as a condition for external financial support led to political openness or liberalism. The World Bank was emphatic when it noted that 'because countervailing power has been lacking, state officials in many countries have served their own interests without fear of being called to account' (World Bank 1989: 60). Failure, in the view of the World Bank, to hold the 'all-powerful state accountable for its systemic failures' (ibid.) led to personalization of political power and the entrenchment of neo-patrimonialism. This position also influenced the imposition of political conditions on aid recipient countries, including Ghana.

The view of the US on political conditions is contained in the following statement: 'Open societies that value individual rights, respect the rule of law, and have open and accountable governments provide better opportunities for sustained economic development than do closed systems which stifle individual initiative' (Nelson and Eglinton 1992: 20). For Barber Conable, 'investors will not take risks, entrepreneurs will not be creative, people will not participate – if they feel they are facing [a] capricious, unjust or hostile political environment' (cited in Olukoshi 1992: 5). Democratization was necessary because 'getting the politics right' for capitalist development, as argued by Sandbrook, 'is as essential as getting the prices right' (Sandbrook 2000: 12). Downsizing overextended governments and removing constraints on market forces, according to Sandbrook, will amount to nothing if certain institutional conditions that will create an enabling environment for the private sector are not created. 'Democratization should re-establish the rule of law, open up policy debates, reduce governmental waste and capriciousness through enhanced accountability, and empower coalitions supporting market-based reforms' (ibid.: 13). The need for a liberal governmental set-up was thus felt across Africa after the collapse of communism and the end of the Cold War, among other things, to facilitate economic development and growth by ensuring a congenial political atmosphere in which individuals could freely contribute their quota. How has the liberal Ghanaian state coped with the challenges of economic growth and development? Chapter 3 by G. Kwaku Tsikata tackles this all-important issue. The author has no doubt in his mind that, notwithstanding the comprehensive pursuit of structural adjustment under the supervision of the Bretton Woods institutions, economic growth constituted and continues to constitute a crucial challenge to national governments since political independence. Drawing inferences where appropriate from Malaysia and South Korea, he argues strongly that developmental leadership, as opposed to power-hungry leadership, is required if Ghana is to attain sustainable economic growth.

9

His evidence further strengthens the fact that the liberal culture is conducive to investment and growth and must of necessity be sustained.

The idea that the pursuit of neoliberal economics and liberal democracy are antithetical has been hotly debated in the literature. Does the logic of the market lend itself to the dictates of democratic norms? How does the liberal state perceive the market? In *Democracy and the Markets*, Adam Przeworski argues that 'the most rational and humane economic system is one that relies on regulated markets to allocate resources and on the state to assure a minimum of material welfare for everyone' (Przeworski 1991: xi). Przeworski's stand flies in the face of the core strand of neoliberalism and the Washington consensus which calls for a minimal role by the state in economic activities. The components of neoliberal economics noted above and the postulates of the Washington consensus, to me, are two sides of the same coin. The position of the Washington consensus has been strongly attacked by Stiglitz. The Washington consensus advocates – and proponents of neoliberalism committed the cardinal error of extolling – a 'one-size-fits-all' policy approach to the economic problems of the developing world. Given the dynamic interplay of markets and technological advancement as well as other essential externalities, the governmental role in market processes should not be underestimated. While this was obvious to the successful East Asian countries, the Washington consensus policies did not see things in these terms (Stiglitz 1998). There have been doubts about the efficacy of Washington consensus strategies on account of their abysmal failure in Sub-Saharan Africa and Latin America. Stiglitz further enumerates some of the failures of the Washington consensus policies/strategies as follows:

- Undermining the role of the state in the market was erroneous and at odds with the success of the East Asian countries.
- Policy conditionalities imposed on developing countries had too narrow a focus and stressed the liberalization of agricultural prices without adequate attention to the necessary requirements to enhance agricultural productivity such as credit availability and infrastructure, especially road network.
- The insistence on static comparative advantage led to the fallacy of composition whereby increasing exports of commodities by many countries led to collapse in their prices.
- Financial sector reforms were focused excessively on making interest rates market-determined in very thin and rudimentary markets leading often to prolonged periods of very high interest rates without the availability of credit.

- Failure to focus on the factors that contributed to market volatility such as capital market liberalization.
- Wrong mindset that perceives government as the problem with markets as the solution.
- Countries were given short deadlines to reform social security programs or to privatize or change the charter of their central banks, to engage in reforms that the democracies of many advanced industrial countries had rejected.
- Excessive belief in market fundamentalism. (Stiglitz 1998)

Interestingly, advocates of the Washington consensus 'could always find something that was wrong, and add something to the increasing long laundry list of what countries should do' (Stiglitz 1998). International financial institutions have thus created unfair rules and keep shifting the goalposts any time a policy measure ends in a failure.

In light of the foregoing, it is appropriate to ask whether or not the market has performed creditably in the liberal Ghanaian state. What have been the relations between democracy and the market? These issues are discussed in Chapter 4 by Kwame A. Ninsin. There should be what he terms 'welfare compromise' if democracy is to be achieved and sustained in a market economy. It is when the welfare of the people is balanced with market demands, taking into consideration equity and justice, that the democracy project can succeed. The state is strongly urged by Ninsin, along the lines of the thinking of Adam Przeworski, to intervene in the market to minimize inequality and ensure a balanced distribution of societal goods. This approach will create the conditions for effective citizenship, which is defined as 'the capacity to freely exercise the volition (free will) to participate in or influence public affairs'. Both the NDC and the NPP were committed to market reforms but stayed aloof, to a large extent, to the social implications of such reforms. In spite of the country's commitment to the structural adjustment programmes, the per capita income of Ghanaians still remained at $390 at the time the NDC lost the 2000 elections and by the end of 2003, Ghana's average GDP had not gone beyond 5 per cent. The skewed income and wealth distribution in the country has been sharpened on account of market reforms. The liberal Ghanaian state, in the view of Ninsin, 'is too weak to protect society from the ravages of capitalism' and this is because the market is inefficient in wealth creation for society at large. The major challenge, then, is to ensure that equity and justice for the generality of the people are part and parcel of the ongoing market reforms. This is critical because of the glaring socio-political as well as economic inequities that characterize the operations of most liberal states, thus diluting the sacrosanct values inherent in liberalism. Greven and Pauly assert in this regard that 'as modern capitalism has deepened, as corporate and financial power has become more salient, as regulation has become more technical, and as economic rewards have become more tightly correlated with specialized skills, even political equality has become more and more unattainable' (Greven and Pauly 2000: 2). The inequity argument put forward by Ninsin finds further grounding in the words of Robert Dahl, who arguably is the 'dean' of contemporary studies of democracy. Dahl argues:

> When authoritarian governments in less modernized countries undertake to develop a dynamic market economy, they are likely to sow the seeds of their own ultimate destruction. But once society and politics are transformed by market-capitalism and democratic institutions are in place, the outlook fundamentally changes. Now the inequalities in resources that market-capitalism churns out produce serious political inequalities among the citizens. (Greven and Pauly 2000: 2)

It is explicit from Ninsin's exposition that the inequities in political resources and access to political resources are yet to be fully addressed by the liberal Ghanaian state.

One major layer of reforms that has gained currency also from the Bretton Woods institutions and other development partners is reforming institutions, including public institutions. Nicholas Amponsah appraises institutions in the liberal state in Chapter 5. The objective for strengthening institutions, as also pointed out by the Commission for Africa Report, is to ensure that they are capable of delivery and are more accountable (Commission for Africa Report 2005: 358). Political institutions are important when analysing the progress a country has made in consolidating democracy. In other words, political institutions 'play an essential role at the macro level' when countries are the unit of analysis (Bratton et al. 2005: 331). According to Michael Bratton and others, when it comes to judging the extent of democratic and market regimes on the performance of the economy, citizens tend to look at the performance of the president, the delivery of political rights, and the *trust* in state institutions (ibid.: 287). Amponsah argues that the credibility of democratic institutions is crucial in the quest for democratic consolidation. Good intentions and desirable ends fall far short of the strict test for democratic growth. Institutionalized mechanisms offer the support needed for economic development. Several economic and democracy goals could be achieved by the nation if effective and credible institutional mechanisms are put in place. The issue of enhancing private investment, ensuring transparency and regime accountability, as well as strengthened democratic structures, is dependent, to a large extent, on credible institutions. He concludes that the weak institutions of the liberal state explain why, in spite of a good policy regime, economic growth and development have been very slow.

Conflict without consensus by the political elite has been a serious drawback in the development of Africa. The quest for market-oriented development will lead nowhere in the absence of social peace and political stability. Where interminable conflict becomes the order of the day, development is arrested and the liberal state finds it difficult to find its proper level in the international system. Many African countries have had to contend with destructive intra-state conflicts that eventually engulfed whole regions such as in Somalia, Rwanda, the Congo DR, Liberia, Sierra Leone and Côte d'Ivoire. Few people will argue about the relative peace in Ghana but the question is why has Ghana been able to steer its affairs away from polarizing conflicts? In Chapter 6, Alexander K. D. Frempong takes us through various forms of conflict situations that the liberal Ghanaian state has had to contend with since the democratization process got under way in January 1993. He explains the underpinning theoretical postulates of liberal democracy, political conflict and elite consensus. The transition process, the 1992 elections and their effects on the creation of the liberal state are well covered. The ability of the liberal state to navigate around all potential explosive electoral disagreements and misunderstandings could be attributed to the ability of the Electoral Commission to achieve elite-level complementarities/consensus. The formation of the Inter-Party Advisory Committee (IPAC) in 1994 was instrumental in achieving consensus. This explains why in the face of several contested issues, such as Value Added Tax (VAT), election-related violence created by the leading political parties since December 1992 came under control. Finally, the peaceful change of government through the ballot box in 2000, the first since the country attained independence in 1957, attests to the fact that democracy has come to stay.

The question of leadership and development has assumed greater importance in Africa. Ineffective, unaccountable, rapacious and dictatorial leadership is often blamed, among other factors, for Africa's persistent underdevelopment. It also accounts for the glaring crisis of confidence in the ability of the African state to deliver appreciable economic growth and development. The World Bank is also of the view that a good example set by a country's leadership can minimize those corrupt practices that have also undermined Africa's development (World Bank 1989: 61). Roland Hope notes that 'the considerable lack of exemplary ethical leadership' exhibited by African leaders has not only exacerbated corruption in Africa but also engendered political instability and underdevelopment (Hope 2000: 22). African leaders have by commission or omission pointed to leadership crisis since independence as a major constraint on development. In the New Partnership for Africa's Development (NEPAD), the authors of the document unequivocally state that 'we recognize that failures of political and economic leadership in many African countries impede the effective mobilization and utilization of scarce resources into productive areas of activity in order to attract and facilitate domestic and foreign investment' (Organization of African Unity 2001: 8). According to Tony Blair's Commission for Africa Report, 'it is Africa's actions and leadership that will be the most important determinant of progress in generating a resurgence in Africa, advancing standards and taking forward the fight against poverty' (Commission for Africa Report 2005: 359). Joseph R. A. Ayee discusses the question of leadership in the liberal Ghanaian state in Chapter 7. The Fourth Republic has produced two distinct leadership types as personified by the styles of former President Jerry Rawlings and the current leader J. A. Kufuor. The context of Ghanaian leadership, according to Ayee, is influenced by four factors: namely, the challenge that faced political leaders; the neoliberal environment within which the leaders worked; culture; and the media. African leaders are generally confronted with the singular challenge of meeting expectations with meagre resources and continued dependence on an exploitative international economic order. Political leadership could be assessed within the framework of (i) maintaining the cohesion of the administration; (ii) developing a strategic policy direction aimed at contributing to change; (iii) the relationship between politicians and bureaucrats; and (iv) the personal dimension or style. Within the foregoing context, Ayee discusses the performance of leadership in the liberal Ghanaian state using Jerry Rawlings's two-term NDC rule and the one term of J. A. Kufuor as case studies. He concludes by drawing some lessons from his study. He confesses to the difficulty of measuring political performance on account of structural constraints and points out that an open and personal style of leadership does not guarantee citizen involvement or institution building. Also, leaders are vulnerable to the forces unleashed by neoliberalism, the quest for administrative cohesion, developing strategic policy direction, and so on. Most Ghanaian leaders cannot boast of having undergone seasoning and mentoring because of recurrent political instability.

The spate of instability that has affected the nation's leadership is equally a pointer to the fact that the security set-up capable of defending the sovereignty of the state from marauding military adventurers has been very weak. Chapter 8 by Kumi Ansah-Koi deals with security issues in the liberal state.

Ansah-Koi briefly recounts the role the security services have played in destabilizing the nation through frequent military interventions. The current structure of national security is outlined in the Security and Intelligence Agencies Act, 1996. An innovation was the establishment of security councils at the district levels. These regional and district security councils operate as wings of the National Security Council. The objective for this decentralization of powers of officials dealing with security is to arrest any form of conflict with the potential to destabilize the nation as quickly as possible. According to Ansah-Koi, the liberal state has been able to assert civilian control over the security services and to enhance civil–military relations. Currently, there is a parliamentary oversight over the military even though, for security reasons, parliament is restricted from perusing the military budget. Enhanced service conditions for the security agencies as well as logistical support, especially for the police, have equally had a positive impact on combating crime and defending the territorial integrity of the nation.

A virile workforce with focused targets contributes in no small measure to the development of a nation. Chapter 9 by Abeeku Essuman-Johnson gives an overview of organized labour in a liberal Ghanaian state. In his view, the liberal state has overseen the downsizing of labour by adhering resolutely to the dictates of the Bretton Woods institutions. Rigid adherence to privatization by the state provoked reactions, especially from the Civil Servants' Association and the Trades Union Congress. The spate of IMF-inspired redeployment compelled the TUC to venture into business aimed at creating employment, especially for those workers retrenched as a result of government policies. The setting up of the Labour Enterprise Trust (LET) was one venture aimed at creating jobs for members of organized labour. The passage of the Labour Act in 2003 was an attempt to streamline the operations of labour by the state. The act liberalized the formation of labour unions by ensuring freedom of association. Arguably, the liberal Ghanaian state has conformed to constitutional stipulations by addressing the urgent need of informal workers who want to join organized unions through the Labour Act of 2003.

To a large extent, the ability of the liberal state to survive also depends on forging good relations with other actors in the global system. This is crucial in a world of growing interdependence and globalization, leading to changes in how nations relate to each other within the international system. According to Ikenberry and Doyle, two main reasons account for this. First, few theories attempt to explain such a development because a lot of changes happen outside 'the parameters of the system – and states simply respond to it in the form of balancing actions that follow shifts in the distribution of power' (Ikenberry and Doyle 1997: 273). Existing theories rather account for the continuity and repetition of world politics over long stretches of history. Second, the sudden demise of the Eastern bloc and the end of the Cold War underpinned the limitations of existing theories in their predictive capabilities. But the fact remains also that in most developing countries, such as Ghana, which are trying to strengthen democratic structures, such sudden changes at the international level could not be predicted. In most cases, too, successor governments had no choice but to follow the external policies of their predecessors simply because the world is no longer divided between East and West. For a developing country, whether the nation is aligned to the East or West is irrelevant. What is important is an alignment stimulating economic development and growth that will enhance the living conditions of the generality of the people. Chapter 10 by Kwame Boafo-Arthur deals with the liberal state in the international system at a time of growing interdependence and globalization. The state must of necessity carve out survival policies, given the poor living conditions of its people. This explains why the NDC continued with PNDC's pragmatic external policies of positive relationships with the international community, especially with the nation's development partners and the Bretton Woods institutions. Even though the pursuit of IMF policies did not ensure a sustainable economic growth, the NPP had no choice other than to continue with such policies because of Ghana's weak economic base and the fact that the party claims to be liberal democratic. Interestingly, the NPP laid stronger emphasis on economic diplomacy which was initially mooted by the NDC. It is incontrovertible that the liberal state, in its dealings with the international community, is informed by the sole interest of the people. One other rationalization for the seeming continuity of policies of previous governments is the fact that, in ideological terms, they all espoused neoliberalism in both economic and political terms, regardless of the fact that the antagonistic ideological blocs are no longer in existence. Nevertheless, there has been a distinctive departure from the antagonistic stance of the NDC with regard to its immediate neighbours; in its place the NPP pursues a policy of neighbourliness which has ensured positive relations with its immediate neighbours. With the international system generally, the NPP has concentrated on economic diplomacy and the development of the private sector as the engine of economic growth. The debilitating impact of debt and debt servicing compelled the government on assuming power to join the Highly Indebted Poor Countries (HIPC) club. It appears that positive benefits have accrued to the state, especially after reaching the HIPC completion point, with the cancelling of debts by most of its creditors.

16

Women have played a critical role in the politics of Ghana since the onset of the liberal state in January 1993. Without doubt, few of them have been inducted into national politics because of cultural inhibitions, but the few who have ventured into political office or ended up in public life are giving it their best shot. Beatrix Allah-Mensah discusses the dynamics of the role of women in the liberal state in Chapter 11. After a brief historical overview that starts in 1956, Allah-Mensah concentrates on the role of women in the making of the 1992 Constitution. She examines the role women have played in local-level politics and their participation in national politics between 1993 and 2003. Women have equally played key roles in political party organization and she highlights such roles in the leading political parties. The number of women in both local and national politics has been on the increase, demonstrating that the traditional cultural inhibitions preventing participation in politics in particular and public life in general are easing.

Conclusion

Donald Rothchild makes the point that 'to achieve self-sustaining development, the state as a political manager must complement and reinforce the state as an economic manager' (Rothchild 1991: 15). I do not think the liberal state could be an economic manager in a vacuum. It is indisputable that the Washington consensus and neoliberal adherents just want to see the state making laws for the operation of the market but not participating in the market itself. How a state can know what needs to be done if it is only a law-maker and not an active participant in economic activities is baffling. Thus, the wholesale marginalization of the state in the management of the market is the wrong approach in my view.

The chapters in this volume make it clear that much has been achieved in this era of liberalism. Human rights, high on the agenda of most democratic states, have not been toyed with. Even though the economy appears to be still in a coma, the hope is that policy measures implemented with the support of the Bretton Woods institutions will, in the long run, assist in resuscitating the economy. The increasing distancing of the state from direct economic management, as underlined by the extra attention paid to private sector development, is bound to impact negatively on the vulnerable in society. One cannot give a free rein to neoliberalism and expect an equitable distribution of societal resources. The point is that general societal interests are often marginalized in market economies and when this happens it is the vulnerable groups who find themselves at the receiving end. This is why it would be highly beneficial for the market to be regulated by the state so as to ensure an equitable allocation of resources and minimum

17

welfare for the majority of the people. The liberal state has successfully dealt with societal conflicts, especially those pertaining to electoral politics. Since most intrastate conflicts in the West Africa sub-region emanated from partisan political activities and rumblings that came to the fore after national elections, it could be argued that the state has been able to keep conflict at bay through effective conflict resolution mechanisms and the proverbial gentleness of the Ghanaian populace. Credit must also go to the role of the reinvigorated state institutions and other constitutional bodies with the mandate to resolve societal crises.

For Ghana to have been under democratic governance for more than a decade is an achievement and one has to congratulate the strenuous efforts made to educate the security agencies into appreciating the essence of democratic governance. That there has been no successful coup d'etat since Ghana's redemocratization is also a pointer to the growing assertion of civil control over the military and the realization by the military that its corporate future does not lie in destabilization. Another important issue in the liberal state is the kind of leadership style adopted. Through democratization, Ghanaians now have a firm base to compare leadership styles across the board. This is important in the sense that a nation is often judged in international terms by its style of leadership. Notwithstanding the fact that this is not an appropriate yardstick, the political performance of leaders of the liberal state offers the chance for a lasting study of political leadership in the country. A positive fall-out from the liberal state is the opportunity for political mentoring and grooming, unlike in the past when military men with no political experience took over the mantle of leadership through the barrel of the gun. Not all needs have been satisfied by the liberal state but it cannot be disputed that peace, stability, transparency, accountability, respect for human rights and the rule of law have been its enduring features.

Sources

Biro, P. L. (2002) 'Some Thoughts About a Liberal Legal Culture', mimeo (Toronto).

Bratton, M., R. Mattes and E. Gyimah-Boadi (eds) (2005) *Public Opinion, Democracy, and Market Reform in Africa* (Cambridge: Cambridge University Press).

Clift, J. (2003) 'Beyond the Washington Consensus', *Finance and Development* (September).

Commission for Africa (2005) *Our Common Interest*, Report.

Dunn, J. (ed.) (1992) *Democracy: The Unfinished Journey, 508 BC to AD 1993* (Oxford: Oxford University Press).

Folson, K. G. (1993) 'Ideology, Revolution and Development – the Years of

J. J. Rawlings', in E. Gyimah-Boadi (ed.), *Ghana Under PNDC Rule* (Dakar: CODESRIA).

Fukuyama, F. (1992) *The End of History and the Last Man* (New York: Avon Books).

Greven, M. T. and L. W. Pauly (eds) (2000) *Democracy Beyond the State?* (Toronto: University of Toronto Press).

Hoffman, S. (1995) 'The Crisis of Liberal Internationalism', *Foreign Policy* (Spring): <www.ub.edu.ar/facultades/feg/crisis.htm> (accessed 22 November 2004).

Hope, K. R. Sr (2000) 'Corruption and Development in Africa', in K. R. Hope Sr and B. C. Chikulo (eds), *Corruption and Development in Africa: Lessons from Country Studies* (New York: St Martin's Press).

Ikenberry, G. J. and M. W. Doyle (1997) 'Continuity and Innovation in International Relations Theory', in M. W. Doyle and G. J. Ikenberry (eds), *New Thinking in International Relations Theory* (Boulder, CO: West View Press).

Kane-Berman, J. (2004) 'Empowerment: The Need for a Liberal Strategy', <www.fnf.org.za/New/empower.htm> (accessed 20 November 2004).

Lowry, C. (2000), 'A Defence of Individual Autonomy in a Multination Liberal State', *Prolegomena*, Winter: <www.philosophy.ubc.ca/prolegom/papers/Lowry.htm> (accessed 20 November 2004).

Macpherson, C. B. (1997) *The Life and Times of Liberal Democracy* (Oxford: Oxford University Press).

Nelson, J. M. and S. J. Eglinton (1992) 'Encouraging Democracy: What Role for Conditioned Aid?', Policy Essay no. 4 (Washington, DC: Overseas Development Council).

Ninsin, K. A. (ed.) (1995), *Ghana: Transition to Democracy* (Accra: Freedom Publications).

Nugent, P. (1995) *Big Men, Small Boys and Politics in Ghana* (Accra: Asempa Publishers).

Olukoshi, A. (1992) 'The World Bank, Structural Adjustment and Governance in Africa: Some Reflections', mimeo (Dakar: CODESRIA).

Organization of African Unity (OAU) (2001) *The New Partnership for Africa's Development (NEPAD)* (October).

Przeworski, A. (1991) *Democracy and the Market* (Cambridge: Cambridge University Press).

Robinson, M. (1996), 'Economic Reform and the Transition to Democracy', in R. Luckham and G. White (eds), *Democratization in the South: The Jagged Wave* (Manchester and New York: Manchester University Press).

Rothchild, D. (1991), 'Ghana and Structural Adjustment: An Overview', in D. Rothchild (ed.), *Ghana: The Political Economy of Recovery* (Boulder, CO: Lynne Rienner).

Sandbrook, R. (2000) *Closing the Circle: Democratization and Development in Africa* (London: Zed Books).

Shillington, K. (1992) *Ghana and the Rawlings Factor* (London: Macmillan).

Spiegel, S. L. (1995) *World Politics in a New Era* (New York: Harcourt Brace).

Starr, P. (2004) 'The New Life of the Liberal State: Privatization and the Restructuring of State–Society Relations': <www.princeton.edu/-starr/ newstate.html> (accessed 22 November 2004).

Stiglitz, J. E. (1998) 'Post Washington Consensus, Initiative for Policy Dialogue', mimeo, Colombia University.

Williamson, J. (1990) 'What Washington Means by Policy Reform', in J. Williamson (ed.), *Latin American Adjustment: How Much Has Happened?* (Washington, DC: Institute for International Economics).

— (2000) 'What Should the World Bank Think About the Washington Consensus?', *The World Bank Research Observer*, Vol. 15, no. 2 (August).

World Bank (1989) *Sub-Saharan Africa: From Crisis to Sustainable Growth* (Washington, DC: World Bank).

Yeebo, Z. (1991) *Ghana: The Struggle for Popular Power* (London: New Beacon Books).

2 | Trends in the promotion and protection of human rights under the 1992 Constitution

KOFI QUASHIGAH

Human rights as a significant element of good governance

The preamble to the 1948 UN Universal Declaration of Human Rights states, *inter alia*, that 'it is essential, if man is not to be compelled to have recourse, as a last resort, to rebellion against tyranny and oppression, that human rights should be protected by the rule of law'. The importance of respect for human rights in guaranteeing good governance is beyond doubt, for governments are instituted for the generally accepted purpose of working for the protection of the personal liberties of the people and the improvement of their economic and social lives. Anything short of that would give credence to Kelsen's comparison of the government to a band of armed robbers, with the distinction, however, that the 'government of a state has as its legitimizing basis the authority of the state which is manifested through the ability to legislate to give legal authority to its decisions and also to enforce such decisions' (Kelsen 1979: 44). Definitely, the idea of government carries with it the inherent conception of some modicum of respect for human dignity and human welfare. Any system of government that rejects this is an aberration and does not have the legitimacy to continue to govern.

The events leading to the promulgation of Ghana's 1992 Constitution and the very foundation of the Fourth Republic that is based on it are all deeply rooted in the essence of human rights. Respect for human rights is one of the fundamental principles on which the Constitution is built, as for instance is clearly announced in the preamble to the Constitution and in the Directive Principles of State Policy which prescribe the general philosophical principles according to which governance should be ordered.

A national survey undertaken by the National Commission for Democracy (Afari-Gyan 1995) revealed a clear demand by the people of Ghana for a system of government that has inherent in it the principle of respect for human rights. The 1992 Constitution was the product of this expressed desire for the establishment of a liberal state to replace the military-backed Provisional National Defence Council (PNDC) that had ruled from 31 December 1982 to 6 January 1993. The PNDC era was based on a system of administration according to which the deserts of ordinary citizens were determined by individuals who were not themselves limited by any measures; the PNDC administration of the period wielded absolute power under which individual rights were not guaranteed.

The preamble to the Constitution proclaims the people as the source of authority; that the people derive that authority from God who grants them their natural and inalienable rights. It further states that the people, in the exercise of that God-given authority, have given to themselves the present Constitution which has among its prime commitments 'the protection and preservation of Fundamental Human Rights and Freedoms'. In keeping with this commitment, the Constitution makes provision for an array of guaranteed fundamental human rights and freedoms and also makes provision for their protection and preservation by the courts and a national human rights institution, the Commission on Human Rights and Administrative Justice (CHRAJ).

This chapter analyses the extent to which the fundamental human rights and freedoms guaranteed under the 1992 Constitution have in practice been realized.

A sketch of trends in human rights prior to the 1992 Constitution

Ghana, like all other former British dependencies, except India and Nigeria, was ushered into independence without an elaborate provision of fundamental human rights guaranteed in the constitution. Until recently the classical doctrine of the supremacy of parliament held sway in Britain with the consequent presumption that 'constitutional guarantee of principles of civil and political liberty is unnecessary' (Jennings 1953: 48, 54). Earlier, Dicey had contended that the protection of human rights through the common law affords greater protection than through constitutional instruments because while the former focuses on the availability of remedies the latter emphasizes the mere existence of rights. This perception underlay Dicey's assertion that 'The Habeas Corpus Acts declare no principle and define no rights, but they are for practical purposes worth a hundred constitutional articles guaranteeing individual liberty' (Dicey 1959: 199). The British had absolute confidence that parliament would respect and protect fundamental rights; this view was echoed in the observation of Lord Wright in the case of *Liversidge v Anderson* (AC 1942: 261) that the greatest 'safeguard of British liberty is in the good sense of the people and in the system of representative and responsible government which has been evolved'. This perception influenced the nature of the Independence Constitution of Ghana in the sense that no elaborate provision of human rights was included in it. That constitution was put to test in the case of *Re Akoto* (GLR 1961: 523) when the Supreme Court was confronted with the question of the constitutionality of the Preventive Detention Act (PDA) as it related to the 1960 Constitution.

The Supreme Court upheld the constitutionality of the PDA in the *Re Akoto* case and thereby, by implication, supported the emasculation of any protective authority that the 1960 Constitution might have contained. The decision provided judicial support to the Nkrumah regime's unbridled trampling upon the rights of citizens; and many Ghanaians, both prominent and not so prominent, were incarcerated without trial.

When the 1969 Constitution was being drafted, a conscious step was taken to entrench fundamental human rights as a means of avoiding the abuse of rights that had been experienced under the Nkrumah regime. That was one of the steps taken to return the country to a liberal democratic system. The entrenchment of fundamental human rights provisions has thus become a regular feature of the subsequent Ghanaian constitutions.

The 1969 Constitution was abrogated by the military in a coup d'etat led by General Acheampong in 1972.[1] In 1979 the country was returned to democratic rule under the 1979 Constitution, which in its turn was terminated in a coup d'etat led by Flight Lieutenant Rawlings.

The period immediately preceding the coming into effect of the 1992 Constitution was one of military rule by the Provisional National Defence Council headed by Rawlings. It was a period of unconstitutional rule; the 1979 Constitution had been abrogated and justice was dispensed according to the whim of the military leadership and their civilian collaborators. That was the situation until the return to constitutional rule on 7 January 1993.

Human rights under the 1992 Constitution

The nature of the rights protected under the 1992 Constitution Article 12(2) makes the fundamental human rights and freedoms guaranteed both vertically and horizontally applicable in the sense that they are enforceable against both the government and against individuals and private institutions.

The rights guaranteed are a reflection of the liberal democratic underpinnings inherent in the various democratic constitutions since 1969. The basic liberal democratic principles of protection of the right to life, protection of personal liberty, respect for human dignity, protection from slavery and forced labour, equality and freedom from discrimination, protection of privacy of home and other property, the right to a fair trial, protection from deprivation of property, the right to freedom of speech and expression including freedom of the press and other media, freedom of thought, conscience and belief including academic freedom, freedom to practise

23

any religion, freedom of assembly and demonstration, freedom of association, right to information and freedom of movement. In addition there are other equally progressive rights such as the guarantee of the property rights of spouses, guarantee of fair administrative justice, guarantee of economic rights, especially the right to work under satisfactory, safe and healthy conditions, and to receive equal pay for equal work. It also guaranteed the right to education, cultural rights and practices, the rights of women, children's rights, rights of the disabled and rights of the sick. All these rights are described as fundamental human rights and freedoms and enshrined under Chapter 5 of the Constitution. Redress for breach or anticipated breach of any of these rights can be sought in the High Court which has the authority to issue such directions or orders it may consider appropriate – Article 33(1)(2).

In addition to Chapter 5, other provisions of the Constitution guarantee some other specific rights; one such example is Chapter 12 that guarantees the 'freedom and independence of the media'. Also worth mentioning is Article 42 which guarantees to every citizen of Ghana of eighteen years of age or above and of sound mind the right to vote.

These are very impressive rights on paper but in practice illiteracy, inadequate court systems and other logistical problems have operated to deny many, especially the politically, socially and economically underprivileged, the benefits of these elaborate liberal rights.

In addition to the specific provisions already mentioned there is also Chapter 6 which covers the Directive Principles of State Policy; it sets out the various basic objectives that functionaries of the state and individuals should use as focus in taking and implementing policy decisions for the establishment of a just and free society. The objectives mentioned include political, economic, social, educational and cultural objectives. The legal import of these objectives is discussed below.

The human rights jurisdiction of the High Court and Supreme Court The Constitution has vested in the High Court and the Supreme Court original jurisdiction in the determination of any matter relating to the enforcement of the fundamental human rights and freedoms guaranteed; these are so stated in Articles 33 and 130 respectively. In the case of *Edusei v Attorney-General* (SCGLR 1996–97: 1) the plaintiff invoked the original jurisdiction of the Supreme Court for the enforcement of his fundamental right to freedom of movement freely to leave and enter Ghana. The Attorney-General raised the preliminary objection that since the plaintiff was seeking the enforcement of his right to freedom of movement, it was the High Court and not the Supreme Court that was vested with jurisdiction to entertain the suit. The court ruled in support of the Attorney-General's position that, taking the totality of the relevant articles into account, the Supreme Court's original jurisdiction could not be invoked in this case because no issue of interpretation was raised; that the Supreme Court's original jurisdiction can properly be invoked only if the parties are really contending the meaning of a particular provision of the Constitution or urging different or diametrically opposed views as to the actual meaning of the said provision.

With that decision it was clearly settled that the High Court has the original jurisdiction in the judicial enforcement of the fundamental human rights guaranteed under the Constitution.

The ability of the average citizen to access the High Court for the enforcement of his/her fundamental human rights is, however, a different matter; it is common knowledge that the court process is slow and expensive and therefore not within the means of the majority of Ghanaians. Hence the importance of the protective role of the CHRAJ.

The importance of Article 33(5) Article 33(5) of the Constitution creates an important nexus between the constitutionally provided rights in Chapter 5 and the other rights that are inherent in democratic systems of governance. Article 33(5) provides that: 'The rights, duties, declarations and guarantees relating to the fundamental human rights and freedoms specifically mentioned in this chapter shall not be regarded as excluding others not specifically mentioned which are considered to be inherent in a democracy and intended to secure the freedom and dignity of man.' This provision therefore links constitutional provisions on human rights to the ever-growing number of rights at the international level. The implication herein is that the individual's rights extend to cover those that are inherent in or accepted in democratic societies. In addition, it is an indication to the judiciary, and therefore to the CHRAJ, to adopt interpretative attitudes that will bring the rights guaranteed in line with the conception of those rights in the international community. As between the judiciary and the CHRAJ, it would appear, so far, that the CHRAJ is the more flexible of the two in allowing human rights trends in other democratic jurisdictions to influence its decisions.[2]

The interpretative approach of the courts

Civil and political rights The coming of the Constitution in 1992 gave a renewed spirit and human rights conscience to the courts; it became possible for the courts to pronounce decisions that seek to enhance the human rights guaranteed under the Constitution. In the case of *Coffie v Heman* (Ghana

Quarterly Law Journal [hereafter GQLJ] 1997: 8), the court was confronted with a situation where the police, in order to compel a man who was wanted in connection with a case to give himself up, arrested and detained his son. This was a practice that was rife under the previous military administration. The court took the opportunity to deprecate the practice: 'we know no law which permits the police to arrest a wife when they are looking for her husband, a son when looking for the father or vice-versa. Such practice constitutes negation of the fundamental rights of the individuals involved; and is unsupported by law and the constitution' (GQLJ 1997: 8). This was a direct attack on a practice that the law enforcement authorities had adopted without restraint during the military period when even children were picked up to compel the appearance of their fathers.

Another important decision of the Supreme Court in the direction of the enhancement of the enjoyment of the fundamental rights guaranteed was the decision in the *NPP v Inspector-General of Police (The Public Order Case)* (2GLR 1993–94: 459) in which the Public Order Decree that required a police permit for assembly and demonstration was declared unconstitutional in view of Article 21(1)(d) of the 1992 Constitution. The Supreme Court proceeded to order that the Inspector General of Police should ensure that the decision be posted at all police stations throughout the country for the information and guidance of police personnel.

A test of economic and social rights Unlike India, the legal profession in Ghana has not developed the aptitude of fashioning personal rights in terms of economic and social rights; the Ghanaian courts have therefore also not developed the expertise needed for the handling of economic, social and cultural rights. The courts in Ghana have so far been presented with few opportunities to deliberate on and pass judgment on these rights. An opportunity arose in the case of *Issah Iddi Abass & others v Accra Metropolitan Assembly and another (Sodom & Gomorrah case)* (Unreported Misc. 1203/2002, 2002); it was a case in which the plaintiffs sought to assert their rights to a number of economic and social rights provided for in the 1992 Constitution and in international human rights instruments ratified by Ghana.

Sodom and Gomorrah is an unapproved shanty settlement at Accra. It occupies an area that has been described as a water zone, sprawling on the banks of the Korle Lagoon. It is not earmarked for residential purposes. The plaintiffs by their own admission were squatters. The Accra Metropolitan Assembly (AMA), owners of the land, initiated a project intended to restore the Korle Lagoon to its former state and to check flooding in parts of the city of Accra; the project was known as the Korle Lagoon Ecological Restoration Project. As required by law, an environmental and social impact statement of the project was prepared; this proposed certain mitigating and enhancing measures to be undertaken by the defendants, including relocation or resettlement of the people of Sodom and Gomorrah. The AMA requested the squatters to vacate the area to make way for the unimpeded execution of the project. The squatters did not. It was evident that the plaintiffs/squatters had been given ample time to vacate the place.

When it became obvious that the AMA (first defendant) was going to carry out an eviction exercise in the area, the plaintiffs/squatters filed a writ in the High Court claiming that the defendants must be bound by the requirements of the environmental and social impact statement that said that the residents of Sodom and Gomorrah should be resettled and that any unplanned eviction of the residents would constitute an infraction upon their right to life which includes the right to a livelihood, the right to housing and shelter and the right to human dignity. In addition, it was argued that the rights of the plaintiffs' children to education and adequate shelter would be affected if the plaintiffs were to be thrown on to the streets without the provision of adequate shelter. The plaintiffs relied on various provisions of Chapter 5 of the 1992 Constitution including Articles 12(1) and 33(5). Also included was Article 23 which imposes a mandatory duty on administrative bodies and officials to act fairly and reasonably.

The judge accepted the contention of counsel for defendants that the plaintiffs were trespassers and should therefore not be permitted to benefit from their act of lawlessness. He distinguished the social problem of homelessness that pertains in India and South Africa as non-existent in Ghana and accordingly rejected the invitation to adopt a position similar to what had been decided in India. He rather preferred to follow various English decisions and accepted the view of Lord Denning that:

> If homelessness were once admitted as a defence to trespass, no one's house could be safe. Necessity would open a door which no man could shut. It would not only be those in extreme need who would enter. There would be others who would imagine that they were in need, or would invent a need, so as to gain entry. Each man would say his need was greater than the next man's. The plea would be an excuse for all sorts of wrongdoing. So the courts must, for the sake of law and order, take a firm stand. (2 All ER 1971: 179)

In the view of the court, the only argument that could be urged in favour of the plaintiffs was that the way in which an eviction is carried out can constitute an infringement of their rights as human beings; he accordingly entreated the first defendant to allow plaintiffs another grace period of two weeks from the date of judgment to enable them to organize themselves and vacate the land peacefully; and should an eviction become inevitable, it should be carried out in a humane manner.

This approach has not advanced jurisprudence in Ghana towards the international idea that individuals have some basic rights to housing that the state must guarantee when the requisite conditions become prevalent.[3]

The debate over the nature of the Directive Principles of State Policy Chapter 6 of the 1992 Constitution touches on what are labelled the 'Directive Principles of State Policy'. According to Article 34(1), these are intended to guide all citizens, parliament, the president, the judiciary, the Council of State, the cabinet, political parties and other bodies and persons applying or interpreting this Constitution or any other law and in taking and implementing any policy decisions, for the establishment of a just and free society. The exact import of this provision became a matter of controversy in the Supreme Court in a number of cases.[4]

Generally, the traditional view had been that these provisions are non-justiciable in the sense that they are not enforceable in the courts; they are meant to serve as political standards according to which those in authority must rule. This is the traditionalist view as expressed in the Indian Constitution (Austin 1966: 75) and the 1979 Constitution of Nigeria.

The 1979 Constitution of Nigeria was clear enough in its categorization of the Directive Principles as non-justiciable in the courts of law. Article 13 of that constitution made it the 'duty and responsibility of all organs of government, and all authorities and persons exercising legislative, executive or judicial powers to conform to, observe and apply the provisions of this Chapter' (i.e. Chapter II on Directive Principles of State Policy). Nevertheless, Article 6(6)(c) explicitly excluded the jurisdiction of the courts in undertaking judicial inquiry or enforcement with respect to those provisions. The Indian Constitution also, in Article 37, makes the Directive Principles non-justiciable yet fundamental in the governance of the nation. If we were to follow these positions, it might be assumed that the Directive Principles of State Policy in the 1992 Constitution of Ghana are equally non-justiciable, perhaps until the Supreme Court decision in the case of *New Patriotic Party v Attorney-General (31st December Case)* (2 GLR 1993–94: 35).

In the 31 December case, different opinions were expressed on the legal nature of the Directive Principles of State Policy by Adade JSC and Bamford-Addo JSC who was supported in her opinion by Hayfron Benjamin JSC. Bamford-Addo JSC adopted the traditionalist view that the Directive

Principles are not justiciable and that no cause of action can therefore be based thereon. According to her, 'the principles are included in the Constitution for guidance of all citizens, parliament, the President, Judiciary, the Council of State, the Cabinet, political parties or other bodies and persons in applying or interpreting the Constitution or any other law and in making and implementing any policy decisions, for the establishment of a just and free society' (2 GLR 1993–94: 35). In arriving at this conclusion she depended heavily on the 1991 Committee of Experts' Report, paragraphs 94–97, wherein the Directive Principles were explained as 'spelling out in broad strokes the *spirit* or *conscience* of the constitution'. The Committee of Experts acknowledged the tradition of the non-justiciability of the Directive Principles and in a rather forthright manner stated categorically that:

> The Directive Principles of State Policy are for the guidance of Parliament, the President, the Council of Ministers, Political Parties and other bodies and persons in making and applying public policy or the establishment of a just and free society. The Principles should not of and by themselves be legally enforceable by any Court. The Courts should, however, have regard to the said Principles in interpreting any laws based on them. (Committee of Experts Report 1992: 96)

Contrary to this strong assertion coming from the Committee of Experts was the position taken by Adade JSC that:

> this idea of the alleged non-justiciability of the Directive Principles is peddled very widely, but I have not found it convincingly substantiated anywhere. I have the uncomfortable feeling that this may be one of those cases where a falsehood, given sufficient currency, manages to pass for the truth. I do not subscribe to the view that Chapter 6 is not justiciable: it is. (2 GLR 1993–94: 35)

His line of argument started from the premise that the Constitution as a whole is a justiciable document and that if any part of it is to be labelled as non-justiciable, this must be so stated by the Constitution itself; he does not, however, see 'anything in Chapter 6 or in the Constitution 1992 generally, which tells me that Chapter 6 is not justiciable' (ibid.).

Justice Adade further based his argument on the second premise that Articles 1(2) and 2(1) of the Constitution seek to render all inconsistencies with the Constitution unconstitutional. The two provisions read as follows:

> 1(2) This Constitution shall be the supreme law of Ghana and any other law found to be inconsistent with any provision of this Constitution shall, to the extent of the inconsistency, be void.

2(1) A person who alleges that –

a) an enactment or anything contained in or done under the authority of that or any other enactment; or

b) any act or omission of any person is inconsistent with, or in contravention of a provision of this Constitution, may bring an action in the Supreme Court for a declaration to that effect.

In his view, since these two Articles made no exceptions in favour of Chapter 6, it cannot be claimed that the Directive Principles are non-justiciable.

Adade JSC's third consideration was based on his interpretation of Article 34(1) of the Constitution, quoted above. He found it difficult to appreciate how else the principles can *guide* the judiciary in applying or interpreting the Constitution 'if not in the process of enforcing them' (2 GLR 1993–94: 67). He was not unaware of the statement of the 1991 Committee of Experts to the effect that 'by tradition Directive Principles are not justiciable' (ibid.: 68). He argued, however, that it is clear that the 'tradition' which the Committee of Experts relied on was the 1979 constitutional provision, but that an examination of the parliamentary history of the relevant Chapter 4 of the 1979 Constitution would show that when the Constituent Assembly put forward the issue of whether the Directive Principles should be justiciable or non-justiciable, the House voted for justiciability. It is from this observation that he espoused the view that the Directive Principles are justiciable, especially in the absence of any specific intention of the Consultative Assembly to make them non-justiciable. In his estimation, not even the use of the phrase 'shall guide' in Article 34(1) of the 1992 Constitution could be interpreted as implying that the Directive Principles are not meant to be justiciable for, 'after all, all laws are for our guidance, but they are not on that account non-justiciable' (ibid.: 67).

The legal status of an interest is a matter for the legal system to determine. The justiciability or non-justiciability of a particular interest is not a matter of general consideration; specific consideration must be given to each interest in determining whether or not the legal regime accords justiciability to it. Nothing prevents a constitution from making the right to health, shelter and food justiciable; legally speaking, all it takes is the proper formulation.

It may be simplistic to posit the problem as one simply of differences in enforcement procedures (Addo 1988: 1423); it could be one of procedure but, essentially, it is the juristic implications of the end results of the procedure that matter. The aspect relating to the end result has much to do with the dichotomy between the consequences of a legal right and that of a mere moral or political right. A legal right is amenable to the judicial procedure and the final determination is legally enforceable, i.e. the law gives binding force to the determination reached on the right claimed. On the other hand, the claim might be morally or politically enforceable but not legally justiciable in the sense that the courts would not accord direct legal binding force to it; the citizen can enforce it indirectly through the electoral process by voting out of office any government which does not respect those claims.

The history of the development of human rights has so far shown them to be a dynamic force. This is not surprising as human rights deal with ideas and human circumstances, which are constantly changing in consonance with human consciousness and means. In the words of Van Hoof, human rights concern the very foundations of society and 'are therefore influenced by developments in that society. Particularly in present times which witness far-reaching changes, the law of human rights finds itself in a state of more or less permanent development' (Van Hoof 1984: 97).

There was a time when it was argued that economic, social and cultural rights could not form the subject matter of legal rights. The traditional reasons adduced for this were as formulated by Bossuyt (quoted ibid.):

(1) the economic, social and cultural rights require a financial commitment by the State while the civil and political rights do not demand much economic expenditure.

(2) that the civil and political rights 'require non interference on the part of the State, whereas the implementation of economic, social and cultural rights requires active intervention by the State'.

(3) deducible from (1) above is the argument that while the civil and political rights can be conceived to have some basic minimum content, the economic, social and cultural rights will vary from country to country taking into account the varying economic circumstances of each country.

Perhaps the conceptual distinction needs to be made between an obligation to protect and an obligation to promote. An obligation to protect obviously carries the action of doing something to prevent an abuse of the right to be protected; essentially through the court process. In the 1992 Constitution of Ghana, therefore, we find a provision made in Article 33(1) that: 'Where a person alleges that a provision of this Constitution on the fundamental human rights and freedoms has been, or is being or is likely to be contravened in relation to him, then, without prejudice to any other action that is lawfully available, that person may apply to the High Court for redress.' The provision seeks to infuse the idea of protection into the character of the rights found in Chapter 5 and, in fact, the side note to the particular section reads, 'Protection of Rights by the Courts'. All rights under Chapter 5, including even those of economic, social or cultural character in Articles 24, 25 and 26, are subject to protection by the courts; they are justiciable. Without doubt, therefore, the fundamental rights and freedoms in Chapter 5 are justiciable.

On the other hand, the Directive Principles of State Policy contained in Chapter 6 are described as a *'guide'* to 'all citizens, Parliament, the President, the Judiciary, the Council of State, the Cabinet, political parties and other bodies and persons *in applying or interpreting this Constitution or any other law* and in taking and implementing any policy decisions, for the establishment of a just and free society'. The guide to our understanding the true nature of the Directive Principles lies in our appreciation of the philosophical objectives of the whole Constitution, the implications of Chapter 6 itself and, of course, the words used in the above-quoted Article 34(1). Clearly, that Article is meant to be a *guide* to all and sundry, including the judiciary, in any exercise of applying or interpreting the Constitution or any other law. This view finds support with Bimpong-Buta:

> Under article 34(1) of the Constitution, the Directive Principle of State Policy as stated in articles 35–41 (and these include the political, economic, social, educational and cultural objectives of the State) 'shall guide' not only all citizens, Parliament, the President, the Council of State, the Cabinet and political parties but also the Judiciary 'in applying or interpreting the Constitution or any other law.' The word 'guide' in article 34(1) must be construed in its ordinary meaning as: directing or conducting another on the way. In effect, the Directive Principles of State Policy are aids to construction or interpretation of the Constitution, ie or any other legislation. (Bimpong-Buta 1995: 128)

In the more recent case of *New Patriotic Party v Attorney General (CIBA Case)* (SCGLR 1996–97: 729) the Supreme Court again had the opportunity to determine the constitutional implications of the Directive Principles of State Policy. The Supreme Court therein held that the Directive Principles have the effect of providing goals for legislative programmes and being a guide for judicial interpretation but were not of and by themselves legally enforceable by any court. In that case, Bamford-Addo JSC had the opportunity to reiterate her position in the earlier 31 December case that:

> In general therefore, it is correct to say that the Directive Principles are principles of state policy which, taken together, constitute a sort of barometer by which the people can measure the performance of their government. They also provide goals for legislative programmes and a guide for

judicial interpretation but are not of and by themselves legally enforceable by any court. However, there are exceptions to this general principle. Since the courts are mandated to apply them in their interpretative duty, when they are read together or in conjunction with other enforceable parts of the Constitution, they then, in that sense, became enforceable. (SCGLR 1996–97: 745)

In support, Akuffo JSC had this to say:

The essence of these paragraphs is that the Directive Principles are intended to function as the 'core principles around which national, political, social and economic life will revolve.' They spell out 'in broad strokes the spirit or conscience of the constitution' ... where it is intended that specific Directive Principles are to be justiciable, they have been specifically stipulated in other parts of the Constitution as substantive articles. (SCGLR 1996–97: 802–3)

Definitely no one can seriously assert that the provisions in Chapter 6 do not have judicial consequences; they have, in the sense that any application or interpretation of the Constitution which does not conform to Chapter 6 would be unconstitutional. If that happens, a court of law, i.e. the High Court or the Supreme Court as the case might be, could be called upon to exercise its judicial functions to have the proper thing done.[5] The provisions of Chapter 6, therefore, do not stand by themselves as guaranteed rights which can be enforced independently in the courts; they rather serve as adjuncts to the fundamental rights and freedoms in Chapter 5 in particular and the whole Constitution and other laws in general. If we like, these Directive Principles can be explained as an attempt by the Constitution to determine for the judiciary and all others in this country how they should think and behave when confronted with particular practical situations.

It is, therefore, possible to assert without fear of contradiction that the Directive Principles of State Policy are enforceable through the fundamental human rights and freedoms provisions of the Constitution. One might take, for instance, the rights of the disabled under Article 29(6)[6] which provides that: 'As far as practicable every place to which the public has access shall have appropriate facilities for disabled persons.' In the interpretation of this fundamental right provision, the court must take into account the Directive Principles provision in Article 35(3) that: 'The State shall promote just and reasonable access by all citizens to public facilities and services in accordance with law.'

It is clear that Article 35(3) reinforces Article 29(6). Again, we find in Article 17 the guarantee of equality and freedom from discrimination stated thus: '(1) All persons shall be equal before the Law. (2) A person shall not be discriminated against on grounds of gender, race, colour, ethnic origin, religion, creed or social or economic status.' As a complement, we find in Article 35(5) under the Directive Principles the provision that: 'The State shall actively promote the integration of the peoples of Ghana and prohibit discrimination and prejudice on the grounds of place of origin, circumstances of birth, ethnic origin, gender or religion, creed or other beliefs.' In these examples, Articles 35(3) and 35(5), therefore, become justiciable only in the sense that they respectively qualify Articles 29(6) and 17.

In the subsequent case of *New Patriotic Party v Attorney General (CIBA Case)* (SCGLR 1996–97: 729) Bamford-Addo JSC drew this link between fundamental rights and Directive Principles of State Policy as follows:

> There are particular instances where some provisions of the Directive Principles form an integral part of some of the enforceable rights either because they qualify them or can be held to be rights in themselves. In those instances they are of themselves justiciable also ... This present case provides a good example of the special case where a provision under Chapter 6 can be said to be an enforceable right. Article 37(2)(a) and (3) regarding associations, read together with article 21(1)(2), undoubtedly mean that every person in Ghana has 'the freedom of association free from state interference ... ' The words 'rights of people to form their own association free from state interference' in article 37(2)(a) can only mean what they clearly say. In effect, they create a 'right' and can be held as qualification of article 21(1)(e) in respect of freedom of association protected under article 33, though it does not come under Chapter 5. (SCGLR 1996–97: 745–6)

The Directive Principles are, therefore, dependent upon the fundamental rights and freedoms for their realization. In other words, the Directive Principles can be used to 'promote' the 'protection' of fundamental rights and freedoms. The controversy between Justice Adade and Justice Bamford-Addo need not have arisen; all that needs to be done is a conscious attempt at always viewing the fundamental rights and freedoms through the eye of the Directive Principles of State Policy. When this is done a beautiful synthesis could be achieved and the spirit of the Constitution would prevail. This approach has become very popular in India where, irrespective of Article 37 of the Indian Constitution which expressly precludes the courts from judicial application of the Directive Principles of State Policy, the Supreme Court has over the years shifted from a confrontational interpretation as between fundamental rights and freedoms on the one hand and the Directive Principles on the other to an approach of mutual complementarity. The present position in India has been described as follows:

(iv) The Supreme Court has gone through various phases in interpreting the relationship between fundamental rights and directive principles. Initially there was a firm adherence to the supremacy of fundamental rights. After several constitutional amendments, public debate and disputes over court decisions, the Supreme Court has adopted a more balanced and integrated approach in order to interpret harmoniously the two chapters.

(v) The current attitude of the Supreme Court is that fundamental rights should be understood within the framework of directive principles. Legislation which may limit fundamental rights is upheld if it is reasonable, in the public interest and shows a clear nexus with the directive principles. (Steiner and Alston 1996: 308)

It is through this interpretative approach that our courts, especially the High Court and the Supreme Court, can transform the Constitution into a living social charter which would satisfy the aspirations of the people.

It is when we make these Directive Principles of State Policy actually realizable that we will begin to move away from just paying lip-service to human rights.

The developing jurisprudence through the Commission on Human Rights and Administrative Justice

In addition to the courts charged with the protection of the rights guaranteed, there is also the Commission on Human Rights and Administrative Justice (CHRAJ) whose establishment is mandated by Article 216 of the Constitution. In keeping with that mandate, therefore, Act 456 was passed in 1993 to establish the CHRAJ. According to the Long Title of the Act, it was intended to:

establish a Commission on Human Rights and Administrative Justice to investigate complaints of violations of fundamental human rights and freedoms, injustice and corruption; abuse of power and unfair treatment of persons by public officers in the exercise of their duties, with power to seek remedy in respect of such acts or omissions and to provide for other related purposes.

Access to the commission is virtually free; no fees are charged for its services. The significance of this to the delivery of justice to the majority indigent members of the community will be appreciated when considering the low levels of income in the light of the relatively expensive and very slow court litigation process.

The CHRAJ received a total of 10,523 complaints in 2001, 9,347 of which were disposed of.

Although the CHRAJ is not a court and therefore not vested with judicial authority, it has in its decisions been gradually assisting in the development of a human rights jurisprudence that may in the future serve as the basis for the interpretation of constitutional provisions on human rights. In the case of *Morgan and another v Ghana International School (No. 1)* (CHRAJ 1994–2000: 293) for instance, the CHRAJ took advantage of the nature of the case to expound on the constitutional provisions relating to equality and freedom from discrimination.

The CHRAJ's interpretation of some provisions of the Constitution was not as revolutionary as might have been expected. This was the case with respect to its interpretation of the right to food and shelter. The relevant case in this respect was a complaint lodged by a young woman that her right to an adequate standard of living, including the provision of food, shelter and clothing, had been denied her. She was abandoned by her parents when she was a baby and, through the Department of Social Welfare, adopted by a couple from Cape Coast. Unfortunately, the couple died in a motor accident and left her without a guardian. She travelled to Côte d'Ivoire where, being destitute, she got into prostitution. While there she married a Camerounian with whom she had two children. Subsequently the man ran away with the two children. She returned to Ghana and reported to the Department of Social Welfare for assistance. The department accommodated her at its Rehabilitation Centre but forced her out after six days. Hence her complaint to the CHRAJ, contending that the department had a duty to help her obtain accommodation and secure a job because, as she put it, 'I am a Ghanaian and have got the right to survive in my country' (CHRAJ 1995: 44). According to the commission's report, the petitioner appeared to have abandoned her complaint because she did not show up thereafter; in any case, the commission concluded that, even if she had shown up, 'it could not direct that the Department should provide accommodation for her since the law as it stands now did not guarantee the right to food and shelter' (ibid.). This is a positivistic interpretation that does not seem to have taken into consideration Article 33(5) of the Constitution.

Legislative initiatives

Since the coming into force of the 1992 Constitution, the country has ratified a number of important international human rights instruments whose existence seems previously to have been ignored; perhaps this could be interpreted as one of the steps towards liberalism. Significant among those instruments are the International Covenant on Economic, Social and Cultural Rights and the International Covenant on Civil and Political Rights, both of which were ratified on 7 September 2000.[7] These human rights instruments are in addition to others such as the African Charter on Human and Peoples' Rights, the Convention for the Elimination of All Forms of Discrimination Against Women and the Convention on the Rights of the Child that had been ratified earlier on.[8]

Various pieces of new and amended legislation have been brought into being in order to realign the laws with the human rights demands of the new Constitution and obligations under international law. The Children's Act and the Criminal Code (Repeal of Criminal Libel and Seditious Laws) (Amendment) Act are respective examples of this type of legislation.

Mention may here be made of the Labour Act 2003, Act 651 that in section 10 sets out the rights of the worker to:

a) work under satisfactory, safe and healthy conditions
b) receive equal pay for equal work without distinction of any kind
c) have rest, leisure and reasonable limitation of working hours and periods of holidays with pay as well as remuneration for public holidays
d) form or join a trade union
e) be trained and retrained for the development of his or her skills
f) receive information relevant to his or her work.

These are in accordance with the country's obligations under international law and also as required under Chapter 5 of the Constitution. Note should be taken, however, of the fact that, just as in Article 24 of the Constitution, the right to work itself is not categorically guaranteed.

Some of the legislative initiatives are still at the bill stage; examples are the Freedom of Information Bill and the Domestic Violence Bill. The Freedom of Information Bill is intended to support the system of democratic governance that entails active participation by all in the governance of the country. It follows from the realization that it is only when those who are to participate in governance are well informed that they can contribute meaningfully to governance and that this can be achieved only if they have access to the relevant information.[9] According to the Memorandum to the bill: 'The purpose of the Bill is to give substance to the Constitutional provision in article 21(1)(f) on the right to information by providing for (a) access to official information held by government agencies and private bodies, and (b) the qualification and conditions under which such access should be obtained.' The coming into being of this proposed legislation will definitely enhance the enjoyment of the right to information as is contained in Article 21(1)(f) of the Constitution and will therefore improve participatory democracy.[10]

The Domestic Violence Bill 2002 is intended to prohibit persons in domestic relationships from subjecting others to acts of domestic violence.

The prohibition extends to cover sexual, psychological, physical and economic abuse. Examples of these are given as forcible confinement or detention of another person such as spouse or a child and the deprivation of another person of access to food, shelter and clothing (WAJU 2003: 14). Also suggested for protection under the bill are housekeepers, husbands, wives, children in the same household and also co-tenants.[11]

The bill is the private legislative initiative of a coalition of human rights NGOs campaigning against domestic violence. One problematic provision of the bill is the portion that seeks to create the crime of marital rape which would make it possible for a husband to be convicted for the rape of his wife. The bill is now before parliament.

Children's Act Parliament enacted the Children's Act 1998 with the main objective of bringing the country's legislation on children into conformity with its obligations under the CRC, ratified in 1990, and also to satisfy the requirements of Article 28 of the Constitution which guarantees the rights of children. The long title to the Act explains that it was intended 'to provide for the rights of the child, maintenance and adoption, regulate child labour and apprenticeship, for ancillary matters concerning children generally and to provide for related matters'.

The Children's Act is a very detailed piece of legislation that seeks to effect some positive changes in the rights of children. The Act sets the age of a child as up to eighteen years; this is in conformity with the CRC. In addition, the Act mentions other rights of the child which are to be protected as, first, that the interest of the child shall be paramount in any matter concerning a child. Generally, as is provided by the Act, the child is entitled to the following:

• not to be discriminated against
• to a name and nationality
• the right to grow up with parents
• the right to parental property
• the right to education and well-being
• the right to social activity
• disabled children to be given special care
• the right to an opinion
• protection from exploitative labour
• protection from torture and degrading treatment
• the right to refuse betrothal and marriage

Parents also have duties and responsibilities.

38

Criminal libel The 1992 Constitution ushered in a new era of constitution-ally guaranteed rights; nevertheless, some of the pieces of legislation that had derogated from a number of the rights remained in place under the National Democratic Government (NDC) administration. Of significant interest was the criminal libel law that the NDC administration found useful in curbing the unbridled intrusion of the media. The law on criminal libel remained on the statute books until the coming into office of the New Patriotic Party (NPP) administration in 2000. It was a campaign promise of the NPP to repeal the criminal libel laws.

Irrespective of the provisions of the Constitution guaranteeing free-dom of expression and the media, together with the general appeal of the Constitution to upholding democratic principles, the NDC administration found the existing sections of the Criminal Code on Libel relevant for its purposes; these include sections 112–19, 182A, 183, 183A and 185. These provisions together operate to impose extensive limitations on the right to freedom of expression and therefore the media; sections 112–19 seek to punish criminal libel; section 182A empowers the president to prohibit any organization whose objects or activities are contrary to public good or are being used for purposes prejudicial to the public good; section 183 permits the president to prohibit the importation or publication of newspapers that in his opinion would be contrary to public interest. Section 183A in particular is inimical; it seeks to punish any publication intended to bring the President hatred, ridicule or contempt. Section 185, which became notorious in its application under the 1992 Constitution, punishes any false statement or report which is likely to injure the credit or reputation of Ghana or the government and which is known or believed to be false. This particular provision became the subject of the well publicized case of *Republic v Tommy Thompson Books Ltd (No.2)* (GQLJ 1998: 5). Unfortunately, the Supreme Court itself found that piece of legislation relevant, even under the Constitution, and held that section 112 of the Criminal Code 1960 Act 29 was not inconsistent with the 1992 Constitution.

In keeping with its campaign promise, the NPP administration, upon coming into office in January 2001, was able to secure an amendment to these provisions of the Criminal Code on 17 August 2001 through the Criminal Code (Repeal of Criminal Libel and Seditious Laws) (Amendment) Act 2001, Act 602. The Act repealed sections 112–19, sections 182A, 183, 183A and 185. In addition, it provided for the immediate cessation of pro-ceedings in respect of any prosecution instituted under any of the repealed sections and, more than that, any person who had already committed an offence under any of the repealed sections would not be prosecuted. In the long title to the Act it is stated that the objective of the amendment was to 'bring the laws on expression and the media into conformity with the provisions of the Constitution'.

Some specific rights considered

Personal liberty There has been considerable improvement in the area of the right to personal liberty; especially upon the coming into force of the 1992 Constitution. Requests for money as precondition for bail continue to exist, especially at police posts in rural areas. The regular inspection of prisons by the CHRAJ is a very positive approach to ensuring that prison reforms are effected. Financial constraints have, however, hindered efforts towards comprehensive reforms within the prison system (CHRAJ 2001). The situation of persons on remand is also not the best; it was reported in June 2004, for instance, that a total of 1,270 remand prisoners whose warrants had expired were in prison custody nationwide (*Daily Graphic*, 10 June 2004, p. 1).

From time to time, cases of excessive use of force by the police against citizens are reported (CHRAJ 2001: 43). On a positive note, the police administration has often demonstrated its commitment to punish any police officer who goes beyond the limit in the exercise of force.

Media freedom Media freedom as guaranteed by the Constitution received added support with the repeal of the criminal libel law (Republic of Ghana 2001, Criminal Code [Repeal of Criminal Libel and Sedition Laws] [Amendment] Act 602). As indicated above, there is, in addition, a bill now before Parliament that seeks to open up access to information. All these will enhance the performance of the media, which is essential for the effective protection and promotion of human rights and for guaranteeing accountability.

Right to education Since independence, the importance of education as a human right and as a requisite for national development has been realized. The Education Act 1960, Act 87, had made basic education free and compulsory. Subsequent constitutions, the 1979 and 1992 Constitutions also reiterated this and in addition made adult literacy a constitutional objective. The 2002 Population and Housing Census Summary Report provided that 53.3 per cent of over-fifteen-year-olds were literate. The total population stood at a total of 18,912,079. Of that number 11,105,236 were over fifteen years. The gender ratio put women at a greater illiteracy level than the men; women number 5,669,407 out of the total of 11,105,236 literates, but 54.3 per cent of their number were not literate (Republic of Ghana 2002: 27).

The quality of education has continued to decline significantly, especially in the rural areas. Poverty and lack of motivation are contributory factors.

Rights of children Traditional practices such as female genital mutilation and *Trokosi* (female slavery) still persist even in the face of legislation aimed at criminalizing them. Various pieces of legislation have been tightened to guarantee greater protection for the rights of the child; these include the Criminal Code (Amendment) Act 1998, Act 554. That Act enhanced the punishment for rape and defilement of children and also criminalized the practice of *Trokosi* and proscribed early marriages. As a complement the judiciary responded by the imposition of severe punishments for convictions for child abuse and defilement.

Statistics indicate improvements in health and educational levels since the ratification of the Convention on the Rights of the Child (CRC); infant mortality decreased from 103:10,000 in 1990 to 56.7:10,000 in 1998. During the same period the under-five mortality rate decreased from 155:10,000 to 108:10,000 (Republic of Ghana 2003). These successes were attributed to the influence of the country's first National Programme to Action on the Follow-up to the World Summit for Children which sought to focus the activities of governmental institutions on child survival protection, participation and development. Media coverage and publicity on children's rights, together with the contributions of child-rights-focused NGOs, also accounted for the success. Nevertheless, it is believed that much more could be achieved taking into account the low level of expenditure on health and education which are put at 2 per cent and 2.8 per cent of GDP respectively; these are admitted as being much lower than African averages (ibid.: ii).

It should be noted that the figures mentioned above as national figures do not represent a uniform trend throughout the country; it is reported that 'infant mortality in the three northern regions is generally higher than in the south' (ibid.).

There still exists the intractable issue of child labour. The incidence is very widespread. Reports of trafficking in children for use as labourers and prostitutes are rife.

The Women and Juveniles Unit (WAJU) of the Police Service has extended its branches to all the regional capitals and intends to establish its presence in all districts in the country. Lack of adequate resources is, however, an impediment to rapid expansion. The existence of WAJU has improved the level of police protection of the rights of women and children in relative terms, especially in the urban areas where branches of the Unit are currently located.

Rights of women With the objective of strengthening the structures that work for the protection of women and children, the current administration created a Ministry of Women and Children's Affairs. As a matter of policy Ghana acknowledges the underprivileged position of women and therefore has shown a readiness to implement affirmative policies where needed. The Constitution, in Article 17(4), authorizes parliament to enact laws that are reasonably necessary for the implementation of 'policies and programmes aimed at redressing social, economic or educational imbalance in the Ghanaian society'.

Particular attention is being paid to girl children to correct the neglect that the education of females has suffered over the years. Parliament has not as yet formulated any law that specifically addresses the issue; nevertheless, some government agencies have adopted policies that seek to correct this historical imbalance. The Ministry of Education has, for instance, created a Girls' Education Unit within the Basic Education Unit of the Ghana Education Service to focus on improving girls' education. The public universities have also been implementing a policy of affirmative action in favour of female applicants in their admissions.

A legislative bill intended to legislate out the incidence of domestic violence is currently being discussed by the Ministry of Women and Children's Affairs and interested NGOs.

HIV/AIDS Controlling the further spread of HIV/AIDS and ensuring adequate treatment to people living with HIV/AIDS is a national policy that is being pursued relentlessly. It has to do with the right to live in dignity.

The government has established a Ghana Aids Commission under the Ghana Aids Commission Act 2002, Act 613, the main functions of which are to formulate a national HIV/AIDS policy, develop programmes for the implementation of the policy and direct and coordinate the programmes and activities in the fight against HIV/AIDS.

There is the observable indication that the Commission is doing a lot to raise public awareness about the prevalence of the disease and the need for the public to treat those afflicted with dignity.

Environmental rights Environmental rights are protected through a call, in Article 41(k) of the Constitution, to all citizens to protect and safeguard the environment. The response to the protection of the environment, especially by the mining companies and those who exploit the forests, is not in the best interests of the country. The rights of many rural dwellers to survival, including those of future generations, are derogated from especially by the damaging effects of surface mining. The result is the frequent displacement of local farming communities and the poisoning of bodies of water, thus endangering the lives of communities living along the banks of the rivers.

Rights of the vulnerable and excluded The Ministry of Employment and Social Welfare estimates that about 10 per cent of the population suffers from one disability or other. There is recognition of the need to protect the interests of the vulnerable in society. The Constitution, for instance, recognizes the rights of the disabled and expects parliament to legislate to give specificity to the rights guaranteed in that respect. Unfortunately, parliament has proved reluctant to take positive action in this respect. A draft bill on the interests of the disabled, in fact, exists but parliament has been lethargic in its consideration because of the possible financial implications that the passage of the bill will involve. This lethargic attitude forced the association of the disabled on to the streets in January 2004, calling for the passage of the Disability Bill. In response, cabinet suggested administrative measures to address the concerns of the disabled in society until the passage of the bill through parliament: all new public buildings being constructed were to ensure access for the disabled while the new Labour Law made provisions for special allowances for disabled employees (Ghana News Agency, 27 January 2004). The bill is now before parliament.

The spectre of 'streetism' is becoming a reality; the number of children and adults living on the streets is rising. Poverty, with its attendant collapse of families, is blamed for this. Admittedly, the government has a policy for street children and there are ongoing learning and training projects for them at Accra, Kumasi, Sekondi-Takoradi and Tamale (Republic of Ghana 2003: 52).

Economic social and cultural rights It has been acknowledged that for the past ten years Ghana has experienced growing and deepening poverty; five out of ten regions had more than 40 per cent of their population living in poverty in 1999 (Republic of Ghana 2003: ii). As a matter of general policy, the main policy focus of the present administration is poverty reduction and all ministries, departments and agencies are required to formulate strategies that fall in line with this broad objective.

Policies by themselves might not be sufficient but it is worthy of note that the government has in place policies to replace what is known as the 'cash and carry' system in the health sector; according to that system access to medical services was dependent upon the ability to pay on the spot. A national health insurance scheme is being promoted to make basic medical care accessible to the whole population. To that effect the National

Health Insurance Act 2003, Act 650, has been enacted. In addition, there is an ongoing fee exemption policy for maternal deliveries in four of the most deprived regions in the country (ibid.: 52).

The Constitution guarantees the right to work under satisfactory, safe and healthy conditions; the CHRAJ has in many of its decisions endeavoured to protect individuals against employers who abuse these rights.

The transitional provisions and national reconciliation

The transitional provisions A coup d'etat is an unconstitutional means of effecting a change of government; it is always a threat to the liberal democratic system of government. Standing by itself, it is treason, which is a crime, and like all crimes it remains punishable at any time. A government founded upon the success of a coup d'etat remains, at least in principle, a potentially illegitimate government and its actions are likewise subject to challenge on the basis of lack of legal foundation. In addition, experience in Africa has shown that the fundamental rights of individuals come under strain during those periods of military rule that follow any successful coup d'etat. It has also been the experience over the years that various acts of indiscretion that are in themselves abuses of the right to personal liberty and the property rights of individuals are also often indemnified. It is to pre-empt challenges to the legitimacy of the whole enterprise of the coup d'etat as well as the various illegalities committed during the periods of its existence that the indemnity clauses are inserted in the various constitutions that replace the military periods.

In all cases, the indemnity clauses are contained in the transitional provisions which are inserted as the first schedule of each constitution. The general trend in their formulation is that they seek to oust the jurisdiction of the courts from entertaining any action instituted against any person for the very act of overthrowing constitutional authority and also protect all executive, legislative or judicial actions taken or purported to have been taken on behalf of the particular government.

In the case of *NPP v Attorney-General* (2 GLR 1993–94: 35) an opportunity presented itself for the Supreme Court to deliberate on the scope of the indemnity clause in the transitional provision of the 1992 Constitution. In that case the NPP, which was a political party, questioned the legality of the celebration of 31 December[12] as a public holiday using public funds. This the defendant interpreted to mean an attempt by the plaintiff 'to question the constitutionality and legality of 31 December revolution, and the events which gave rise to that revolution on 31 December 1981 which should not be entertained by the court by virtue of section 34, particularly section 34(2) of the transitional provisions of the Constitution, 1992' (2

GLR 1993–94: 45). By a decision of five to four, the Supreme Court upheld the plaintiff's argument that the celebration of 31 December as a public holiday was unconstitutional.

In the earlier 1981 case of *Kwakye v Attorney-General* (GLR 1981: 44), the transitional provision was given an interpretation by the majority of the Supreme Court that supported the near absolute indemnity of any illegalities committed.[13]

The experience, as shown elsewhere, has been that courts are not best suited to be trusted with redressing injustices committed during military periods of government. It is contended that:

> One particularly troubling aspect of transition is what role the existing legal system can and should play. Courts in newly constituted or re-emerging civilian regimes must contend with a legacy of a lack of independence, ties to the old regime, mistrust, fear and corruption, or the inexperience of newly appointed personnel. Under these conditions, some have suggested that courts are not a suitable vehicle for doing justice. (Roht-Arriaza and Gibson 1998: 845)

It is claimed that this was the opinion of the Salvadoran Truth Commission (ibid.). Examples exist of various countries in which different judges have achieved different results on the issue of legality of impunity provisions, using different approaches including resort to international law provisions (ibid.: 862). We can see the same divergent trends in various cases that attempted to pass judgment on the indemnity provisions

The National Reconciliation Commission The indiscretions committed against human rights during the various military regimes have remained unremedied because of the transitional provisions inserted into the various constitutions. The transitional provisions seek to indemnify the perpetrators of various human rights transgressions. Impunity essentially implies absence of punishment for the guilty (Tyagi 1993: 76). According to François JSC: 'An indemnity suggests exemption from penalties. It is the closing of a chapter ... In constitutional terms and with the relevance of our own circumstances, an indemnity connotes a perception of a bright future with all past errors consigned to the archives of history' (2 GLR 1993–94: 86). This view, according to Rev. Father Aguire, assumes that the wounds have been closed; in his view, they have not and the 'only way to close them is to achieve a genuine national reconciliation based on truth and justice with regard to the past' (Aguire 1993: 114).

In the opinion of Kumado: 'The indemnity clauses provide the victims no hope. Besides, the security they appear or purport to offer the beneficiaries is a false one ... it can only be maintained by power not law' (Kumado 1995: 85).

The National Reconciliation Commission Act 2002, Act 611, was promulgated with the following objective:

> [to] seek and promote national reconciliation among the people of this country by recommending appropriate redress for persons who have suffered any injury, hurt, damage, grievance or who have in any other manner been adversely affected by violations and abuses of their human rights arising from activities or inactivities of public institutions and persons holding public office during periods of unconstitutional government.

The nine-member commission's recommendations are intended, to some extent, to assuage the hurt feelings of many. The process could be seen as a partial circumvention of the impediments posed by the transitional provisions; it is in itself a process for addressing past human rights abuses.

If it were to be made possible for individuals to pursue such matters through the court process, the fear is that the lapse of time might affect the effective marshalling and presentation of evidence before the courts. In any case, what about those perpetrators who have died? And those victims who are also dead? To a large extent a truth commission becomes the best alternative means of assuaging the hurt feelings of the individuals and their family members. On 13 October 2004, the NRC presented its final report to the President of the Republic, and the government responded by publishing a White Paper on the report, accepting all its recommendations. No concrete steps have yet been taken, however (due to financial considerations), to compensate victims as recommended.

Conclusion

The reinstatement of constitutional rule under the 1992 Constitution has led to the re-emergence of the liberal state, a relative improvement in the level of enjoyment of human rights and an increasing feeling of freedom. Some legislative reforms have been undertaken to bring laws into line with the human rights requirements of the 1992 Constitution and also the country's responsibilities under international law.

There is, however, a need for greater commitment, especially from the executive and also the courts, to working for the realization of civil, political, economic, social and cultural rights. It must nevertheless be admitted that the worsening world economic situation, which tends to affect third world countries more severely, also derogates from the capacity of the state to satisfy the human rights demands of the people, especially economic, social and cultural rights.

Notes

1 General Acheampong was removed in a palace coup by General Akuffo who was himself removed from office by Flight Lieutenant Rawlings in a coup d'etat on 4 June 1979.

2 This is reflected in the number of decisions mentioned under the CHRAJ and its development of a human rights jurisprudence.

3 Case law in India and South Africa, for instance, is in that direction.

4 Examples are the *New Patriotic Party v Attorney-General (31st December Case)* [1993–94] (2 GLR 35); and also the *New Patriotic Party v Attorney-General (CIBA Case)* [1996–97] (SCGLR 729).

5 The High Court has jurisdiction if the complaint relates to a fundamental right or freedom; otherwise, if it is a matter of pure interpretation which has nothing to do with fundamental rights then it is a matter within the jurisdiction of the Supreme Court. See *Edusei v Attorney-General* [1996–97] (SCGLR 1).

6 This falls under Chapter 5, Fundamental Rights and Freedoms.

7. See <www.ohehr.org/english/countries/ratification/3.htm>, accessed 24 May 2005.

8 They were ratified on 24 January 1989, 2 January 1986 and 5 February 1990 respectively.

9 See Memorandum to the bill on right to information.

10 As at April 2006, the bill was yet to be considered by parliament.

11 The bill is yet to be finalized by the Attorney-General's Department for presentation to parliament.

12 December 31 1981 was the day that the PNDC military government overthrew the government elected to office under the 1979 Constitution.

13 The transitional provisions under consideration in this case were similar to the 1992 constitutional provisions.

Sources

Addo, M. K. (1998) 'The Justiciability of Economic, Social and Cultural Right', *Commonwealth Law Bulletin* (October).

Afari-Gyan, K. (1995) *The Making of the Fourth Republican Constitution of Ghana* (Accra: Friedrich Ebert Foundation).

Aguire, L. P. P. (1993), 'The Consequences of Impunity in Society', in ICJ (eds), *Justice Not Impunity* (Geneva: ICJ).

Alston, P. and K. Tomasevski (eds) (1984) *The Right to Food* (Dordrecht: Martinus Nijhoff).

Austin, G. (1966) *The Indian Constitution: Cornerstone of a Nation* (Bombay: Oxford University Press).

Bimpong-Buta, S. Y. (1995) *The Law of Interpretation in Ghana* (Accra: Advanced Legal Publications).

CHRAJ (Commission on Human Rights and Administrative Justice) (2001) Prisons Inspection Reports.

— (1995) *Second Annual Report.*

De Villiers, B. (1992), 'The Socio-economic Consequences of Directive Principles of State Policy: Limitations on Fundamental Rights', *South African Journal of Human Rights*, Vol. 8: 188–98.

Dicey, A. V. (1959) *The Law of the Constitution*, 10th edn (London: Macmillan).

Gyandoh, S. O. (1996) 'The Constitutional Protection of Human Rights in Developing Nations', Bangkok World Conference on World Peace Through Law.

Jennings, I. (1953) *Some Characteristics of the Indian Constitution* (Madras and New York: Oxford University Press).

Kelsen, H. (1979) *Pure Theory of Law* (Berkeley: University of California Press).

Kumado, K. (1995) 'Forgive Us Our Trespasses: An Examination of the Indemnity Clause in the 1992 Constitution of Ghana', *University of Ghana Law Journal*, Vol. 19.

Quashigah, E. K. (1999), 'Legitimate Governance in Africa: The Responsibility of the International Community', in E. K. Quashigah and O. C. Obiora (eds), *Legitimate Governance in Africa: International and Domestic Legal Perspectives* (The Hague, London and Boston: Kluwer Law International).

Republic of Ghana (2002) Population and Housing Census Summary Report of Final Results (March).

— (2003) *Ghana Poverty Reduction Strategy 2003–2005: An Agenda for Growth and Prosperity*, Vol. 1.

Roht-Arriaza, N. and L. Gibson (1998) 'The Developing Jurisprudence on Amnesty', *Human Rights Quarterly*, Vol. 20: 843–85.

Steiner, H. J. and P. Alston (eds) (1990) *International Human Rights in Context* (Oxford: Clarendon Press).

Tyagi, Y. K. (1993) 'Pardon, Oversight, Revenge, Equitable Punishment, Responsibility', in ICJ (eds), *Justice, Not Impunity* (Geneva; ICJ).

Van Hoof, G. J. H. (1984) 'The Legal Nature of Economic, Social and Cultural Rights: A Rebuttal of Some Traditional Views', in P. Alston and K. Tomasevski (eds), *The Right to Food* (Dordrecht: Martinus Nijhoff).

WAJU (Women and Juvenile Unit of the Ghana Police Service) (2003) *WAJU News* (December).

3 | Challenges of economic growth in a liberal economy

G. KWAKU TSIKATA

The problems of economic growth and development in Ghana have puzzled many economic analysts since the 1960s. A country with a per capita income at independence (1957) higher than that of some of the fast-industrializing countries in South East Asia, Ghana has been relegated to a land of declining living standards since the mid-1960s. The cogent question that can be posed is: why is a country such as Malaysia, for example, enjoying accelerated growth and development while Ghana's performance record can be at best described as sluggish, even though both nations became independent from England at almost the same time? Equally important in the development process is the issue of equitable distribution of incomes. While poverty continues to recede during the development process in most of the newly industrializing countries (NICs), notably in South Korea, Ghana's growth process has generally been accompanied by a growing disparity in incomes and an overall escalation in poverty.

The importance of economic growth in the development process is well embedded in one of the commonest definitions of economic development: economic growth plus structural changes in the economy (Meier 1976). The concern for economic growth is universal and, as Todaro (1989) reminds us, 'economists and politicians of all nations, rich and poor, capitalist, socialist, and mixed, have worshipped at the shrine of economic growth ... "Growthmanship" has become a way of life.' Thus, the importance of economic growth in the development process is unchallengeable; what is unclear, however, is the extent of government intervention that can be considered optimal in Ghana, and Sub-Saharan Africa in general, in an era of democracy and emphasis on free market principles. One major concern is that markets in LDCs are generally imperfect and cannot be relied upon entirely to effect acceptable levels of income distribution.

Ghana's disappointing growth performance over the years is captured in Table 3.1 below. In trying to address the monumental growth problem of the late 1970s and early 1980s, Ghana embarked on the Economic Recovery Programme (ERP) in 1983, which then subsequently led to a structural adjustment programme (SAP). The Bretton Woods institutions spearheaded the financing of the reform effort and the negative growth

Box 3.1 Important politico-economic events in Ghana (1957 to present)

Year Regimes and events

1957 Attainment of independence with Kwame Nkrumah as prime minister.

1960 Attainment of republican status with Nkrumah as first president.

1964 Single-party (socialist) government declared.

1966 Military coup deposes Nkrumah and a junta, the National Liberation Council (NLC), is established with General J. A. Ankrah as chairman; Ankrah later replaced by General A. A. Afrifa.

1969 K. A. Busia assumes office as prime minister after democratic elections in August.

1972 Busia government overthrown by Col. I. K. Acheampong in a military coup; National Redemption Council (NRC) established with Acheampong as chairman.

1975 Acheampong replaces NRC with Supreme Military Council (SMC) consisting of all military officers.

1978 SMC replaces Acheampong with General F. Akuffo as chairman of SMC II.

1979 Abortive coup attempt by Rawlings in May; SMC II replaced in June with Armed Forces Revolutionary Council (AFRC); elections scheduled prior to the coup finally held in July and won by Dr Hilla Limann who assumes office in September.

1981 Rawlings stages a second coup and establishes Provisional National Defence Council (PNDC).

1983 Economic Recovery Programme launched.

1992 Multi-party elections held and won by Rawlings under the banner of the National Democratic Congress (NDC).

1993 Rawlings assumes office as civilian head of state (president).

1995 Ghana-Vision 2020 launched as economic management to make Ghana a middle-income country by 2020.

1996 Rawlings wins a second four-year term as president.

2000 New Patriotic Party (NPP) wins elections.

2001 J. A. Kufuor assumes office as president.

2003 Ghana Poverty Reduction Strategy (GPRS) launched.

2004 Kufuor wins second term.

trends were reversed to register an average rate of growth of about 5 per cent from 1984 to 1991.

After a decade of ERP/SAP reforms in what could be described as a revo-military environment, Ghana's reform effort has received mixed reviews. In general, the Bretton Woods institutions, especially the World Bank, have assessed the outcomes as successful: 'The program was successful in arresting the deteriorating economic situation and introducing a modest recovery. Ghana witnessed positive per capita income growth for the first time since 1978, although per capita incomes remain well below levels observed at Ghana's independence' (World Bank 1988: 78). An opposite view, provided by Kraus, states: 'The economic gains have not made a significant difference in the living standards of most Ghanaians. This is not simply because of the depth of Ghana's economic depression in 1977–83, but largely because the architects of the reform program have been relatively indifferent to core sources of growth' (Kraus 1991: 151).

One disappointing aspect of Ghana's growth picture is that the projected 8 per cent per annum rate of growth targeted in Ghana's Vision 2020 strategy – a strategy aimed at lifting the economy to upper-middle-income level by the year 2020 – appears to be merely an illusion. Even the 5 per cent average growth rate achieved during the reform era of the 1980s seems difficult to attain in recent years. There was a commendable outcome in 2003 when the growth rate reached 5.3 per cent, exceeding the target of 4.7 per cent.

Economic growth therefore constituted and continues to constitute the most crucial challenge to all governments since independence.

Another key consideration is that, as in most Sub-Saharan African countries, political stability and the nature of government cannot be separated from Ghana's history of economic growth and development. Political instability has been one of the key factors that has had a negative impact on economic growth (Fosu 1992). Tsikata (1996), using dummy variables, found a high and statistically significant negative correlation between political instability and economic growth. The study also found that a democratic form of governance has a positive and significant relationship with growth. Some relevant politico-economic events are listed in Box 3.1 to help convey the complexities of economic and political management of the country.

Objective

This chapter aims to examine the key challenges to the economic growth process in Ghana in an era of democratic governance and market liberalism. The key issues to be analysed include: the role of developmental

51

TABLE 3.1 Key macroeconomic indicators, 1970–81

	1970	1971	1972	1973	1974	1975	1976	1977	1978	1979	1980	1981
GDP (current cedis billion)	2.259	2.501	2.815	3.502	4.666	5.283	6.526	11.163	20.986	28.231	42.853	72.626
Real GDP growth (%)	6.78	5.56	2.5	15.3	3.39	12.9	3.52	2.29	8.48	7.82	6.25	3.5
BOP (US$ million)												
Trade accounts	52	-32	161	213	-29	150	89	29	113	263	195	-243
Current accounts	-68	-146	108	127	-172	17	-74	-80	-46	122	29	-421
Overall balance	NA	NA	NA	109	-142	106	137	-9	-46	36	-30	-289
Narrow fiscal deficit (cedis billion)*	-31	-58	-122	-248	-190	-122	-592	-1,212	-1,678	-1,875	-3,041	-4,606
(as % GDP)	-1.4	-2.3	-4.3	-7.1	-4.1	-8.0	-9.1	-10.9	-8.0	-6.6	-7.1	-6.4
Money supply growth rate (broad money) (%)	22.2	27.3	33.1	12.2	33.9	22.4	25.7	37.3	54.4	25.6	47.7	43.3
Inflation CPI (%)	3.5	5.1	20.3	1.6	24.3	41.2	41.2	121.2	73.2	54.4	50.1	116.5
Exchange rate (cedis/US$)	1.02	1.03	1.33	1.149	1.149	1.149	1.149	1.149	2.75	2.75	2.75	2.75
Real interest rate (%)	3.3	-3.4	-3.5	-7.5	-6.7	-24.3	-47.2	-93.9	-79.0	-41.5	-45.4	-104.5
Fixed gross capital formation (as % GDP)	12.0	12.4	8.7	7.6	11.6	11.9	9.8	9.4	6.5	6.7	6.1	4.7

TABLE 3.1 Key macroeconomic indicators, 1982–93

	1982	1983	1984	1985	1986	1987	1988	1989	1990	1991	1992	1993
GDP (current cedis billion)	86.451	184.038	270.561	3,430	5,110	7,460	1,056	1,417	2,032	2,575	3,009	3,949
Real GDP growth (%)	6.92	4.56	8.0	5.1	5.2	4.8	5.6	5.1	3.3	5.3	3.9	5.0
BOP (US$ million)												
Trade accounts	18.3	-61	33	-185	-171	-300	-305	-399	-523	-554	-740	-964
Current accounts	-109	-174	-39	-263	-204	-225	-264	-315	-432	-454	-592	-815
Overall balance	-10	173	-144	115.5	-56.8	138.1	124.8	127.2	118.0	170.8	-124.3	-41.3
Narrow fiscal deficit (cedis billion)*	-4,364	4,514	-4,050	-5,453	2,966	2,966	9,894	18,047	12,874	48,560	-95,302	-91,875
(as % GDP)	-5.1	-2.5	-1.5	-1.5	0.6	1.2	0.9	1.3	0.6	2.0	-3.4	-2.5
Money supply growth rate (broad money) (%)	38.9	122.8	39.6	65.0	66.5	57.1	50.0	60.6	22.6	69.2	50.0	23.0
Inflation CPI (%)	19.2	128.7	2.6	10.4	24.6	39.8	31.4	25.2	37.2	18.0	10.1	25.0
Exchange rate (cedis/US$)	2.75	30.0	50.0	54.4	106.4	162.4	202.4	270.0	330.0	375.0	437.0	649.0
Real interest rate (%)	-9.3	-120.9	-22.3	-42.5	-14.8	-12.5	-6.8	-10.7	14.1	18.9	6.1	3.3
Fixed gross capital formation (as % GDP)	3.5	3.8	6.0	9.6	6.4	10.4	11.3	13.3	14.4	15.8	12.8	14.8

TABLE 3.1 Key macroeconomic indicators, 1994–2003

	1994	1995	1996	1997	1998	1999	2000	2001	2002	2003
GDP (current cedis billion)	5,186	7,752.6	11,339.2	14,113.4	17,296	20,579.8	27,152	38,014	47,764	65,262
Real GDP growth (%)	3.8	4.1	4.6	4.2	4.7	4.4	3.7	4.2	4.5	5.3
BOP (US$ million)										
Trade accounts	-626	-235.7	-336.9	-638.3	-805.7	-1,222	-842.9	-848.3	-641.2	-672.2
Current accounts	-466	-114.7	-324.7	-549.7	-443.1	-932.5	-1,283	-161.5	15.6	40.8
Overall balance	163.4	247.2	-20.4	26.7	107.9	-89.6	-258.5	144.1	39.8	367.3
Narrow fiscal deficit (cedis billions)*	103,950	66,762	-318,990	-296,381.4	-1,055,056	-1,337,687	2,199,312	-1,672,616	-2,953,125	-2,349,432
(as % GDP)	2.1	0.9	-3.0	-2.1	-6.1	-6.5	-8.1	-4.4	-6.3	-3.6
Money supply growth rate (broad money) (%)	46.0	33.4	32.1	46.3	21.2	16.2	38.3	46.1	61.0	NA
Inflation CPI (%)	24.9	60.0	46.5	27.9	15.7	12.4	25.2	35.0	32.9	15.9
Exchange rate (cedis/US$)	956.6	1,200	1,637.2	2,050.2	2,314.1	2,669.3	5,455.1	7,170.8	7,932.7	8,724.1
Real interest rate (%)	1.0	-32.8	-11.1	9.1	13.2	11.2	1.5	-1.2	1.8	2.4
Gross fixed capital formation (as % GDP)	15.9	21.1	20.6	23.6	22.8	24.0	20.2	19.8	18.2	23.0

Sources: IMF Balance of Payments Yearbook; World Bank 1988; World Bank 1995 Statistical Appendices; ISSER (1995–2003).

Note: * Narrow fiscal deficit excludes expenditures financed by foreign loans and grants.

leadership, political stability, the market and its limitations, the structure of the economy, the out-turn of selected macroeconomic variables in the growth process, sectoral and international considerations and selected non-growth-promoting practices.

In terms of organization, the next section provides analyses of the key issues and challenges of economic growth since the re-establishment of democratic governance and market liberalism. The final section looks at the conclusions from the study and gives suggestions about the way forward in the growth and development process of the country.

The challenges of economic growth

Background At this juncture, it would perhaps be appropriate to look at a snapshot of the macroeconomic landscape at the dawn of the democratic dispensation. This would provide us with the appropriate material to assess the performance of the economy and thereby identify the major challenges it has encountered and continues to encounter.

In general, the reform programme of the 1980s led to a turn-around in the economy by 1992. An average real rate of growth of about 5 per cent was attained and, from $274 in 1982, the GDP per capita rose to $441 by 1992. The inflationary rate that had reached triple digits (123 per cent) in 1983 fell to 10 per cent by 1992. However, the remarkable achievement of maintaining budgetary surpluses for the six previous years gave way to a huge deficit, equal to 3.4 per cent of GDP. In terms of the external balance, the balance of payments (BOP) remained in deficit at $124.3 million. Despite the modest improvements in the macro variables, at the sectoral level the structure of the economy remained virtually unchanged, with the agricultural sector still accounting for about 40 per cent of GDP. Savings and investment remained low and this was problematic for the growth effort. By 1992 it had become clear that the reform effort was not geared explicitly to simultaneous reduction in poverty. It operated on the untested hypothesis of the Bretton Woods institutions that economic growth would trickle down to the poor. There was every indication that poverty had escalated, rather than abated.

Against the backdrop of the above analysis, we consider below the various aspects of the objectives outlined above.

DEVELOPMENT GOAL As indicated above, Ghana, after almost a decade of the Economic Recovery and structural adjustment programmes (ERP/SAP) within a controlled economy, embarked on a liberalized form of economic management with the objective of attaining the status of an upper-middle-income country by the year 2020. In addition, the objective of

55

the government was vigorously to pursue measures to ensure the equitable distribution of the wealth that would be created in the process of development. This development perspective, christened Vision 2020, emanated from a twenty-five-year perspective planning concept which was given a philosophical expression in *Ghana – Vision 2020: The First Step (1996–2000)*. The framework was to consist of a set of five-year medium-term plans, the first of which was launched as the *Ghana – Vision 2020: The First Medium-term Development Plan (1997–2000)* in July 1997.

The plan strategy covered five priority areas of development: economic growth, human development, rural development, urban development and the creation of an enabling environment for growth and development.

The advent of the New Patriotic Party government extended the focus from outright growth and its developmental characteristics to a set of explicit poverty-reduction goals, as contained in *Ghana Poverty Reduction Strategy (2003–2005)*, launched in February 2003 as 'An Agenda for Growth and Prosperity'. In more specific terms, the document stipulates that the strategy is to 'ensure equitable growth, accelerated poverty reduction and the protection of the vulnerable and excluded from within a decentralized, democratic environment'.

By and large, some measure of progress has been, and continues to be, made. The economy continues to record positive growth rates, albeit below annual projected rates that will warrant the attainment of the primary goals of the *Vision*. Through fiscal and monetary measures, macroeconomic stability has been partially restored. However, lack of coordination between the ministry of finance and economic planning and implementing ministries and agencies constitutes a major obstacle to the success of the planning process.

It is largely in the context of the above propositions that the economic growth challenges identified below must be viewed.

ANALYTICAL APPROACH Analyses will be undertaken to assess the performance of the economy and, when data and information are available, international comparisons will be provided. As stated earlier, the common colonial heritage and similarities in the structure of their economies render comparison between Ghana and Malaysia an insightful exercise. In a few selected instances, South Korea will be included as an analytical control case.

Democratic environment and the problem of growth The analysis of growth and development in Ghana and, to a large extent, Sub-Saharan Africa in general, cannot be plausibly tackled in the Solow-type of neoclassical economic growth framework (Solow 1956). This framework applies more to mature democratic political systems where capital and technology, as engines of growth, are abundant. The complexities of the growth problem in Sub-Saharan Africa are such that political factors can at times play an overriding role in the determination of the type and direction of resource allocation for growth and poverty reduction. In the foregoing regard, the fundamental challenge during the period under review was the identification of leadership qualities that would be conducive to economic growth. Specifically, with regard to the Rawlings era, the challenge was simply how to metamorphose from a long-standing dictatorship into a democracy.

In the case of the Kufuor administration, the (presumably unexpected) election victory posed two challenges: (a) the need to pursue bold policy initiatives, despite the inexperience of the majority of cabinet members; and (b) the need to transform the economy from rent-seeking capitalism and conspicuous consumerism into a system that embraced venture capitalism.

A challenge common to both the Rawlings and Kufuor dispensations was/is how to maintain political stability and operate the growth process in an environment of virtually frictionless political debate and respect for property and human rights, as enshrined in the Constitution. This condition is of paramount importance, especially in situations where strong political will is required to formulate and implement unconventional but necessary long-term policies.

In addition, leadership dynamism was/is required to anticipate and, thereby, minimize the incidence of coups d'etat. In this respect, we posit that the transformation of the Rawlings regime – the Provisional National Defence Council (PNDC) – into the National Democratic Congress (NDC) administration did not provide any serious cause for national security alarm.

The foregoing stable political environment for economic growth could not be equally applied to the time the New Patriotic Party (NPP) unexpectedly took over from the NDC. The history of governance in Ghana would seem to indicate that such an unexpected and euphoric electoral victory would have had to be hastily accompanied by the provision of public and quasi-public goods to ensure the lasting support of interest groups, especially those within the armed forces and voter coalitions. So far, this concern poses a crucial challenge to and policy preoccupation of the Kufuor administration.

A subsidiary challenge that Vision 2020 growth policy-makers cannot run away from is the fact that almost all the newly industrializing countries (NICs) in Asia (also known as the Asian Tigers) and other fast-growing

57

Asian economies that Ghana wants to emulate, especially Malaysia and South Korea, emerged from poverty to their present status through the application of a degree of dictatorship and government interventionism in the market. The big question, therefore, is whether there could evolve an optimal application of the democracy process that would entail suitable elements of benevolent dictatorship for the attainment of the stated goals of growth and development.

Additionally, it must be noted that the NICs had the following commonalities that a potential replicator must take into account: high savings and investment; export promotion as a priority; and the availability of appropriate manpower (educated and skilled) for the development effort.

The degree of market orientation and government intervention The concept of the market as a promoter of efficiency in economic activity has been well established since Adam Smith posited the concept of the invisible hand of the market. In neoclassical terms, market engenders competition which in turn promotes efficiency in the allocation of resources and, therefore, economic growth and wealth creation. However, the market does not guarantee equitable distribution of incomes and the reduction of poverty.

Under the World Bank/IMF reforms of the 1980s, market orientation became a conditionality for aid during the multi-party democracy era. A large degree of market orientation of the economy, therefore, existed before the Kufuor administration declared its dispensation as 'the golden age of business'. For analytical reasons, let us assume a hypothetical optimal level of market orientation which engenders economic growth and simultaneously reduces the incidence of poverty. In this regard, the Rawlingsian dispensation must be construed as emerging from a revolutionary background that favoured a market orientation to the left of the optimal market set-up while the Kufuorian market orientation concept seems to have been to the right of the optimum and, as such, having the potential for income inequity. Thus, the challenge has been – and continues to be – how to make a fine-tuned determination of the optimal level of market orientation and how to attain that optimum. The foregoing constitutes an intellectual challenge and a conundrum of empirical investigation for policy formulators and researchers.

DIAGRAMMATIC EXPOSITION OF THE GROWTH–MARKET ORIENTATION CORRELATION We provide below a cursory depiction of the impact of market orientation on economic growth during the period under consideration. For this purpose, we disaggregate GDP into: (a) total government

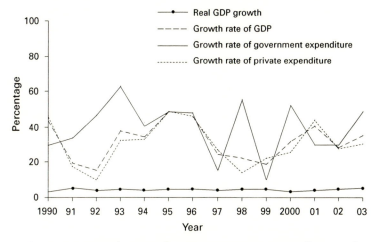

Figure 3.1 Growth rates of GDP, government expenditure and private expenditure in Ghana, 1990–2003

expenditures as proxy for public sector activity (controlled economy); and (b) private sector activity (as proxy for market orientation). The growth rates of the two disaggregates are graphed along with the real GDP growth rates and the nominal GDP growth rates in Figure 3.1.

Diagrammatically, the correlation between the real GDP growth rate and private sector expenditure growth is not easily discernible. However, nominal GDP growth rates can be observed as showing a positive correlation with the degree of market orientation, especially notable from 1992 to 1995 and again from 2000 to 2001. In sum, it could be said that there exists at least some positive correlation between market orientation and economic growth.

THE TRAJECTORY OF, AND CONSTRAINTS ON, GROWTH: GENERAL ANALYSIS OF THE TRENDS Even though the reform exercise in the 1980s enabled the reversal of negative rates of growth in previous years, growth performance has had a chequered history since the country was returned to constitutional rule in 1992. The democratic process itself has been extremely costly, especially in terms of conducting the general elections and establishing the organs of democratic governance (including parliament and the Electoral Commission). As stated earlier, after six years (since 1986) of budgetary surpluses, a huge budgetary deficit (narrow budget, i.e. excluding grants) amounting to 3.4 per cent of GDP was recorded in 1992. The magnitude of the deficit could be categorized as a fiscal shock that adversely affected the growth process. One of the ramifications of the shock was the crowding out of investors (denying them funds which could have been used to build businesses) and the consequent fall in the real rate of growth from 5.3 per cent in 1991 to as low as 3.9 per cent in 1992. In a poor country where resource constraints had long prevented accelerated growth, it was tempting for analysts, especially those who were socialist revolutionaries, to question both the financial and social cost-effectiveness of the democratic process. However, it has been shown empirically that a democratic environment actually enhances the growth process (Tsikata 1996).

We examine below some of the salient issues that have been raised by the policy-making establishments and research analysts as constituting the constraints on and, therefore, the challenges of economic growth in Ghana.

Out-turns of selected macroeconomic variables From Table 3.1, period averages of key macroeconomic variables have been computed to enable us to compare out-turns during the controlled and liberalized periods (see Table 3.2). The infusion of capital during the ERP/SAP led to a remarkable average growth of about 5 per cent from 1983 to 1991, compared to a slow-down in the liberalized period of 1992–2000 (Rawlings era) in which the economy grew at an average rate of about 4.3 per cent per annum. The latter out-turn was partly due to the fact that donor financing had substantially declined while the private sector remained stagnant in growth-promoting activities. This has been followed by a slight recovery of almost 4.7 per cent during the 2001–03 period (Kufuor era). This could be explained by improvements in cocoa (due to the crisis in Côte d'Ivoire) and gold earnings and, probably, the gradual growth of investor confidence in the 'golden age of business'.

The rapid depreciation of the currency (the cedi), which occurred during the controlled period, gave way to a relatively more stable currency during the liberalized period. On average, the cedi depreciated by 37 per cent per annum. There was further stability during the 2001–03 period; on average, the exchange rate variations dropped from 37 per cent to 17 per cent. This was because improvements in foreign exchange earnings, remittances from Ghanaians abroad and market interventions by the Bank of Ghana eased pressure on the cedi. In sum, the cedi was more stable from 2001 to 2003 than in the earlier periods. The assertive autonomy that the Bank of Ghana has assumed recently and the establishment of the Monetary Policy Committee (MPC) to superintend the monetary issues in the economy pose a challenge of sound monetary management that should confer further stability on the cedi.

TABLE 3.2 Period average out-turns of selected macroeconomic variables

	1983–91	1992–2000	2001–03
Average real rate of growth	4.62	4.27	4.66
Exchange rate: average rate of change (%)	146	37	17
Inflation CPI	39.43	35.62	26.93
Narrow fiscal deficit	0.11	-3.19	-4.77
Balance of payments: overall balance	21.06	1.23	231.77

Source: Author's calculations from Table 3.1.

The transition from a controlled to a liberalized economy has not had a substantial impact on inflation. In the former case, the annual average stood at almost 40 per cent. It dropped to about 36 per cent during the 1992–2000 period and 27 per cent from 2001 to 2003. Thus, the rather lofty goal of attaining a single-digit inflation rate has been impossible to achieve.

The budgetary deficit stands out as one fiscal item that has deteriorated over the entire period of liberalization. As we observed earlier, operating the democratic system per se entails costly expenditure outlays which are not matched by revenue growth. The revenue-generating quota for the revenue agencies to attain has always been exceeded, making it a conjectural exercise. The inherent challenge is, therefore, to devise a realistic quota system that will engage the ingenuity of tax formulators and administrators not only to widen the tax net, but also optimally to maximize the tax returns. As in most Sub-Saharan African countries, adequate incentives for tax officials will constitute the quid pro quo for a meaningful outcome.

The structure of the economy Changes in the structure of an economy constitute a major indicator as to whether or not an economy is on the path of development. The potency of structural changes is premised on the fact that flexibilities in structures of the economy enable resource mobility from low productivity areas to high growth-promoting areas; the resource transfers could be inter- or intra-sectoral. Even though the Ghanaian economy has undergone measured growth since the reforms were initiated, the structure of the economy has remained virtually the same. In the context of our definition – economic growth plus structural changes – there has been economic growth without the structural changes that could technically qualify the economy as being on a development path. As far back as 1965, Szereszewski observed that ever since the economy

61

Challenges of economic growth

of Ghana had undergone structural changes between 1891 and 1911 (as the result of the introduction of cocoa and mining industries), not much subsequent transformation had taken place. Indeed, Killick (2000) and Aryeetey and Fosu (2004) have further emphasized the fact that the sluggish growth of the economy has emanated from the lack of structural changes in the economy over the last four decades. On annual average, agriculture, industry and the services sectors contributed 36.6 per cent, 25 per cent and 28.6 per cent, respectively, to total GDP. In a dynamic economy that is undergoing development, the share of agriculture will normally decrease while the shares of industry and services increase. Despite the growing market orientation of the economy, the dominant contributor in the services sector has been government services, which contribute about 11 per cent out of the sector's 29 per cent.

The total factor productivity (TFP) problem Raising factor productivity is crucial in the growth process. Market orientation tends to promote gains in factor productivity (productivity of capital, labour, land and other resources), mainly through the firm pursuit of profits and competition in the market, both of which encourage the efficient allocation of resources. We adopt the method used by O'Connell and Ndulu (2000) and Aryeetey and Fosu (2004) – that is, the Collins and Bosworth growth accounting table – in analysing TFP growth during the period. Outcomes for Ghana and Sub-Saharan Africa (SSA) are compared in Table 3.3.

It can be observed in the Table that, although output per worker during the entire period (1960–97) fell by 0.12 per cent, it rose by 1.27 per cent during the period of analysis (1990–97). It is, however, interesting to observe that output per worker growth in the controlled period (1985–89) was much higher (2.32 per cent) than that in the period of analysis, thus indicating a lower performance of market forces. In both periods, the Ghanaian economy on average performed much better than the economies of SSA as a whole. The contribution of physical capital per worker in the liberal period (0.75 per cent) was higher than the previous period's value (which was in addition negative: -0.40 per cent). For the whole period (1960–97), SSA countries as a group performed better than Ghana, 0.61 per cent growth compared to 0.51 per cent. The results for education were the reverse for the periods. Contribution of education per worker during the controlled period (0.72 per cent) was higher than in the liberal period (0.41 per cent). This could be explained by the fact that the gradual curtailment of government subvention for education had impacted negatively on quality and productivity of new labour market entrants. The impact of education on the labour force in Ghana is, however, larger than the average for all

TABLE 3.3 The Collins and Bosworth growth accounting-based decomposition of sources of growth, Ghana vs. SSA [in brackets]

Period	Growth in real GDP per worker	Contribution of physical capital per worker	education per worker	residual
1960–64	1.56 [1.26]	3.02 [0.86]	0.49 [0.14]	-1.96 [0.26]
1965–69	-0.28 [1.60]	0.94 [1.03]	0.78 [0.18]	-2.01 [0.39]
1970–74	2.41 [2.29]	0.40 [1.22]	0.20 [0.20]	1.81 [0.87]
1975–79	-4.22 [-0.10]	-0.13 [0.81]	0.23 [0.27]	-4.32 [-1.18]
1980–84	-3.94 [-1.28]	-0.93 [0.41]	0.66 [0.30]	-3.66 [-1.99]
1985–89	2.32 [0.64]	-0.40 [0.06]	0.72 [0.30]	2.01 [0.28]
1990–97	1.27 [-1.55]	0.75 [-0.14]	0.41 [0.18]	0.11 [-1.59]
Total: 1960–97	-0.12 [0.41]	0.52 [0.61]	0.50 [0.23]	-1.15 [-0.42]

Sub-Saharan African countries. As Aryeetey and Fosu (2004) maintained, the latter might be due to the large investments made by Ghana during the post-independence era. The challenge in terms of raising total factor productivity will be to ascertain areas where there are market failures requiring government intervention. Once this is achieved, the onus will again rest on the government to intervene in the market, especially in the provision of the social infrastructure that will facilitate long-term investments in directly productive activities (Hirschman 1958).

The human capital formation problem It is now an accepted development paradigm that human capital constitutes the most important ingredient of economic growth (World Bank 2000). There are three key ingredients taken into account in the human capital formation process: education, health and nutrition. Because of the cost and long gestation period, especially in terms of education, human capital formation has doubtlessly been one of the most difficult policies to implement in Sub-Saharan Africa. In highly depressed rural areas, the opportunity cost of schooling is the loss in output and/or productivity on the farm.

Ghana, since independence, has invested comparatively more than most Sub-Saharan Africa (SSA) countries in education, especially at the secondary and tertiary levels. However, there have been cracks in aspects of the educational system which render it inconsistent with the goals of rapid growth and development. This is especially the case at the secondary level. We provide below selected aspects of the educational system that posed challenges during the period under review.

THE SECONDARY SCHOOL SYSTEM A critical challenge to the educational system stems from quality of products from the secondary schools. The three-year senior secondary school (SSS) system churned out huge numbers of pre-university students whose academic credentials constituted a source of worry for university officials, especially in the sciences, mathematics and functional English. To arrest the declining trends, the Kufuor administration has now fully endorsed the four-year concept advocated by many educationists. It is hoped that the new system will provide the requisite foundation for tertiary education that in turn will produce the calibre of professionals needed for the growth and development of the country. This constitutes a challenge which must be met with dedication and backed by adequate budgetary commitments.

THE TERTIARY EDUCATION SYSTEM The rapid growth of private tertiary education poses a challenge to the public tertiary institutions which must adopt measures to retain qualified lecturers/personnel and to attract young and promising lecturers with the right conditions of service. This brings into sharp focus the need for the sensitization of the general public to the positive correlation between quality education with appropriate facilities and funding.

The savings gap, capital flight and transformation problems and venture capitalism Growth models in general have emphasized the role of savings in capital formation. A case in point is the Harrod-Domar-type of model in which, given an incremental capital–output ratio (ICOR), specified saving ratios will generate various growth rates. In the South East Asian countries that are experiencing some of the fastest growth rates in the world, the saving habit is well entrenched in the people from Confucian teachings. Low incomes and, to some extent, a high propensity to consume instead of save and invest in most of Sub-Saharan Africa have often led to a savings gap that has to be filled to accelerate growth. Compounding the savings problem is the growing incidence of capital flight in which the rich and famous search for safe havens to keep their money abroad. The problems of development emanating from the deficit have, at times, been lessened through external sources of finance. In this regard, the challenge that the economy faced during the period under review, and continues to face now, has been how to cultivate an appropriate savings habit through financial market operations and/or moral persuasion of the rich to keep their money in Ghana.

Another aspect of the problem is the situation where savings are available but transforming them into the required capital for development is difficult because the capital market tends to be imperfect in poor countries.

Conceptually, the transformation problem in Ghana can be attributed to either the lack of opportunities for productive capital formation or the cultural underpinnings which encourage rent-seeking activities. In the extreme case scenario, the savings gap problem stems from the tendency towards risk avoidance based on the history of expropriations during the revolutionary era. The challenge here is how to foster the emergence of authentic venture capitalists whose vision will transcend rent-seeking commercial activities. Such people would have the motivation to undertake hardcore directly productive activities with new technological innovations. As Aryeetey and Fosu (2004) maintain, there has been sparse technological investment in the economy because the source of investment has not been the private sector but rather government provision of basic infrastructure.

Conspicuous consumerism versus venture capitalism Another major constraint on growth in the era of liberalization is the lack of capacity to control conspicuous consumption. Experience has shown that trade liberalization without adequate fiscal policy safeguards results in foreign goods flooding the market which, eventually, tends to choke off local producers. With rent-seeking (abnormal profit-seeking) behaviour, windfall gains find their way into conspicuous consumption at the expense of productive capital formation. This seems to be underpinned by an emerging Ghanaian concept of the need for instantaneous acquisition of wealth and the consequent materialist interpretation of any financial success thereof. Sumptuary taxes (taxes on luxuries) have had limited success because of loopholes and compromises by tax administrators and politicians. A good case in point is the inflow of upper-end luxury goods (such as expensive cars) which do not correlate with economic growth; in fact, this trend rather creates external diseconomies that constitute a drain on public expenditures. Another pervasive occurrence is the prioritization of some social phenomena which are growth dampening. A classic example is the proverbial Ghanaian spirito-material consideration of the dead and the attendant elaborate funerals. The labour-intensive and productivity-reducing *one-week, forty-day etc.* celebrations, aimed at adding value to the respect accorded the dead, impose time and resource constraints on the growth effort. The growth challenge here is simply the ability to muster political courage to devise optimal fiscal instruments that will either coerce or entice people to reprioritize expenditures in favour of growth-promoting investments. However, at times, politicians themselves are among the most guilty. They seemingly want to exude what might aptly be described as politico-economic Veblenism – looking politically rich and famous. In

65

this instance, the politician faces the challenge of adopting a growth-and-development-oriented attitude towards consumption.

Business growth and investment/ownership challenge The growth of business is key to sustainable economic growth and development. An economy accelerates its pace of industrialization as businesses evolve from sole proprietorship, through partnership, to limited liability companies. In Ghana, most of the limited liability companies have a majority or substantial foreign equity component. The development of strictly home-grown companies from sole proprietorship to partnership is not very common. Possible reasons include: (a) the desire to maintain freedom of operation; (b) the tendency to take parochial positions in family businesses in order to ensure family financial security; and (c) the desire to avoid rivalry and conflicts concerning business policy and property rights. The culture of business growth through partnership formation and business mergers is therefore impeded by these factors. The lack of this basic foundation for industrial growth poses a challenge that must be vigorously addressed, especially at a time that has been declared 'the golden age of business'.

Sectoral considerations

We now consider the performance of the leading sub-sectors within the agricultural, industrial and service sectors and their impact on macro-economic growth during the period under review.

Growth in the agricultural sector The case for productivity and output increases in the agricultural sector in Ghana derives from mainstream development economics. It is posited (Johnston and Mellor 1961; Kuznets 1966) that increases in agricultural productivity and output can lead, inter alia, to:

- the generation of jobs and accompanying incomes for rural dwellers
- increases in total food supplies and the dampening of inflationary pressures and agitation for higher wages by urban workers
- foreign exchange earnings through exports of the surplus output
- capital acquisition for investments in directly productive activities and infrastructural development.

These instrumental values of agriculture pose the most fundamental challenge to the development process in most less developed countries (LDCs). Ironically, however, they have often been accorded limited attention in many Sub-Saharan African countries, including some of the countries with fast-growing populations and vast tracks of fertile agricultural land.

Countries lucky enough to possess strategic resources such as oil simply neglect the sector – a tendency referred to as 'Dutch disease'.

Ghana's agricultural sector has some distinct features which impose constraints on productivity and increases in output. In general, agriculture is rain-fed and as the seasonal rain patterns change, at times reaching drought proportions, agricultural productivity and output are negatively affected. As Nyanteng and Seini (2000) pointed out, fluctuations in agricultural output and growth are basically determined by fluctuations in the weather, especially the rainfall pattern. Second, the poor condition of access roads to producing centres has been a major hindrance, especially during bumper seasons that coincide with the periods of heavy rainfall. Third, the unilateral removal of subsidies on agricultural inputs, especially those on food crops for domestic consumption, has not only adversely affected agricultural productivity, but also has helped to fuel inflationary pressures to the detriment of the poor, especially workers in the urban areas. This is a policy initiative that has been criticized on the basis that, even in mature and market-based economies such as the United States of America and Japan, some subsidies have been retained as safety nets for poor farmers.

COCOA SUB-SECTOR Growth in the cocoa sub-sector in particular was due to the positive response to price incentives provided under the reform exercise. A good example of using price incentives to boost production of cocoa was provided during the 1998 crop season when the world price of cocoa was falling. Government maintained the producer price at C2.25 million per tonne. That amounted to an average producer price of approximately 68 per cent of the freight-on-board (fob) price. Despite the price adjustment initiative over the period, the producer price in Ghana was always below the prices offered in neighbouring countries, a strategy that encouraged the smuggling of significant quantities of cocoa across the borders. Table 3.4 shows the trends in output and producer prices during the period.

One can observe the oscillatory pattern of production growth. In the 2000/01 crop season, for example, output fell by 2 per cent (from 436,600 tonnes) partly due to severe blackpod disease. It declined further by almost 13 per cent in the next season. Despite government intervention through mass spraying and producer price increases, the official target of 700,000 tonnes by 2009/10 seems currently out of reach and would require extensive policy adjustments to achieve. Although the incidence of smuggling has been difficult to determine, producer price differentials between Ghana and neighbouring countries, especially Côte d'Ivoire, have been partially blamed for the declines in output recorded. By implication, the price effect on producers is yet adequately to manifest itself in terms of output increases.

TABLE 3.4 Cocoa production trends and nominal producer prices, 1990/91–2002/03

Year/period	Cocoa (tonnes)	Cedis per tonne
1990/91	293.4	224,000
1991/92	242.8	251,200
1992/93	312.1	258,000
1993/94	254.7	308,000
1994/95	309.5	700,000
1995/96	403.9	840,000
1996/97	322.5	1,200,000
1997/98	409.4	1,800,000
1998/99	397.7	2,250,000
1999/00	436.9	2,250,000
2000/01	389.8	3,475,000
2001/02	340.6	6,200,000
2002/03	496.8	8,500,000
Average 1989/90–1993/94	279.6	–
Average 1994/95–1998/99	368.6	–

Source: Cocobod.

ISSER (2002) suggests that the declining output resulting from smuggling indicates that the goal of getting the 'price right' is not being achieved.

It is worth noting that producer price determination has been based on three key factors: (a) price increases in the world market; (b) price trends in Côte d'Ivoire (to minimize the incidence of smuggling); and (c) depreciation of the cedi.

From the analysis above, the sub-sectoral growth challenges would, therefore, include, inter alia, the task of not only getting the right price that would substantially raise productivity and output as well as curtail smuggling, but which would also leave revenue residuals for fulfilling budgetary obligations.

It is worth pointing out that besides cocoa and timber (traditional exports), there is a gradual growth in non-traditional agricultural exports, especially pineapples and tuna. See Table 3.5 for trends in export earnings from non-traditional exports. The challenges posed during the period under study include (a) accessing markets with the products; (b) raising quality and quantity of Ghanaian products in competing markets; and (c) honouring contracts, for example, timely deliveries of perishable exports to their destinations. Proximity to the European market confers a huge advantage in the foregoing regard. A limited government intervention in terms of

TABLE 3.5 Foreign revenue from non-traditional agricultural commodities

Year/period	Total non-trad. ($ million)	Agric. non-trad ($ million)	% agric. non-trad
1995	159.7	27.4	17.2
1996	275.6	50.3	18.2
1997	329.1	57.4	17.5
1998	401.7	77.8	19.4
1999	404.4	84.5	20.9
2000	400.7	74.5	18.6
2001	459.6	82.0	17.8
2002	504.3	85.7	17.0
Average 1990–94	77.0	29.9	38.8
Average 1995–99	314.1	59.5	18.9

Source: Ghana Export Promotion Council.

adjustment in regulations and financial support to access markets might in the long run have a positive impact on the national budget.

THE AGRICULTURAL SECTOR AND RURAL DEVELOPMENT NEXUS The challenges of agricultural growth in the context of the overall growth of the economy cannot be divorced from the challenges of rural development. This is primarily because 65–8 per cent of Ghanaians live in the rural areas where agriculture is the main source of income. Also, the major challenges of growth and development – poverty, illiteracy and disease – are mainly rural phenomena. The more human capital formation features prominently as the most important source of growth (World Bank 2000), the more the onus rests on government to find the resources to provide at least some minimum level of education and health standards that will raise agricultural output and productivity. Ironically, the relatively educated and vibrant youth, especially those who acquire education in the urban areas, resent returning to rural life where their marginal productivities would be higher in agriculture than in most urban endeavours.

The need for effective mobilization of skilled manpower to utilize the country's rich resources in the rural area has been fully recognized by the various governments. A good reference point in this regard is the *Ghana – Vision 2020* document (Ghana Government 1995: 66). The primary challenges for accelerated rural development outlined in the document include, inter alia, the need to:

- reduce disparity between urban and rural areas
- upgrade rural areas economically, socially and environmentally
- reduce hard core poverty and deprivation in the rural areas
- increase monetization, savings and investment among the rural dwellers.

The establishment of the rural and community banks (RCBs) was partially aimed at solving some of the problems outlined above, especially the problem of saving and investment in activities that enhance productivity and growth. However, despite control mechanisms enforced by the Bank of Ghana, mismanagement remains rife. By September 2003, 115 RCBs were in operation, out of which 100 were classified as 'satisfactory' and 15 as 'mediocre'. As at the end of September 2003, their combined assets stood at C1,066.1 billion.

Second, the District Assembly Common Fund (DACF), established by parliament as a development-oriented scheme to promote participatory development, has also been fraught with controversies between district chief executives (DCEs) and parliamentarians of the districts in terms of control of funds and priority development activities where the funds could be channelled.

There is no doubt that both the RCBs and the DACF constitute important sources of development finance. The key problem of lack of effective monitoring and local politics will have to be addressed in order for the institutions to confer maximum growth impact on the rural economies.

Growth in the industrial sector Rapid industrial growth has been of the utmost concern to government since the early days of independence. Nkrumah (rather unrealistically) indicated that even though it took the developed countries over one hundred years to industrialize, it was imperative for Ghana to shorten the development timeframe to ten years. Import substitution industrialization strategy was chosen as the means to achieve directly that lofty ambition. State-owned enterprises (SOEs) were established for manufacturing and ancillary services. Management criteria were determined more by political expediency than by the fundamental efficiency conditions that would enable the corporations to at least break even. In some of the ailing corporations, operating costs such as salaries had to be paid from government subventions. In sum, the SOEs were not as active in propelling the growth and industrialization process as had been expected. Meanwhile, the private sector was being muzzled and became lethargic because of the long history of outright expropriation or forced equity participation by government. The prospect of long-term investment in the real sector was viewed with much trepidation.

TABLE 3.6 Real GDP and sectoral growth rates (%), 1995-2002

Year/period	Real GDP	Agriculture	Services	Industry
1995	4	3.7	4.2	4.1
1996	4.6	5.2	4.2	4.2
1997	4.2	4.3	6.5	6.4
1998	4.7	5.1	6	3.2
1999	4.4	3.9	5	4.9
2000	3.7	2.1	5.4	3.8
2001	4.2	4	5.1	2.9
2002	4.5	4.4	4.7	4.7
Average 1990-94	4.3	1.1	7	4.4
Average 1995-99	4.4	4.4	5.3	4.7
Average 2000-02	4.13	3.5	5.07	3.8

Source: ISSER (1995-2003).

The advent of democratic rule and liberalization of the economy brought a ray of hope for industrial sector growth. Ironically, short-term rent-seeking investments (especially trading) became and, indeed, continue to be more attractive and viable than growth-promoting ventures. As a result, there has been sluggish growth in the industrial sector. Table 3.6 shows that in the second half of the past decade, growth rates in the industrial sector in two out of six years (1996 and 1998) were below the respective GDP growth rates. Even in the years in which industrial sector growth rates were higher than GDP growth, the difference could not be regarded as significant enough to propel the economy to the projected annual rate of 5 per cent or more, not to mention the targeted annual industrial growth rate of 9.3 per cent under the *Ghana – Vision 2020: The First Step (1996-2000)*.

An example of the effort of the government to deepen the economy's market orientation could be found in the divesture of the SOEs. Many of the enterprises had become a drain on public finances and, also influenced by donor insistence on acceleration of the pace of liberalization of the economy, the government decided to privatize most SOEs. In general, the sale of SOEs to the private sector was slow partly because: (a) potential investors were wary of future changes in government policy and their repercussions (especially the confiscation of company assets); (b) there was low demand in the domestic market for products because of competition from domestic importers of 'superior' foreign goods at cheaper prices, a direct result of the liberalization programme; and (c) some of the assets were virtually non-assets because they were in poor operational condition.

Challenges of economic growth

71

Based on the issues raised above, the challenge to government is to demonstrate its credibility with strict adherence to the constitutional provisions protecting private property in order to create the requisite confidence in the market. In addition, social cost–benefit analyses may have to be undertaken to ascertain the degree to which government may have to assist in recapitalizing the assets to render them financially viable and attractive in the market.

The monetary outcome of sales was not as lucrative as might have been expected. However, the privatization exercise has substantially curtailed government expenditure on subventions. There was also a financial turn-around for some of the ailing firms. Perhaps the most significant impact of this exercise is the ongoing expansion in output, capital formation and employment generation in the privatized enterprises.

Available information indicates that employment generation in some of the enterprises was quite significant. For example, ISSER (1999) observes that, within or after four years of privatization, a number of important divested firms increased their employment levels significantly; for example, the Tema Steel Company increased its number of employees from 130 to 584, representing a rise of almost 350 per cent.

IMPACT OF THE MINING SUB-SECTOR The mining sub-sector, led by the gold industry, has continued to dominate exports in its contribution to foreign exchange earnings since it took over the leading position from cocoa in 1990. Table 3.7 indicates sub-period averages in output and earnings spanning the period 1970 to 2003. During the pre-reform period (1970–82), output growth on average was negative (-5.8 per cent) but this trend was reversed in the reform era, which recorded strong growth of almost 13 per cent during the 1983–92 period. On average, there was a slow-down in output growth (8.6 per cent) during the liberalized period because it coincided with a decline in ore discoveries, distortions in electricity supplies that reached their peak during the energy crisis in 1998, the offloading of gold reserves by European central banks, the IMF and the Russians on the market which, in turn, forced prices downwards. All of these had a negative impact on output and revenue generation in the gold industry.

The overriding importance of the mining sector in the economy is not adequately matched by forward and backward linkages to other economic growth-promoting activities. This is because, with the exception of the semi-skilled labour force, most of the inputs are imported and the mineral products are exported with little or no value added. In other words, the multiplier effect that will constitute a major push factor for accelerated

TABLE 3.7 Period averages of gold production and revenues

Period	Average output (oz)	Output growth (abso)	Average output growth rate	Average revenue	Average revenue growth rate	Average price (p/oz)	Average price change
1970–82	25,926.29	-31,450.02	-5.77	62,392.85	14.66	213.3	44.41
1983–92	467,220.86	66,115.28	12.9	147,241.80	12.1	385.4	-3.72
1993–2003	1,991,438.84	118,058.23	8.64	640,907.82	8.58	327.38	5.63
2000–03	2,325,512.75	-63,532.75	-2.49	709,782.50	4.69	329.13	7.69

Source: Author's computation from Minerals Commission and Bank of Ghana data.

growth is lower than would be the case if mining activities were properly integrated into the economy. This, therefore, constitutes one of the two main challenges – the other being environmental considerations – that require policy initiatives to address.

ENVIRONMENTAL CONSIDERATIONS Closely linked to mining activities is the problem of environmental degradation and consequent food insecurity in affected areas. The advent of surface mining in the gold industry in the mid-1980s added a crucial environmental dimension to the growth problem. Surface mining in major mining areas such as Tarkwa and Abosso in the Western Region entails the degradation of large tracts of fertile agricultural land and, at times, contamination of rivers through chemical spillage (mercury and cyanide). The implications transcend just the outcomes of compensation for displaced people and ruined farms. The intergenerational inequity problems pose a challenge for a 'win-win' approach in which mining activities are allowed to generate resources for growth, but appropriate restoration programmes are undertaken for future agro- and forest-based activities (Songsore et al. 1994). It must be conceded that the Environmental Protection Agency (EPA) has been quite active in its supervision of mining activities. However, the perennial foreign exchange demands on the economy often tend to take precedence over acceptable environmental requirements for sustainable growth. The overall sluggish growth of the economy and the horizontal and vertical escalation of poverty would indicate that the challenge of sustainable growth (growth with environmental sustainability) might be difficult to attain, at least for some time to come.

THE SIGNIFICANCE OF THE SALT INDUSTRY The government of Ghana has for some time recognized the huge potential of the salt industry in the diversification and growth of the economy. This vast potential of the industry in transforming the economy through foreign exchange earnings has earned the mineral the accolade of being the 'white gold' of the economy. Indeed, among the several ongoing 'presidential initiatives' for growth and development, the salt initiative appears to be the one with most promise. Regrettably, the political economy of the industry's actors has retarded the full exploitation of this strategic resource.

At the root of the problem is the lack of cohesion among the local chiefs of Ada (the main producing area in the country) over property rights and royalties, which has made the Songhor Lagoon salt deposits a controversial asset over the years. The government take-over of Vacuum Salts Limited, the operating company, during the PNDC administration, provided a brief respite. The advent of the Kufuor administration resuscitated the long-standing agitation by the local people to repossess all production rights. Resolving the key production issues in all the production areas constitutes one of the key challenges to the administration.

This is especially imperative because of the potential impact of the industry on the economy. Conservative estimates put long-term output at over 2 million tons per annum. Attainment of this goal should reorder the contribution of industry to GDP significantly and help to reduce poverty in the Ada area. Proximity of the Nigerian oil industry, a major consumer of salt, provides unique locational advantages which must be fully exploited.

The services sector In the services sector there are two major issues that have posed, and continue to pose, challenges in the process of growth: development of the tourism sub-sector and the alarming brain drain phenomenon. Analyses of these two areas of concern are given below.

TOURISM Tourism is the third largest foreign exchange earner in the economy. Prior to achieving this status (that is, before 1995), the sub-sector was largely underexploited due to lack of facilities, especially hotel accommodation and restaurants, which could appeal to a foreign clientele. In response, the government put in operation the Master Tourism Plan in 1996 and tried to promote private sector investment in the industry. There are indications that the North American, European (especially British) and Caribbean markets are underexploited and, therefore, can constitute a huge source of tourist inflow to boost the country's foreign exchange earning capacity. Against the backdrop of foreign exchange earning difficulties in the country, the projected earnings in 2003 ($600 million) constitute a substantial input to the development effort. This amount would be five times the earnings in 1991.

Besides vigorous overseas promotion of Ghana as a good tourist destination, the challenge will be to inculcate in the youth and the middle class the essence of domestic tourism and, therefore, the need optimally to allocate some of their time and income to undertake local tourism expeditions. A major concern of tourism observers is the unprofessionalism at times demonstrated by officials at vantage points such as the airport and tourist destinations. In general, good attitudes are a crucial determinant of the potential viability of tourism expansion and therefore constitute a challenge that Ghana must vigorously address in order to succeed as a major destination in Africa.

TABLE 3.8 Brain drain of health workers, 1995–2002

Main cadres	1995	1996	1997	1998	1999	2000	2001	2002	Total
GPs/medical officers	56	68	59	58	68	50	60	68	487
Dentists	2	3	3	3	4	2	2	2	21
Pharmacists	29	27	35	53	49	24	58	77	352
Nurses*	195	182	174	161	215	207	205	214	1,553

*Includes general nurses, midwives, public health nurses, intensive care nurses and peri-operative nurses.
Source: Ministry of Health.

THE BRAIN DRAIN AND BRAIN GAIN ARGUMENTS Despite the recent cracks in the junior and senior secondary school systems as indicated earlier, the comparative proficiency of professionals from Ghana's tertiary educational system has been acknowledged in the sub-region, East Africa and, to some extent, in North America and Britain. Shortages of personnel in the health sub-sectors of North America and Britain and the attractive conditions of service available have created opportunities for Ghanaian professionals seeking greener pastures, much to the detriment of the country's development effort. The health delivery system has been a major victim of the brain drain, as depicted in Table 3.8. The rate of exodus of medical officers and nurses paints a gloomy picture of the future of the health delivery system in the country.

From 1995 to 2002, a total of 487 doctors left the country, an average of over 60 doctors per annum. During the same period, 1,553 nurses, an average of 194 per annum, also went abroad to practise. Various efforts made to arrest the situation through incentives have not kept pace with expectations of health professionals. As a partial solution, Cuban medical workers have been imported for some time now, to minimize the impact of the loss of personnel.

It has been argued that the exit of Ghanaian professionals should not be construed narrowly as being unpatriotic since they make substantial remittances home to ease the foreign exchange pressure on the economy (the so-called 'brain gain' concept). Although the argument sounds plausible, a more complete picture would require a social cost–benefit analysis between the financial impact made on the economy from the said remittances and the impact health professionals practising in Ghana would have made (the counterfactuals). In general, it appears doubtful that the country can afford to train professionals, including health workers, with scarce resources only to lose them to advanced economies in exchange for remittances without proper assessment of the socio-economic net gain to the economy.

International perspectives of the growth problem

GLOBALIZATION AND EXPORT-LED GROWTH As far back as 1776, Adam Smith, in *The Wealth of Nations*, recognized the need for countries to expand into the export market and specialize in the production of particular goods. Today's globalization of the world's economy implies competitive efficiency in virtually all international transactions. Quality requirements in industrialized markets, against the backdrop of falling commodity prices, make it imperative for Sub-Saharan countries such as Ghana to penetrate new markets with new exports produced under highly efficient conditions. Tariffs and quotas, despite the various declarations for free trade, constitute a disincentive to the growth of exports. The general case for Africa's active participation in the globalization of its economies stems from the continent's marginalization which, in turn, can be attributed to 'isolationist policies and close-economy approach to development, such as high tariff barriers and import substituting strategy ... The appeal to open up to global markets is based on a simple but powerful premise: economic integration will improve economic performance' (Ajayi 2000). In the light of the foregoing, the modest strides made in the development of non-traditional exports (NTEs) should provide an indication that a concerted approach to research and development of other NTEs will go a long way to boost the country's export earnings. The classic case of the Malaysians who came to Ghana to understudy oil palm development some two decades ago in their effort to diversify their export base should open the eyes of policy-makers. Whereas in Ghana the sub-sector is fraught with bottlenecks, Malaysia is now the world's largest exporter of palm oil. The remarkable progress that the Malaysian economy has made in export-led growth can serve as a learning experience for Ghana. Some relevant statistics are shown in Table 3.9 to compare the cases of Ghana and Malaysia to underpin our proposition.

From 1980 to 1990, there was an average deceleration of 15.3 per cent in the growth of export volume in Ghana. During the same period, exports from Malaysia underwent a rapid growth of over 14 per cent. However, Ghana enjoyed a positive export growth of 9.1 per cent in the following decade, mainly due to increases in gold and various non-traditional exports. Malaysian exporters further expanded their output by 15.8 per cent during the same decade.

On the basis of export values, both economies performed much better in the 1990s than in the previous decade (10.85 per cent growth for Ghana in the 1990s compared to -0.2 per cent growth in the 1980s; 12.7 per cent

77

TABLE 3.9 Growth of merchandise trade (average annual % growth)

	Ghana	South Korea	Malaysia
Export volume			
1980–90	-15.3	11.5	14.3
1990–99	9.1	15.3	15.8
Import volume			
1980–90	-17.5	11.0	5.8
1990–99	7.2	9.5	11.2
Export value			
1980–90	-0.2	14.9	8.6
1990–99	10.8	10.1	12.7
Import value			
1980–90	2.8	11.8	7.6
1990–2000	9.1	6.6	9.9

Source: World Bank, World Development Indicators (2002).

growth for Malaysia in 1990s compared to 8.6 per cent growth in the 1980s). By every indication, there is the need aggressively to revamp Ghana's export drive if the country is to replicate the Malaysian mini-miracle. A policy approach that must not be overlooked is the fact that Malaysia supplemented market-determined policies with interventions aimed at correcting distortions in the market. South Korea provides another example where protective barriers against imports were enforced and where interest rates were maintained below the market rates to favour investors. These measures were used as an incentive regime that served to encourage venture capitalists to enter the export market. The challenge here is the examination of the current status of the market and ascertaining the extent to which variants of these practices can be integrated into the growth process.

THE EXTERNAL DEBT BURDEN AND AID DEPENDENCY The external debt burden constitutes a major impediment to growth in Sub-Saharan Africa. A country such as Nigeria, despite the vast natural and human resources, has not been able to reduce significantly its foreign indebtedness because of mismanagement of the economy and widespread corruption. Without ruling out at least a moderate contribution from both factors, Ghana's problem with indebtedness can be ascribed mainly to the following factors:

- the ineffectiveness of some of the loans in correcting distortions in priority sectors, due to poor feasibility studies
- the contracting of loans based on political survival rather than on the facts of growth and poverty reduction

78

TABLE 3.10 Aid dependency

	Ghana	South Korea	Malaysia
Net official development assistance or official aid ($ million)			
1995	651	57	109
2000	609	-198	45
Aid per capita ($)			
1995	38	1	5
2000	32	-4	2
Aid dependency ratios (aid as a % of GNI)			
1995	10.3	0.0	0.1
2000	12.1	0.0	0.1
Aid as a % of gross capital formation			
1995	50.3	0.0	0.3
2000	49.5	-0.2	0.2
Aid as a % of imports of goods and services			
1995	28.8	0.0	0.1
2000	17.6	-0.1	0.0
Aid as a % of central government expenditure			
1995	–	0.1	0.6
2000	–	–	–

Source: World Bank, World Development Indicators (2002).

- loan-financed projects/programmes with an urban bias
- the disparity between export growth and the incidence of loan contraction.

As at the end of 1999, Ghana's external debt stood at $5.9 billion and steadily rose to slightly above $7 billion by 2003, of which 84.4 per cent and 8.8 per cent were in the form of long-term and medium-term loans, respectively. However, total debt repayments (including IMF facilities) diminished substantially at the same time from $564.20 million to $127.10 million. This was because Ghana was successful in negotiating with donors/development partners to convert some of the loans into concessional loans. Despite objections from opposition parliamentarians who reasoned that it might constitute a debt stigma, the Kufuor government's relegation of Ghana to the status of a highly indebted poor country (HIPC) made it possible to access debt relief which, in turn, culminated in a slowdown of debt service and the cancellation of some of the external debts.

The comparative statistics on aid dependency are shown in Table 3.10. The Malaysians have kept aid dependency low (0.1 per cent in 1995 and 2000) compared to Ghana (10.3 per cent in 1995 and 12.1 per cent in 2000).

A more striking aid dependency assessment can be discerned from the high level of aid as a percentage of gross capital formation: 50.3 per cent and 49.5 per cent in 1995 and 2000 respectively for Ghana as compared to Malaysia's 0.3 per cent and 0.2 per cent for the respective years. It is difficult to visualize sustainable long-term growth that is based on such an extent of aid dependency. Malaysia and Korea provide vital examples which would indicate that rapid sustainable growth cannot depend on aid dependency in perpetuity and that a sense of purpose and direction is essential in managing public debt that will eventually have to be serviced at the expense of the taxpayer and export revenues. Against the backdrop of declining aid flows, there is a compelling need to seek domestic sources of development financing. In addition, efficient utilization of available aid for the intended purpose(s) would become paramount. Again, cultivating a saving culture is imperative.

Foreign direct investment and the growth problem Foreign direct investment (FDI) has, since the mid-1980s, been accepted as a complement to other sources of development finance. This has been in sharp contrast to the early part of the revolutionary era when FDI was seen by high-profile socialists in the country as a channel for the neocolonialist domination of Ghana by transnational corporations. By the time the country returned to constitutional rule in 1992, it had made modest gains in attracting FDI, especially into the mining industry. Research has shown (Tsikata et al. 2000) that for FDI to be instrumental in the economic growth process, certain key determinants of inflows must be addressed. The results were based on econometric and survey outcomes. The key results were:

- uncertainty about the economy emerged as the most crucial concern of investors
- the investment climate must be congenial
- democratic governance is crucial to investors, due to the inherent guarantees against expropriation and due regard for the rule of law
- a liberal trade regime must be maintained
- export orientation has a significantly positive impact on FDI mainly because of investment activities in the mining sector
- high interest rates have a negative impact on local FDI partners.

The factors outlined above constitute formidable challenges that confront most least developed countries (LDCs). Furthermore, of special significance is the fact that foreign investors normally look at how local entrepreneurs are treated as an indication of the seriousness of a government that proclaims an existing investor-friendly environment. This is of course reminiscent of the old adage that 'charity begins at home'. Threatening statements and deprecation of local businessmen and their general characterization as crooks have a negative impact on foreign investor confidence.

If our analysis of the FDI and growth nexus is allowed to include redistributive aspects of growth, then the concentration of FDI in the Accra-Tema area over the years constitutes an additional challenge to the development process. Unfortunately, there seems to be no reliable mechanism to disperse new investment to depressed areas. The problem of environmental degradation has already been analysed in the section on mining.

Favouritism and corruption Lip-service to meritocracy and dedication in governance has led to non-optimal exploitation of the vast resources of Sub-Saharan Africa. Consequently, the benefits that should accrue to enhance the growth process have been limited. Of equal concern are the pervasive favouritism, cronyism and outright corruption which constitute a major drain on resources. Although the case of Ghana has been (and is) far from the classic cases of some of the countries in Sub-Saharan Africa, no government since independence has been able significantly to reduce their practice and consequences on growth. The crusade of the Kufuorian dispensation – 'zero tolerance of corruption' – is yet to bear observable results. Some analysts, including Gyimah-Boadi and Jeffries (2000) and Aryeetey and Fosu (2004), have rationalized the incidence of corruption as the consequence of poor policies. Bureaucrats use corruption to minimize the negative effects of poor policies on their living standards while politicians see it as an opportunity to acquire resources to enhance their socio-political and economic status. By implication, good policies that promote growth are therefore likely to minimize the incidence of corruption. Simply stated, it might be plausible to consider the challenge of good governance and policies as a partial solution to the corruption problem.

Conclusion

It is clear from the analyses above that economic growth poses the strongest challenge to the overall development of Ghana. The economy has to grow in order to create wealth for 'equitable' distribution. Unfortunately, there is nothing in the literature to indicate that sustainable growth is easy and cheap to attain in Sub-Saharan Africa as a whole. The set of issues that may be regarded as constituting the 'stylized facts' about the challenges of economic growth in Ghana may be summarized as follows.

Fundamentally, economic growth is the most intricate and overriding component of the development process and, therefore, must be of foremost consideration in the allocation of resources to attain targets of accelerated development. The sluggish growth that occurred over the years has been the result of bad policies and the misallocation of resources in both the public and private sectors.

The leadership factor is critical to the attainment of development goals. All the examples in South East Asia, especially the Malaysian case, of rapid economic growth and development that Ghana is enthusiastic about replicating, had strong and enlightened visionaries at the helm. Indeed, they could be described as having provided the requisite developmental leadership. Consequently, the economic growth problems analysed in this chapter beg the question as to whether Ghana has, so far, had the right developmental leadership and the requisite technocratic class that could have pushed the growth agenda forwards from 1992.

Closely related to the leadership challenge is the essence of human capital formation. The educational system has been faced with formidable challenges in terms of quality at all levels. The intellectual rehabilitation of the secondary school system (both JSS and SSS) will require adequate planning and inputs.

An interesting question to pose about the growth process itself is whether there exists an appropriate growth-promoting culture in Ghana. The low propensity to save, the preference for short-term investment and a rent-seeking syndrome have all served to hinder the promotion of long-term directly productive activities with high employment-generating capacity. In addition, conspicuous consumerism as an indication of material success has led to either the misprioritization and misallocation of resources or the sheer dissipation of productive time, for example, the inordinate amount of time spent on funeral preparations. On the other hand, the country's de facto role model – the Malaysians – are high savers, saving about 38 per cent of GDP as compared to Ghana's 8 per cent. The labour force is disciplined, committed and prepared to make sacrifices for investment in children's education and, therefore, is capable of creating intergenerational family wealth.

Empirical evidence shows that the democratic dispensation, although costly to implement, has had a positive impact on investment and growth, and needs to be sustained.

It is imperative to ascertain empirically the extent of market orientation that would optimally promote growth. Market failure in critical areas of the economy, for example, in education, the labour and capital markets and in social services, makes fine-tuning of government intervention imperative in enhancing market performance.

The structural foundations of the economy are virtually static in terms of factor mobility that will ensure efficiency in the allocation of resources. If the declaration of 'the golden age of business' implies enhancement of market performance, then it is imperative to explore areas with the potential for accelerating economic growth, especially in the industrial sector.

At the sectoral level, agriculture remains vital to the growth process in terms of food production and exports. The cocoa sub-sector and an expanding non-traditional export sub-sector provide some stimulus for growth. The excellent economic policy performance and the private–public sector harmony in investment which characterizes Malaysia should constitute a challenge worth emulating for effective expansion in the productive sectors. A case in point is the expansion in the palm oil industry to enhance the foreign exchange earning capacity of the economy.

Despite the relaxation of various aspects of the investment code, including the lowering of corporate taxes, there has not been much change in the contribution of the industrial sector to GDP. Apprehensions that gripped investors, especially in the manufacturing sub-sector, during the revolutionary years have remained largely in place. It is therefore necessary to create an investment climate that generates confidence in the policy-making establishment and an enlarged market as stimulus for both local and foreign direct investors.

Ghana, indeed Africa, cannot escape the wind of global economic changes. Export-led growth is at the forefront of the South East Asian growth miracle. The challenge is to explore new export sources and to add value and volume to the old. In this regard, the recent 'salt production initiative' aimed at developing the industry as a major foreign exchange earner may go a long way towards the restructuring of the industrial base of the economy.

Finally, it must be re-emphasized that attainment of sustained economic growth traces its origins to factor productivity. In the case of Sub-Saharan African countries, including Ghana, the overriding political factor productivity issue pertinent to the growth process is the need to move from a power-hungry leadership style to a visionary/developmental leadership. The former regards the economy as a fat cow that must be milked till it is dry, leaving the majority of the people in abject poverty. In sum, the future of economic growth and development of the country resides in the quality and philosophical resiliency of politico-economic leaders, the appreciation of human capital as the fuel in the engine of growth, the fine-tuning of economic policies that can lead to economic growth and simultaneous reduction in poverty levels, the minimization of extraneous reward systems and the commitment of policy managers to the development effort as a whole.

Sources

Ajayi, S. I. (2000) 'Globalisation and Africa', *Journal of African Economies*, Vol. 12 (Supplement, Oxford University Press).

Aryeetey, E. and A. K. Fosu (2004) 'Economic Growth in Ghana: 1960–2000', Paper presented at the International Conference on Ghana's Economy at the Half Century, University of Ghana's ISSER and Cornell University.

Fosu, A. K. (1992) 'Political Instability and Economic Growth: Evidence from Sub-Saharan Africa', *Economic Development and Cultural Change*, Vol. 40, no. 4: 829–41.

Gyimah-Boadi, E. and R. Jeffries (2000) 'The Political Economy of Reform', in E. Aryeetey, J. Harrigan and M. Nissanke (eds), *Economic Reforms in Ghana: The Miracle and the Mirage* (Oxford: James Currey and Woeli Publishers).

Hirschman, A. O. (1958) *The Strategy of Economic Development* (New Haven, CT: Yale University Press).

ISSER (1995–2003) *The State of the Ghanaian Economy*.

Johnston, B. F. and J. W. Mellor (1961) 'The Role of Agriculture in Economic Development', *American Economic Review*, Vol. 51: 566–93.

Killick, T. (2000) 'Fragile Still: The Structure of Ghana's Economy (1960–94)', in E. Aryeetey, J. Harrigan and M. Nissanke (eds), *Economic Reforms in Ghana: The Miracle and the Mirage* (Oxford: James Currey and Woeli Publishers).

Kraus, J. (1991) 'The Political Economy of Stabilization and Structural Adjustment in Ghana', in D. Rothchild (ed.), *Ghana: The Political Economy of Recovery* (Boulder, CO: Lynne Rienner).

Kuznets, S. (1966) *Modern Economic Growth* (New Haven, CT: Yale University Press).

Meier, G. M. (1976) *Leading Issues in Economic Development* (New York: Oxford University Press).

Nyanteng, V. and A. W. Seini (2000) 'Agricultural Policy and the Impact on Growth and Productivity: 1970–95', in E. Aryeetey, J. Harrigan and M. Nissanke (eds), *Economic Reforms in Ghana: The Miracle and the Mirage* (Oxford: James Currey and Woeli Publishers).

O'Connell, S. and B. Ndulu (2000) 'Africa's Growth Experience: A Focus on the Sources of Growth', mimeo, AERC, Nairobi.

Republic of Ghana (1995) *Ghana – Vision 2020 (The First Step: 1996–2000)*, Presidential Report to Parliament on Coordinated Programme of Economic and Social Development Policies, 6 January (Accra: National Development Planning Commission).

— (1997) *Ghana – Vision 2020: The First Medium-term Development Plan (1997–2000)* (Accra: National Development Planning Commission).

— (2002) *The Coordinated Programme for Economic and Social Development of Ghana* (Accra: National Development Planning Commission).

— (2003) *Ghana Poverty Reduction Strategy (2003–2005)* (Accra: National Development Planning Commission).

Solow, R. (1956) 'A Contribution to the Theory of Economic Growth', *Quarterly Journal of Economics*, Vol. 70, no. 1: 65–94.

Songsore, J., P. W. K. Yankson and G. K. Tsikata (1994) *Mining and the Environment: Towards a Win-Win Strategy*, Report for the Ministry of Environment, Science and Technology and the World Bank.

Szerezewski, R. (1965) *Structural Changes in the Economy of Ghana: 1891–1911* (London: Weidenfeld and Nicolson).

Todaro, M. P. (1989) *Economic Development* (New York and London: Longman).

Tsikata, G. K. (1995) *The Gold Sub-Sector and Economic Growth and Development in Ghana*, Report for the Minerals Commission and the World Bank.

— (1996) *Economic Growth in Ghana: Some Stylized Facts*, Legon Economic Series (Legon: Department of Economics, University of Ghana).

Tsikata, G. K. and Y. Asante and E. M. Gyasi (2000) *Determinants of Foreign Direct Investment in Ghana* (London: Overseas Development Institute and University of Ghana).

World Bank (1988a) *Adjustment Lending: An Evaluation of Ten Years of Experience*, Policy and Research Series (Washington, DC: World Bank).

— (1988b) *World Development Report 1988: Public Finance in Development* (New York: Oxford University Press).

— (1995) *World Development Report 1995: Workers in an Integrating World* (New York: Oxford University Press).

— (2000) *The Quality of Growth* (New York: Oxford University Press).

— (2002) *World Development Indicators 2002* (New York: Oxford University Press).

4 | Markets and liberal democracy

KWAME A. NINSIN

The current wave of democracy in Ghana followed the failure of the stringent economic reforms to overcome the severe economic crisis into which the country had been plunged. By the close of the 1980s – that is, after about eight years of diligent pursuit of economic reforms – Ghana's per capita income had remained at about US $390, which placed it among the poorest countries in the world. The authoritarian state, presided over by the government of the Provisional National Defence Council (PNDC), had failed to overcome poverty. The social implications were grave; there was need therefore to accelerate the rate of reform if growth was to be achieved and poverty brought under control. There were political reasons as well: the failure of the authoritarian state had resulted in widespread disillusionment coupled with growing demands for political reform towards greater openness and enhanced citizen participation in public affairs. In the meantime, the World Bank had reached the conclusion that state power should be democratized and good governance practices, including greater transparency and accountability, adhered to (World Bank 1989). A political arrangement based on checks and balances, a free press and open debate, openness and accountability in public affairs, an independent judiciary, political pluralism, guarantees of the fundamental rights of the citizen, and other democratic principles would be necessary to provide greater legitimacy for government, and generally secure an enabling environment for sustainable economic growth and prosperity for all and sundry. Democracy alters the distribution of political power in favour of the poor and marginalized, and makes government responsive and accountable to them. The market reforms should therefore proceed in tandem with political reforms towards democratic governance. In general, the claim was that the democratization of political power facilitates the growth of a free market economy which in turn generates prosperity for all (Dunn 1992). The flip-side of this argument was that capitalism promotes the growth of freedom and equality which strengthens the growth of democratic institutions (Friedman 1982). Exponents of market democracy among Africanist scholars also reiterated this claim, that the growth of the market, private enterprise, especially small and medium enterprises, enhances the growth of freedom and the collapse of authoritarianism. African governments came under considerable pressure to implement reform policies that would expand the market and civil society at the expense of the state. The declared principle was: more of the market and civil society and less of the state, and society will secure freedom and democracy.

Since the return to constitutional rule in January 1993, under the 1992 Constitution successive Ghanaian governments have pursued the required market reforms while ensuring the consolidation of democracy. In this chapter I test the postulate that the market (i.e. capitalist) economy enhances the growth of democracy; that the two – market and democracy – more than complement each other; they are symbiotically related. I examine the extent to which the current market reforms in Ghana have promoted the growth of a democratic society. I argue that a successful democratic state can be achieved only on the basis of a 'welfare compromise' by which the welfare of the people is carefully balanced with the demands of the market (Palma 1997: 292); although the market may be efficient in promoting wealth in general, it is inefficient in promoting equity and justice. In fact, market reforms have been found to lead to the deterioration of the material conditions of many groups and thereby undermine liberty, equity and justice, especially where the economy is dependent and the state is too weak to intervene to correct the imperfections of the market in the distribution of access to the resources necessary for effective citizenship. I define effective citizenship as the capacity freely to exercise the volition (free will) (Lindley 1986) to participate in or influence public affairs – that is, to exercise self-determination. This capacity is enhanced where individuals are 'provided with the resources they require to secure equal access to the advantages they need in order to live the life they have reason to value' (Callinicos 2003: 108). Where economic reforms are known to exacerbate inequality, it is the responsibility of the state to intervene in the market with policies that redistribute resources to improve the quality of life of its citizens. In other words, the state must intervene in the market to maintain the conditions for effective citizenship if groups and individuals are to develop sustained faith in democratic institutions to process their interests (Przeworski 1995: 11–12).

The chapter is divided into five sections. The first is a narration of the impressive achievement of formal democracy as indicated by the expansion in media freedom, freedom of expression, and in the orderly transfer of power. The second examines the importance of effective citizenship in realizing democracy. In the third section, I argue that the rise in poverty among Ghanaians as a result of the market reforms explains the weak capacity of Ghanaians in exercising effective citizenship. The result is a particular form of democracy, 'democratic elitism', in which democracy means periodic elections and the enjoyment of negative rights. In the fourth section I argue that the logic of the market has forced the state to surrender its functions and sovereign powers which have been appropriated by civil society organizations, particularly NGOs. Today, government is struggling to govern while NGOs actively contest its claim to represent society and function as society's sovereign agent for development and the assurance of good governance. In the fifth and final section I conclude that democracy is more than procedures, the freedom to choose and express civil and political liberties. Pervasive poverty arising from the failure of the market and the failure of the state to correct the ravages of the market have weakened people's capacity to function effectively as citizens; and democracy has been reduced to a form of government by periodic elections mediated by a proliferation of civil society organizations.

Democratic consolidation since 1993

The most significant achievement in Ghana's transition to democracy is the orderly transfer of power, through the 2000 election, from the National Democratic Congress (NDC) governments led by J. J. Rawlings to the New Patriotic Party (NPP) government led by J. A. Kufuor. In a continent which is notorious for unconstitutional changes of government and controversial elections, Ghana's 2000 general election vindicated liberal democracy as the only political form that has the mechanism for a peaceful, orderly and legitimate transfer of power.

The 2000 election represented the triumph of democracy in another sense. By enabling Ghanaians to express their sovereign will to choose who should govern them, it affirmed the principle of government by consent. In a democracy sovereignty resides in its free and equal agents who are called upon to express their sovereign power to choose their representatives at general elections held periodically. Recently, Ghanaians have been able to express this sovereign power on three successive occasions: 1992, 1996 and 2000. By the third election, the electoral process had stabilized and achieved a significant measure of credibility and legitimacy, so that Ghanaians could confidently claim to have a democratically elected government. The country's elites had also worked assiduously towards this end. Immediately after the controversial 1992 election, they laboured through tortuous negotiations to reach consensus on the rules of the electoral process and agreed to accept its outcome as legitimate (Ninsin 1998a: 184–202).

Furthermore, civil society was resurgent, having grown in scope and self-confidence in its determination to preserve freedom and ensure good governance. The print and electronic media are outstanding among those that have become vociferous in defence of democracy and human rights.

There has been dramatic growth in media pluralism, especially in respect of FM stations and newspapers. No fewer than sixty-seven FM stations, most of them private, have started operating (Amoakohene 2004) and at least five private TV stations are also broadcasting. Regarding the print media, 'about 40 [newspapers and magazines] were published between 1991 and the general elections of November-December 1992 ... Between 15 and 20 newspapers were started from mid-1991; but later ceased operation' (Karikari 1998: 165). The newspapers were owned by individual entrepreneurs who had responded to the new wave of freedom sweeping the country, and the additional impetus provided by the repeal of the Newspaper Licensing Law 1985 in May 1992. By 2003, following greater political opening in the country, and the repeal of the criminal libel law, many more private newspapers came into circulation, significantly increasing the total number of newspapers operating in the country. According to the National Media Commission, sixty-seven newspapers, including news magazines, had registered with it by 2003.

Media pluralism progressively added to the pressure for greater political opening up in the country. From 1992 onwards, the content of newspapers became 'critical, polemical, and combative. [In particular,] the independent press raised [issues such as] morality and accountability in public life, especially issues which involved members of the PNDC government and its functionaries' (Karikari 1998: 175). They did not constitute an 'alternative press'; nor did they pose any 'fundamental and critical questions about ... economic and political policies and programmes'. They were merely consistent advocates of 'the conventional ideas and institutions of liberal democracy' (ibid.: 179). By 2002, the press had deepened their commitment to liberal democracy by becoming a platform for Ghanaians from all walks of life and across the political spectrum freely and openly to engage public officials on public affairs, strive to ensure good governance and protect the nation against the abuse of power and office. Compared to the 1992 and 1996 general elections, when the limited media pluralism coupled with the application of repressive laws scared the media into allowing the ruling party to recycle itself in power, the media had gained sufficient courage and confidence by 2000 to ensure a free and transparent election in that year.

Democracy institutions such as the National Media Commission, National Electoral Commission, and Commission of Human Rights and Administrative Justice (CHRAJ) also gradually accumulated confidence and relative autonomy to perform their functions in a reasonably free and impartial manner. The number of development NGOs and human rights organizations playing advocacy roles in public affairs – especially in the area of human rights, including the rights of children and women – also increased substantially during this period. In 1999, the directory of NGOs published by the Ghana Association of Private Voluntary Organizations in Development (GPVOD) recorded just 450 NGOs and INGOs. A statement issued more recently by the Ministry of Manpower Development and Employment (*Daily Graphic*, 25 February 2004, pp. 1, 3) gave the number of NGOs in the country at the end of 2002 as more than 3,000. The Private Enterprise Foundation, established in 1994, had emerged as the umbrella advocacy body for the Association of Ghana Industries, Ghana Employers Association, Federation of Associations of Ghanaian Exporters, Ghana Association of Bankers, and the Ghana Chamber of Mines. In sum, Ghanaians enjoyed a significant measure of 'negative rights' (Berlin 1969) by 2003.

Democracy and agency

For democracy to flourish, citizens must be advocates of their own cause, and at the same time be able to act in cooperation with others to engage the state in defence of their rights, including the right to social and economic security. Article 1(1) of the 1992 Constitution affirms that 'The Sovereignty of Ghana resides in the people of Ghana in whose name and for whose welfare the powers of government are to be exercised.' Article 42 provides the instrument – the franchise – for establishing a government and ensuring that, once established, government would exercise its powers for the welfare of the people. It seems that from the 1992 election, Ghanaians became more and more civic conscious. A study of the 2000 election conducted by the Department of Political Science, University of Ghana (see Ayee 2001 Vol. 2) concluded that the National Democratic Congress (NDC) lost the election because Ghanaians disapproved of its policies (Anebo 2001: 69–88; Dunn 1975; Jefferies 1980; Chazan 1987; Ninsin 1993).

First, there is supposition that there is a *common good* that is discernible by the people. This view is consistent with the classical theory of democracy: that the people have the capacity to arrive at the common good through rational argument. Second, an election is the 'institutional arrangement for arriving at political decisions which realizes the common good by making the people ... decide issues through the election of individuals who are to assemble in order to carry out [the people's] will' (Schumpeter 1950: 250). This view, that the people usually have the capacity to make rational choice through elections, needs to be interrogated. Do citizens normally have the capacity to engage in rational discussion upon which to arrive at the best interests of society? I am inclined to Schumpeter's view that the mundane concerns of people are mostly private and rather intimate matters; people are much less concerned with matters in the public domain. Even at the local or community level where public issues are easily within the grasp of citizens and they are therefore expected to identify with, and show interest in, them, there is a 'reduced power of discerning facts; reduced preparedness to act upon them; and a reduced sense of responsibility' (ibid.: 260). Naturally, therefore, a sense of volition and responsibility diminishes as citizens are confronted with public issues of national concern.

Can citizens discern the common good, and independently act as the best judges in concert with others, for example, at an election? In a harsh economic and social environment, the people tend to be preoccupied with their own survival, and have no time for public affairs. They easily become 'bad and corrupt judges' (ibid.) even if they have to decide on clear issues presented to them at an election, and even if they have access to prolific information about alternative public issues. Consequently, in a democracy where the political process is an infinitely complex jumble of individual and group influences, actions and reactions, the decisions arising from the electoral and other political processes would lack democratic credentials; they can only represent the 'manufactured will' of the people produced by political entrepreneurs, the media and other forces that are external to them (ibid.: 263). The power of such external forces over the political choices of the Ghanaian electorate is overwhelming, and expresses itself as clientelism or 'big man small boy' syndrome in politics (Nugent 1995).

The great issues of politics are not settled at elections. They are settled in the policy arena where various interests compete to have their cause succeed and embodied in a public policy instrument. It is at this level that democracy, as the expression of the common will of the people, can be manifested in the form of organized citizens' actions or contestation to shape public policy. A crucial test of the democratic credentials of the citizens of a democratic society is how they have engaged the state during the inter election period. Such engagement would take the form of pressure group activities, or lobbying of varying magnitude. For this mode of action to occur, the citizens should be capable of effective volition in public affairs.

During the period 1993–99, when the civilian government of the NDC applied certain authoritarian methods that were reminiscent of the PNDC era, there were only sporadic political interventions organized by civil society. Among the few civil society actions were (a) the protests staged against the imposition of value added tax under the Value Added Tax Act 1994 (Act 486); (b) protests against the serial killing of women; and (c) the mobilization of a network of domestic election monitors to monitor and observe the 2000 election.

The VAT had instantly inflated prices and precipitated a further drop in the living conditions of the majority of Ghanaians (Osei 2000: 266–8). In response the Alliance for Change organized two major nationwide protest marches. The first (*Kume preko*) was organized in Accra on 11 May 1995; and the second (*Sieme preko*) in Kumasi on 25 May 1995. A third mass protest was organized in Takoradi on 22 June 1995.

Second, for over a year there was what appeared to be serial killings of mainly young women in the Accra metropolis. The state appeared unable to solve the riddle of those killings or stop them. Various women's groups organized protest marches in Accra to draw the government's attention to those criminal acts, demand punishment for the culprits and, in addition, adequate security, especially for Ghanaian women.

The third civil society action was against the recurring malpractices and manipulations that had characterized the electoral process from 1992. The need to ensure the integrity and credibility of the electoral process, and to establish an orderly regime for changing or choosing government, led to the growth of election monitoring groups which came together to form the Network of Domestic Election Observers (NEDEO). NEDEO fielded between 4,100 and 5,500 (Boafo-Arthur 2004) election observers nationwide to monitor the 2000 elections.

The effect of these civil protests was the instant suspension of the VAT law until 1998 when the value added tax was reintroduced under the Value Added Tax Act 1998, Act 546. The intervention of civil society organizations in the 2000 election as observers and monitors produced a substantially transparent and fair election in which the incumbent party, the NDC, was defeated by the NPP. The women's protest, however, failed to produce any actions or reactions at the policy level.

In general, organized action by citizens to bring vertical pressure on the state to ensure the good of society was rare. As the successful protests clearly show, political action by citizens was mediated by civil society groups. The anti-VAT protests were organized and led by the Alliance for Change, a coalition of nine opposition political parties. The election monitoring and observation exercises were executed under the auspices of NEDEO, an umbrella organization of civic, religious, professional and human rights bodies (Ninsin 1998a: 192). The two protests that were spearheaded by organized civil society groups were successful compared to the abortive women's protests which were not led by similar groups. This suggests that successful citizens' intervention in the political process was made possible only through the mediation of civil society organizations. But for such mediation, the people would not have engaged in those actions of their own volition.

The period from January 2001 to 2003 of the government of the New

Patriotic Party (NPP) has also been characterized by political inertia on the part of the people despite the fact that that period was not without harsh and controversial policies, some of which had a deleterious effect on the material situation of the people. Examples of such policies are: the government's decision to release for mining purposes portions of forest reserves in the Western Region of the country; degradation of the environment by mining companies, both big and small; hefty increases in electricity and water tariffs as well as the 100 per cent increase in fuel prices; and the proposed privatization of water. These harsh policies occurred or were proposed when there was further deterioration in the quality of life of most Ghanaians under the regime of market reforms. Yet, whenever the government proposed new market reform policies it became the responsibility of advocacy groups and individuals to intercede on behalf of the citizens. Otherwise the citizenry would remain aloof, grumbling only in their private cells. For example, the Third World Network (Africa Office), in conjunction with one or two environmental NGOs, became the voice of the communities adversely affected by the activities of mining interests; and the National Coalition Against the Privatization of Water, the Integrated Social Development Centre (ISODEC) and others agitated on behalf of Ghanaians against the government's plans to privatize water. When the government made public its intention to privatize the Ghana Commercial Bank, it was the diligence of the Trades Union Congress (TUC) and the relentless agitation by a few individuals against the proposal[1] that persuaded the government to suspend its decision to privatize. In general, the public always grumbled privately or complained loudly through the country's numerous radio talk-shows, but showed no inclination to engage in organized public action to press their concern about those policies.

This general lack of engagement with the state has been ascribed to the dominant authoritarian culture of power that pervades it. According to Osei (2000: 265–6), the NDC government's 'inherited authoritarian mindset' undermined the democratic policy process which the 1992 Constitution had guaranteed. The government became 'a serious impediment to plural politics'; it was not just reluctant to open the policy process to broader participation; it had also retained on the statute books such draconian laws as the Preventive Custody Law 1982 (PNDCL 4), and Habeas Corpus Amendment Law (PNDCL 91) to punish those who held critical or dissenting views. The two successful citizens' actions to which I have referred above were motivated by the need to remove this dictatorship. When in late 1994 the NDC government closed down a private FM radio station (Radio Eye) the same political impetus moved a few citizens to embark on a street protest on 13 December 1994 against that state action. Though that action

Markets and liberal democracy

was suppressed (Ninsin 1998b: 68), it added to the pressure on the NDC government to behave in accordance with the norms of democracy and the 1992 Constitution. Admittedly, this authoritarian political culture was an important factor inhibiting citizen engagement in the political process; but it does not explain the absence of organized citizens' action against unjust policies, especially in an increasingly open political environment. A probable explanation is that those sporadic mass actions were part of the opposition politics of the moment whose aim was either to force the NDC government to liberalize further or be removed from power. They were therefore not driven by citizens' free will to effect policy changes.

Schumpeter attributes this to the citizens' lack of the will to act which is 'the psychic counterpart of purposeful responsible action' (Schumpeter 1950: 261). I would argue that at the turn of the last century the growing poverty among the majority of Ghanaians had severely impaired citizens' capacity to exercise the will to act in public affairs. Poverty has the power to disempower individuals and communities, and diminish people's self-confidence; it 'negates the realization or enjoyment of human rights. There is no real possibility of enjoying rights, whether civil, political, social economic or cultural, without resources such as food security, education, physical safety, health, employment, property, access to justice, and due process' (CHRI 2001: 15). The sense of physical, social and economic insecurity which poverty engenders among people produces a sense of powerlessness over their political, social and economic environment, and makes them feel vulnerable in the face of the powerful political forces they have to contend with. This feeling of powerlessness is manifested as withdrawal from public affairs, as apathy or as indifference. As such, the poor can only act, when they have to, as clients of their political patrons rather than as autonomous political agents. The clientelist mode of political action is what a long tradition of studies into the electoral and general political behaviour of Ghanaians has established (Austin 1975; Dunn 1975; Chazan 1987; Jefferies 1980; Ninsin 1993). The proliferation of advocacy NGOs, which claim to be the voice of the voiceless and the power of the powerless, is a response to the disempowerment of the vast majority of the people during the last two decades.

Economic growth and citizenship

Freedom of speech and expression (including freedom of the press and other media), freedom of association, choice and assembly as well as the civil liberties that Ghanaians enjoy are important democratic rights. But, as Przeworski emphasized:

democracy is a system of positive rights; it does not automatically generate the conditions required for an effective exercise of these rights, as well as obligations. In particular, the material security and education, as well as access to information, necessary to exercise citizenship are not guaranteed to everyone by the mere existence of democratic institutions. Hence, in many countries, some groups remain incapable of exercising their rights and obligations. [The result is] democracies without an effective citizenship for large sections of the political community. (Przeworski 1995: 34)

It is the responsibility of the state to ensure that all individuals enjoy basic social and economic entitlements that will make the exercise of effective citizenship feasible.

During the period under review, the Ghanaian economy has been progressively freed from the old regime of controls while the state has remained almost aloof from its adverse effects on society. The result has been a substantial growth in poverty which, in my view, accounts significantly for the growing political inertia among Ghanaians. For, as argued by Przeworski and colleagues (ibid.), there is an unambiguous connection in liberal political theory and practice between the capacity to form opinions on public matters and effective volition on one hand, and education and material security on the other. This capacity grows when individuals enjoy positive rights. Because the market is reluctant to allocate the factors required to make effective citizenship feasible, the state must intervene to create and allocate them.

In 1992 the World Bank had offered the following authoritative prognosis on the prospects for poverty reduction in the country.

With a population growth rate of about 3 per cent per annum, and national income growth of 5 per cent per annum, income per capita will grow at 2 per cent per annum. If the average poor person's income also grows at this rate, then it will take 20 years for him or her to cross the poverty line. ... Consider those in extreme poverty with a standard of living half that of the average poor person ... For this extreme poverty level, per capita income growth of 2 per cent per annum would put the cross-over time in an incredible 53 years. In other words, at present growth rates the alleviation of extreme poverty would not occur for more than half a century ... Ghana should aim for accelerated growth [in order to get out of this poverty trap]. (World Bank 1992: 10)

When a civilian government took office in 1993, it was clear that the copious market reforms had not resolved the economic crisis facing the country. The newly elected government of the NDC, and its successor in

2001 (the NPP), were obliged to pursue the market reforms with much greater diligence. In the case of the NDC the imperatives of electoral politics had led to policy compromises which undermined the integrity of the entire reform programme. In particular, the process of transforming the PNDC from a military government into a political party (the NDC) that would exercise power only through the ballot box, had 'shifted power from technocrats to political brokers more concerned with patronage and less with market rationality. As these "carpetbaggers" ... tightened their grip on the party, corruption ... became a marked feature of the programme ... The NDC and the [state] bureaucracy increasingly descended ... into cronyism and corruption' (Hutchful 2002: 2). The NPP on the other hand remained doggedly focused on ensuring macroeconomic stability in spite of the temptation embedded in electoral politics.[2]

Notwithstanding differences in commitment to reform policies demonstrated by the two successive governments, the goal of these policies remained unchanged. Fundamentally, the aim was to remove the distortions in the economy in order to facilitate the growth of a market economy in which trade and investment would be liberalized and the role of the government would 'change from owner and regulator of economic activity to a facilitator through infrastructural investment and institutional changes' (ISSER 1994). By reducing the power of the central government and promoting the free market economy, the scope for the individual actor as an autonomous economic agent would also be enhanced. A free market produces a free citizen. It yields economic freedom which is the precondition for political freedom; because 'capitalism and the existence of private property ... [provide some] checks to the centralized power of the state' (Friedman 1982: 10).

In the social sector the reform policies were also driven by liberalism – by the claim that the free market is the best system for producing the free citizen 'as the ultimate entity in society' (ibid.). Accordingly, the reforms aimed at transforming 'the conditions of social reproduction' (Hutchful 2002) from one in which the state was the main agent to one in which individuals and private organizations would assume that responsibility. Several arguments were adduced to justify and legitimize such reconfiguration of life's opportunities available to Ghanaians; but central to the prevailing economic policy was the need to promote the free market to a hegemonic position.

By 2003 Ghana's average GDP growth per annum had still not exceeded 5 per cent. Meanwhile, the state had continued actively to put in place institutional and other measures aimed at ensuring that the emerging market would operate freely to accrue optimum benefits to the private investor.

At the same time, Ghanaians were made to pay for services they consumed. In the agricultural sector, for example, the withdrawal of state support led to a decline in credit by the banking sector and in budgetary support (Hutchful 2002), resulting in a decline in performance. Growth averaged some 2.5 per cent during the 1990s; and its share of the GNP fell from 53 per cent in1983 to 40 per cent in 1998. The sector was plagued by a host of problems, including deteriorating terms of trade, a sharp rise in rural inequality, decline in productivity, reduced use of farm inputs such as fertilizer, etc. (World Bank 1992). Additionally, the small and medium enterprises which dominate Ghana's industrial sector, accounting for about 92 per cent of the labour force, were also faced with severe problems, including access to credit and unequal competition from imports (Hutchful 2002: 89).

These structural problems and the commoditization of goods and services, especially the progressive withdrawal of state subsidies on various services – water, electricity, rent, telephone, fuel, transportation and health – and the liberalization of wage policy had two broad social effects. First, inequality in the distribution of wealth and income within the industrial sector and urban society in general increased sharply. Second, the social safety net that the state and private sector employers had provided for formal sector workers was removed so that Ghanaians came face to face with the challenges of individual survival.

Formal sector workers suffered most. Even those in the financial sector, who generally benefited from the economic reforms, felt the pinch. Their income levels remained generally low, or declined, in real terms despite improvements in real earnings recorded in 1992 (of about 43 per cent as a result of the 80 per cent pay increase awarded to civil servants) and 11 per cent in 1993 (Hutchful 2002: 90). From the 1990s onwards, unemployment became a prominent urban phenomenon: about 13.4 per cent compared to 5.5 per cent in rural Ghana (ISSER 2004: 182–5). Because of the low economic growth rate of about 4.7 per cent since 1984 which, above all, yielded fewer new jobs compared to the rapid increases in the labour force of about 5.8 per cent per annum, formal sector unemployment shot up. It is estimated that the economy could absorb just about 2 per cent of the 230,000 young people who joined the labour force annually. Thus, by 2000 unemployment had reached about 10.4 per cent, affecting mostly Ghanaians in the fifteen-to-twenty-five-years age bracket.

In short, Ghanaian society was increasingly divided by extreme inequality in the distribution of wealth and income: a growing majority was becoming poorer while a small minority was getting richer. In 1991–92 about 51 per cent of Ghanaians were defined as poor; by 1998–99 the figure had fallen to about 43 per cent; but the drop was grossly misleading. Accra

97

and the communities in the forest belt were the main beneficiaries of the growth in income and wealth. 'In the remaining localities, both urban and rural, poverty fell only very modestly, apart from urban savannah, where the proportion of the population defined as poor increased during the period. In both periods, poverty ... [was] substantially higher in rural areas than in urban areas. Within both urban and rural areas, poverty ... [was] disproportionately concentrated in the savannah' (World Bank 2000: 6). There were substantial regional variations as well. The Western, Greater Accra, Volta and Brong Ahafo regions benefited most from the reduction in poverty while the Central, Northern, Upper East and Upper West 'experienced large increases in poverty between these two years'. The remaining regions showed very little change in poverty levels (ibid.: 8–9). By 2000 the pattern of poverty in the country had changed for the worse. Income inequality had widened: 'the 20% of the individuals in the lowest quintile ... [had] only 5.7% of total expenditure, while the top 20 percent ... [had] almost 46% of total expenditure' (Ghana Statistical Service 2000: 83). Regional differences had also worsened. The Greater Accra Region had the highest per capita income, followed by Ashanti and Western regions: 'All the other regions ... [had] an average per capita expenditure below the national average.' The Central, Volta, Northern, Upper West and Upper East [had] 'an average per capita expenditure of less than half of that of Greater Accra Region' (ibid.: 84). That poverty had rapidly become an intractable social crisis during the decade 1992–2003 is underscored by the frantic search for a solution to it. Between 1992 and 2003 the following initiatives were taken to mitigate poverty.

- The Child Cannot Wait, 1992
- Revised Population Policy and Population Action Plans, 1994
- National Action Programme for Poverty Reduction, 1995
- Extended Poverty Study 1988–1992, 1995
- Medium-Term Health Strategy, 1995
- National Plan of Action: HABITAT II, 1995
- Free Compulsory Universal Basic Education, 1996
- Highly Indebted Poor Country Initiative, 2000
- Ghana Poverty Reduction Strategy, 2002

Milton Friedman (1982) has argued that the extension of economic freedom is the most effective way to promote equality and welfare. The evidence adduced above shows that the promotion of economic freedom benefited just a minority; the market could not promote either sufficient economic growth or equality and welfare. The majority of the people became progressively more impoverished.

The failure of the market to function efficiently is not fortuitous. It is characteristic of an economy that is prone to hyperinflation; an economy that has 'systemic weaknesses', and 'continues to suffer from anaemic growth'; is subject to a cycle of 'macroeconomic imbalances' – an economy that alternates between decelerated growth and stagnation as well as high levels of unemployment (CEPA 1996). For example, rising unemployment has been a permanent feature of the Ghanaian economy since the inception of the economic reforms, due largely to persistently sub-optimal growth rates. According to 1991–92 estimates, 'only about 15 percent of approximately 250,000 young people coming out of the school system would find regular paid employment. The rest ... [had] to be absorbed by the informal rural and urban sectors' (World Bank 1992: 25). According to the Ghana Living Standards Survey (GLSS) the youth (fifteen to twenty-four years) had the highest rate of unemployment (15.9 per cent), followed by those within the twenty-five to forty-four age bracket, with 7.4 per cent unemployment. The majority of the youth, according to the World Bank (1992: 25), were likely to enter the agricultural sector while the others would engage in productive activities, as well as trading and services at the ratio of 4:3. This segment of the Ghanaian population forms part of the more than 40 per cent that are poor and vulnerable, and are concentrated in the rural sector of society, mainly in the three northern regions, as well as the Central and Volta regions. They also form the bulk of the electorate and the proportion of the citizens that is expected to be most active in the economy and politics.

The various studies, which were conducted using the government's foremost instrument for studying poverty, the GLSS, have established a strong correlation between poverty and self-employment. This is to be expected in an economy characterized by jobless growth (Ninsin 1991: 100). For the poor, self-employment in the informal sector becomes, in the words of Kilby (1969: 310), 'a quasi-sponge' for the unemployed, 'a low equilibrium trap'. Poverty is more prevalent among the illiterate and semi-literate than their better-educated counterparts. A low level of education, or lack of it, has also been found to be a factor that forces labour into the informal sector (Ninsin 1991: 88). Cobbe (1991) found in his study of education and employment patterns in Ghana that the less educated tend to become self-employed. Self-employment declines among persons with higher educational attainment levels. He estimated from the GLSS data that self-employment declined from 92 per cent of those with no education to about 21 per cent of those with university education or its equivalent. Trends in the education system show that a large number of Ghanaians have little or no formal education because of impediments embedded in the social structure (Addae-Mensah 2000). The poor and the very poor form the bulk of this group. Also, the poor usually have the least or no access to a range of social, cultural and economic factors that are necessary to ensure a life of dignity, security and freedom. This is the depth of poverty that has diminished the capacity of the majority of citizens, and forced them into a culture of powerlessness and political inertia.

Governance as democracy

I have argued that citizens usually lack effective volition to exercise sovereign judgement in public affairs. Poverty further weakens their will to act. Where they act at all, civil society organizations mobilize them. Increasingly, democracy is becoming a method by which civil society speaks for society when self-determination by citizens has come to mean the assumption of direct responsibility for their welfare. The law of cause and effect is at work. The market reforms have made Ghanaians poorer both as individuals and as communities or groups such as workers, farmers and so on. A variety of private organizations, especially development NGOs, local as well as foreign, have to intervene to provide access to life's essentials such as water, health and education; to create employment and establish income-generating ventures because the state is barred from providing these – it is either incapable of or inefficient in providing them. This is why, during the last twenty years or so, such private interests have progressively assumed responsibility for social reproduction instead of the state. Part of the responsibility for social reproduction has also been transferred to district assemblies and communities under the guise of decentralization: that is, since 1987, even though district assemblies are financially and institutionally too feeble to be able to discharge these responsibilities effectively. The single most important justification for the transfer of responsibilities for social reproduction from the state is that the market, rather than the state, must decide in the allocation of values, including life's opportunities.

Responsibility for development goes with the exercise of political power. Private interests are therefore quietly appropriating the political space (and political power) relinquished by the state at a time when states are under pressure to become liberal, lean and allow for the participation of a broader spectrum of private interests in public affairs. The result is that, in spite of the provisions of the 1992 Constitution concerning the unitary character of the state, there is a de facto diffusion of power into private hands, however subtle this might be.

The sharing of the state's sovereign power and responsibilities with private interests is the shape of the emerging governance structure which links the central government to local communities as well as NGOs (national and international) in a network of so-called development partners. In reality, the country's development partners have become part of the emerging structure of national power: a synergy of private powers and public powers presumably working towards a common goal – the good of the people. It is significant that, like the national government, NGOs, especially those engaged in grassroots development, also claim to represent the people, and act as the people's voice in order to bring development to those who are poor and marginalized and cannot defend their rights against the forces of the evolving market society. In a nutshell, the idea of governance is not just about 'influencing [public] policy but taking over the business of government' (Stoker 1998: 19–21, 23).

The emerging idea that democracy *is* good governance raises fundamental questions about the meaning and prospects for democratic practice. By whose mandate do the private interests or civil society organizations exercise the power of government? To whom are they responsible and accountable? In a democracy, elections and other structures like citizens' associations ensure that the government would at least exercise legitimate power and is accountable to the citizens. Citizens know who represents them, how they can communicate their grievances, or how they can achieve policy change. In contrast, the private interests or civil society groups exercise the power to govern without the mandate of the citizens. This is contrary to the norms of liberal democracy, and blurs the lines of responsibility between the governors and the governed. Additionally, the citizens lose the sovereign power that is vested in them to exercise moral and political control, overtly or otherwise, over those who should normally have the authority to govern them. If those who now exercise governmental authority over the citizens' lives are not bound to society by the contractual obligation embedded in the Constitution of the Republic, to whom do the citizens turn, or hold accountable, in case there is abuse of trust or power?

Conclusion

Democracy is more than the freedom to choose one's political leaders periodically. It is also more than the freedom of speech and expression, including freedom of the press and other media to thrive. During the last decade the articulate sections of Ghanaian society have exercised these political freedoms in a robust and healthy manner, determined to ensure accountable and responsible government, combat corruption and prevent abuse of power. They have exercised these freedoms through the media whose autonomy and freedom have been boosted by the 1992 Constitution and the market.

For these freedoms to endure, the country would need educated, informed, vigilant and autonomous citizens who are able freely to exercise their will to preserve the freedoms guaranteed by the 1992 Constitution, because all the civil and political rights enshrined in Chapter 5 of the Constitution are expendable. Where citizens cannot act in the public sphere as autonomous agents, a tyrannical regime could easily redefine or manipulate freedom of the press and the individual to pursue its own hegemonic agenda. I have argued that poverty is a threat to democracy in the sense that it weakens the will of the people to exercise effective volition in public affairs. The market accounts for the exponential increase in Ghanaians who are poor. As pointed out above, poverty dominates the most active members of the Ghanaian population – those between fifteen and twenty-four years of age who are concentrated in the urban centres of the country from which political activity of any kind gravitates. Evidently poverty has restrained this politically strategic section of the Ghanaian population from exercising effective citizenship resulting in a democracy 'without an effective citizenship' (Przeworski 1995).

One of the central arguments of Milton Friedman in his defence of capitalism is that monopolies limit freedom; they 'destroy a free society' (Friedman 1982). What he did not admit is that capitalism also breeds monopolies and thereby limits competition, leading to the abolition of private property (Schumpeter 1950). It is at its monopoly stage that capitalism commits its worst outrages against members of society. In the developed capitalist societies, the state intervenes periodically to protect society from such excesses. Ghana's development experience of the last ten years shows that the state is too weak to protect society from the ravages of capitalism. Capitalism could commit such excesses against Ghanaians because, first, the market is inefficient in creating wealth for the benefit of society. Second, though the constitutional state is the guarantor of citizenship, and has responsibility to empower civil society (Di Palma 1997: 292), the Ghanaian state is so weak in the face of the raging market forces that it is unable to intervene to protect society from the excesses of the market. This is why under the market reforms poverty has become endemic, afflicting not less than 40 per cent of Ghanaians, and diminishing their will for effective citizenship.

The problem of building a democratic society in Ghana is rooted in this accumulation model in which the market is both inefficient and powerful and operates with the complicity of a weak state. This model, as the evidence shows, can generate only low rates of growth. It creates very little wealth, distributes the little wealth it creates in an extremely unequal manner, and weakens the political will of the citizens to exercise their sovereign power in participating in their own governance and holding their leaders accountable.

All this leaves liberal democracy a distant pedigree of its classical form. Schumpeter's definition of democracy as 'that institutional arrangement for arriving at political decisions in which individuals acquire the power to decide by means of a competitive struggle for the people's vote' (Schumpeter 1950: 269) fits Ghanaian democracy very well. A Ghanaian taxi-driver restated the same view in less sophisticated but thoughtful words.

> The seat of government is not like the Asantehene's stool which one person or group of persons can occupy till death. If we vote you on to the seat of government, you can only govern for a period of two successive terms. After this you should give way to another person or group of persons; because governing cannot be the preserve of one group of persons; it should be exercised by different people from time to time. After all, no single group of persons has monopoly over wisdom. It is therefore important to leave the seat of government after serving your term. That's why I voted for — in the last election; and that's why I shall vote for — in the next election.[3]

Undoubtedly, Ghanaians believe that democracy as freedom to choose one's leaders through the ballot subsumes freedom of speech, which they have adeptly defined as *'ka bi ma me nka bi amambu'* (speak and let me also speak form of government), and other civil and political rights. The last decade of Ghana's democracy has been characterized by unqualified expression of the freedoms of speech and choice. This notwithstanding, the greatest test for the nation is whether democracy will succeed. Whether or not democracy can be preserved depends on the extent to which ordinary citizens and their leaders will show commitment to democratic values and principles. For the ordinary citizens, commitment to preserve democracy will grow if the institutions of democracy are perceived as effective in providing their basic social and economic needs. Where democratic institutions fail in this regard, instilling the democratic norms and procedures that should govern political action becomes problematic and a welcome justification for a faction of the political elite to exploit popular disenchantment to corrupt democratic institutions or subvert them. Therefore the challenge facing government is to ensure that the pursuit of equity and justice for the people of this country forms an integral part of market reforms.

Notes

1 Individuals spoke against the proposed privatization mainly through the press.

2 Aware of the grave damage done by the PNDC/NDC government to the economy through 'reckless' spending on the eve of the 1992 elections, the NPP government has consciously reminded the country of its resolve not to

allow itself to be lured into undermining the level of macroeconomic stability it has achieved so far because it wants to please the electorate.

3 A friendly taxi-driver whom I engaged in a conversation on his assessment of the present government and its policies, and about voters' choice in the December 2004 elections.

Sources

Addae-Mensah, I. (2000) *Education in Ghana (A Tool for Social Mobility or Social Stratification)* (Accra: Ghana Academy of Arts and Sciences).

Amoakohene, M. (2005) 'Assessment of Advertising and Sponsorship Trends in the Ghanaian Electronic Media', *Ghana Social Science Journal*, Vol. 3, nos 1 and 2 (June and December).

Anebo, F. (2001) 'The Ghana 2000 Elections: Voter Choice and Electoral Decisions', *African Journal of Political Science*, Vol. 6, no. 1 (June).

Austin, D. and R. Luckham (eds) (1975) *Politicians and Soldiers in Ghana 1969–1974* (London: Frank Cass).

Berlin, I. (1969) 'Two Concepts of Liberty', in *Four Essays on Liberty* (Oxford: Oxford University Press).

Boafo-Arthur, K. (2004) 'Election Monitoring in Ghana: The Case for Domestic Monitors and Observers', in S. E. Quainoo (ed.), *Ghanaian Lenses* (Binghamton, NY: Vestal International Press).

Callinicos, A. (2003) *An Anti-Capitalist Manifesto* (Cambridge: Polity Press).

CEPA (Centre for Policy Analyses) (1996) *Macroeconomic Review and Outlook* (Accra: CEPA).

Chazan, N. (1987) 'Anomalies and Continuity: Perspectives on Ghanaian Elections Since Independence', in F. M. Hayward (ed.), *Elections in Independent Africa* (Boulder, CO: Westview Press).

CHRI (Commonwealth Human Rights Initiative) (2001) *Human Rights and Poverty Eradication* (New Delhi: CHRI).

Cobbe, J. (1991) 'The Political Economy of Educational Reform in Ghana', in D. Rothchild (ed.), *Ghana: The Political Economy of Recovery* (Boulder, CO, and London: Lynne Rienner).

Di Palma, G. (1997) 'Markets, State and Citizenship in New Democracies', in M. Midlarsky (ed.), *Inequality, Democracy and Economic Development* (Cambridge: Cambridge University Press).

Dunn, J. (1975) 'Politics in Asunafo', in D. Austin and R. Luckham (eds), *Politicians and Soldiers in Ghana 1969–1974* (London: Frank Cass).

— (ed.) (1992) *Democracy, the Unfinished Journey, 508 BC to AD 1993* (Oxford: Oxford University Press).

Friedman, M. (1982) *Capitalism and Freedom* (Chicago and London: University of Chicago Press).

Ghana Statistical Service (2000) *Ghana Living Standards Survey: Report of the Fourth Round (GLSS 4)* (Accra: Ghana Statistical Service).

Hutchful, E. (2002) *Ghana's Adjustment Experience: The Paradox of Reform* (Geneva: UNRISD/Woeli/Heinemann/James Currey).

ISSER (Institute of Social Statistical and Economic Research) (1994) *The State of the Ghanaian Economy in 1993* (Legon: ISSER, University of Ghana).

— (2004) *The State of the Ghanaian Economy in 1993* (Legon: University of Ghana).

Jefferies, R. (1980) 'The Ghanaian Elections of 1979', *African Affairs*, Vol. 79, no. 318 (July).

Karikari, K. (1998) 'The Press and the Transition to Multi-Party Democracy in Ghana', in K. A. Ninsin (ed.), *Ghana: Transition to Democracy* (Dakar: CODESRIA/Freedom Publications).

Kilby, P. (1969) *Industrialization in an Open Economy, Nigeria 1945–1966* (Oxford: Oxford University Press).

Lindley, R. (1986) *Autonomy* (London: Macmillan).

Midlarsky, M. I. (ed.) (1997) *Inequality, Democracy, and Economic Development* (Cambridge: Cambridge University Press).

Ninsin, K. A. (1991) *The Informal Sector in Ghana's Political Economy* (Accra: Freedom Publications).

— (1993) 'The Electoral System, Elections and Democracy in Ghana', in K. A. Ninsin and F. K. Drah (eds), *Political Parties and Democracy in Ghana's Fourth Republic* (Accra: Woeli).

— (1998a) 'Civic Associations and the Transition to Democracy', in K. A. Ninsin (ed.), *Ghana: Transition to Democracy* (Dakar: CODESRIA/Freedom Publications).

— (1998b) 'Postscript: Elections, Democracy and Elite Consensus', in K. A. Ninsin (ed.), *Ghana: Transition to Democracy* (Dakar: CODESRIA/Freedom Publications).

Nugent, P. (1995) *Big Men, Small Boys and Politics in Ghana* (Accra: Asempa Publishers).

Osei, P. D. (2000) 'Political Liberalization and the Implementation of Value Added Tax in Ghana', *Journal of Modern African Studies*, Vol. 38, no. 2 (June).

Przeworski, A. (1995) *Sustainable Democracy* (Cambridge: Cambridge University Press).

Schumpeter, J. A. (1950) *Capitalism, Socialism and Democracy*, 3rd edn (New York: Harper).

Stoker, G. (1998) 'Governance as Theory: Five Propositions', *International Social Science Journal*, no. 155 (March).

World Bank (1989) *Sub-Saharan Africa: From Crisis to Sustainable Growth* (Washington, DC: World Bank).

— (1992) *Ghana 2000 and Beyond: Setting the Stage for Accelerated Growth and Poverty Reduction* (Washington, DC: World Bank, West Africa Department).

— (2004) *Country Assistance Strategy for Ghana 2000–2003* (Accra: World Bank, Ghana Office).

5 | Institutions and economic performance: Ghana's experience under the Fourth Republic, 1992–2002

NICHOLAS AMPONSAH

The search for a durable democratic system of governance in many less developed countries has always concentrated on the more formal aspects of democracy. Attention is usually focused on the holding of free elections and their regularity. Once that has been attained, attention is shifted to how free and fair these elections are. Thus, Bratton and van de Walle note that 'a transition to democracy is held to have occurred with the installation of a national government chosen on the basis of one competitive election, as long as that election is freely and fairly conducted within a matrix of civil liberties, and all the contestants accept the validity of the election results' (Bratton and van de Walle 1997: 12). Even though analysts agree that the people for whom democratic governance is instituted judge the performance and sustenance of democracy in terms of the substantive benefits that accrue to them, they contend that democratic consolidation implies the presence of a certain minimal set of procedures provided to citizens to chose their leaders (ibid.).

The formal institutional aspects of democracy are necessary but not sufficient for ensuring the sustainability of democracy in emerging nations. Democracies must deliver in performance as well. As Przeworski et al. (1996: 43) note: 'Once democracy is in place, affluence is a sufficient condition for it to survive regardless of anything else.' The efforts of the various regimes under Ghana's Fourth Republic to secure a modicum of stability, development and the eradication of mass poverty will yield no dividends in the absence of functionally credible political and economic institutions that facilitate vibrant and productive economic activities leading to growth and development. The World Bank (2001a) aptly posited this issue, noting that the ability of democratic regimes to deliver more effectively to their citizens depends on the accountability and responsiveness of state institutions.

Today it can be said that democracy in Ghana is irreversible. The people of Ghana are concerned with how to deepen it and make it deliver the desired benefits of social and economic well-being. This is what calls for good governance. Good governance implies establishing credible institutions, with transparent rules that are known, internalized and above all enforced. We note that the quality of political and economic institutions determines and affects the capacity of a less developed country such as Ghana to ensure economic diversification, transformation, growth and development.

This chapter examines how the institutions of state under the Fourth Republic work to promote the socio-economic well-being of the people of Ghana. I argue that the sustenance of Ghana's nascent democracy is significantly related to the effective and efficient workings or application of the institutions established for managing the affairs of state, especially in the economic realm. Two dimensions of institutional analysis serve as the focus for this chapter. The first relates to the much more mundane institutional analysis which conceives institutions not merely as the presupposition of the existence of the rule of law under constitutional government. Far more than that, it conceives of institutions including the application of the principles of the rule of law in functional terms, to mean 'that a country's formal rules are made publicly known and enforced in a predictable way through transparent mechanisms' (World Bank 2001a: 102). The second relates to the functioning of the more formal institutional structures including the legislative, executive and the judiciary. It also examines the capacity of the state system to streamline bureaucratic procedures to avoid problems of bureaucratic bottlenecks. The former is of particular interest in this study.

The chapter is developed along the following lines: section two defines and explains the institutionalist perspective and emphasizes the significance of institutions for the consolidation of democracies. Section three reviews the flow of private investments during the 1992–2004 period under the neoliberal state. It examines the factors militating against the capacity of the liberal state to deliver in substantive economic terms. Emphasis is placed on those institutional variables that relate to the economic environment. Utilizing a variety of empirical data including a field survey, section four examines the functioning of state institutions especially in relation to property rights protection, the efficacy of the bureaucratic machinery, as well as state actions or inactions in relation to the upholding of the rule of law and contractual obligations. This is done with the view to assessing the prevalence or otherwise of institutional credibility in the liberal state in Ghana. The fifth section draws conclusions.

Significance of institutions in creating an enabling economic environment

Unlike the leadership of the highly performing Asian economies (HPAEs), African governments are often less motivated to seek the cooperation of civil society and private business in contributing their input towards the national endeavour through taxes and other resources, but, rather, are more content with rent-seeking and patronage (Bates 1999: 86). At best, African governments ignore civil society actors, especially private economic entrepreneurs, considering them simply as malevolent; at worst, they tyrannize them out of existence (Tangri 1992: 97–111). How can these critical actors – state functionaries and societal economic entrepreneurs – cooperate for the mutual benefit of their nation's economic growth and development? How can Ghana's democratic regime under the Fourth Republic secure the cooperation of private economic actors who have been duly recognized as the engine of growth and development so as to be able to deliver in terms of economic performance? Recent works of social scientists demonstrate that cooperation is facilitated and democracy consolidated by the prevalence of *credible institutions* (Keefer and Knack 1997: 590–602).

Institutional credibility implies the existence of formal and or informal rules, regulations, procedures and processes that are known, accepted and internalized by all actors in the process of shared growth. It is within the framework of such known, accepted, internalized and enforceable principles and procedures of social and political conduct that nations are rated as having high or low levels of transparency in governance. It connotes the prevalence of rights to own property and do business, the certainty that there would be no expropriation, and the assurance that governmental enforcement of 'the rules of the game', and honouring of contractual obligations is predictable. This last aspect of institutional prerequisites is of special importance for our purposes in appraising Ghana's performance under the Fourth Republic. This is because: 'In matters of governance, "good intentions" and "desirable ends" are not enough' (Prempeh 2002).

A major objective in this sphere is to examine the extent to which a stable, consistent and predictable regulatory environment prevails under Ghana's neoliberal Fourth Republican dispensation. On the other hand, the lack of credible institutions in a society, and in particular the enforcement and adherence to rules and contractual obligations by regimes, manifests itself in increasing doubts in the minds of private actors both at home and abroad about the goals, objectives and actions of the authorities, especially in the area of bureaucratic bottlenecks, and the application of the due process of law. These are also the forces that breed an atmosphere of corruption and indiscipline, all of which hinder progressive socio-economic development. So that, where there is increasing suspicion by society, and especially by entrepreneurs, about the implicit and explicit actions of the authorities, there is undoubtedly no institutional credibility.

A consideration of institutional credibility entails not only an examination of the extent to which a state system provides clearer and specific definition and allocation of rights to own property and do business. More than that, we are interested in the extent to which these rights, rules and regulations are protected by the state system and are accepted and internalized, thereby lowering the uncertainties in social and business interactions. In state systems lacking institutional credibility, problems related to the allocation and definition of property rights are pervasive, discretionary action by state actors is rampant, and the costs of obtaining legality in the formal state system in terms of delays and productive time lost are extremely high. Furthermore, the policy environment is so volatile because the rules, procedures and processes are very ambiguous or complicated. At the same time, there is little trust for the state's adherence to contractual obligations both by domestic actors as well as external economic actors as manifested in the low levels of foreign direct investment (FDI) in Ghana.

The way institutions of the state work is very important, yet most studies on the rebirth of democracy in the new states of Africa do not focus attention on the workings or application of the 'rules of the game'. A constitution, for instance, is created as the basic institution of every state for several purposes. Indeed, it is to serve as the basis for translating the wishes and aspirations of the people into reality and to forestall their fears. It is therefore important that the institutions of state, underpinned by the constitution, work to sustain the wishes and aspirations of its people.

Exploring the literature on institutions, investment and economic performance

How can African democrats seize the opportunity provided in the liberal state and begin the process of constructing stable democracies? The biggest threat to the consolidation of democracy in Sub-Saharan Africa is likely to be the continent's continuing economic crisis. For democracy to be consolidated and deepened in new democracies such as Ghana, it is imperative for the political leaders to find ways that facilitate economic growth and stability. Van de Walle notes: 'The survival and consolidation of democracy in sub-Saharan Africa will depend on the ability of the new democratic leaders to find ways to promote and maintain economic stability' (Van de Walle 1996: 128–41). He continues: 'Economic performance is a significant factor in citizens' evaluations of their government and, consequently, strongly affects any democratic regime's long-term prospects', adding that, 'Africans may well value democratic government as an end in itself and be more forgiving of the new democratic leaders than they were of their authoritarian predecessors in this regard, but it would be naive to think that any of the new governments will long escape blame if economic progress is not forthcoming' (ibid.).

In fact, the specific economic policies that these regimes adopt are ultimately less important than whether they embark on the process of building institutionalized mechanisms, in both government and civil society, that support economic development. Such policies are most likely to be implemented if and when a nation succeeds in combining a professional and impartial public bureaucracy with a consensus regarding the general outline of economic policy. Building strong political institutions will go a long way towards ensuring both economic renewal and the consolidation of democratic rule. Various analysts (Herbst 1993; Sarpong 1996: 73–1000) have duly recognized the importance of the institutional framework for assuring and sustaining democracy and development via a private-sector-led strategy. Yet the emphases have always been on the formal aspects of political and economic institutions. Sarpong (1996), for example, provides a list of preconditions for ensuring performance under the liberal state in Ghana. Among the important preconditions he enumerates are: 'A regulatory framework favorable to enterprise development; access to finance suitable to the peculiar requirements of firms; effective trade liberalization; availability of adequate physical infrastructure; access to required technology; availability of capable manpower and technical personnel; and, positive government attitude towards the private sector.'

Institutional strength in this regard refers to the extent the political system is able to create mechanisms that guide, facilitate and strengthen the ability of its domestic as well as foreign investors to utilize initiative and cooperate in the national development endeavour. Such an institutional paradigm disperses authority by deliberately avoiding the centralization or concentration of authority. The case for institutional credibility is particularly important not only in a country's search for foreign investors, but for mobilizing domestic investment as well. For it is these twin forces that propel economic growth and development often attributed to modern liberal states.

Various regimes in Ghana have approached the issue of investment, both domestic and foreign, through what might be termed the 'tea-party' approach. In their bid to woo investors, especially foreign direct investment (FDI), the various regimes utilized the 'delegation' or 'mobilization' strategy by which regime leaders toured the globe beckoning investors to make Ghana their destination. Just as the Provisional National Defence Council (PNDC) regime, the National Democratic Congress (NDC) and the New Patriotic Party (NPP) administrations sent several delegations throughout the world including North America, Europe and East and South East Asia.

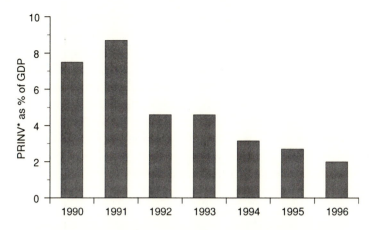

Figure 5.1 Private investment flows under the liberal state, 1990–96 (*Source*: Tsikata et al. 2000: 7)

The latter is noted to have made the most strenuous efforts in terms of air miles travelled. The Limann administration in the Third Republic had followed the same approach of 'globe-trotting', to no avail.

On the assumption of office, the New Patriotic Party administration declared a 'golden age' for private business. During the following forty-two months, the regime toured most parts of the globe in a fruitless search for investors. In due recognition of the sluggish pace with which the private sector was actually responding to the call to invest in this 'golden age' of business, the government launched yet another strategy. Thus, in mid-July 2004, barely six months before the end of the regime's tenure, the government launched its medium-term private sector development strategy. The president intimated that the launch of the strategy, by way of providing access to venture capital to prospective private investors, reflected the actions government intended to take to promote private sector investments and remove the constraints on their competitiveness and growth (*Daily Graphic*, 19 February 2002). To be sure, the numerous efforts by various regimes in Ghana to woo private investors, as elsewhere in Africa, appear not to have convinced or enticed private economic actors to commit their investment resourses to gainful investment. Figure 5.1 provides the most vivid picture of private investment flows in Ghana during the period 1990 to 1996 under the liberal dispensation.

While the most recent data on investment trends in the period under study are not available, the indications from Bank sources show that the trends have not witnessed any upward progression (World Bank 2003: 24). Worse still, the available data consist of the aggregate of both domestic and foreign private investment. As for domestic private investment, there is little if anything significant to write about. As noted, governments in Africa, including Ghana, following the dictates of neoliberal economic theory espoused by the international financial institutions (IFIs) and the advanced industrialized countries (AICs), have approached the problem of investment and development through the 'mobilizational' or 'promotional' strategy which has not yielded dividends. On the contrary, such an approach to securing a modicum of investment has brought little if any investment. There is a need to examine the root causes of the problem of securing investors both at home and abroad. To be sure, several factors, including institutional uncertainty, explain the lukewarm attitude of would-be investors.

Among the critical factors found to have a negative impact on prospective investors, Tsikata et al. (2000: 15) note poor infrastructure, especially in power, transportation and communication. Others include the trade and exchange rate regime, and the extent to which it is liberal-oriented, as well as political stability. On these counts, Ghana may be said not to be wanting. Thus, the question to ask is, why has the country had such a hard time securing investment so as to promote development? Among the unresolved issues that dissuade investors, Tsikata et al. (ibid.) reiterate the historical record of the credibility of the regime in terms of trust. In their view, the likelihood that a country will gain significant investment 'all boils down to the question: has country X been sufficiently FDI-friendly to past investors to warrant new investors?' In addition to this is the nagging issue of whether the regime can be trusted to honour contractual obligations, especially on matters that border on the supremacy of the constitution and the adherence to the principles of rule of law. They conclude that the 'Lack of predictability in terms of the government's respect for its own laws and regulations ... discourage[s] foreign investors' (ibid.) as well as domestic investors.

Institutional credibility and private investment: analysis from survey data

Utilizing a variety of empirical data including field surveys, I examine the functioning of state institutions, particularly in relation to property rights protection, efficacy of the bureaucratic machinery, as well as state action or inaction in relation to contractual obligations. The theory and practice of the functioning of other formal state institutions, including the hybrid legislature, the executive and the judiciary, are also reviewed. This is done with a view to assessing the prevalence or otherwise of institutional credibility in the liberal state in Ghana. The study employs survey data on the perceptions of Ghanaian private entrepreneurs about the institutional climate. While urging caution in the use of surveys, Tsikata et al., however, note that 'survey data (via questionnaires and/or interviews) that analyze the key motivations of investors are ideally suited for studying qualitative factors which may be difficult to incorporate into an econometric model' (Tsikata et al. 2000: 15).

There is general agreement that the various administrations in Ghana under the liberal democratic dispensation have performed creditably in terms of rationalizing the country's macroeconomic imbalances. In fact, the NPP administration may be said to have chalked up the most gains in macroeconomic management, in terms of fiscal discipline and inflation control as mandated by the IFIs. Nevertheless, these successes have had no positive impact on the readiness of private investors to commit their resources to investment in the liberal state as neoliberal theory anticipates. Lewis (2004: 16–17) hit the nail on the head when he intimated that although Ghana had pursued sound macroeconomic policies, 'the most important issue [is] not the policy regime but how to improve the institutional regime to improve growth'. In what he referred to as 'the paradox of Ghana's development initiatives', Lewis noted that the country had a good policy regime but, contrary to expectations, slow economic growth. The missing link clearly seems to be the absence of a predictable or credible atmosphere for economic transactions and the rules of the game pertaining to doing business and honouring contractual obligations.

The role of government in helping establish credible institutions necessary for cooperative endeavour cannot be overemphasized. This is particularly so in societies with little history of stable institutional development and cooperative endeavour. The long-established institutional practices, traditions and norms of relationships between state agencies and private entrepreneurs, and between state governments and domestic and foreign businesses, are considered critical for enhancing or dissuading entrepreneurial endeavour. The way state structures and institutions, including rules of practice, laws, norms and procedural regulations, have operated on and influenced entrepreneurial ventures in the past always serves as the basis for making any long-term business decisions. Again, the trust that prospective business entrepreneurs both at home and abroad have for the government's adherence to the rules of the game, and particularly in honouring contractual obligations, plays a significant role in the flow of investments. Vigorous entrepreneurial activity will emerge in an atmosphere where experience based on the existing rules of institutions points to abundant opportunities for unfettered business development. If the interplay of the rules regarding business transactions and contractual obligations are unpredictable because they are cumbersome, the task of securing investors will be difficult.

Ghanaian private business entrepreneurs were surveyed on two sets of questions related to aspects of the traditions and norms of social interaction that prevail in their dealings with the authorities. These traditions and norms reflect the institutional and regulatory environment and serve as the basis of trust for the entire state system. They include, first, the security of businesses and property, including land; and, second, the pervasive discretionary power of the state. These issues are related to the level of trust that exists in any modern society.

Private business and the problems of property rights and expropriation in Ghana We have noted that economic performance, especially in terms of private investment flows, is highly related to the level of institutional credibility. This is how Borner, Brunetti and Weder put it:

> The common view on economies in transition is almost identical, but it stipulates that institutional reforms be the first essential step in any reform package. In economies making the transition from central planning to a free market approach, the importance of developing institutions that provide credible legal support for the growth of a private sector-driven market economy is clearly recognized. However, the need for institutional reform in LDCs is not widely discussed by most policy-makers, let alone given priority. (Borner et al. 1995)

Campos and Root (1996) also identified the prevalence of credible political and economic institutions, especially in terms of the certainty of the available rules for economic transactions, as a major factor for private sector trust of the economic environments in the highly performing Asian economies (HPAEs), and their eagerness to invest in those economies. Can the same be said about the poorly performing African economies (PPAEs) such as Ghana, even under the neoliberal state? In the latter case, contempt for private business, especially under the NDC administration (1992–2000), created a wide gulf between the state and private entrepreneurs (Tangri 1992).

On the other hand, even where the state authorities profess to advocate private business, as under the New Patriotic Party (NPP) administration, there is a tendency to assume that merely demonstrating commitment and support for private business – adhering strictly to the dictates of market rationality through the maintenance of a robust macroeconomic regime – would deliver the desired objectives of increased investment, especially from private actors. In either case, there is a tendency to take for granted the critical imperative for reforming the institutional regime. Referring to a similar situation that confronted the post-communist states of East Asia, Stein notes: 'the ex-communist countries are advised to move to a market economy and their leaders wish to do so, but without the appropriate institutions no market economy of any significance is possible' (Stein 1994). It is in the light of this that we probe the levels of institutional credibility in Ghana's liberal state and its possible relationship with the state's economic performance. The first area of institutional credibility examined here relates to the problems of property rights protection and the potential for expropriation.

Entrepreneurs were asked a series of questions to find out to what extent such problems – relating to property, business, and contractual rights and bureaucratic bottlenecks – constitute a hindrance to doing business. Table 5.1 summarizes the views expressed by Ghanaian private business persons on these institutional problems. The problem of property rights protection in nascent nations takes various forms; there may be direct or wanton confiscation or surreptitious obstruction by the authorities, especially in the public bureaucracy where most requirements for initiating a business commence. We probed the issue of property rights protection with a direct question: 'Do you think that the state can seize your business or property at any time without any justification?' (Q. 2a). As the responses indicate, a significant number of respondents said that outright confiscation of an individual's property or business by state authorities was not very likely. When this same question was asked five years later, the answer was a more emphatic 'no'. Thus, the narrow definition of property rights protection seems to have gained currency in Ghana. The reason, according to some entrepreneurs, was due to the façade of democratization, which has ushered in a proliferation of business associations and relatively critical media.

There was consensus, however, that certain subtle actions by the state authorities could impede an individual's freedom or ability to carry on productive economic activities. Asked whether the authorities could act in certain oppressive ways that would impede or halt the productive activities of an entrepreneur (see Q. 2c), a significant majority of respondents (63.1 per cent) answered in the affirmative, 35.9 per cent strongly so, and 27.2 per cent moderately so.

The view of Ghanaian private entrepreneurs generally supported the belief that the Ghanaian regime of the first two administrations was intrinsically antagonistic to private business people (Tangri 1992; Hutchful 1995: 303–17). Even though five years later the situation seemed to have improved, only half of the entrepreneurs surveyed thought that covert or surreptitious harassment from state authorities was unlikely (see Q. 2c,

TABLE 5.1 Private business entrepreneurs and problems of property rights and expropriation in Ghana

Question	Survey data I: 1997–98[1]							Survey data II: 2003–04[2]						
	Yes	(%)	No	(%)	Don't know	(%)	Total	Yes	(%)	No	(%)	Don't know	(%)	Total
Q. 2a: Do you think the state can seize your business/property at any time without any justification?	222	49.9	223	50.1	–	–	445	40	9.9	365	90.1	–	–	405
Q. 2c: Do you think the state can act in some surreptitious ways to harm your business operations?	281	63.1	153	34.4	11	2.5	445	170	41.3	207	50.1	36	8.6	413
Q. 4e: Are the levels of bureaucratic authorities to traverse in order to formalize or start up a business reasonable?	173	40.4	243	56.7	12	2.8	428	235	54.6	180	41.8	15	3.4	430
Q. 4q: Do you agree that 'rules of the game' are always adhered to in formalizing or starting up business operations?	174	39.0	267	59.8	5	1.1	446	201	47.6	210	49.7	11	2.6	422

Sources: Survey data I: Amponsah 2000: 8–34; Survey data II a repeat of Survey data I, conducted autumn 2003 and spring 2004.

Survey data II in Table 5.1). To be sure, there are still people who, for one reason or another (especially those who are not in the good books of the incumbent administration), acknowledge the possibility of harassment from certain state authorities.

Aryeetey et al. (1994) note that in Ghana the ability of a private enterprise to grow is 'constrained by inadequate access to finance, or other market factors, product markets, and licenses needed to operate legally'. These constraints thus make private business persons highly risk-averse in terms of investment ventures. Nevertheless, such mundane obstacles on business operations are not considered property rights problems in official circles. Whenever the ruling elite are confronted with an observation pointing to the need for institutional reforms they are always quick to rebut it by answering that under the democratic dispensation these institutions do exist. In the recent past, when Ghana was under military dictatorships, a common occurrence had been the capricious seizure of the properties of certain entrepreneurs, most often by state fiat. Under the liberal state's programmes of economic liberalization and democratization, which began in 1992, such rapacious practices were supposed to be a thing of the past.

There is another conception of the property rights problem that is much more common, and more subtle. This relates to situations in which the authorities commit certain surreptitious acts, often extra-legal, that impede or completely halt business operations. Political authorities in a reforming or democratizing third world country may not directly or openly confiscate property as they did in the past praetorian political order prior to reforms, but they could act covertly in much the same way. Borner et al. (1995) observed a similar situation in Nicaragua where the political and bureaucratic elite referred to instances of outright confiscation of property as the only property rights problem.

The results of this study corroborate Aryeetey's (1994: 1211) speculations that risk-averse behaviour probably accounts for the reason why potential private investors shy away from long-term investment commitments. It is apparent from this study that a reasonable number of Ghanaian private business entrepreneurs still perceive the illiberal, neopatrimonial and predatory tendency of the state and its bureaucratic agencies to be omnipresent despite the democratization façade. They believe that even if the state in Ghana cannot overtly expropriate or seize businesses and property outright, there are several subtle or covert ways in which the actions of the state could interfere or halt the smooth operation of business. The weakness of the institutional climate in pre-empting any perceived potential predatory governmental actions is, therefore, very serious, and a major

117

inhibiting factor for market liberalization or democratization to achieve the desired goals. The most serious arena of institutional uncertainty is in the area of bureaucratic ineptitude.

Encountering state institutions in Ghana

This section examines the functioning of state institutions including the public bureaucracy, the legislature, the executive and the judiciary. I also examine the propensity of the Ghanaian state to honour contractual obligations. These issues, which border on institutional credibility, also constitute the hallmark of a liberal democratic state.

There is unanimous agreement among Ghanaian private entrepreneurs that, because of several years of experience with wanton expropriation, they do not trust that such incidents will not recur. The existence of trust among a host of economic agents and between them and the state authority (Putnam 1993) explains the success of economic enterprises, their growth and development. When a regime provides a stable administrative and institutional environment that facilitates coordination and cooperation for mutual benefit, it creates a healthy economic atmosphere for prospective economic and social actors as they acquire a sense of trust and cooperative spirit. Thus, the propensity for individuals living in a society to join together to engage in issues of mutual concern is indicative of the presence of credible institutions in that society. The success of economic performance in the liberal state in Ghana therefore depends on the extent to which a credible institutional environment, including a trusted and efficient bureaucracy, prevails. The efficacy of the public bureaucracy is probed in the framework sketched above.

Bureaucratic bottlenecks and 'kalabule' The difficulty that faces an entrepreneur in either initiating a business venture or maintaining and consolidating such a business may in part be the result of bureaucratic bottlenecks. In fact, most analysis of variations in political capacity among nations is essentially about the differences in the efficiency of public bureaucracies. Thus, Evans describes the archetype of the developmental state as characterized by exceptional competence and coherence in organization, while the archetype of the predatory state is typified by the rapaciousness of officialdom and moribund bureaucratic organization, which in itself places bottlenecks on the economic decisions of private actors (Evans 1995: 43–50). In Ghana, bureaucratic bottlenecks and malpractices that give rise to various forms of rent-seeking behaviour, such as corruption, are referred to in common parlance as *kalabule*.

Bureaucratic bottlenecks, here, means those procedures and processes that present entrepreneurs with requirements that are unreasonable or extremely difficult to comply with. We hypothesized that under the liberal state in Ghana these troubling impediments should be withering away if not entirely absent. Where there are numerous hierarchies of authority, all of which must be consulted in order to initiate or remain in an industry, the difficulties faced by entrepreneurs become even more complicated than usual. The resultant problem of 'complexity of joint action' has been identified by policy analysts as a major obstacle preventing policies, programmes and government economic development projects, as well as individual entrepreneurs, from being successful and achieving their goals (Pressman and Wildavsky 1973: 87–124). Thus, an effective and efficient bureaucracy that functions professionally becomes a critical prerequisite for institutional stability. If, in fact, bureaucratic practice itself constitutes a constraint on business activity in the liberal state in Ghana, then the prospects of private sector investment would be slim, since private productive business transactions would become very costly.

In fact, the issue of bureaucratic bottlenecks and the general uncertainty regarding the costs of regulations need to be clarified. In less developed and institutionalized societies such as Ghana, such problems can appropriately be characterized as issues related mostly to the formalization or normalization of business operations from an ostensibly informal status. Indeed, if one were to ask most business operators in Ghana or in several other less institutionalized African societies whether they considered regulations for business start-up, per se, as obstacles, the answer would most likely be 'no'. To be sure, most businesses emerge as informal entities, initiated without official documentation. When asked, 'What is your attitude towards the so-called "informal" sector of the economy?' a Ghanaian minister for trade and industry said:

> The informal sector is usually characterized as one where the operators are small, unrecognized and do not pay tax. In Ghana it includes a series of unstructured economic activities that are largely labor-intensive, depending mainly on rudimentary technology and involving only marginal production. Informal operators can emerge in almost any economic field, as a response to unmet needs, and thriving on their own instincts for survival. The contribution of this sector to the Ghanaian economy has gained wide acceptance. (*Courier* 1994: 29)

Thus, even the most important spokesperson for the government of Ghana (1992–2000) recognized that businesses in Ghana emerge without official sanction or registration. Generally, therefore, when asked whether the regulations for business start-up constitute a hassle (Q. 4a), many business people will answer in the negative. They know that they must, of necessity, begin without official rules, regulations and procedures, which are not enforceable anyway. For prospective business-starters in Ghana, therefore, the problem is not getting started but, rather, how to remain in operation without interference, and more important, how to secure a speedy response to urgent needs when dealing with state bureaucrats. Thus, most issues on business-related regulations in Ghana must be considered more in the realm of formalization of business and transactions with the public bureaucracy.

Levels of bureaucratic authority To find out the extent to which bureaucratic practice in Ghana may have been an impediment to formalizing or maintaining private business ventures, we asked private entrepreneurs several questions. Their responses are summarized in Figure 5.2 and Table 5.1. We asked about the number or levels of hierarchical bureaucratic authorities a business person has to go through in order to formalize or constitute a business enterprise, as well as the procedural steps that have to be followed at each level.

Typical official transactions that might require certain cumbersome procedures include the issue of licences, allocation of building permits, and the registration of business and/or machinery. The more cumbersome, complicated or numerous these administrative hierarchies and procedures, the more costly it is to transact business legally and formally. Under such circumstances, prospective entrepreneurs may operate with or without appropriate legal requirements. Or they may decide to buy their way (however illegal) into operation.

On the other hand, prospective entrepreneurs might resort to mechanisms such as go-betweens that enable them to circumvent these procedures. The state system must guard against such neopatrimonial practices in order to encourage and promote legal and expeditious economic activity. Table 5.1, Q. 4c and 4q probe the level of bureaucratic certainty in liberal Ghana. We also gauge the levels or hierarchy of authority a prospective business person has to traverse in order to initiate or formalize his/her business (see Figure 5.2), and the extent to which entrepreneurs find this hierarchy relatively reasonable or not (see Table 5.1, Q. 4q).

The hierarchy of bureaucratic authorities necessary to transact a particular official business is considered very important because it represents conditions that may be costly to an entrepreneur in terms of access to the attainment of official requirements necessary for continued productive activity. They are important also because these have serious consequences for bureaucratic inefficiency and bottlenecks that lead to red tape, bribery

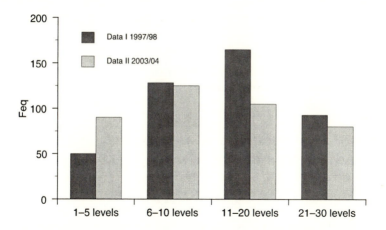

Figure 5.2 Levels of bureaucratic authority to be traversed in order to constitute or formalize a business (*Source*: Survey data I: Amponsah 2000; Survey data II, autumn 2003 and spring 2004)

and corruption. Bureaucratic practice is of particular importance in societies such as Ghana where the basic communications and information infrastructure of telephones, fax facilities, transportation and even postal systems are poorly developed or inefficient. Under such circumstances, higher and cumbersome levels of bureaucratic authority complicate an already bad situation.

Ghanaian private entrepreneurs were asked to enumerate the number of hierarchical official bureaucracies which must be consulted in order to meet legal requirements necessary for formalizing or constituting a business, as well as their continued legal existence in that business. The levels of authority were divided into four. Those situations with levels of authority ranging from 1 to 5 were considered as 'very good' and indicative of institutional certainty with respect to the public bureaucracy, while those with 21–30 were considered as the 'worst-case' scenario. The results are summarized in Figure 5.2. Only a few entrepreneurs (11.5 per cent) felt that the levels of bureaucratic authorities were good enough during the first survey (1997–98). Five years later, the figure, though improved, was still insignificant: only 21 per cent.

In all the cases, the majority of entrepreneurs felt that there were too many levels of bureaucratic authorities to be negotiated. The situation as intimated to me by one businessman in the timber industry is even more complicated by the over-centralized bureaucracy in that sub-sector. In a nutshell, many entrepreneurs believe that because the levels of bureaucratic authorities one has to traverse constitute a great deal of hassle, prospective

The Fourth Republic

business persons fall prey to neopatrimonial and patron–clientelist practices. Many entrepreneurs share the view that the levels of bureaucratic authority constitute a problem and, thus, in transacting business with the state bureaucracy, the 'rules of the game' are scarcely adhered to (Table 5.1, Q. 4q). In other words, there is a great deal of uncertainty in bureaucratic transactions in Ghana.

The persistent land issue and investment prospects That land constitutes the most fundamental prerequisite for productive industrial investment start-up and development cannot be overstated. Yet this fundamental asset has found no credible institutional foundation in the liberal state in Ghana, though it has in many other African countries. Several recent studies (World Bank 2001b; Desewu 2004; Dogbevi 2002) support the proposition that land policy in Ghana has continued to be a major stumbling block to FDI and development as there are no certain or credible institutional mechanisms for its procurement. Not only is land acquisition generally shrouded in a host of confused and insecure processes, often with several parties, there is also the risk that there may be several claimants to a piece of land even when it is perceived to have been legitimately acquired. This is not to mention the propensity for landowners to make arbitrary additional financial demands within the lease period. In most agreements or negotiations on land acquisition, the legal status of the particular land may be problematic precisely because there are few certain or clear and transparent institutionalized rules pertaining to land.

In the absence of any cadastral survey, or credible institutionalized procedures for land acquisition, buyers are at the mercy of the good-will of the local communities with concomitant higher risks and transaction costs. It is not uncommon for agreements made with a local chief about a parcel of land to be broken upon the de-stoolment or death of the old chief and the en-stoolment of a new one. To be sure, 'obstacles to land acquisition for business projects have been a major drawback to business development and growth' in Ghana (Desewu 2004: 1). In Côte d'Ivoire, where a modicum of clearer land tenure rules allows for easier acquisition of land by investors, horticultural exports such as pineapples have grown rapidly, to the benefit of the national economy. Indeed, the most serious institutional problem here is the inability to offer land, the most fundamental physical capital for collateral, due to the uncertainty of the security of title (World Bank 2001b: 47). It comes as no surprise that private businesses in Ghana, even under the liberal state that purports to be committed to a 'golden age of business', lament the ambiguous and uncertain institutional arrangements pertaining to land acquisition. Thus, private business in Ghana urges the need for simplifying and rationalizing the process of land acquisition to ensure its reliability and credibility (Desewu 2004).

Trust for the primary institutions of governance By far the most crucial aspect of the problem of institutional uncertainty that faces nascent democracies such as Ghana relates to the extent to which the primary political institutions, including the judiciary, the legislature and especially the executive, can be trusted to uphold not only the letter, but also the spirit of the principles of the rule of law. Having parliaments, judiciaries and elected executives formally established and ostensibly in operation may be one side of viewing the liberal state. The realization of the purposes and functions of these ostensibly democratic institutions in practice is another. In other words, these institutions would matter, only to the extent that they can be trusted and seen as credible. It is this latter aspect that has been a matter of concern to democracy observers all over the world. And it is also this aspect that has the potential to persuade or dissuade prospective economic actors

As Gyimah-Boadi rightly observed: 'Parliaments in Africa have been resurrected at least, formally ... attempts are being made to enforce accountability in government ... But serious barriers to representative government remain' (Gyimah-Boadi 1998: 10). As he notes, the deficiencies in political institutions arise because of the tendency for African presidential executives to dominate and control all sources of authority in their states including legislative and judiciary institutions. The Ghanaian parliament under the liberal state, for example, is noted in several instances as being a 'mere rubber stamp' of the executive. Thus, the Ghana Centre for Democratic Development (CDD) pointed to the failure of Ghana's legislature to exercise due diligence over an IFC/$1 billion loan, a débâcle that ended in a fiasco. Such instances, as the CDD noted, demonstrate that the Ghana legislature exists only in name 'and does not serve any useful public interest' (CDD 2002: 3).

A state may nominally be said to be democratic as the liberal state in Ghana is perceived to be, but its institutions of democracy may be a façade and thus have serious consequences for its development prospects. In addition to the empirical field data presented here, several instances of manifestations of institutional uncertainty, and lack of faith that the government will honour contractual obligations, abound in Ghana, and in part explain why it has been an uphill struggle for the liberal state to make gains in the economic realm in terms of investment. For example, immediately after the change in administration occurred in Ghana in 2002, the minister for communication, by mere word of mouth and without

123

due protocol, bluntly indicated the new regime's intention to abrogate a contract entered into by its predecessor, the NDC regime, with Telecom Malaysia, even before the formal tenure of the agreement had actually expired (*Daily Graphic*, 19 February 2002).

Another instance that called into question the government's commitment to ensuring institutional certainty and trust for the regime relates to the handling of affairs bordering on the rule of law. The president, taking advantage of certain loopholes in the Constitution (the absence of a constitutional ceiling on the size of the Supreme Court), appointed new Justices to the Supreme Court resulting in the overturning of an already decided crucial case in the government's favour, reminiscent of 'court packing'. Such instances cast a slur on the credibility of such august institutions as the Supreme Court and make a mockery of the intentions of good governance in a liberal democratic state. Such incidents are particularly lamentable under Ghana's Fourth Republic in which strenuous efforts are being made to adhere to upholding the principles of rule of law and accountability. This is Ghana's fourth attempt at democratization so any display of surreptitious acts that tarnish the credibility of legal institutions, especially the Supreme Court, and parliament, is worrisome. Yet, such occasions have cropped up, raising the question of whether the nation is up to the challenge of deepening its democracy. As Prempeh rightly noted: 'A government committed to rule of law must show as much concern for "means" as it does for "ends."' And, again, it is in the light of these that he concludes: 'The culture of the Ghanaian political elite, retains strong elements of *illiberalism* [emphasis mine] and patrimonialism and thus continues to adversely affect the quality and progress of constitutionalism in Ghana' (Prempeh 2002: 2); the intrinsic relationship between effective institutions and economic performance cannot therefore be overemphasized. In the words of Saffu: for Ghana's economy 'to perform effectively every public organization or institution is in need of urgent and radical reform' (Saffu 2004: 7).

Conclusion

The liberal theory that correlates democratization with economic diversification and development is being confounded in Ghana. Contrary to expectations, the liberal state under the Fourth Republic has failed to deliver in economic performance, as manifested in the lack of response by prospective private investors to a 'golden age of private business', while the state lies prostrate in self-accepted defeat as a highly indebted poor country (HIPC). The problem of poor economic performance even in the liberal state of Ghana continues to baffle many in government as well as in business circles. This is what has been referred to as the paradox of Ghana's development initiatives: the country has a relatively sound or good policy regime but, contrary to expectation, a slow economic growth and development. How do we explain this paradox?

The explanation must be sought in the institutional regime, as this chapter vividly shows. The outward and cosmetic manifestations of the liberal state – elections, parliaments, media pluralism, etc. – do not in themselves translate or promote economic diversification and growth. Indeed, the predictability, credibility and certainty of economic transactions and their relationship to transaction cost matter in all societies. But they matter the more in transitional economies with turbulent economic past histories. The fact that land acquisition title continues to be a troubling matter even in a liberal state that proposes a 'golden age of business' should therefore explain some of the reasons why the liberal state has had a hard time securing investors both at home and abroad. For the liberal state to deliver the desired economic impact, it must demonstrate the certainty and credibility of its political and economic institutions, especially in relation to property and land title rights, efficiency and credibility of public bureaucratic institutions, the legislature and the judiciary and a demonstrable commitment on the part of the state to honour contractual obligations.

The 'war' that the liberal state needs to wage in its struggle for economic growth and development should be against pervasive institutional uncertainty. Only the crafting and maintenance of credible institutions will ensure investment flows. Growth and development will occur only in state systems where there is institutional credibility. And institutional credibility exists only where social actors are confident that all state actions follow predictable laid-down procedures and norms. They are predictable because of the trust that has been built up over the years while cooperating to achieve social goals. As Putnam (1993) intimated, for a variety of reasons, life is easier in a community blessed with a substantial stock of credible institutions – *social capital*. This is because they allow dilemmas of collective action to be resolved.

Notes

1 Survey data I collected in autumn 1997 and spring 1998. Osei Kwadwo and Adansi-Pipim, both graduate students of the Department of Political Science, University of Ghana, assisted in the data collection, as did Akwasi Addai-Boateng and Yaw Adjei-Sarkodie of Sunyani, Ghana. See Amponsah (2000).

2 Survey data II collected in autumn 2003 and spring 2004, as a follow-up to provide a time series analysis of trends in Ghana's institutional regime.

Sincere appreciation again goes to K. Addae-Boateng of Sunyani, Bugumah Mohammed, M.Phil Candidate, Department of Political Science, as well as Daniel Appiah, a teaching assistant, also in the Department of Political Science, University of Ghana.

Sources

Amponsah, N. (2000) 'Ghana's Mixed Structural Adjustment Results: Explaining the Poor Private Sector Response', *Africa Today*, Vol. 47, no. 2 (Spring).

Aryeetey, E. (1994) 'Private Investment Under Uncertainty in Ghana', *World Development*, Vol. 22, no. 8.

Aryeetey, E., A. Baah-Nuako, T. Duggleby, H. Hettige and W. F. Steel (eds) (1994) *Supply and Demand for Finance of Small Enterprises in Ghana* (Washington, DC: World Bank).

Bates, R. H. (1999) 'The Economic Bases of Democratization', in R. Joseph (ed.), *State, Conflict and Democracy in Africa* (Boulder, CO: Lynne Rienner).

Borner, S., B. Aymo and B. Weder (1995) 'Policy Reform and Institutional Uncertainty: The Case of Nicaragua', *Kyklos*, Vol. 48, no. 1: 43.

Bratton, M. and N. van de Walle (1997) *Democratic Experiments in Africa: Regime Transitions in Comparative Perspective* (Cambridge: Cambridge University Press).

Campos, J. E. and H. L. Root (1996) *The Key to the Asian Miracle: Making Shared Growth Credible* (Washington, DC: Brookings Institution).

CDD (Centre for Democratic Development) (2002) *Democracy Watch,* quarterly Newsletter of Ghana Centre for Democratic Development.

Courier (1994) 'Country Report, Ghana: Striving to Keep Up the Momentum', *Journal of the African-Caribbean-Pacific and European Union*, Vol. 44 (March/April).

Desewu, E. E. (2004) 'Private Sector Proposals for Trouble-free Land for Investments', *Ghana Business Week*, no. 069, 21–27 June.

Dogbevi, E. (2002) 'Land Management in Ghana: Some Knotty Issues,' *FOELINE*, Vol. 15 (January–March) Friends of the Earth magazine, Accra.

Evans, P. (1995) *Embedded Autonomy: States and Industrial Transformation* (Princeton, NJ: Princeton University Press).

Gyimah-Boadi, E. (1998) 'Representative Institutions', in *Democratic Consolidation in Africa: Progress and Pitfalls*, conference report (Johannesburg: Center for Policy Studies).

Herbst, J. (1993) *The Politics of Reform in Ghana, 1982–1991* (Berkeley: University of California Press).

Hutchful, E. (1995) 'Why Regimes Adjust: The World Bank Ponders Its "Star Pupil"', *Canadian Journal of African Studies*, Vol. 29, no. 2: 303–17.

Jeffrey, H. (1993) *The Politics of Reform in Ghana, 1982–1991* (Berkeley: University of California Press).

Keefer, P. and S. Knack (1997) 'Why Don't Poor Countries Catch Up? A Cross-national Test of an Institutional Explanation', *Economic Inquiry*, 25 July: 590–602.

Lewis, P. (2004) 'American Economist Calls for Improved Institutional Environment', lecture delivered at conference organized by the Ghana Centre for Democratic Development (CDD), *Daily Graphic*, 24 July.

Prempeh, K. H. (2002) 'Rule of Law, Constitutionalism and Human Rights', Ghana CDD Briefing Paper, Vol. 4, no. 4.

Pressman, J. L. and A. Wildavsky (1973) *Implementation: How Great Expectations in Washington are Dashed in Oakland* (Berkeley: University of California Press).

Przeworski, A., M. Alvarez, J. A. Chebub and F. Limongi (1996) 'What Makes Democracies Endure?', *Journal of Democracy*, Vol. 7, no. 1.

Putnam, R. D. (1993) *Making Democracy Work: Civic Traditions in Modern Italy* (Princeton, NJ: Princeton University Press).

Saffu, Y. (2004) 'Deepening Our Democracy: The Functioning of Our Democratic Institutions', *Governance Newsletter* (Accra: Institute of Economic Affairs) (March).

Sarpong, K. (1996) 'Institutional Framework and Policies for Private-sector-led Development', in *Agenda '96: Preparing Ghana for the 21st Century: Some Economic and Social Issues* (Accra: Friedrich-Naumann-Stiftung).

Stein, H. (1994) 'Theories of Institutions and Economic Reform in Africa', *World Development*, Vol. 22, no. 12.

Tangri, R. (1992) 'The Politics of Government–Business Relations in Ghana', *Journal of Modern African Studies*, Vol. 30: 97–111.

Tsikata, K. G., Y. Asante and E. M. Gyasi (2000) *Determinants of Foreign Direct Investment in Ghana* (London: Overseas Development Institute).

van de Walle, N. (1996) 'Crisis and Opportunity in Africa', *Journal of Democracy*, Vol. 6, no. 2.

World Bank (2001a) *World Development Report: Attacking Poverty* (New York: Oxford University Press).

— (2001b) *Ghana, International Competitiveness: Opportunities and Challenges Facing Non-Traditional Exports*, Country Report no. 22421 – Africa Region (Washington, DC: World Bank).

— (2003) *Africa Development Indicators* (Washington, DC: World Bank).

6 | Political conflict and elite consensus in the liberal state

ALEXANDER K. D. FREMPONG

Ghana returned to constitutional rule in 1993 after eleven turbulent years of the authoritarian military-cum-civilian Provisional National Defence Council (PNDC) under the chairmanship of Flight Lieutenant Jerry John Rawlings who eventually became the first president of the Fourth Republic. He was leader of the National Democratic Congress (NDC) which had been formed to contest the multi-party elections held in 1992. Rawlings completed his two constitutional terms of eight years as president but his party lost the 2000 elections.

It may be argued, and justifiably so, that a decade is a relatively short time to assess the successes and failures of a democratic experiment. But for Ghana this is the first time in its nearly fifty years that constitutional governance has crossed the ten-year finishing line. It has witnessed a civilian government completing its two terms of office and a change of regime (or is it a shift in the balance of power?) from one political party to another. The very fact that this latest attempt at democracy began on very shaky foundations but has succeeded thus far is a short story in itself. This achievement is made even more dramatic, first, because the process of democratization in post-Cold War Africa has witnessed deadlocks, reverses, failures and mounting complexities (Conteh-Morgan 1997: 1) and, second, because Ghana is in a sub-region which has recently been far better known for violent civil conflict than for democracy and development. The extent to which this feat has been achieved through the interplay of political conflict and elite consensus is the thrust of this chapter.

Theoretical issues

Liberal democracy A major postulate of liberal democracy is that for the management of state affairs, there should be an open and free field for members of society to compete to exercise the power to control and manage the material resources of the state for and on behalf of the entire population, irrespective of race, religion, gender or political conviction (Hagan 1995: 83). Again, all governments rest on some mixture of coercion and consent but democracies are unique in the degree to which their stability depends upon the consent of a majority of those governed (Diamond et al. 1995: 9).

More significant for our purposes here is the fact that democracy has as its central paradox *conflict* and *consensus*. This is manifested in several forms:

- While democracy entails a set of rules for managing conflict, this conflict must be managed within certain limits and result in compromises, consensus or other agreements that all sides accept as legitimate. An overemphasis on one side of the equation can threaten the entire undertaking. Democracy, therefore, must find a mechanism to mitigate conflict and cleavage with consensus (Diamond and Plattner 1999: xiii).
- Democracy is by nature a system of institutionalized competition for power. Without competition and conflict, there is no democracy. But any society that sanctions political conflict runs the risk of becoming so conflict-ridden that civil peace and stability can be jeopardized.
- In between elections, citizens must be able to influence public policy through various non-electoral means such as interest group associations and social movements, which invariably involve cooperation and competition among citizens.
- Democracy implies dissent and division, but on the basis of consent and cohesion. It requires that citizens assert themselves, but also that they accept the government's authority.
- A democratic society needs the commitment of citizens who accept the inevitability of conflict as well as the necessity for tolerance. To develop a democratic culture, individuals and groups must be willing, as a minimum, to tolerate each other's differences, recognizing that the other side has a valid right and a legitimate point of view.
- Coalition building is the essence of democratic actions. It teaches interest groups to negotiate with others, to compromise and to work within the constitutional system. By so doing, groups with differences learn how to argue peaceably, how to pursue their goals in a democratic manner and ultimately how to live in a world of diversity.

In short, in a democracy, a balance must be found between competing values; and political actors must cooperate in order to compete. To be effective and stable, there must be the belief in the legitimacy of democracy, tolerance for opposition parties, a willingness to compromise with political opponents, pragmatism and flexibility, trust in the political environment, cooperation among political competitors, moderation in political positions and partisan identifications, civility of political discourse and efficacy and participation based on the principles of political equality (Diamond et al. 1995).

Political conflict Conflict has traditionally been viewed as dysfunctional, destructive and damaging, a generally undesirable by-product of life. But conflict is an inevitable and inescapable reality; a normal and even healthy part of life. As a result, all stable societies evolve legitimate organizations, rules, norms and procedures for conflict management. In a democracy, the established institutions mediate conflict in a systematic way with the aim of achieving consensus through dialogue and bargaining. Political parties, pressure groups, parliaments, elections and the judiciary are among the overarching institutions that mediate the wide variety of conflicts in such societies. Political institutionalization, therefore, is strongly related to the stability of democracy. According to Diamond et al. (1995): 'institutions structure behaviour into stable, predictable and recurrent patterns; institutionalized systems are less volatile and more enduring, so are institutionalized democracies'. However, culturally heterogeneous societies present particularly difficult problems in the design of institutions that would channel conflicts into the framework of a rule-governed interplay of interests (Przeworski et al. 1995: 107).

The most important intra-elite conflict is the competition for political power that usually takes the form of electoral competition using the party system. In older democracies, where these issues have been settled long ago, disagreements related to them are resolved administratively by the authorities responsible for elections; the rules governing competition have been institutionalized; and the pursuit of power is not a zero-sum game and therefore not fatally divisive. In new democracies, however, the most ordinary issues are often politicized; the contest for power itself is a winner-takes-all (Ninsin 1995: 66). Under such circumstances, the vicious cycle of political distrust and coercion remains intact because to cooperate with one's 'enemies' is to invite one's own destruction (Higley and Burton 1988: 115). The tensions and acrimony that characterize the electoral process in new democracies, then, are largely due to institutional vacancy; lack of the required level of institutionalization of intra-elite conflict management (Higley and Burton 1988: 115; Ninsin 1995).

Hagan (1995: 83) also makes the following insightful points about political conflict in the context of liberal democracy:

- That the existence of diverse and conflicting values and interests creates severe cleavages in society as social forces align themselves and confront each other for power and dominance in the quest to satisfy their needs. But then 'all conflictual features of democratic governance reach a climax in a free democratic election, the event par excellence that gives a democratic system its unique and peculiar character'.

- That citizens' freedom and power to reject rulers in an election does not only engender strife, but also releases tensions and suspense and creates collective catharsis that provides communal healing and reduces conflicts.

- And that in a democratic election, the enacted battle should be with ballots and not bullets to ensure that the vanquished survive with the victors, leaving open the possibility of turning fortunes around. The contest should not be such that the victors leave their opponents prostrate, unable to stand and mount a credible challenge.

On the whole, while democracy makes conflicts inevitable it provides a system for managing and settling disputes through articulation and exchange of views and the possibility of peaceful change.

Elite consensus Theorists argue that the cohesion of a state's elite helps to determine the state's democratic progress (Gould and Szomolanyi 1997). They emphasize that a prerequisite of stable democracy is that elites agree on the parameters of the democratic political system and that where they fail to unify behind the concepts of democratic norms and procedures as the 'only game in town', the viability of democratic institutions is endangered creating a situation where some elites may prefer to attempt to rule by non-democratic means rather than forgo their claims to power (ibid.).

Elites, according to Burton and Higley (1987: 295), 'are people who are able, by virtue of their authoritative positions and powerful organizations and movements of whatever kind, to affect national political outcomes regularly and substantially'. It is because of elites' disproportionate power and influence that they matter most for the stability and consolidation of democracy, not only in their behaviour but also in their beliefs.

Elite beliefs and norms are usually important because, first, they are more likely to have elaborate systems of political beliefs; more likely to be guided in their actions by their beliefs and have more influence over political events. Second, elites also play a crucial role in shaping political culture and in signalling what kinds of behaviour are proper. Third, elites lead partly by example, good or bad; when they are contemptuous of the rules and norms of democracy their followers are more likely to be as well (Diamond and Plattner 1999: 66). But it must be emphasized that the political culture of bargaining, accommodation and constitutionalism must not be confined to the elite level; rather, the elites must reach out to the masses and to raise their political consciousness, develop democratic practices and mobilize participation (ibid.: 20).

Elite consensus measures elites by the extent to which they share similar

131

views and by their degree of access to crucial decision-making. At the two extremes are *strongly unified elites* and *divided or disunified elites* (Burton and Higley 1989: 9). Strongly unified elites are characterized, first, by tacitly shared consensus about the rules and codes of political conduct and restrained partisanship; and second, by relatively reliable and effective access to each other and the most central decision-makers. They view politics as a positive-sum game, which if played by the rules will lead to benefits in the long run, even in the face of setbacks at the polls (ibid.). The two features above are virtually absent among weakly unified elites. They retain neither shared understanding of the rules of the game, nor consistent and reliable access to key decision-makers. They are either 'in' or 'out' and, for them, politics is a zero-sum game that must often be 'waged' as vigorously and brutally as on a battlefield. Between the two extremes lies a whole range of mixed motive games and behaviour including temporary alliances, balances of power and log-rolling of interests at the expense of the rest of society (Gould and Szomolanyi 1997).

Scholars of the New Elite framework further contend that until settlement between elites is achieved, either by one-time historic compromise or through gradual transformation, a stable democracy is unlikely. Thus, divided elites must struggle over and settle on procedural consensus before the prospects for sustainable democracy will exist. Under the circumstances, political opponents do not necessarily have to like each other, but they must tolerate one another and acknowledge that each has a legitimate and important role to play. The ground rules of society must encourage tolerance and civility in public debate. No matter who wins elections in a democratic system, both sides must agree to cooperate in solving the common problems of society. The losers must know that they will not lose their lives or go to gaol. Instead, the opposition must continue to participate in public life in the knowledge that its role is equally essential; and that it is loyal to the fundamental legitimacy of the state and to the democratic process itself. Higley and Burton put this more succinctly: 'Although the groups are forever quarrelling, an operational code of "give to get" eschews mutually destructive struggles' (Higley and Burton 1998: 98).

Transition from an authoritarian regime towards a democratic order presupposes progress in the direction of elite consensus in the form of an elite pact. O'Donnell and Schmitter define a pact as: '[A]n explicit but not always publicly explicated or justified, agreement among a select set of actors which seek to ... redefine rules governing the exercise of power on the basis of mutual guarantees for the vital interest of those entering it' (O'Donnell and Schmitter 1986: 37).

An elite pact may come about as a result of a decline in the ability of the ruling group to control society by force or the broader elite realization that continued entrenched positions among the elites serve nobody's interest. But the important fact is that it seeks to reconcile the core values of contending factions in society. Again, such a pact may have undemocratic elements such as the granting of amnesty to the incumbent/outgoing regime, but at the core is a negotiated agreement by key political contenders to abide by the newly crafted democratic framework. It is in these respects that an elite pact represents a significant step towards elite consensus. However, it does not necessarily mean that actual elite consensus has been achieved. This is because elites can come to a tactical compromise out of mutual self-interest without reconciling their fundamental values and beliefs. This can render pacts mere short-term tactical agreements among elites. Thus, while elite pacts or settlements may generate tacitly accommodative and overtly restrained practices among competing political elites, they may continue to hold on to their most cherished beliefs (Higley and Burton 1998: 115; O'Donnell and Schmitter 1986: 37; Gould and Szomolanyi 1997).

Consensus is more than the sum total of the ideas of the individuals in a group. During debate, ideas build one upon the next, generating new ideas until the best decision emerges. This dynamic is called the creative interplay of ideas. Creativity plays a major part in discussing what is best for the group and the more people are involved in this cooperative effort, the more ideas and possibilities are generated. In this respect, the persistent, indiscriminate and uncompromising application of parliamentary majority (that has characterized both the NDC and NPP administrations) is inherently confrontational and not consensual. The goal has often been winning the vote, regardless of an alternative choice that might be in the interests of the whole group; it resorts to the power of domination instead of persuasion. When the will of the majority supersedes the concerns of the minority, it is inherently conflictual. Consensus strives to take into account every disagreement and resolve them all before a decision is made. More importantly, this process encourages an environment in which everyone is respected and all contributions are valued.[1]

The foregoing theoretical discourse provides a framework for assessing issues of conflict and consensus among the political elites in the first decade of Ghana's Fourth Republic.

Brief historical background

Ghana's post-independence history began in March 1957 with a liberal democratic rule which soon degenerated into a quasi-dictatorship; and as a result, the first military coup of 1966 (Gyimah-Boadi 2000: 2). In the subsequent decade and a half, Ghana made two other brief attempts at liberal democracy – between 1969 and 1972 and 1979 and 1981 – each overthrown after twenty-seven months. In the latter instance, Flight Lieutenant Jerry Rawlings, who assumed the reins of power for 112 days in 1979 and handed over to the civilian administration of President Hilla Limann and his People's National Party (PNP), staged a comeback on Christmas Eve 1981. The new ruling group, the Provisional National Defence Council (PNDC), also under Rawlings's chairmanship, in spite of its name stuck to power for eleven years until 7 January 1993 when Ghana embarked on the current experiment under the 1992 Constitution, and whose first decade is under scrutiny in this book. The PNDC, unlike the various military regimes before it, had, almost from the beginning, given a strong indication of wanting to stay much longer in power. It doggedly refused to bind itself to time, choosing to refer to itself and its actions as part of an indefinite political process ostensibly to implement a so-called participatory, grassroots democracy that had a disdain for multi-party politics (Gyimah-Boadi 1991: 35).

Against this background, the PNDC only reluctantly conceded to constitutional rule under pressure from external and domestic forces, in the early 1990s. On the international front, the pro-democratic trend of the post-Cold War era had begun to have a contagious effect across Africa (Ninsin 1998: 14); while locally there were persistent and increasing demands from various civil society groups for change and political reform after the almost decade-long culture of silence under PNDC rule. The PNDC leaders then were unwilling coverts bent on ensuring that they crafted a transition programme that would leave their interests virtually intact. In addition, given its abysmal human rights record, the regime had genuine fears for its physical security once it surrendered power. This explains to a large extent the deliberate slowness, foot-dragging and evasiveness that characterized the latest Ghanaian transition to constitutional rule. The special interest the incumbent regime had in the outcome of the transition produced the heightened tensions and the unprecedented lack of compromise that became the hallmark of the process. It should thus be clear that the ruling elite in Ghana coopted democracy to the service of its political ambitions. And the whole scenario fits what Ake has aptly described as 'the paradox of democratization': '[T]hat those who have power tendentially have no interest or inclination to democratize, for democratization entails the redistribution of power against those who are in power and those who are privileged. When such people support democracy it is usually for some countervailing compulsion' (Ake 2000: 70).

The transition programme

One major area of conflict in a transition process is agreeing on its modalities. In the Ghanaian context, this was a very contested matter. It was characterized by inconsistencies, biases and uncertainties. The PNDC refused to spell out a clear timetable for the transition. It packed the constitution-drafting Consultative Assembly with pro-government 'identifiable bodies' to the virtual exclusion of those with anti-government views. It also refused to grant a general political amnesty, release political detainees or repeal repressive laws; and it kept a tight control of the whole process by refusing to place it in the hands of any other body apart from its own National Commission on Democracy (NCD) (Gyimah-Boadi 1991: 37–40).

Conteh-Morgan (1997: 77–80) argues that when the need to cooperate to democratize becomes a *fait accompli*, the incumbent regime must find a means of managing the inhibiting effects of political insecurity. Operating in a situation of adversarial cooperation, an incumbent regime may assess the transitional arrangements in the context of worse-case projections and take measures that yield it the greatest absolute gains at the expense of its rivals. In the context of the transition programme under review, the threat to the incumbent PNDC regime was aggravated by the ultra-conservative utterances of the opposition. Under such political uncertainty, the PNDC also decided that the incumbent military ruler, for the first time in the country's history, should contest the presidency. This in effect turned the incumbent regime into a referee and a player at the same time. For the PNDC, therefore, the transition programme was a preparation for self-succession.

The PNDC in line with its agenda took several actions in 1990–92 without consultation. These included organization of regional fora to collate views on a new democratic order; the drafting of a new constitution; the establishment of the electoral body; the political parties' law and dates for various phases of the transition (Bluwey 1998: 105–11).

Political and civil society groups, no doubt, protested against several, if not all, of those unilateral decisions. But more significant was the consensus that such protests brought among groups of varying backgrounds and sometimes traditional political foes. For instance, the Movement for Freedom and Justice (MFJ), vocal critics of the transition process, had in its leadership elements of the two political traditions of Nkrumahists and Danquah-Busiaists as well as elements of political groups ranging from those with moderate to extreme left-wing orientations (Ninsin 1998: 58). The PNDC government, operating with towering political power and with the muscle of the paramilitary organs, blithely ignored all these protestations and demands. Yet the opposition forces, like the PNDC, campaigned during the April 1992 referendum for the acceptance of the Constitution; hoping, rather naïvely, that they could still compete fairly and wrestle power from the PNDC.

The position of the opposing forces was further weakened following the lifting of the ban on party politics. The various political groups and civic associations that had hitherto been active and vociferous in the politics of the transition metamorphosed into different political parties, largely along their traditional orientations. The net effect was that, later, when several of the new parties came together to form a loose Alliance of Democratic Forces, to oppose the PNDC-created National Democratic Congress (NDC) and its allies demanding, inter alia, the formation of an interim government, dissolution of the PNDC paramilitary organs, replacement of the electoral register and the reconstitution of the INEC, they had lost too much steam to be effective.

This discussion of the politics of the transition process forms the bedrock of issues of conflict and consensus that occupied the following decade.

The 1992 elections and their aftermath

The November 1992 presidential election resulted in a 58.3 per cent victory for Rawlings and the NDC which had gone into electoral alliance with the National Convention Party (NCP) and the Every Ghanaian Living Everywhere (EGLE). The other contesting parties – the New Patriotic Party (NPP), People's National Convention (PNC), National Independence Party (NIP) and People's Heritage (PHP) – denounced the presidential contest as fraudulent. The immediate post-presidential election situation was chaotic. The results triggered a spate of violence and left a trail of widespread mistrust of the electoral process.

The four defeated political parties stuck together and made fresh demands for a more even playing field as their condition for participating in the then pending parliamentary elections. The demands included an interim government to supervise the rest of the transition, a new voters' register, a new electoral commission whose membership would include representatives of the political parties (Oquaye 2001). In the midst of the confusion, a high-powered government delegation met the opposition parties for the first time in an attempt to achieve consensus. This was facilitated by the National House of Chiefs and Christian and Muslim religious bodies (*Pioneer* 1992). This attempt at reintegrating the opposition into the political process did not succeed because of entrenched positions on both sides but, at least, it indicated an acknowledgement of the need for some basic agreement.

The parliamentary election, originally scheduled for the first week of

December, was shifted to the end of that month, but the opposition parties, which had jointly announced their withdrawal, carried out their threat and boycotted it (Jonah 1998: 78). As a result, the three parties forming the Progressive Alliance (NDC, NCP and EGLE) stood and two independent candidates were returned to the 200-member parliament.

This state of affairs had many implications for both the ruling alliance and the defeated parties. It was a clear manifestation of a flawed transition that risked disrupting the cherished democratic order. For instance, the opposition was absent from the inaugural ceremony on 7 January 1993. Thus, the first government of the Fourth Republic was born out of bitter controversy and its inauguration was a distinctly partisan affair (Bluwey 1998: 118). At the same time, the boycott put pressure on the various stakeholders to secure some form of consensus. This, to some extent, explains why political conflict in the first term in the Fourth Republic did not become as acrimonious and destabilizing as the immediate post-election indicators showed.

On the part of the government, the boycott produced a virtual one-party parliament, since the three parties that contested the election were offshoots of the same family tree. On the surface this looked good for the consolidation of power by the government, but the exceptionally low voter turn-out of 29 per cent in the parliamentary election reduced the legitimacy of the whole transition process. It became obvious that if the young political order was not secured on the basis of consensus among the political elites, the new government, like its predecessor, would suffer from a crisis of legitimacy. Above all, the vacuum arising from the lack of consensus could encourage another group of adventurers to seize power again and reverse the whole process.

For the opposition parties, withdrawal from the parliamentary election had two broad outcomes: a greater pressure on them to achieve consensus with the NDC government; and the need for alternative strategies to enhance their political effectiveness. In the first instance, consensus was needed on the rules of the electoral contest to ensure a smooth transfer of power from one leadership to another in future and also to inspire confidence in the multi-party system. Continued or prolonged disagreement over the rules of electoral politics and elite succession could lead to militant and radical action from sections of the lower classes. There was also the possibility that if the stand-off with the Rawlings government remained unresolved, the government might seize the opportunity to perpetuate itself in power (Ninsin 1998: 187).

Second, the withdrawal effectively excluded the opposition from the central political platform of the new constitutional order. The right to vote

137

against objectionable legislation was forfeited and the chance to put up staunch opposition to unacceptable policies of the executive was lost. They therefore needed to adjust to their self-exclusion to get the government to listen to them, to influence government policy and prevent the creation of a one-party state by default (Jonah 1998: 87).

It was against this background that, early in 1993, the defeated parties came up with an Inter-Party Coordinating Committee and promised the nation a 'shadow cabinet' outside parliament to monitor the activities of the government. They appealed to the government to consult them on major national issues and urge their supporters to accept the NDC government and post-election situation for the sake of peace (*Uhuru* 1993). These initial collective moves did not produce much positive response, however, and soon the opposition groups went their separate ways along the traditional political divide: the Danquah-Busia NPP on its own and the Nkrumahist parties (PHP, NIP, PNC, etc.) going into a series of unity talks.

The NPP in the meantime had issued a report, *The Stolen Verdict*, which contained hundreds of detailed allegations of irregularities in one hundred of the two hundred constituencies; but the main opposition party established its relevance in the first year and made up for its absence from parliament by waging its battles in the courts. This in effect turned the judiciary into a theatre for political struggle (Jonah 1998: 88). The fact is that with the stymied political process, the role of the Supreme Court became crucial as issues which would ordinarily be mediated through the political process had to be 'legalized' and 'constitutionalized' and through the mediation of the judiciary (Kotey 1995: 279).

The NPP in several constitutional cases obtained favourable Supreme Court rulings. Four of these rulings were outstanding (ibid.: 288–302):

• The case of the *New Patriotic Party v Ghana Broadcasting Corporation* related to the obligation of the state-owned media to be fair to all shades of opinion and to afford equal opportunity for the expression of a plurality of views and divergent opinion. The GBC had failed to cover the NPP's response to the 1993 budget after it had for two days broadcast a forum on the same budget by the finance minister. The Supreme Court unanimously upheld the claims of the NPP and ordered the GBC to offer the NPP the same facilities that it had previously given the government.

• The *NPP v Inspector General of Police* involved the interplay of public order and the excesses and misuse of police powers and the right to freedom of assembly and political activity guaranteed under the Constitution. The Supreme Court again adjudged that the system of permits under the Public Order Decree was inconsistent with the 1992 Constitution.

- In the *NPP v Electoral Commission & Annor*, the Supreme Court declared by unanimous vote that the district assemblies as constituted in 1993 were not competent to hold elections for approving candidates for appointment as district chief executives.
- In the *NPP v Attorney General*, the NPP sought an order to stop the celebration of 31 December (the date of Rawlings's revolution) as a public holiday. The Supreme Court, by a majority of 5:4, ruled that the public commemoration and financing of an event that signified the violent overthrow of a constitutionally elected government was against the letter and spirit of the Constitution. This last decision triggered a series of events that weighed heavily on the judiciary itself through the Abban affair (discussed below).

By these victories the NPP established clearly that, while not in parliament, it still possessed the capacity to influence or check the political conduct of the government. In Jonah's view, it was as if the NPP was telling the NDC: 'You got us at the polls; we've got you in court' (Jonah 1998: 88).

The legal battles notwithstanding, the strongest signal, in the first year of constitutional rule, of opposition willingness to dialogue with the NDC government came from NPP when its leadership floated the idea of 'doing business with the government'. By this the NPP indicated its willingness to settle its differences with the NDC through negotiation rather than confrontation and non-cooperation, and in so doing to build the necessary consensus over the rules of political competition and elite succession. The main reason for the pursuit of dialogue, according to NPP chairman da Rocha, was to search for genuine and sincere national reconciliation (Boafo-Arthur 1995: 220).

This 'Doing Business' strategy provoked strong criticisms from within the party and ridicule from the other opposition parties. Given the (P)NDC's track record of non-cooperation and non-compromise, the general perception was that the NPP initiative was misguided. But it was generally in line with the view that:

> The birth of democracy creates a dilemma for the opposition: how much to oppose and by what means. If the opposition does oppose vigorously, democracy may be threatened … [an] intransigent opposition may create an ungovernable situation. As a result political forces often seek to establish a pact, an agreement that distributes offices [or] to pursue particular policies. (Przeworski et al. 1995: 54)

The NPP and the NDC held a couple of meetings at which the electoral process, inter-party relationships and the mass media were discussed and joint committees proposed. By the end of 1993, however, the new-found friends fell apart amid accusations and counter-accusations. The NPP accused the NDC of foot-dragging and the utilization of the dialogue as a gimmick to score cheap political points. For the NDC, the whole thing was a non-starter when the NPP refused to withdraw *The Stolen Verdict*. Under the circumstances, the presence of a mediator of some sorts would have been useful. Worse still, the two parties could not take substantive decisions on most issues discussed in the absence of the other political parties (Boafo-Arthur 1995: 220–5). In spite of its shortcomings, the NDC–NPP dialogue became the forerunner of the Inter-Party Advisory Committee that achieved so much elite consensus before the 1996 elections (see below).

On their part, the defeated Nkrumahist parties (PNC, PHP and NIP) together with other groups such as the Concerned Nkrumahist Unity Caucus and the People's Party for Development and Democracy (PPDD), which had not registered in 1992, sought to unify their ranks. A technical committee was established for the purpose of creating a new united Nkrumahist party. But unity would elude the group for a long time. For instance, Dr Hilla Limann, the leader of the PNC, did not join the unity talks but several leading members of his party did (Jonah 1998: 88). When eventually a new party was minted in the form of the People's Convention Party (PCP), it was made up of the groups which began the unity talks and a large section of the NCP led by Vice President Arkaah who had abrogated its alliance with the NDC. The PNC continued to stay out.

The electoral commission and consensus building

Against the background of the disputed 1992 election and with key political actors and their supporters deeply mistrustful of the electoral process, the election authorities faced formidable challenges of building both confidence and credibility.

With the inauguration of the Fourth Republic, the life of the largely discredited INEC officially came to an end; a new seven-member electoral commission was inaugurated in August 1993. Its composition and powers were provided for in the Constitution and amplified by statute. Apart from its responsibility for conducting elections, delimiting electoral constituencies, compiling and updating of voters' register, voter education and registration of political parties, it was empowered to make regulations by constitutional instrument for the effective performance of its functions. The existence of a body of laws and explicit rules and regulations provided the electoral commission with a measure of insulation and put it in a stronger position lawfully to resist undue external pressures and interference in its work. Above all, the laws formed the framework for the resolution of the electoral conflicts.

These changed circumstances and donor assistance enabled the EC to embark on a comprehensive programme of reforming the electoral process and enhancing credibility. But suspicion and mistrust of the election authority as an independent and impartial arbiter lingered, in part because the procedure for appointing the commissioners still allowed for a significant degree of presidential influence but more so because a deputy chairman, Dr K. Afari-Gyan, and a commissioner, David Kanga, both of the defunct INEC, were 'promoted' to chairman and deputy chairman respectively of the new EC.

The EC saw a clear need for electoral reforms with a view to achieving greater transparency in all aspects of the election process and sought to create popular faith in the ballot and to build confidence in the EC itself. Thus the EC, like the government and the opposition parties, as earlier indicated, was under some pressure to seek consensus. The most important mechanism for managing distrust of the EC by the opposition parties and among the various political parties was the innovative Inter-Party Advisory Committee (IPAC). The EC, through the IPAC, coopted the parties into the process of election management from March 1994. The IPAC brought together representatives of the political parties to regular monthly meetings with the EC to discuss and build consensus on contested electoral issues (Ayee 1997: 10).

The IPAC offered a two-way channel of information for both the EC and the parties. It enabled the EC to discuss all aspects of its programmes and activities with the parties, elicit inputs and address problems, protests and disagreements whenever they were aired. And the parties were able to express their views freely and openly about EC programmes and activities and to bring their concerns to the table. The IPAC process, no doubt, had its hiccups but it succeeded in achieving compromise solutions to such contested matters as a single day for both parliamentary and presidential elections; photo ID cards, transparent ballot boxes; and gained the active involvement of party agents in the registration exercise as observers (ibid.: 10–11). It must also be emphasized to the credit of the EC that although the IPAC was purely advisory and non-statutory and its decisions not binding on the EC, it gave serious attention to those decisions that were practical, legal and cost-effective.

By succeeding in bringing the 'warring factions' to the 'peace' conference table, therefore, the EC through IPAC fulfilled one of the prerequisites for consolidated democracy – elite consensus, i.e. a disposition towards compromise, flexibility, tolerance, conciliation, moderation and restraints among elites through both formal and informal communication networks.

Contested issues (1993–96)

The consensual state of affairs at the IPAC had a moderating influence on the 1996 elections. Meanwhile, there were several other contested issues in the 1993–96 period.

VAT, AFC, Kume Preko In a democratic society, citizens have a right to gather peacefully and protest about the policies of their government or the actions of other groups with demonstrations, marches, petitions, boycotts, strikes and other forms of direct citizen actions. Protests, indeed, are a testing ground for any democracy. The ideals of free expression and citizen participation are easy to defend when everyone remains polite and in agreement on basic issues. But protesters and their targets do not agree on the basic issues and such disagreements may be passionate and angry. The challenge, then, is one of balance: to defend the right to freedom of speech and assembly, while maintaining public order and countering attempts at intimidation or violence. To suppress peaceful demonstrations in the name of order is in a sense repressive; to permit uncontrolled violent protest is to invite anarchy. There is, however, no magic formula for achieving this balance. To a large extent, it would depend on the dominant forces of the day.

It is against this background that we examine the three related issues of the introduction of the Value Added Tax (VAT) bill, the formation of the Alliance for Change (AFC) and its *Kume Preko* demonstrations of the first half of 1995. The NDC government had introduced as part of its budgetary policy for 1995 a new tax system, VAT, which imposed a 15 per cent tax on selected goods and services. But because it was implemented with little or no public education, sellers of exempted goods such as food increased their prices in the name of VAT. The resultant hardships led to the formation of Alliance for Change (AFC) – a coalition of opposition forces from the Nkrumahist and the Danquah-Busiaist camps – to protest against VAT. On 11 May 1995, the AFC began the first in a series of peaceful demonstrations scheduled to take place in all regional capitals dubbed *Kume Preko* in Accra. The delicate balance between the citizens' right to demonstrate and the government's responsibility to maintain order received a heavy blow when an alleged government-sponsored counter-demonstration led to the death of four of the protesters in cold blood. Though the AFC eventually succeeded in getting the government to withdraw VAT, the deaths were never fully investigated. More significantly, the successes of the AFC brought to the fore the need for an alliance of all opposition forces to contest Rawlings and the NDC in the 1996 elections.

The Arkaah factor The composition of the first parliament following the opposition boycott of the 1992 election meant that the rivalry and conflictual relations that had existed between parliament and executive in the Third Republic were virtually absent. The NCP tried to play the role of the minority in parliament, unsuccessfully because of its small size (eight members) and its role as a junior partner in the ruling alliance. Thus, most often the only discordant voices that could be heard were those of two independent candidates. But perhaps in a balancing act, this near-perfect consensus between the executive and the legislature was matched by interpersonal acrimony of unprecedented proportions within the presidency between President Rawlings and Vice President Arkaah.

Arkaah had in 1992 cunningly wrested the leadership of the NCP from its founder Kwaku Boateng and virtually sold it to the NDC in an alliance which earned him the vice presidency. But the vice president found his party increasingly sidelined by the NDC; himself in a relationship with the president that was never cordial; and his position bereft of its powers. Not only was he denied his constitutional right of chairing the cabinet in the absence of the president but he did not even have an official residence. He survived a sex scandal – the Jemima Yalley affair. But on the fateful 28 December 1995, in a clear manifestation of the bad blood between them, Rawlings assaulted Arkaah at a cabinet meeting. This last act was reportedly in reaction to a speech Arkaah had delivered critical of the government. This had intensified earlier calls for his resignation, but, in an uncompromising manner, Arkaah had argued against resigning, saying, in the first instance, that he had taken an oath to serve the people of Ghana and, in the second instance, calling on his assailant, the president, to resign first. By sticking to his guns, Arkaah in 1996 made history as the sitting vice president who also became the running mate on the opposition ticket.

The Abban affair Another issue that raised controversy was the appointment of Justice I. K. Abban as chief justice in 1995. Article 144(1) of the 1992 Constitution provides that the chief justice 'shall be appointed by the President acting in consultation with the Council of State and with the approval of Parliament'. The appointment of Abban, an able jurist who had served previously as a High Court and Appeals Court judge and also as Chief Justice of the Seychelles, did not breach this constitutional provision. But it attracted, for other reasons, fierce partisan opposition and objections from the Ghana Bar Association (GBA) (Prempeh 1999: 3, 24).

The president, having consulted the Council of State, quickly got parliament to sit in an emergency session to approve the nomination on the lame excuse that with the resignation of the previous chief justice, the position needed to be filled immediately (Oquaye 2001: 25). But what prevented the most senior judge from acting for a period so that the substantive justice could be appointed without indecent haste?

The answer lay in the fact that the government was anxious to make the incoming chief justice owe it a debt of gratitude and thereafter make him malleable (ibid.). At the time of his appointment, Abban was embroiled in controversy, allegedly for doctoring his judgment on the case on the celebration of 31 December as public holiday. This had in turn led to the trial and imprisonment of a journalist, Mensah Bonsu, who had exposed him, for publicly attacking the integrity of a judge (Prempeh 1999: 2). The GBA went to the unusual extent of filing a lawsuit seeking a declaration from the Supreme Court that Abban, on account of his conduct that precipitated the Mensah Bonsu case, was not fit for the office of chief justice. The GBA had based its claim, inter alia, on the provision in Article 128(4) of the 1992 Constitution limiting the high judicial office to persons of 'high moral character and proven integrity'. But the case was summarily dismissed by the Supreme Court on the ground that the petitioners' claim raised a non-justiciable political question (ibid.: 24). Prempeh describes this as 'the Ghanaian judiciary's continuing fidelity to the jurisprudence of an authoritarian past' in spite of the adoption of a liberal democratic constitution (ibid.: 4).

The 1996 elections

The success of the IPAC in producing consensus on several key areas of electoral politics in the two years preceding the 1996 elections enhanced the confidence of all the key actors and ensured that the conduct and outcome of the elections would be accepted by the contending parties as free and fair (Ninsin 1998: 190). This notwithstanding, the path leading to the elections had been strewn with several issues of conflict and consensus within and among political parties.

The undercurrents The NDC, which lost its major partner in the 1992 alliance, the NCP, found a replacement in the low-key coastal-based Democratic People's Party which later played the role of 'propaganda par excellence' for Rawlings's campaign (Aubynn 1997: 21). Two other issues that confronted the ruling NDC were the choice of a new running mate and the need to strengthen the quality of its parliamentary representation. With the embittered Arkaah out of the way, there were several options open to

Rawlings. He could select a northerner not only for the purpose of striking a geographical balance in the north–south equation but more as a reward for the three northern regions for their loyalty and unflinching support for him; or he could select a long-time ally from the PNDC days. But Rawlings sprang a surprise by selecting the hitherto politically unknown internal revenue commissioner, John Atta Mills.

The need for the NDC to improve the quality of its MPs in 1996 was more urgent. In 1992, thanks to the boycott, there were several NDC MPs who won their seats for lack of serious competition (Aubynn 1997: 34) and indeed twenty-three had gone unopposed (Badu and Larvie 1996: 17). In 1996, it was clear that the race was going to be keener and if the NDC did not act, the poor quality of its MPs could be used as an issue against the party. Stated differently, the ability of the NDC to shed 'stop-gap' candidates and rejuvenate its ticket with more qualified and more popular candidates was going to have an impact on the party's electoral fortunes. The issue was a delicate one, for if care was not taken to placate the incumbents, the party could be in disarray.

The NDC, with the advantage of incumbency and access to resources, managed it well. In the end about eighty MPs lost their positions. But with the single exception of the MP for Mampong, George Akosah, who in 1995 had stirred the ethnic hornets' nest (Frempong 2001: 147), the NDC MPs who were replaced stood solidly behind the party. The cue was that they were quickly compensated with cash awards, ostensibly to campaign for the party, and promises of lucrative jobs in the party and state organizations if they remained loyal. Other incentives were the end-of-service gratuities and the chance to purchase on very favourable terms their government-rented estate houses at Sakumono in Accra.

The NDC had some problems with its alliance partners, EGLE and DPP, over parliamentary representation. Against the expectation that the Progressive Alliance would put up a single candidate in each constituency, the NDC found itself vying with EGLE in eight constituencies and the DPP in thirteen according to the official list of the EC. But this paled into insignificance compared to what transpired in the Great Alliance.

On the other side of the political divide, the issue of an alliance of the traditional political adversaries, the Danquah-Busiaist NPP and the Nkrumahist PCP, had become not only a crucial electoral strategy but also the main preoccupation. On the face of things, this represented elite consensus of sorts. The successes of the AFC in 1995 had created the impression that with a united opposition front the NDC could be defeated. But lack of consensus on the modalities created friction within and across the opposition parties.

In the NPP, the rumbles had begun in 1995 when Kwame Pianim started his campaign of 'reconciliation', calling for the rejection of the 1992 NPP flag-bearer, Adu Boahen, for a 'compromise' candidate who would be acceptable to the two traditions. There was every indication that the focus was on Pianim himself. By the time he was disqualified by the Supreme Court for his earlier conviction for treason against the PNDC, he had succeeded in discrediting Adu Boahen and paving the way for John Kufuor. There was still deep-seated disagreement within the NPP about the alliance. While former chairman B. J. da Rocha had publicly decried the alliance with the support of several party faithfuls, Wereko-Brobbey, a leading NPP member and a frontliner of the AFC, had left the party because the alliance agenda was not being pursued (*Daily Graphic*, 15 July 1996).

The PCP also had its internal squabbles and lacked consensus on the alliance deal. The party's national chairman, Asuma Banda, had questioned the viability of alliance as a political strategy (Aubynn 1997: 22), since it created the impression that neither the PCP nor the NPP by itself could defeat the NDC. In addition, the PCP was only a fraction of the Nkrumahist family with the PNC on its own and a chunk of the former NCP in the NDC fold. But the worst baggage that the PCP brought to the alliance was the election in June 1996 of Arkaah as its presidential candidate. Clearly he had ridden on the crest of his 28 December ordeal.

The alliance of the NPP and the PCP had agreed in principle to field common candidates in both the presidential and parliamentary elections. The conventional wisdom was that the NPP, given its strength on the ground, its relative unity and stability, would be given the upper hand. Thus, the NPP had expected that the PCP flag-bearer would readily accede the alliance presidential candidacy to its own leader, Kufuor; but the choice of Arkaah, the self-acclaimed 'Stubborn Cat', changed all that. The bitter but somewhat muted struggle between Arkaah and Kufuor for the alliance top slot delayed the consummation of the alliance until September, barely three months before the election.

Far worse was the struggle over parliamentary seats. The PCP in spite of its weaknesses on the ground made an initial demand for 50:50 share of the seats. When the 112–86 formula was eventually agreed on, the two parties had in many places registered separate candidates and it was difficult getting some to step down; the battle, therefore, raged till election day. A cursory look at the allocation of the alliance seats proved that the leadership was not on the ground. For instance, two of the three seats in the NPP stronghold of Kwahu South (this writer's home district) had been allocated to the PCP. The net effect of all this was disastrous. The NDC capitalized on the wrangling and raised the possibility of instability and chaos should the government lose to the bickering opposition alliance (Ayee 1997: 15). In places such as Ayawaso Central, where the PCP's Kwesi Pratt and the NPP's I. C. Quaye both claimed to be alliance candidates, they openly traded insults and their supporters exchanged blows (Aubynn 1997: 22). In the Birim North constituency, the minority leader, Owusu Agyekum of the PCP, lost his seat to the NDC because of the challenge of NPP's Owusu Ahinkora. Their combined votes amounted to 52.5 per cent compared to the winner's 46.5 per cent (Ephson 2003: 125). In both Abetifi and Nkawkaw constituencies in the Kwahu South district, had the electorate not defied the alliance and voted for the NPP instead of the PCP (which was virtually non-existent), victory would have gone to the NDC. An even more tragic aspect of this comedy of alliance was the premature bickering over ministerial posts before the elections were held.

The poll These intra- and inter-party wranglings did not seriously affect the general conduct of the polls except that it gave the NDC considerable advantage at both the parliamentary and presidential levels. The voter turn-out was an impressive 73.5 per cent compared to 48.3 per cent in 1992. In the three-way presidential contest, Jerry Rawlings (NDC/Progressive Alliance) obtained 57.4 per cent; John Kufuor (NPP/Great Alliance) 39.6 per cent; and Edward Mahama (PNC) 3 per cent. For parliament, the NDC won 133 seats (one short of a two-thirds majority), NPP won sixty-one, PCP five, and PNC one (Ayee 1997: 17; Ninsin 1998: 185).

The general mood following the election confirmed the fact that the contending political leaders had agreed upon the basic rules of electoral politics (Ninsin 1998: 194). Unlike 1992, the defeated presidential candidates, Kufuor and Mahama, conceded defeat and congratulated the winner; Rawlings in turn congratulated the losers for their competitive spirit. Kufuor, for instance, declared that there would be no 'Stolen Verdict' on the 1996 elections and he conceded that the NDC and Rawlings had emerged as a potent 'Third Force' in Ghanaian politics. At Rawlings's second inauguration also, Kufour, Mahama and their top party executives were present and the two candidates publicly shook hands with President Rawlings (Ayee 1997: 12–13).

Rawlings's acceptance speech as quoted below was conciliatory:

> I wish to thank each and everyone for making the election peaceful, fair
> and transparent. Together we have established the tradition of orderly
> democratic procedure and every Ghanaian should take satisfaction in its
> accomplishment ... I congratulate Dr Edward Mahama ... and Mr. John
> Agyekum Kufuor ... for their competitive spirit. For me, all political rivalry

147

came to an end when Ghanaians cast their vote on 7th December ... It is my hope therefore that in all we say or publish, we will stress more the things that unite us as a people than those that tend to divide us. In the true spirit of reconciliation, I wish to assure the nation that we bear no grudges ... I pledge the government's commitment to draw upon the experience and expertise of all men and women of integrity, no matter their political leanings, in our common effort to improve upon our national performance. (Ninsin 1998: 190–1)

Rawlings implied that his second victory was going to facilitate a smoother, albeit protracted, transition away from the quasi-militarized authoritarianism of the PNDC on which he first rode to power. The continuity entailed in the second electoral triumph, it was generally believed, would gently ease Rawlings into his ultimate retirement at the end of the constitutionally mandated second term (Gyimah-Boadi 1999: 412).

Another dividend of the 1996 election was that candidates who had complaints expressed their intention to seek redress through the EC and the courts rather than resorting to more dubious tactics. Significantly, this cut across the political parties. They included the two independent candidates, Hawa Yakubu (Bawku Central) and John Achuliwor (Navrongo Central); Isaac Amoo (NPP, Ayawaso West Wuogon), Odoi-Sykes (NPP, Odododiodio), Ibn Chambas (NDC, Bimbilla), Said Sinare (NDC, Ayawaso Central) and John Ndebugre (PNC, Bolgatanga) (Gyimah-Boadi 1999; Ayee 1997: 13). The defeated political parties and their supporters seemed geared up for Election 2000. This indicated a broad consensus that the ballot box was the sole legitimate instrument for seeking power (Gyimah-Boadi 1999: 412).

But these conciliatory gestures, however, should not make us oblivious to some issues that pointed to the fragility of the new democratic order:

• The NDC government had refused to accede to the request of the EC to provide all the contesting parties with vehicles as was done in 1992. Clearly, the belief that politics is a game of the strongest and must be played to the disadvantage of the weaker persisted (Ayee 1997: 16; Ninsin 1998: 194).
• The NDC exploited incumbency to commandeer state resources for its electoral victory, perhaps, far worse than in 1992. Money widely attributed to kickback on state contracts was channelled into the coffers of the ruling party. Its campaign was a lavish affair but there were no reliable mechanisms in place to enforce post-election accountability (Sandbrook and Oelbaum 1997: 617; Gyimah-Boadi 1999: 419–20).
• The indiscipline and violence in certain areas as well as the uncertainty about the intentions of the political leaders that characterized

the electioneering campaign led to mass hysteria on the eve of voting. There was real fear as to what would happen if Rawlings and the NDC were to lose (Ninsin 1998: 194). Significantly, the PNC leadership had said it 'took note of the verdict in the interest of peace and stability and decided to trade peace for injustice in spite of the gross abuse of incumbency by the presidential candidate of the NDC' (*Ghanaian Chronicle*, 11 December 1996: 6–7).

- Irregularities and malpractices were also detected. This caused the leader of the great alliance to note that the acceptance of the results was: 'without prejudice to the normal legitimate protests against the many incidents of molestations, malpractices and irregularities during and after the election, which were being reported all over the country for redress by the appropriate authorities' (ibid.).

On the whole, the 1996 election produced a far more favourable outcome than its much-contested predecessor of 1992; suggesting, rather paradoxically, that even a flawed transition could set the stage for democratic progress.

The renewed mandate

Government Any hopes for the formation of an 'all-inclusive government' that were raised as a result of Rawlings's post-election gestures soon fizzled out. Though a few new faces such as Muhammad Mumuni and Ekwow Spio Grabrah were brought on, Rawlings's new cabinet still contained holdovers from the PNDC days such as Obed Asamoah, Iddrissu Mahama and Totobi-Quakyi. More significantly, the junior partners in the Progressive Alliance were not represented in the cabinet, much less the opposition groups.

Parliament As illustrated in Table 6.1, the face of parliament, however, had changed. The two vibrant independent candidates lost out, the former NCP lost all of its eight seats and the single EGLE MP did not return. The NDC's representation had reduced from 189 to 133, sixty-four of whom were new, leaving only sixty-nine from the previous parliament (Badu and Larvie 1997: 44). Added to this were sixty-one from the NPP, five from the PCP and one from the PNC.

Clearly, the ruling NDC had a controlling majority and most of its members were educated professionals, but the minority bloc was studded with relatively more experienced and more vocal politicians. J. H. Mensah (the new minority leader) and C. O. Nyanor on the NPP bench were veterans from the Busia era while Frederick Blay (the second deputy speaker) and Kojo Armah from PCP came from families with a rich history in politics. Nana

149

TABLE 6.1 Party composition of first and second parliaments

Party	No. in first parliament	No. in second parliament	New members
NDC	189	133	64
NCP	8	–	–
EGLE	1	–	–
Independent	2	–	–
NPP	–	61	61
PCP	–	5	5
PNC	–	1	1
Total	200	200	131

Source: Derived from parliamentary election results, 1992 and 1996.

Akufo Addo, Konadu Apraku, Papa Ankomah, and others, were a new breed of well-educated and vociferous politicians. Their presence was expected to enliven parliamentary debate, improve policy-making at parliamentary committee level and boost governmental accountability and transparency (Gyimah-Boadi 1991: 415; Aubynn 1997: 34).

The minority had grudgingly acceded to the continuation of Justice D. F. Annan (an experienced jurist but with PNDC antecedence), as the Speaker of parliament. But the first major point of controversy arose over the proper interpretation and implementation of Article 78(1), which empowered parliament to approve the president's ministerial nominees. Parliament disagreed on whether or not the new parliament should approve ministers in the previous Rawlings government whom he had reappointed. In the first parliament, presidential nominations had attracted casual scrutiny. The majority was insistent that the new parliament should consider the retained ministers, most of whom were holdovers from the authoritarian era, duly vetted and to concentrate on the new nominees. The minority vehemently opposed this view, arguing that given the very changed circumstances, the vetting of the previous parliament could not be binding on the new one. The minority felt compelled by its conviction to stage the first of a series of boycotts of parliamentary proceedings. Indeed, that matter was contested at the Supreme Court, and it was only after the court took a decision that was more confusing than clarificatory that parliament came to a compromise solution.

Following the presentation of the 1997 budget, the minority's insistence on producing an alternative budget created further controversy. From then on parliamentary work proceeded uninterrupted, but, as usual, marked by cooperation and dissent. On the one hand:

- The representation of different shades of ideological and political opinion and the quality of deliberations in the legislative body improved considerably. Some of the bills enacted by parliament, such as the Serious Fraud Office bill, were vastly improved versions of the original bills – a clear manifestation of the quality of inputs that went into the legislative process at the committee stage and in the House (Gyimah-Boadi 2000: 4).
- The second parliament did a better job in discharging its constitutional and democratic obligation of overseeing the executive. Presidential nominees were more vigorously vetted; ministers were posed more probing questions before parliament; the budget was subjected to closer scrutiny and the auditor general's report carefully reviewed (ibid.: 5).

At the same time:

- Some of the bills (like the Office Holders Declaration bill) betrayed shoddiness and pedestrian treatment and others (like the Emergency Powers Act in particular) had dubious democratic validity. The former bill stepped out of contemporary best practice by exempting spouses and the military and making declarations almost inaccessible to the public. And the latter not only conferred wide discretionary powers on the president but also placed them beyond legal scrutiny (ibid.).
- In spite of the presence of the strong minority contingent, parliament failed to initiate private members' legislation and limited itself to the role of considering, amending and passing bills initiated by the executive (ibid.).
- The exercise of parliamentary oversight was greatly inhibited by the prevalence of crude partisanship in the House. The ruling party over-exploited its majority, allowing the minority to have its say while the majority had its way. Under the circumstances, parliamentary consensus was rare.

With the presence of the minority in parliament the frequent judicial battles over constitutional matters eased a great deal. Similarly, within the presidency cordiality prevailed between the president and the new vice president.

Political succession One major political issue that cast a long shadow on the Ghanaian political scene during the early part of Rawlings's second term was whether or not he would abide by the constitutional term limit and relinquish power at the end of 2000. Indeed, one of his troubleshooters, Vincent Assisseh, had tested the political waters with the suggestion of a prolonged term of office for the president. In an era where the third-term presidency was coming back in vogue across Africa, this could not be taken lightly.

Other factors made the spectre of a 'third coming' hang like an albatross around the necks of Ghanaians. Rawlings retained the assets of youth, dynamism and popularity; demonstrated unremitting interest in power and influence; and seemingly had a hold on the security agencies. All this, together with his history of coup-making, evoked much apprehension over how he would manage his departure (Agyeman-Duah 2000: 23).

At an NDC rally at Agona Swedru in the Central Region to commemorate the nineteenth anniversary of the 4 June 1979 uprising, Rawlings gave the clearest indication about his departure when he expressed his preference for Vice President Mills as the party's flag-bearer at the next elections. The significance of this seemingly innocuous platform talk was that given the hold that Rawlings had over the NDC and the apparent impregnability of the party at the time, the statement virtually amounted to the 'anointment' of Mills as the next president.

The Swedru Declaration, however, had serious implications for the NDC and contributed in no small measure to its eventual defeat in Election 2000. First, it effectively foreclosed any credible competition from within the party. It, therefore, dashed the presidential ambitions of stalwarts in the government like Attorney General (and the longest-serving foreign minister) Obed Asamoah and defence minister Iddrisu Mahama. Indeed, it was not surprising by NDC standards that at its 2000 congress to choose the flag-bearer, Mills became the only candidate and was elected by acclamation. The net effect, however, was that the support of these veteran politicians who saw themselves outwitted and outpaced by new entrant Mills waned considerably for a while.

Far worse was the split that the declaration created in the NDC. Un-enthused by the undemocratic manner of Mills's anointment, the cadres (the foot-soldiers of the revolutionary era) led by Goosie Tandoh, formed the Reform Movement, initially demanding internal democracy within with the NDC and eventually forming the splinter National Reform Party (NRP). Tandoh, a long-time Rawlings pal, reportedly in contention for NDC running mate in 1996 before the emergence of Mills, apparently had presidential ambitions of his own towards 2000. The emergence of the NRP hurt the NDC in two ways. First, it encouraged the opposition to attack more forcefully the democratic credentials and policies of the NDC. Second, in 2000 the NRP could not win any parliamentary seats but, acting as spoilers, caused NDC defeat (and NPP victory) in six constituencies in six regions across the country: Shama, Krowor, Okere, Damongo-Daboya, Navrongo

Central and Jaman (Ephson 2003: 9–10). A similar attempt by the NDC to impose sitting MPs as parliamentary candidates (another manifestation of lack of internal democracy), led to the emergence of several independent candidates with a similar 'spoiler-effect' in nine other constituencies. For constituencies like Okere, Akropong and Navrongo Central, the margins of defeat were painfully small (ibid.: 10–12). Given that the NPP defeated the NDC in the parliamentary election by 101 seats to 92, the NDC could have at least maintained its parliamentary majority had it effectively managed its internal differences.

The NPP had its fair share of internal differences but the dynamics were quite different and they were also better managed. Reeling under the disastrous effects of the alliance, the party had decided early that it was going to contest the 2000 elections on its own. It also held its primary to choose the flag-bearer two clear years ahead of the elections. The August 1998 contest was between the 1996 defeated candidate Kufuor and a number of parliamentary minority frontliners: Nana Akufo Addo, J. H. Mensah, Kofi Apraku and Alhassan Yakubu. In what turned out to be a two-horse race between Kufuor and Addo, the former had a convincing victory. The early primary had the therapeutic effect of healing internal divisions within the party. More importantly, it exposed the presidential candidate to the public and enabled the party to develop a coherent strategy (Gyimah-Boadi 2001: 108).

At the parliamentary level, the party, generally impressed by the perform- ance of its MPs, retained 90 per cent of them. Only in five constituencies – Amansie West, Bekwai and Offinso South (in the Ashanti Region) and Atiwa and Kade (in the Eastern Region) – were the incumbents replaced. This consensus formula worked well for the NPP. Only in three constitu- encies, Abetifi, Akropong and Bantama, did party-men rebel to stand as independent candidates. And with the single exception of Wulensi, the NPP retained all its 1996 seats in 2000.

Election 2000

The electoral milieu Though Election 1996 had raised high hopes for democratic development, deep distrust and intense acrimony between the ruling party and the opposition characterized the pre-election environment in 2000. Reports of ruling party agents and organs of state intimidating the opposition were rife (Gyimah-Boadi 2001: 104). Ethnic hype was at its worst as the NDC and NPP vowed to cause upset in each other's strong- hold (Frempong 2001: 152). Basic administrative rules governing the game became highly politicized. The registration and inspection of the voters' register generated a great deal of controversy. The effort to choose a date consistent with the Constitution and the religious practices of various groups led to intense bickering between the ruling party and the opposition and vacillation on the part of the EC. But the worst case was the attempt to replace thumbprint voter-identification cards with photographic ones. This simple matter attracted a Supreme Court decision (Gyimah-Boadi 2001: 105). All this, together with doubts about whether the result would be accepted by the incumbent administration, particularly if it lost, created an unprecedented state of public anxiety.

The running mate conundrum The choice of running mates was full of uncertainties and for the two major parties it became a cat and mouse game, each waiting for the other to nominate first. For the NPP, speculations ran in circles from Courage Quashigah, to counter the NDC 'World Bank' status in the Volta Region; through a gender balance with Hawa Yakubu; to an 'own goal' all-Akan ticket with Nana Akufo Addo, before it finally settled on Aliu Mahama, a northerner and a Muslim. In the NDC camp, there were initial speculations that First Lady Agyeman-Rawlings or her close confidante local government minister Cecilia Johnson would be imposed on Mills. But the real contenders were Obed Asamoah and Iddrisu Mahama. Asamoah had waged a long campaign through his association with the Progressive Voluntary Associations and the Verandah Boys and Girls Club. It was therefore one of the ironies of fate that the NDC mantle fell on his deputy attorney general, Martin Amidu, whom Asamoah left to run his office while he went campaigning (Frempong 2001: 153–4). In each camp, the final choice caused some ripples. Within the NDC, Asamoah felt beaten to it twice and one of his staunch supporters, the vociferous Faustina Nelson, was completely lost from the campaign radar of the NDC. In like manner, the second vice chairman of the NPP, Wayo Seini, who had a particular interest in the running mate slot, resigned abruptly from active politics.

The presidential run-off The presidential run-off witnessed far worse divisive, if not dirty, politics. After tasting defeat in the first round and with the six opposition parties 'ganging up' against the ruling party in the form of an electoral alliance, the NDC went all-out to play the ethnic card. The crux of this strategy was to portray Ashantis (Kufuor's people) as wicked and vindictive and to call on the other ethnic groups to join forces to defeat the Ashanti 'invasion'. In this direction:

- The people of the Western and Central regions were chastised for giving their votes to Kufuor (an Ashanti) instead of Mills (a Fanti and son of their soil). Indeed, a team of six chiefs from Volta Region was dispatched to the chiefs in the Central Region to give them lessons on how to support a homeboy.

- Rawlings, at a number of meetings with the chiefs and fetish priests of the Ga Traditional Council, reportedly told them how Ashantis were about to take over Accra through a Kufuor victory. NDC vans also preached the same message in those areas in Accra dominated by indigenous Gas.
- NDC also sought to spread fear and panic by exaggerating alleged incidents of election-related assaults perpetrated against NDC supporters and the indigenes of Volta and the Northern Region by NPP supporters in their strongholds of Ashanti and Brong Ahafo regions.
- Kufuor was also depicted in print and electronic advertisements as a 'ne'er-do-well' – a failed businessman, failed lawyer, failed sports administrator, failed minister in the PNDC government and a failed presidential aspirant in 1996 (Frempong 2001: 156; Gyimah-Boadi 2001: 108–9).

The NPP's response, with the single exception of the revelation of Mills's eleven-year-old son born outside wedlock, was positive. The NPP leadership solicited the help of prominent Ewes to convince Volta Region to come out of its isolation and join the winning bandwagon. A similar appeal was made to the three Northern regions to join the rest for Kufuor for 'positive change'.

The dividends Election 2000 had its liberating effects as well as several dividends for consensus-building and democratic development (Frempong 2001: 156; Gyimah-Boadi 2001: 108–9).

The liberating effect of the opposition victory was multi-dimensional. First, it was celebrated locally as Ghana's 'second independence'. The clear demonstration of the power of the thumb as opposed to the barrel of the gun brought back people's confidence in the ballot box and halted the incipient one-party system that was developing under the NDC. Second, the opposition, particularly the NPP, could congratulate itself for mapping an effective strategy to neutralize the once seemingly invincible NDC. Third, it brought introspection to the defeated NDC, which openly conceded its shortcomings such as abuse of office, lack of internal party democracy and arrogance – a refreshing departure from its culture of official impunity. Its parliamentary group was itself liberated. For the first time it was not going to operate under the tutelage of an overbearing executive. And fourth, for Africa, Ghana's peaceful transfer of power offered some hope that constitutional limits can work on the continent.

No

Election 2000 also offered some lessons in consensus-building. The opposition's show of resilience and fortitude in the face of extreme provocation and the incumbent's gracious concession to defeat and peaceful handing over, were a manifestation of growing elite consensus on the rules of the democratic game. The coalition of opposition forces, particularly for the second ballot, was not only invigorating but, more importantly, demonstrated a degree of consensus-building and a step towards political inclusiveness. The very pivotal role that civil society can play in moderating mounting political tensions was also amply demonstrated in the course of Election 2000. The relentless effort of civil society averted the well-founded fears about election-day violence and its potentially dire implications. The parliamentary outcome, with government and opposition virtually split down the middle, provided an opportunity for increased consensus-building away from the impunity of the majority that characterized the previous parliaments. Lastly, the Ghanaian experience represented a model of 'pacted transition' in which incumbent autocrats are gradually eased out through constitutional means. That model has the advantage of a face-saving device for autocratic rulers and regimes and a reduction in violence that tends to accompany transitions elsewhere in Africa.

The democratic dividend included the fact that, in spite of the ethnic hype, Election 2000, with the exception of the Ashanti–Ewe cleavage, was decided less by ethnicity. The people of Central Region in particular demonstrated that they are perhaps the most detribalized in the country. They rejected their own son because they were not convinced that Mills could deliver the change they desired after almost two decades of PNDC/NDC rule. The outcome of the closely fought election demonstrated the resolve of Ghanaians to exact greater accountability and transparency from the political elite. Election 2000 also brought Ghana closer to completing the process of transition to democratic rule and marked a significant step towards democratic consolidation. Not only was the alternation in power going to test the resilience of Ghana's 1992 Constitution but also the peaceful manner in which it was achieved is rare in Africa.

The post-Rawlings era

The exit of Rawlings posed several challenges that were compounded by the alternation of power. The major challenges included calming political and social tensions flowing from the elections; settlement for Rawlings and his entourage; reorientation, if not restructuring, of the security agencies without a backlash; national reconciliation; and the economy (Gyimah-Boadi 2001: 108–9). The milieu in which to tackle these challenges was at best not conducive. The NDC had yet to come to terms with its defeat while the euphoria surrounding the NPP victory had raised people's expectations too high.

Kufuor's first hundred days and after Within the first hundred days of the Kufuor administration most of the above challenges created controversy.

The ethnic card could not bring victory to the NDC but it succeeded in sharpening ethnic differences. The fact that an Ashanti had become president did not help matters. Kufuor needed to reassure the various groups, which had been 'trained' to be wary of Ashantis – Voltarians, Northerners, Gas and even Fantis – that his administration would not be a threat to them and that each of them would have its fair share of the national cake. Against this background, the regional distribution of cabinet positions was brought under scrutiny more than ever before. The appointment of the new president's brother, Addo Kufuor, and his brother-in-law, J. H. Mensah, to the cabinet raised eyebrows. But the fact is that the two were prominent members of the NPP parliamentary group who would have made it to the cabinet on their own merits, whoever was the NPP president. The initial exclusion of an indigene from the Upper West Region brought back bad memories of the Busia regime's exclusion of the Volta Region under similar circumstances in the 1970s. And attention was also drawn to the Akan (if not Ashanti) dominance in the cabinet; this perception continues to haunt the NPP administration.

The Kufuor administration was virtually plunged into the unfamiliar terrain of an appropriate settlement for Rawlings and his entourage. The issue of Rawlings's post-presidential settlement was always going to be thorny because he and his cohorts were in power for almost two decades but failed to provide appropriate settlement for previous leaders. Indeed, in January 2000, the then minority leader J. H. Mensah had intimated rather sarcastically that a State Settlement Act to provide a settlement for the president be passed. Because, he had argued, at the youthful age of fifty-two and after nearly twenty as head of state, Rawlings would have problems managing his imminent retirement (Agyemang-Duah 2000: 56; *Evening News*, 20 January 2001). But the somewhat unexpected alternation of power and the very limited transition period turned the whole process into a messy affair.

The Joint Transition Team to sort out some of those issues had less than two weeks between the presidential run-off and the inauguration. The number of houses to be given to Rawlings and their locations, whether he was to have military or police guards, the nature of cars former ministers could buy at concessional rates as part of their settlement package, as well as gratuities for MPs were all matters steeped in controversy. Indeed, those

Political conflict and elite consensus

issues put both the new administration and the former government on the defensive. The general perception was that the NPP had struck a bad deal and had became the defendant instead of the prosecutor in the court of public opinion. On its part, the NDC parliamentary group called for a new electoral calendar, in a non-partisan spirit, to ensure an adequate period for a smooth and organized transition that would avoid the embarrassment caused the former ministers over the purchase of cars.

The support the other opposition groups gave the NPP during the run-off provided the NPP with a golden opportunity to form an all-inclusive government. The NRP reportedly declined to be part because it 'represents different social interests, policies and priorities'. Kwesi Ndoum, a defeated CPP parliamentary candidate, was appointed minister of economic planning and regional cooperation, an appointment which proved beneficial to the government. Mallam Isa, then acting chairman of the PNC, was also appointed youth and sports minister but with disastrous consequences. He was dismissed within a month and subsequently tried and gaoled over a $64,000 bonus for sportsmen.

Another interesting dynamic of the immediate post-Rawlings era was the love the NDC developed for the rule of law and due process. Top NDC members, including former deputy attorney general and defeated vice presidential candidate Martin Amidu, contested in rapid succession at the Supreme Court the legality of Kufuor's appointment of his presidential staffers and top brass of the military without consulting the then non-existent Council of State.

The NPP inherited a stagnant economy, depleted national coffers and a huge debt burden which forced the government to declare Ghana a Highly Indebted Poor Country (HIPC) in its first budget of 9 March 2001. Not only was this criticized by the NDC which reportedly resisted international pressures in that direction but there were indications that the government itself was divided over the matter. A week before the budget, Vice President Aliu Mahama had declared that the government would not rush to decide on HIPC. On the eve of the budget, finance minister Osafo Maafo said Ghana could not be an HIPC since the technical committee looking into it had not finished its work, only for him to declare Ghana HIPC the next day.[2] Was it public deception or had the president forced him to announce what he did not believe in?

The Kufuor government has moved away from its initial slips and has been performing creditably in many areas. For instance, it has succeeded in reorienting the loyalty of the military from Rawlings without the expected backlash and has considerably improved the logistical base of the police. But there have been a few instances where its actions have either been controversial or not helped its ambivalent image in the area of transparency and professionalism. In this category are:

- The IFC loan (discussed in the section below).
- The appointment of Justice Afreh to the Supreme Court with the singular purpose of overturning an earlier Supreme Court decision that had declared fast-track courts illegal. Not only did it politicize the judiciary but it also attacked the very roots of judicial independence. Indeed, it was so reminiscent of the Abban affair that the stony silence of the Ghana Bar Association (GBA) on the matter raised eyebrows.
- The government's decisions to privatize water and to sell its shares in the Ghana Commercial Bank which it withdrew midstream under public pressure. While the government interpreted its actions to mean that it is responsive to public opinion, it was interpreted by its detractors as indecision.

The third parliament of the Fourth Republic The situation in parliament was even more intriguing. With their roles reversed it was interesting to see how MPs on either side of the political divide reacted to issues in the first few weeks of the new parliament. First Deputy Speaker Ken Dzirassah swapped positions with Second Deputy Freddy Blay. J. H. Mensah became the new majority leader while the NDC chose Algban Babgin, who had not held ministerial position in the PNDC/NDC era, to lead the minority in the House. Speaker Justice Annan was replaced by a former NPP national chairman Peter Ala Adjetey. Like the NPP in 1997, the NDC had preferred somebody less partisan.

Quite expectedly, the first few months in parliament were marked by disagreements over many issues, with the singular exception of a $20,000 car loan for each MP. Some of the points of disagreement in those hectic days were:

- Whether or not ministerial appointees could assume responsibilities in their ministries before their approval by parliament.
- The use of a presidential jet purchased by the NDC government under none too transparent circumstances.
- An oil purchase agreement (the Sahara affair) and the loan for the purchase of vehicles for the police, both from Nigeria, without parliament's prior approval.
- The non-recognition of the vice president and other non-MPs by the president in his first address to parliament on 15 January 2001. Indeed, whether to call the speech a 'State of the Nation' or a 'Presidential Address' aroused debate.

Political conflict and elite consensus

• The renovation of the president's private residence with state funds.

In all these matters the once vociferous opposition, now on the majority bench, supported the government while the former subservient NDC group vehemently opposed it.

In a rare exception to the rule, the NDC MP for Bimbilla, Mohammed Ibn Chambas, had praised the president's address as containing a 'heavy dose of realism'.[3] Either by fate or design, Chambas was later supported by the NPP government to become the executive secretary of the Economic Community of West African States (ECOWAS). While the NPP trumpeted this as a manifestation of its all-inclusive governance, the NDC saw it as a calculated ploy to weaken the opposition. In the resultant by-election in Bimbilla, the NPP took the seat from the NDC.

After the initial furore, parliament settled down and worked through consensus on several issues. But it must be emphasized that, in 2002 and 2003 respectively, the minority boycotted the debate and voting on the National Reconciliation bill and the National Health Insurance bill. The former sought to deal with unresolved issues of truth, justice and reconciliation; while the latter aimed at replacing the existing 'cash and carry' healthcare system.

The boycott of the bill on national reconciliation was most unfortunate for our purposes here. While both sides agreed on the need for some form of reconciliation for Ghana, they could not agree either on the mode of appointment of the commissioners or the period which their work was to cover. The majority accepted the government's proposal that members be appointed by the president with parliamentary approval, and wanted it restricted to Ghana's unconstitutional governments. The minority preferred a less partisan mode of appointment and the scope to cover all regimes before the Fourth Republic. The majority eventually gave a window of opportunity for complaints for all regimes before the beginning of the Fourth Republic. But the perception that parliament could not set the pace by reconciling itself remained and doggedly haunted the work of the National Reconciliation Commission.

Another issue that amply demonstrated the dangers of non-consensus in parliament was the International Financial Consortium (IFC) loan. The government laid before parliament in the middle of June 2002 an agreement which sought to source a loan worth one billion US dollars from the above-named international private consortium. The opposition and the media raised serious concerns about the loan, but the finance committee, by a majority vote, all members of the minority dissenting, recommended the proposed loan agreement for approval by the House. Parliament in turn, amid intense controversy, 'fast-tracked' the approval process in partisan acquiescence to the wishes of the executive which would not tolerate too many probing but necessary questions. The loan turned out to be a scam (*Democratic Watch* 2002: 1–5).

The lessons from that episode for parliament, particularly the majority, are many:

- that it is part of the role of the majority in parliament even (and perhaps more so) when it is the party in power to help to improve draft documents placed before them by the executive to make the final product more beneficial to all
- that while it is legitimate for MPs to factor the interest of their party into their deliberations, they have a primary responsibility to the people, and that in crucial matters the party interest must be moderated, if not subordinated, to the public interest
- that the parliamentary majority should not, as if in a reflex action, dismiss any and every objection raised by the minority as partisan, unmeritorious or ill-intentioned; rather, it has a responsibility to take those contributions in good faith and examine them on their own merits

Above all, majority rule does not mean that wisdom necessarily and always resides in the majority – a fact that the NPP majority from their experience in opposition should have better appreciated.

The NDC in opposition It should be interesting to examine briefly how the NDC as a party has fared as an opposition party. It was compelled by its defeat, as earlier indicated, to undertake some self-examination. This began soon after the election but formally a revamp team headed by Obed Asamoah was formed in March 2001 to come up with ideas for the reorganization of the party. In this connection, a future role in the party for the ex-president became a bone of contention that has continued to haunt the NDC.

By the time the NDC held its first post-defeat national congress in April 2002, the party had been divided into pro-Rawlings and anti-Rawlings camps. The former were the defenders of the status quo, for whom the party is inseparable from Rawlings and any attempt to diminish his grip on the party would make the NDC something other than the NDC. The latter were the champions of a new and depersonalized NDC advocating an NDC that looked beyond Rawlings (*Democratic Watch* 2002). The April 2002 congress was a Pyrrhic victory for the anti-Rawlings forces: the role of founder of the party became separated from that of leader; and its chief advocate Asamoah squeezed a very narrow victory of 334 to 332 for the national chairmanship at the expense of the pro-Rawlings Iddrisu Mahama. The fact that two regional chairmen announced their resignation at Asamoah's victory indicated further the extent of the rift in the party.

Asamoah had campaigned to bring back to the NDC fold former stalwarts such as Kojo Tsikata, P. V. Obeng and Kwesi Botchwey who had fallen out with the ex-president. It was therefore not surprising that Kwesi Botchwey, for thirteen years finance minister in the PNDC-NDC, would emerge as the only contestant for the party's flag-bearership for the 2004 elections against former vice president Mills. While Mills continued to enjoy his 'anointed son' status, Botchwey campaigned to free the NDC from his dictatorial grasp to create a more democratic and open society. After a keenly conducted campaign, the December 2002 contest resulted in an overwhelming 1,116 to 194 victory for Mills, reportedly amid intimidation, thereby confirming Rawlings's continued dominance of the party and a virtual return to the status quo ante. The Mills victory also effectively turned Election 2004 into a rematch for the 2000 front-runners – Mills and Kufuor.

The relationship between ex-president Rawlings and the ruling party has been conflictual. From June 2001 Rawlings has persistently criticized the Kufuor government to the extent that some of his privileges as former head of state have had to be withdrawn.

Conclusion

It should be clear from the vicissitudes of Ghana's decade of constitutional rule in the Fourth Republic (1993–2003) that this latest experiment at liberal-democratic rule has had its ups and downs. Indeed, a few rough edges remain. The heightened fear and threats to stability that characterize successive elections are a clear indication that the Ghanaian political elite and their followers are yet to imbibe fully the democratic culture. Indeed, it is not one of the norms of democracy to play on the electorate's fear as an electoral strategy. Again, while legislative rubber-stamping of government policies does not serve any useful public interest, the negative tendency of parliamentary subservience to the executive still prevails.

We should nevertheless take delight in the fact that the Ghanaian experience has amply demonstrated, among other things, that:

- The early years of redemocratization must expectedly be tumultuous because there are no quick fixes in transforming institutions and norms of authoritarianism into the norms and structures of democracy. They demand values and attitudes that take years to establish.
- Elite consensus on the rules of the game is vital for democratic devel-

opment. Even a flawed transition could set the stage for democratic progress if the political elites subsequently agree on the basic rules.

• And above all, that peaceful democratic transition is possible in Africa.

Notes

1 See <www.consensus.net/occac1.html>.
2 See <www.ghanaweb.com>.
3 Ibid.

Sources

Agyeman-Duah, B. (2000) *Elections in Emerging Democracies: Ghana, Liberia and Nigeria*, Ghana Critical Perspectives, no. 4 (Accra: CDD).

Ake, C. (2000) *The Feasibility of Democracy in Africa* (Dakar: CODESRIA).

Aubynn, A. K. (1997) *Beyond the Transparent Box: The Significance of the 1996 Elections in Ghana*, Working Paper, no. 5/97 (Helsinki: Institute of Development Studies).

Ayee, J. R. A. (1997) *Ghana's 1996 General Elections: A Post-mortem*, Occasional Paper Series, Vol. 1, no. 1 (Harare: AAPS).

Badu, K. A. and J. Larvie (1996) *Elections 96 in Ghana*, Part 1 (Accra: Gold Type).

— (1997) *Elections 96 in Ghana*, Part 2 (Accra: Gold Type).

Bluwey, G. K. (1998) 'State Organisations in the Transition to Constitutional Democracy', in K. A. Ninsin (ed.), *Ghana: Transition to Democracy* (Accra: Freedom Publications).

Boafo-Arthur, K. (1995) 'Managing Inter-party Conflict in Ghanaian Politics: Lessons from the NDC and NPP Dialogue', in M. Oquaye (ed.), *Democracy and Conflict Resolution in Ghana* (Accra: Gold Type).

Burton, M. and J. Higley (1987) 'Elite Settlements', *American Sociological Review* (June).

— (1989) 'The Elite Variable in Democratic Transitions and Breakdowns', *American Sociological Review* (February).

Conteh-Morgan, E. (1997) *Democratization in Africa: The Theory and Dynamics of Political Transitions* (Westport, CT and London: Praeger).

Democratic Watch (2002) Vol. 3, nos 2 and 3 (September).

Diamond, L. and M. Plattner (1999) *Democratization in Africa* (Baltimore, MD: Johns Hopkins University Press).

Diamond, L., J. Linz and S. Lipset (1995) *Politics in Developing Countries: Comparing Experiences with Democracy* (Boulder, CO: Lynne Rienner).

Ephson, B. (2003) *Countdown to 2004 Elections* (Accra: Allied News).

Frempong, A. K. D. (2001) 'Ghana's Election 2000: The Ethnic Undercurrents', in J. R. A. Ayee (ed.), *Deepening Democracy in Ghana: Politics of the 2000 Elections*, Vol. 1 (Accra: Freedom Publications).

Gould, J. and S. Szomolanyi (1997) 'Elite Fragmentation in Industry and the Prospect for Democracy', *Intermarium*, Vol. 1, no. 2.

Gyimah-Boadi, E. (1991) 'Tensions in Ghana's Transition to Constitutional Rule', in K. A. Ninsin and F. K. Drah (eds), *Ghana's Transition to Constitutional Rule* (Accra: Ghana Universities Press).

— (1999) 'Ghana: The Challenges of Consolidating Democracy', in R. Joseph (ed.), *State Conflict and Democracy in Africa* (Boulder, CO: Lynne Rienner).

— (2000) 'Six Years of Constitutional Rule in Ghana: An Assessment and Prospects of the Executive and the Legislature', in Friedrich Ebert Foundation, *Six Years of Constitutional Rule in Ghana: 1993–1999* (Accra: Gold Type).

— (2001) 'A Peaceful Turnover in Ghana', *Journal of Democracy*, Vol. 12, no. 2 (April).

Hagan, G. P. (1995) 'Democracy as a Conflitual System – the Needed Cultural Premise', in M. Oquaye (ed.), *Democracy and Conflict Resolution in Ghana* (Accra: Gold Type).

Higley, J. and M. Burton (1998) 'Elite Settlements and the Taming of Politics', *Government and Opposition*, Vol. 33, no. 1 (Winter): 98–115.

Jonah, K. (1998) 'Political Parties and the Transition to Multi-party Politics in Ghana', in K. A. Ninsin (ed.), *Ghana: Transition to Democracy* (Dakar and Accra: CODESRIA and Freedom Publications).

Kotey, E. N. A. (1995) 'The Supreme Court and Conflict Resolution in Ghana's Fourth Republic', in M. Oquaye (ed.), *Democracy and Conflict Resolution in Ghana* (Accra: Gold Type).

Ninsin, K. A. (1995) 'Conflict as Pursuit of Liberty', in M. Oquaye (ed.), *Democracy and Conflict Resolution in Ghana* (Accra: Gold Type).

— (ed.) (1998) *Ghana: Transition to Democracy* (Dakar and Accra: CODESRIA and Freedom Publications).

O'Donnell, G. and P. Schmitter (1986) *Transitions from Authoritarian Rule: Tentative Conclusions About Uncertain Democracies* (Baltimore, MD: Johns Hopkins University Press).

Oquaye, M. (2001) *Government and Politics in Contemporary Ghana (1992–1990) – a Study,* Governance Series, Vol. 1, no. 1 (Accra: African Governance Institute).

Pioneer (1992) 26 November (Accra).

Prempeh, H. K. (1999) *The Ghanaian Judiciary and the 1992 Constitution: A Problem of Asymmetrical Jurisprudence*, Ghana Critical Perspectives, no. 1 (Accra: CDD).

Przeworski, A. et al. (1995) *Sustainable Democracy* (Cambridge: Cambridge University Press).

Sandbrook, R. and J. Oelbaum (1997) 'Reforming Dysfunctional Institutions Through Democratization? Reflections on Ghana', *Journal of Modern African Studies*, Vol. 35, no. 4.

Uhuru (1993) Vol. 5, no. 7, February (Accra).

7 | A decade of political leadership in Ghana, 1993–2004

JOSEPH R. A. AYEE

Market forces may create the conditions for success or failure of a state; but a critical factor determining which states succeed and which do not is political leadership. The study of effective leadership is enjoying a period of resurgence at present across the globe (Conger 1989; Handy 1989; Muczyk and Reinmann 1987). One of the most persuasive ideas to emerge from such studies is that, unlike the Asian 'dragons', which have developed transformational leaders to spearhead socio-economic development, African states have not paid sufficient attention to preparing tomorrow's leaders and this, to a large extent, is why so many states have remained largely underdeveloped.

Against this background, this chapter assesses the performance of political leadership, especially of the presidency in Ghana covering the period 1993–2004. It compares the political leadership of the National Democratic Congress (NDC), which was in power from 1993 to 2000, with that of the current incumbent government, the New Patriotic Party (NPP), which came to power in January 2001. The chapter is divided into four sections. It begins by defining leadership and then identifies the leadership challenge in Ghana. The next section assesses political leadership performance based on the following four indicators: (a) maintaining the cohesion of the administration; (b) developing strategic policy direction aimed at contributing to change; (c) the relationship between politicians and bureaucrats; and (d) personal dimension/leadership style. The final section highlights the lessons revealed by the study of political leadership.

Defining leadership

The concept of leadership defies clear-cut definition. It may be defined as:

> creating a vision of the future that takes into account the legitimate long-
> term interests of the parties involved in that activity; of developing a rational
> strategy for moving towards that vision; of enlisting the support of key
> power centres whose cooperation, compliance, or teamwork is necessary to
> produce that movement; and of motivating highly that core of people whose
> actions are central to implementing the strategy. (Kotter 1988: 25–6)

Leadership is a combination of credible authority, persuasion, empowerment of others (Conger 1989), inducement and, perhaps above all, good judgement (Quinn et al. 1989).

Leadership revolves around purpose, and purpose is at the heart of the leader–follower relationship. Indeed, in some cases a compelling statement of mission not only gives direction to a group, but also is its formative experience, shaping the identity of group members by highlighting a shared aim. According to Burns, leaders can be distinguished from their followers:

> Leaders and followers may be inseparable in function, but they are not the same. The leader takes the initiative in making the leader-led connection; it is the leader who creates the links that allow communication and exchange to take place ... The leader is more skilful in evaluating followers' motives, anticipating their responses to an initiative, and estimating their power bases, than the reverse ... Finally ... leaders address themselves to followers' wants, needs and other motivations, as well as to their own, and thus serve as an independent force in changing the makeup of their followers' motive base through gratifying their motives. (Burns 1978: 20)

Although Burns distinguishes between leadership and 'naked power wielding' (ibid.: 427), he sees leadership as a form of power. It is a way of making something happen that would otherwise not take place. Hence Burns offers 'contribution to change' as a test of leadership (ibid.: 20).

From Burns and other scholars, we propose a conception of leadership with three essential elements: (a) leadership is purposeful activity; (b) it operates interactively with a body of followers; and (c) it is a form of power or causation. As succinctly put by Burns, leadership is 'collectively purposeful causation' (ibid.: 434).

An essential ingredient of effective leadership is the establishment of a set of values that will provide the foundation for the development of mutual trust and commitment. Mistrust is the cholesterol of organizational systems; like its medicinal analogy, it clogs and incapacitates the arteries of the organization; it impedes its performance and may ultimately bring about its demise. And like heart disease, it is an epidemic of modern organizational life (Bartolome 1989: 135–42).

The context of political leadership in Ghana

When difficulties arise, a call for leadership is inevitably sounded. The anticipated leader is someone with vision, a plan of action, and perhaps with the ability to summon people to extraordinary effort. Leadership goes to the heart of politics, that is, to the capacity of a people to act together on their shared concerns.

The context of political leadership in Ghana is influenced by four factors; namely, the challenges that face all political leaders, the neoliberal environment within which the leaders work, culture and the media. The challenge to political leadership in Ghana, as in other Sub-Saharan African countries, is daunting. Leaders are faced with a myriad problems including the almost insurmountable challenge of meeting expectations with meagre resources, the need to grapple with continued dependence on an unfavourable international economic order, the need to incorporate a diverse population into a workable whole, and to establish the guidelines for a distinctive Ghanaian path of not only constructive change but also socio-economic development (Pellow and Chazan 1986). Such challenges are acknowledged in Chapter 6 of the 1992 Constitution, the Directive Principles of State Policy, which enjoins political leadership to establish a just and free society and take steps for the realization of basic human rights, a healthy economy, the right to work, the right to good healthcare and the right to education.

The challenge to political leadership has no doubt affected the performance of Rawlings and Kufuor. They have not only acknowledged the prevalence of the challenge in their sessional addresses but also in the budget statements presented to parliament. Ethnic violence has erupted in Northern Ghana and other parts of the country during the regimes of Rawlings and Kufuor, leading to loss of life and destruction of property. Both governments resorted to imposing a state of emergency to curb the violence. The poor state of the Ghanaian economy, human rights issues and unemployment and underemployment have also been key election issues and have cost both the NDC and NPP electoral victories in one way or another. For instance, in 2000, the poor state of the economy and the perception of corruption were contributory factors leading to the NDC losing the elections. Similarly, the NPP lost the Asawase constituency seat in a by-election in April 2005 largely because of harsh economic measures such as the increase in petroleum prices and indirectly because of the decongestion of the city of Kumasi by the Metropolitan Assembly which displaced hawkers. The inability to formulate a comprehensive national wage policy has not only led to strikes and threats of strikes but also to the mistrust that has characterized government–labour relations.

In addition, Rawlings and Kufuor have had to deal with the challenge of insulating national issues from partisan considerations. Discussions on issues, such as the economy, the appointment of people to public offices, parliamentary procedures and the national health insurance scheme, have been politicized. This has led to Rawlings and Kufuor reacting to problems in a knee-jerk fashion that has further compounded them and created problems of legitimacy for their governments.

Dealing with corruption has become a major challenge. Even though Rawlings himself declared that he was not corruptible at the time he left office, his NDC government was perceived as corrupt. Consequently, when Kufuor won the 2000 elections, he announced a policy of 'zero tolerance for corruption' at his inauguration. Five years later, in spite of the promulgation of appropriate legislation such as the Public Procurement Act, the Internal Audit Act and the Financial Administration Act to fight corruption in the country, there was a perception that Kufuor and the NPP government's fight against corruption had become blunted. Dealing with corruption has become a major barometer for measuring the performance of the two leaders in office. Consequently, judging by rankings by Transparency International, neither of the two leaders can be said to have performed well in minimizing the incidence of corruption. This has created serious legitimacy problems for them both.

Since 1983, Ghana has pursued a neoliberal environment (often linked to the so-called Washington Consensus) with emphasis on rolling back or shrinking the frontiers or role of the state, privatization and deregulation, trade and financial liberalization and encouraging foreign direct investment. Under Rawlings's Provisional National Defence Council (PNDC), while the economic recovery programme (ERP) I, 1983–86, focused on exchange rate reform, price decontrol, monetary and fiscal policies, export sector rehabilitation and public sector investment, ERP II concentrated on structural and institutional reforms in the financial sector, state enterprises, education, the civil service, the Programme of Action to Mitigate the Social Costs of Adjustment (PAMSCAD) and the background work on the medium-term agricultural development programme. ERP III, implemented in 1993, unlike ERP I and II, shifted attention from economic recovery to accelerated growth through sustainable development and poverty reduction through private sector development. In January 1995, the then President Rawlings of the National Democratic Congress (NDC) presented a policy document to parliament entitled *Ghana – Vision 2020: The First Step: 1996–2000*, which aimed at an 'open and liberal market economy' and transforming Ghana 'from a low-income to a middle-income country' within one generation through a growth rate in excess of 8 per cent per annum (Republic of Ghana 1995). In addition, *Ghana – Vision 2020* envisaged optimizing economic growth and ensuring the maximum welfare and material well-being of all Ghanaians. These objectives were reinforced by the first medium-term development plan, 1997–2000, which covered five thematic areas, namely, economic growth, human development, rural development, urban development and the development of an enabling environment through decentralization, reform of the public administration system, capacity development and utilization for public sector performance under the National Institutional Reform Programme (NIRP) comprised of: (a) the Civil Service Performance Improvement Programme (CSPIP); (b) the Public Financial Management Reform Programme (PUFMARP); (c) the Legal Sector and Administrative Improvement Programme (LSAIP); (d) a capacity-building programme for private sector development; and (e) science and technology for development (Republic of Ghana 1997).

One of the important outcomes of the various phases of the ERP is the development of a market-oriented economy. The liberalization of the trade and payments system enables entrepreneurs to transact international trade without going through the cumbersome procedures for securing an import licence. In addition, the establishment of the Ghana Stock Exchange has made it possible for private enterprises to access cheap and longer-term funds for expansion (Republic of Ghana 1999). Furthermore, within a decade, the GDP growth rate increased to about 5 per cent per annum and inflation was reduced to an average of 26 per cent per annum (Hutchful 2002: 55–6). However, by the mid-1990s the growth momentum slowed and macroeconomic instability resurfaced. This is demonstrated by declining GDP growth rates (3.4 per cent in 1996), uncontrolled expansion in money supply (47 per cent in 1995) and escalating price inflation (38 per cent in 1995). This has been accompanied by economic hardships, mounting unemployment, a slowing of poverty reduction and an escalation of social tensions (Ayee 1999).

Under the current New Patriotic Party (NPP) government, the neoliberal environment has continued. In the Ghana Poverty Reduction Strategy (GPRS), published in February 2002, the government aims to 'create wealth by transforming the nature of the economy to achieve growth, accelerated poverty reduction and the protection of the vulnerable and excluded within a decentralized, democratic environment'. This goal is going to be achieved by (a) ensuring sound economic management for accelerated growth; (b) increasing production and promoting sustainable livelihoods; (c) direct support for human development and the provision of basic services; (d) providing special programmes in support of the vulnerable and excluded; (e) ensuring good governance and increased capacity of the public sector; and (f) the active involvement of the private sector as the main engine of growth and partner in nation-building (Republic of Ghana 2002).

The 1992 Constitution has buttressed the neoliberal environment with the following provisions:

i. establishment and strengthening of a democratic state, based on the ideals and principles of freedom, equality, regional and gender balance, justice, probity, accountability, transparency and competence

ii. eradication of corrupt practices and the abuse of power

iii. institution-building and reform

iv. establishment of a sound and healthy economy, with a reduction in the role of the state in the economic life of the country through the shifting of more responsibility to the private sector and an environment that encourages investor confidence

v. decentralization of administrative and financial machinery of government to the regions and districts

vi. development of 'value for money' public services (Republic of Ghana 1992)

The neoliberal environment together with the constitutional arrangements have provided opportunites for checks and balances on political leadership. On the one hand, the neoliberal environment has created conditions for patronage while at the same time restricting the leaders through retrenchment, privatization and wage freezes, which have been condemned by the Trades Union Congress (TUC).

The neoliberal environment has assisted the performances of Rawlings and Kufuor. It brought political competition, greater input from civil society, consensus and legitimation, 'increased accountability and scrutiny of fiscal and development policy and government budgeting and spending' (Hutchful 2002: 219). The two leaders, therefore, have a freer environment within which to work. There was limited government which had little effect on the management style of both leaders. In addition, through structural adjustment programmes and the highly indebted poor countries (HIPC) initiative pursued by Rawlings and Kufuor respectively, they had/have financial resources for infrastructural development to reduce the pressure brought by expectations of and agitation from communities for basic services.

Notwithstanding these benefits of the neoliberal environment, the two leaders have been blamed for not pursuing a homegrown development programme but rather succumbed to the dictates of IMF/World Bank conditionalities. In addition, in spite of the neoliberal environment, the country is still faced with

> persistent reliance on the export of a few primary products with little or no added value added (cocoa, gold, timber and others). This has made the economy vulnerable to price fluctuations dictated by buyers in the developed economies. The low earnings from primary products have meant low revenue to the country. This in turn has made it difficult to create meaningful wealth in the country. Per capita income in Ghana today is less than what existed at the time we achieved independence. (Republic of Ghana 2002: i)

This has in one way or another frustrated the two leaders' attempts to use the potential of the neoliberal environment for solving the problems of Ghanaian society. A further dilemma faced by the two leaders is the

> conflict between continued fiscal deflation and democratic 'demand infla-
> tion'; in other words, while democracy can be expected to lead to inflation
> in both demands and the means for articulating them, fiscal deflation
> leads (at least in the short term) to a contraction in the resources available
> to satisfy such demands. If democratization offers reform the mantle of
> political legitimacy, it also imposes an essential constraint in terms of the
> need to reproduce that legitimacy. This has been particularly manifest in
> the so-called 'political-business cycle', in which a government facing an
> election expands spending and stimulates the economy as a way of improv-
> ing its chances of re-election, stabilizing the economy once the election is
> over. (Hutchful 2002: 219)

A third factor influencing political leadership is the media. Political leadership lost its monopoly because private media have flourished since the advent of the Fourth Republic. The media provide an alternative outlet for minority parties and groups to criticize political leadership. This is in contrast to the state-owned media, whose coverage of leadership activities is somewhat skewed in their favour; according to Nana Konadu Agyeman Rawlings, former first lady, 'the state-owned media are supposed to support the government, because they are paid from government resources' (cited in Smith and Temin 2001: 160). The private media's activities, investigation and coverage have strained their relationship with the political leadership, particularly under the Rawlings presidency. Indeed, according to Rawlings's National Democratic Congress (NDC), the party lost the 2000 elections because of negative media coverage. In addition, the investigative journalism exposing corruption and other rent-seeking activities has put the political leadership on its toes.

The media's impact on the performance of the two leaders cannot be overestimated. Rawlings used the legal and coercive apparatus of the state to intimidate, harass and abuse journalists and he employed covert offensives (such as vandalism, smearing of human excreta on the entrance of the *Crusading Guide* newspaper in October 2000); this worked against him to the extent that he became the subject of discussion every day in most of the private media. Even though there is no evidence to show the extent of the impact of this on his performance, he suffered psychological trauma as a result of his negative media image. Some policies and programmes he formulated and implemented were denigrated by the private media because of his tactics. This partly explains why the Rawlings government failed to expunge the criminal libel law which made it a criminal offence for journalists to publish anything that might expose public officials to ridicule and contempt. Kufuor, on the other hand, is in favour of press freedom. When he took over, he held a press conference with journalists in April 2001, scrapped the criminal libel law from the statute books and asked the attorney general to withdraw from the courts all pending criminal libel charges against journalists. Consequently, Kufuor has enjoyed considerable positive media coverage. This has given him and his cabinet 'peace of mind' and an environment in which they are able to concentrate on national issues. The relatively cordial relationship between Kufuor and the media has led to the perception that the media, especially the private media, are 'in bed with' the NPP government and therefore represent a recipe for dictatorship and misrule.

A fourth factor is the cultural underpinnings of the nation, such as kinship and ethnicity. Even though Ghanaian culture places a high value on good character, kinship and ethnicity have tended to have a largely negative influence on the political leadership through the creation of three modes of political patronage: namely (a) the connection between national leaders and local communities through direct links with local leaders; authority figures and prosperous persons who command respect in their communities have been courted by the central political leaders to garner support in their local areas with promises of personal gain, public office or local improvements; (b) so-called popular or democratic organizations have become a key vehicle for the disbursement of benefits, just as membership-card-carrying of the party in power has become one of the main means of access to government resources; and (c) so-called 'mafia' groups that have made and unmade political leaders at the local and national levels. Ruling coalitions have depended heavily on the approval of the ethnic groups that brought them to office. Patrons at the centre have directed state funds and resources to members of this 'mafia' group. In turn, the leaders have hoped to ensure the mafia's support (Ayee 2001). The Ghanaian culture of promoting patronage has reinforced the view that 'When a society's impersonal legal guarantees of physical security, status, and wealth are relatively weak or non-existent, individuals seek personal substitutes by attaching themselves to "big-men" capable of producing protection and even advancement' (Sandbrook 1992: 109).

Consequently, Ghanaian culture has a view of politics that has generated patronage which is essentially extractive. The political arena is seen as a source of benefits with wealth, in its broadest sense, the reward for successful engagement. This kind of thinking by politicians and the electorate has encouraged a vicious cycle of competition for access to and control over national resources. It has also nurtured a zero-sum approach to politics. A winner-takes-all approach has been taken to appease backers of the government and to make use of its position before other patrons take control and divert resources to their own ends (Chazan 1983).

Both the Rawlings and Kufuor presidency have been influenced by these cultural factors. There is a perception that both have relied on patron–client relationships through the appointment of people from their ethnic groups to key positions both in the public service and the armed forces to strengthen their grip over the administration. They have articulated 'symbolic distinctiveness derived from the evolution of social relations around defined modes of production, and expressed through the entrenchment of notions of popular participation. These processes were facilitated by the existence of political institutions with some differentiation and durability' (ibid.: 94).

The interplay of the challenges facing political leaders, the neoliberal environment and the 1992 Constitution, culture and the media, have exposed the peculiarity and distinctiveness of leadership challenges and performance in Ghana. Consequently, they provide important bases from which one can understand and evaluate political leadership in the Fourth Republic.

Leadership performance

Like the definition of leadership, there are no universally accepted criteria for measuring leadership performance. This notwithstanding, four criteria have been generally recognized as providing a useful framework for analysing the development of political leadership. They are: (a) maintaining the cohesion of the administration; (b) developing strategic policy direction aimed at contributing to change; (c) the relationship between politicians and bureaucrats; and (d) the personal dimension or style (Leach and Wilson 2002).

It is important to note that comparing political leadership in Ghana is difficult because Rawlings's National Democratic Congress (NDC) was in power for eight years while Kufuor's New Patriotic Party (NPP) has been in charge of the affairs of the nation only since 2000. In spite of the problem of regime longevity, there is a basis for comparison, particularly when one is not focusing exclusively on the personalities but rather on the regimes that worked or are working within a neoliberal environment.

Maintaining the cohesion of the administration When a majority party is in control, its leadership needs to maintain the cohesion of the party. That is its key task, because if the party group fragments, the viability of the administration becomes threatened. The cohesiveness of the administration depends not only on inter-party solidarity but on how the administration is able to reach out to other groups in an attempt to form an inclusive government. To what extent were the Rawlings and the Kufuor governments able to maintain their cohesion and what mechanisms/structures were in put in place?

Even though both leaders tried to maintain the cohesion of their administration through the state and party structures at their disposal, there were instances of serious lack of cohesion and fracture. In the case of Rawlings, he assaulted his vice-president, Kow Arkaah, at a cabinet meeting on 28 December 1995, bringing some tension to the administration. This led to the resignation of one of the female cabinet ministers who was present at the meeting. The introduction of VAT in March 1995 was also fraught. Revelations by Arkaah indicated that the VAT policy of 17.5 per cent, as implemented in March 1995, was not the policy he presided over at a cabinet meeting. Apparently, there existed an inner core of policy-makers that excluded the vice president. In addition, during Rawlings's second term of office, there was serious controversy over the National Democratic Congress's (NDC) lack of internal democracy before the 2000 elections. This was an issue grossly mishandled by the party executive, as it refused to hold primaries for the parliamentary and presidential elections – in the process confirming or imposing unpopular candidates in the constituencies and producing John Atta Mills as the presidential candidate. When Rawlings openly backed Mills in his famous 'Swedru Declaration', the NDC splintered, with some of its more intellectual forces leaving the party to form the National Reform Party (NRP) – one of the reasons behind the defeat of the NDC in the 2000 elections.

Compared to Rawlings's NDC, Kufuor's administration has a more cohesive administration. The party's internal democracy is vigorous in spite of allegations of vote-buying and intimidation when it comes to primaries to elect parliamentary candidates. This notwithstanding, there have been instances in which cohesiveness has been undermined. The first was the assassination of the Ya-Na Yakubu Andani II on 27 March 2002 and the killing of forty others, crimes that some people believed were politically motivated. They led to the resignation of some of the Abudus (one of the two gates of the Dagbon Skin or Stool) in the government. The second was allegations of corruption against the government. Currently, the opposition thinks that the government is using the prosecution of opposition members to cover up the rot in its own ranks. Some of the allegations include the lack of due diligence by the government to source an elusive billion-dollar loan from the International Finance Consortium (IFC) and another 600 million from Chinese National Trading Company International (CNTCI), a Chinese loan firm whose credibility is in doubt. There have been calls for those involved in the two negotiations to resign from their positions for incompetence and negligence. There were earlier allegations of impropriety by the government in the lifting of oil from Nigeria by Sahara Energy Resources, the reconditioning of the older presidential jet, Fokker 28, in Holland, the renovation of the Castle and the importation of fifty Peugeot cars from Nigeria for the Ghana Police Service without parliamentary approval.

These allegations, whether true or not, saw the cohesion of the Kufuor administration under intense pressure. Most of the time the government did not make any pronouncement because it was overwhelmed by the allegations and seemed to have no strategy to counteract them. This prompted the president to indict the Ministry of Information and Presidential Affairs as being incapable of explaining and commenting on matters of public interest. Not only did this lead to a cabinet reshuffle, but the ministry was split into two: the Ministry of Information and the Ministry of Presidential Affairs.

Developing strategic policy direction This involves the conscious attempt to set out a long-term vision or direction for the country. It could be gleaned from the policy documents of the government such as Vision 2020, the manifestos of the National Democratic Congress (NDC) and New Patriotic Party (NPP) governments and the policies and programmes put in place such as VAT, the HIPC initiative, the National Health Insurance Scheme, and the priorities and legislative programmes. The key questions here are: (a) the nature of policy changes sought and achieved by the government and the extent of institutional change achieved; (b) the nature of the interaction with followers – who is involved, the degree to which followers are actively engaged, and the extent to which they are moved by the leader to see themselves in a different and less narrow way (a programme of citizen involvement).

Both governments formulated and implemented key policies and programmes aimed at reducing poverty and promoting peace and stability (see Table 7.1). Because of the strategic nature of the policies and programmes, they were to have received wider stakeholder participation. In Rawlings's view:

> The phenomenon of 'nation-wide consultation' for policy formulation
> and the implementation of programmes has been an important feature of
> the governance of this country, since the 1980s ... The Economic Recovery

Programme, the District Assembly system of local government, the current constitutional arrangements – to mention a few – were all products of national consultation ... The same consultative process has attended the activities of the National Development Planning Commission. Besides the regional and occupational composition of the NDPC, its Secretariat has an organizational structure that incorporates Cross-Sectoral Planning Groups that enables diverse groups and expertise to provide appropriate inputs into the work of the NDPC. Ghana – Vision 2020 which presents the Government's statement of development aims, objectives and strategies, was a product of this consultative process ... This National Forum on the Economy, therefore, only reinforces what has been a committed pattern of governance. I hope that all institutions, organizations and persons taking part in the deliberations, will do so from a position of objective analysis of issues and the presentation of constructive, problem-solving opinions. We are not interested in arguing over who takes credit for what policy. If there is credit, let us share it as Ghanaians ... There is no shortage of ideas in this country, nor is there lack of will on the part of many towards positive action on the economy. Our problem, however, lies in our part with the lack of discipline and failure to recognize and encourage the talented and positive-minded ones in our midst. These have an impact on the implementation of policies. Our problem is not in knowing what we should do but in doing what we know we should do. (Rawlings 1997: 1–2)

These views on consultation were echoed by the vice president, John Mills, in his closing address, also delivered at the National Economic Forum in 1997. In his words:

Ghana consists of different constituencies, interest groups and stake-holders, but for us to succeed as a nation we need to play like a football team. Each of us must work towards the team effort by playing our different roles in the Team to the best of our ability and not regarding ourselves as being more important than the other players in the Team. (Mills 1997: 1)

There is, however, a feeling that most of the policies and programmes did not receive the much-needed stakeholder participation. Two examples are the introduction of VAT in 1995 and the passage of the National Reconciliation bill in 2002.

In March 1995, the government introduced VAT with a standard rate of 17.5 per cent, after the passage of the VAT bill in December 1994. There was little public debate. For instance, opposition parties were outside parliament because they did not take part in the parliamentary elections of December 1992 in protest against the alleged rigging of the presidential vote by Rawlings and the National Democratic Congress (NDC). The government dismissed opposition misgivings on VAT because it regarded the opposition as a section of embittered pressure groups (Osei 2000). Similarly, the misgivings of other civil society organizations (CSOs) such as the Trades Union Congress, the Association of Ghana Industries, Chambers of Commerce and the Employers' Association fell on deaf ears. In fact, these CSOs publicly declared that they were not consulted by the government. VAT was also condemned by the then vice president, Kow Arkaah, who asked the country to revolt against it during his speech to the country's workers on May Day 1995 (ibid.). When VAT was eventually introduced in March 1995, there was massive public outcry and indignation against it because traders took advantage of it and increased their prices, including on food items which were exempt. In May 1995, a CSO called Alliance for Change (AFC) organized a massive demonstration which led to the loss of four lives. The government was forced to withdraw VAT. The withdrawal demonstrates that a policy has a greater likelihood of successful implementation if the stakeholders are consulted.

Similarly, the National Reconciliation Commission (NRC), established by Act 611 of 2002, began sitting in January 2003 and was dogged by controversy. From the very beginning there were suspicions that the NRC had an agenda and that it was targeted at a particular political tradition. Given the deep antipathy between the NPP and the NDC, the latter feared that the reconciliation process started by the former would be used for political persecution. The NDC emerged from the PNDC which Rawlings headed from December 1981 until the restoration of constitutional democracy in 1993, with Rawlings remaining as head of state until 2000. The NDC was therefore seen as carrying the baggage of the PNDC era. In the initial stages of the discussion on the bill for the establishment of the NRC, there were suggestions from the government side that evidence from the NRC could be used in a court of law for prosecution. The NDC protested, saying that this would lead to self-incrimination. That idea was dropped but another contentious suggestion was made: that the period for investigation and hearing should be limited to the Rawlings eras of June–September 1979 and 1982–92. This did not sit well with the NDC and sections of society which felt that the government was deliberately targeting a specific political tradition, and excluding consideration of abuses outside the selected periods. Eventually, the government capitulated and the period for investigations was expanded to cover all non-constitutional periods, with a 'window of opportunity' for those who suffered under constitutional regimes. This could not, however, erase the intense suspicion and misgivings about the government's intention. Consequently, the NDC MPs refused to vote and walked out of the chamber before the Act establishing the NRC was passed.

The inability to build a consensus on policies by consulting stakeholders through seminars, conferences, workshops and brainstorming sessions reinforces Grindle's assertion that:

> The process of implementing public policies is a focus of political partici-pation and competition in the countries of Asia, Africa and Latin America. This is true because of characteristics of the political systems themselves, such as the remoteness and inaccessibility of the policymaking process to most individuals and the extensive competition engendered by widespread need and very scarce resources ... Thus ... in the Third World a large por-tion of individual and collective demand making, the representation of interests, and the emergence and resolution of conflict occurs at the output stage. (Grindle 1980: 15)

The relationship between politicians and bureaucrats There is no marked difference between the relationship between politicians and bureaucrats under the Rawlings and Kufuor presidencies. Under both the NDC and the NPP regimes, bureaucrats and politicians were involved in policy formula-tion. But while politicians made the ultimate decisions on policy questions, bureaucrats predominated in policy execution. Even in the policy formula-tion stage the influence of the policy-making bureaucrat was consider-able. Interviews held in June 2004 with bureaucrats and some politicians of Rawlings's erstwhile NDC government and Kufuor's NPP government indicate that the relationship between bureaucrats and politicians could be described as a 'love–hate' one. The impression given is that some ministers felt that their bureaucrats knew the rudiments of public policy-making better than they did and therefore did not want the bureaucrats to 'meddle with their affairs'. On the other hand, some bureaucrats felt that they were better educated and more competent than the politicians. It is an open secret that some ministers and their chief directors and directors were not on speaking terms. Some ministers had even asked the head of the civil service to transfer 'their' bureaucrats to 'save their skin'. In spite of this, the politicians failed to do without the bureaucrats because most of the latter were competent, hardworking and conscientious. There was a perception that the bureaucrats were indispensable in public policy-making.

Stretching the point further, the interviews revealed that some ministers in both NDC and NPP regimes were not on speaking terms with their deputies (deputy ministers). Consequently, when they travelled outside the country they refused to allow their deputies to represent them at cabinet

TABLE 7.1 Some key policies and programmes of the NDC and NPP governments

Year	1993	1994	1995	1996	1997	1998	1999	2000	2001	2002	2003	2004
NDC		NIRP	Vision 2020, CSPIP, LSAIP	PUF, MARP, MTEF	VAT, First medium-term development plan		National land policy					
NPP								Zero tolerance for corruption, HIPC	Repeal of Seditious Libel Law, 'Golden age of business'	National Reconciliation Commission Act, Poverty reduction strategy		National health insurance scheme

Key: NIRP = National Institutional Renewal Programme; CSPIP = Civil Service Performance Improvement Programme; LSAIP = Legal Sector and Administrative Improvement Programme; PUFMARP = Public Financial Management Reform Programme; MTEF = Medium-term Expenditure Framework; VAT = Value Added Tax; HIPC = highly indebted poor country.

meetings. Reconciliation had to be undertaken to patch up the differences between the ministers and their deputies.

In spite of the love–hate relationship, there were a few ministers who were on good terms with their bureaucrats. When both politicians and bureaucrats were asked what accounted for the good relationship, the majority indicated that it was a question of personality. In other words, the politicians and bureaucrats had got on well because of good human relations exhibited by both sides.

There is an unhealthy trend under both regimes for some bureaucrats and public servants to campaign on the platform of political parties, or to stand for the two parties in parliamentary elections, or to take up top party posts without resigning their positions. The negative effect of this trend on the supposed neutrality of the public service and its work cannot be overestimated. There is also the possibility of a conflict of interests.

The personal dimension The office of president is the most visible office with access to significant resources, but the personal aims of its occupants may not be conducive to institution-building. The personal dimension involves personal ability, dynamism and creativeness and is both a strength and a weakness. Indeed, it is a two-edged sword. It can imbue the authority of the office with vitality and stimulate follower involvement and growth; but the personal is just that, and the weaknesses and ambitions of individuals impinge on their interaction with their followers and on choices about where and how to direct their energies. The desire for material gain, or for revenge, a hunger for personal glory and a need to be in control are all personal weaknesses. What leadership style did Rawlings and Kufuor exhibit and how does this contribute to our understanding of their regimes?

A leadership style refers to the strategies and behavioural patterns with which a leader seeks to achieve his or her goals. Quite simply, leadership can be exercised in a number of different ways. The factors that shape the adoption of a particular strategy or style are, of course, numerous, the most obvious being the personality and goals of the leader, the institutional framework within which he or she operates, the political mechanisms by which power is won and retained, the means of mass communication available, and the nature of the broader political culture.

In order to discuss the leadership style of Rawlings and Kufuor, it is important for us to look at their background. On the one hand, Rawlings is a retired airforce officer whose Provisional National Defence Council (PNDC) government was in power from 31 December 1981 to 6 January 1993. He is the founder of the National Democratic Congress (NDC). His open dislike for multi-party politics is well known. In one of his speeches, he remarked: 'Even God was unable to practise democracy, that is why when Lucifer rebelled against him, he drove him away from heaven' (cited in Westwood n.d.: i). He also told a parade of the armed forces: 'Constitutional rule makes things difficult ... If we make a mistake and lose power, there is no way we can get it back again. Perhaps we can only get it through another June 4. If June 4, 1979 repeats itself 10 times, I will do what I did then, 10 times over' (ibid.: 139). Furthermore, as president he also complained about 'constitutional anarchy' because democracy had undermined strong executive authority and hence the NDC government's inability to implement policies and programmes:

> A Constitution should make the machinery of democracy run smoothly. But so far, we seem to be bogged down by details, and if we become obsessed by procedural details rather than results, national development can end up as hostage ... The complexities of Constitutional procedures are slowing down government's ability to respond to the concerns of the people ... constitutional government doesn't necessary mean the same thing in Ghana as it might in the United States. In your country, people are educated to a pretty high degree and so everyone has a similar understanding of what the Constitution means. It's part of your culture ... In our situation it can be very costly. The opposition sometimes seems to oppose just for the sake of opposing, not for any particular goal of their own. (Holecek 1993: 173–4)

In addition to this, he is a populist with a penchant for cleaning gutters in Accra but was cautioned by the Council of State to desist from the practice because it was seen as an embarrassment (Oquaye 2001). He seemed also to have a violent temperament as, on numerous occasions when president, he warned people that if it were not for constitutional rule, he would have dealt squarely with certain critics who were undermining his government.

Kufuor, on the other hand, before taking office as president, was a lawyer and a private businessman and had been deputy minister of foreign affairs under Busia's Progress Party (PP) government which ruled Ghana from October 1969 to January 1972, as well as secretary for local government under the PNDC in 1983. He later resigned because of the PNDC's poor human rights record. He attended Prempeh College and belongs to the Danquah-Busia tradition whose belief in democratic culture is not in doubt. He is known as the 'gentle giant' because of his cool and unruffled demeanour. He is a liberal. For instance, while most opposition politicians refused to say anything nice about the PNDC government, Kufuor was charitable: 'No doubt the past few years have recorded some stability and some economic revival, and naturally some of the credit, if not a substantial part of it, should go to the PNDC Government' (Agyeman-Duah 2003: 54). His interview with *Jeune Afrique/L'intelligent* magazine was conciliatory on whether the misfortunes of Ghana can be attributed to the heritage of the Rawlings era: 'My government and myself are fully responsible for any initiatives we take. We will not build a reputation by heaping opprobrium on a regime or a person, whatever mistakes they may have made' (*Daily Graphic*, 12 August 2002: 10). He contested the position of presidential candidate of the NPP on three occasions, lost his maiden bid in 1992 but won on two subsequent occasions in 1996 and 2000.

The Rawlings presidency was a mixture of populism and authoritarian-ism, sometimes marked by unguarded speeches strewn with insinuations and insults. Rawlings's complexion and his fiery and somewhat down-to-earth speeches excited emotions and passions, which won him friends and enemies alike. He was a crowd-pleaser by all accounts. His penchant for speaking extempore, sometimes pushing aside his prepared text, made some of his speeches illogical and pedestrian, even though they were often liked by his audience. As a result of his speeches and behaviour while in office, there was a perception that the image of the office of president sank somewhat under Rawlings. Some people considered his tempera-ment unsuited to the high office of president. His critics believed that, as the longest-serving head of state in the history of the country, he should have behaved in a more fitting manner. His pronouncements at party meetings and public lectures were divisive, and often seen as attempts to create unrest. However, Rawlings saw things differently, claiming that he was misquoted or that his words were taken out of context. On balance, however, under the Rawlings presidency, Ghanaians became accustomed to a certain way of life. The firm grip of a government with dictatorial tendencies bred intimidation.

Unlike Rawlings, Kufuor is not an exciting public speaker. His speeches are dull but easy to follow. He sticks to his prepared speech and on the rare occasions he does digress, he does not go to town. During his visit to the UK in May 2004, some reporters compared him to his predecessor and told him that his speeches were dull and uninteresting. Kufuor retorted that if the dullness brought peace and stability to Ghana, so be it. His general composure, demeanour and public speaking have brought some respect, nobility and dignity to the office of president.

The relationship between Rawlings and the media was frosty. He re-garded the media as his enemies who were always out to write nasty things about him and his family. It is on record that he organized no press confer-ences during his eight years as president. Some have interpreted this media 'phobia' as part of his dictatorial tendencies and his inability to think and reason logically. Kufuor, on the other hand, is seen as media-friendly. His annual people's forum in January to mark the birth of the Fourth Republic and the repeal of the Seditious Libel Law have won him considerable respect within the media fraternity. Indeed, there is a perception that the Kufuor presidency has brought about a more liberal environment. The Castle, the seat of government that used to be a place of terror for civilians under Rawlings, has regained its civilian position, being used for excursions by students. Some people believe that the Kufuor government has not only improved civil–military relations but has also 'demilitarized' the country through his decision to send soldiers, who had a high profile during the Rawlings presidency, back to the barracks. Indeed, under the Kufuor presidency, 'there can no longer be any talk of a culture of silence in the country and people go about their business without fear or intimidation and express their views freely' (Kufuor 2004: 8).

Like his relationship with the media, the relationship between Rawlings and the business community was not cordial. He regarded businessmen as dishonest crooks. He rarely had meetings with the business community, even though his government regarded the private sector as an 'engine of growth'. His poor relationship with the business community may be traced to his intention of being a moral crusader and his inclination for social justice. Shillington regarded Rawlings as someone who had developed a strong moral awareness, constantly searching for philosophical as well as practical answers to the questions which life posed: 'In his early adult life Rawlings had considered entering the priesthood as a means to work for social justice, but he soon realized that he did not have the temperament for the priestly life' (Shillington 1992: 36).

Kufuor's relationship with the business community, unlike that of Rawlings, is cordial. He has organized breakfast and lunch meetings with representatives of the private sector. Having been a businessman before he became president, it is easy for him to relate to the needs and problems of the private sector. In his inaugural address, he promised that his NPP government would promote a 'golden age of business' while his 2004 sessional address to parliament declared 2004 as a 'business-friendly year'. His desire to catapult the country into industrialization and to diversify the economy has led to the creation of Presidential Special Initiatives (PSIs) for cassava, salt, textiles, garments, distance learning and oil palm.

One key question that needs to be asked is whether, with their contrasting personalities, Rawlings and Kufuor were/are able to be on top of the problems facing Ghana while in charge of the administration of the country. There is evidence that both leaders knew the problems facing the country.

In their sessional addresses and other policy documents, issues and problems concerning the economy, poverty, infrastructure, social services and corruption were carefully laid out. There is also evidence to suggest that the two leaders received daily briefings from the chief of staff and personal advisers, even though Rawlings relied more on briefing from his chief of staff and Kufuor on his so-called 'kitchen cabinet'.

As to the question of who is really in charge of the administration of the country, the evidence is patchy. Under the first term of the Rawlings government, the presidential adviser on governmental affairs (PAGA) was the nerve centre of the administration. It was even suggested that most cabinet meetings were chaired by the PAGA. With the exit of the then PAGA, the nerve centre of the administration seemed to have shifted to the office of the chief of staff. This contrasts with the Kufuor presidency under which the nerve centre of the administration used to be the Ministry of Information and Presidential Affairs until its demise in a cabinet reshuffle when it was replaced by a host of presidential advisers, the 'kitchen cabinet'.

It is instructive to note that, under Rawlings, the role of the NDC in influencing the president was minimal because Rawlings was both founder and leader. There was no rapport between the government and the party. In the words of Obed Asamoah: 'The party was being dictated to by the government and therefore, in terms of parliamentary candidates or even the issue of who should be the flag-bearer, the party did not exercise autonomous authority ... Such policy decisions did not help the party as some saw them as imposition and therefore lacked transparency' (*West Africa*, 1–7 July 2002, p. 12). Under the NPP, however, there is some evidence that the government has been influenced in one way or the other by the NPP in certain of its decisions. Even though there has been an attempt by the president to interfere in some party affairs, such as the selection of party officials, it has been kept to the barest minimum.

Overall, Rawlings and Kufuor have exhibited some of the qualities of transactional leadership, such as approaching followers with an eye to exchanging one thing for another: jobs for votes, or subsidies for campaign contributions. However, Kufuor unlike Rawlings is more concerned with upholding the collegiate face of government by negotiating compromises and balancing rival individuals, faction and interests against one another. He has tried to maintain the unity of the NPP and government cohesion more than Rawlings did.

Conclusion: some lessons

A number of useful lessons can be distilled from this chapter. First, measuring the performance of political leadership is a difficult task. In judging political leadership under the Fourth Republic, one should acknowledge structural constraints. None of the leaders has a blank tablet on which to write at will. At the same time, the leadership performances of Rawlings and Kufuor are limited by their personal preoccupations and weaknesses. It is appropriate to look at the negative side of the personal alongside the positive side. Success in meeting the leadership challenge is influenced by the balance between the positive and negative.

Second, the presidencies of Rawlings and Kufuor remind us yet again that elected offices may serve the cause of democracy imperfectly. An open and personal style of leadership by itself is little assurance that policy impact, citizen involvement or institution-building will be substantial.

Third, the challenges faced by the leaders – neoliberalism, culture and the media – have in one way or the other affected political leadership in the four indicators of measurement: cohesion of the administration, developing strategic policy direction, the relationship between bureaucrats and politicians and the personal dimension. The vulnerability of leaders to these forces cannot be overemphasized. They are beyond the reach of leaders who, rather than being transformational, are transactional and therefore do not possess considerable skills of political judgement and vision.

Finally, leaders need to undergo seasoning and mentoring. Few leaders are born but most are groomed over the years through party structures and other state institutions. Unfortunately, this has not been the case in Ghana because of political instability before the advent of the Fourth Republic. With the country enjoying stability and democratic consolidation, it is hoped that future political leaders will be seasoned in party structures and other institutions before they assume the mantle of leadership.

Sources

Agyeman-Duah, I. (2003) *Between Faith and History: A Biography of J. A. Kufuor* (Trenton, NJ and Asmara: Africa World Press).

Ayee, J. R. A. (1999) 'Ghana', in L. Adamolekun (ed.), *Public Administration in Africa: Main Issues and Selected Country Studies* (Boulder, CO: Westview Press).

— (2001) 'Leadership in Contemporary Africa: An Exploratory Study', United Nations University Leadership Academy Occasional Papers, no. 3.

— (2004) 'Leading Large States', in C. Clapham, J. Herbst and G. Mills (eds), *Africa's Big Dysfunctional States* (Cape Toen: SAIIA).

Bartolome, F. (1989) 'Nobody Trusts the Boss Completely – Now What?', *Harvard Business Review* (March–April): 135–42.

Burns, J. (1978) *Leadership* (New York: Harper and Row).

Chazan, N. (1983) *An Anatomy of Ghanaian Politics: Managing Political Recession, 1969–1982* (Boulder, CO: Westview Press).

Conger, J. A. (1989) 'Leadership: The Art of Empowering Others', *Academy of Management Executive*, Vol. 3, no. 1.

Grindle, M. (1980) 'Policy Content and Context in Implementation', in M. Grindle (ed.), *Politics and Policy Implementation in the Third World* (Princeton, NJ: Princeton University Press).

Handy, C. (1989) *The Age of Unreason* (London: Hutchinson).

Holecek, B. (1993) 'Paying the Piper: Conversations with Jerry Rawlings', *Transition*, Vol. 62.

Hutchful, E. (2002) *Ghana's Adjustment Experience: The Paradox of Reform* (Geneva: UNRISD).

Kotter, J. P. (1988) *The Leadership Factor* (New York: Free Press).

Kufuor, J. A. (2004) 'Judge Me by My Works', *Ghana Review International*, no. 104 (February).

Leach, S. and D. Wilson (2002) 'Rethinking Local Political Leadership', *Public Administration*, Vol. 80, no. 4: 665–89.

Mills, J. E. A. (1997) Closing Address delivered by H.E. The Vice President Prof. John E. Atta Mills at the National Economic Forum, Accra International Conference Centre, 2–3 September.

Muczyk, J. P. and B. C. Reinmann (1987) 'The Case for Directive Leadership', *Academy of Management Executive*, Vol. 1, no. 4: 301–11.

Oquaye, M. (2001), *Government and Politics in Contemporary Ghana (1992–1999) – a Study*, Governance Series, Vol. 1, no. 1 (Accra: African Governance Institute).

Osei, P. D. (2000) 'Political Liberalisation and the Implementation of Value-Added Tax in Ghana', *Journal of Modern African Studies*, Vol. 32, no. 2: 255–78.

Pellow, D. and N. Chazan (eds) (1986) *Ghana: Coping with Uncertainty* (Boulder, CO: Westview Press).

Quinn, J. B., H. Mintzberg and R. M. James (1989) *The Strategy Process* (Englewood Cliffs, NJ: Prentice-Hall).

Rawlings, J. J. (1997) Keynote Address delivered at the National Economic Forum, Accra International Conference Centre, 2–3 September.

Republic of Ghana (1992) *The Constitution of the Republic of Ghana, 1992* (Accra: Ghana Publishing Corporation).

— (1995) *Ghana – Vision 2020: The First Step, 1996–2000*, Presidential Report to Parliament on Coordinated Programme of Economic and Social Development Policies, 6 January 1995 (Accra: National Development Planning Commission).

— (1997) *Ghana – Vision 2020: The First Medium-Term Development Plan (1997–2000)* (Accra: National Development Planning Commission).

— (1999) *A Framework Draft Comprehensive Development Framework Towards Ghana – Vision 2020*, Tenth Consultative Group Meeting, Accra, 23–24 November.

— (2002) *Ghana Poverty Reduction Strategy, 2002–2004: An Agenda for Growth and Prosperity: Analysis and Policy Statement* (Accra: National Development Planning Commission).

Sandbrook, R. (1992), 'Patrons, Clients and Factions: New Dimensions of Conflict Analysis in Africa', *Canadian Journal of African Studies*, Vol. V, no. 1.

Shillington, K. (1992) *Ghana and the Rawlings Factor* (London: Macmillan).

Smith, D. A. and J. Temin (2001) 'The Media and Ghana's 2000 Elections', in J. R. A. Ayee (ed.), *Deepening Democracy in Ghana: Politics of the 2000 Elections*, Vol. 1 (Accra: Freedom Publications).

Soudan, F. (2002) 'John Kufuor : le gentil géant de l'Afrique', *Jeune Afrique/ L'intelligent*, no. 2162: 28–35 (17 to 23 June).

Westwood J. (n.d.) *The Amazing Dictator and His Men: A Story of Intrigue, Murder, Presidential Zealousness, Mayhem in Ghana* (Accra: NETRESCO).

Political leadership, 1993–2004

8 | The security agencies and national security in a decade of liberalism

KUMI ANSAH-KOI

Security personnel and agencies have always been of prime concern in issues pertaining to security and national politics in Ghana. In February 1948, when Ghana was still a British colony, a march by disgruntled ex-servicemen led to rioting and subsequently set the whole nation ablaze with such nationalist fervour and strident anti-colonial agitation that it led to the ultimate decolonization of the country in March 1957. Just a year after independence, there was a serious national security scare revolving round army Captain Ahwaitey's alleged (opposition-inspired) plot to overthrow the democratically elected constitutional government of the CPP. Security personnel, in the persons of senior military and police officers, were at the centre of the plots and activities that culminated in the successful overthrow of Ghana's first republican government. Security personnel were similarly central in the plots and activities which culminated in the overthrow of Ghana's second and third bouts of republican rule.

The various regimes put in power after the overthrow of each of those republican dispensations strongly reflected the security personnel's key role in the fall of the republics; and security personnel clearly constituted the single dominant group in the ruling junta then established.

In between republican rule in Ghana, security personnel dominated government and politics. They were in the thick of things in the countless efforts made to topple regimes; just as they were in efforts geared at countering such intended forced regime changes. Security personnel issued a public warning on Ghana's third attempt at republican rule, in 1979, that the incoming government of Dr Hilla Limann was on probation and would be expected to continue with the 'house-cleaning revolutionary agenda' the military had set while holding political power. A little over two years later, security personnel, in the persons of serving and retired military officers and men, capriciously 'failed' that republican government too and forcefully threw it out of power via a coup d'etat.

So involved have security personnel been in violent regime-change and rule in Ghana that many analysts and observers, until very recently, saw in the country a depiction of a modern-day variant of a 'praetorian polity', with the security personnel serving as the 'praetorian guards'.

Praetorianism apart, frequent intra-security agency clashes and conflicts and repetitive widespread abuse of civil and political rights marked government and politics in Ghana prior to the institution of the fourth republic's liberal-democratic dispensation.

The events and circumstances that culminated in Ghana's fourth attempt at republican and democratic rule in April 1992 need not detain us here (Ninsin and Drah 1993; Ninsin 1996, 1998). Suffice it to say that, as a result of the historical legacy highlighted above regarding security personnel and their politics of regime-change and forced rule in the country, there was some trepidation and cynicism regarding the viability of this fourth attempt.

How would the 'transition' from the authoritarian rule of security personnel and their cohorts to the democratic, republican and constitution-regulating rule of elected civilians be effected?

Would the military, a key component of the security sector, submit to 'civilian control'? Can parliament, newly instituted after a long break, succeed in exercising effective oversight of the military and other sectors of Ghana's security apparatus? How would security personnel and the security agencies adapt to the restrictions and limitations inherent in constitutionalism and to the mandatory imperatives of democratic, republican rule? Would Ghana's 'game of musical chairs', which involved republican rule being forcefully aborted and replaced by the rule of security personnel, continue to play itself out?

In November 2004, Ghanaian and the international mass media announced the arrest in Ghana of retired and serving military personnel on suspicion of their engagement in activities meant to disrupt the scheduled December 2004 presidential and parliamentary general elections and to topple both the democratically elected incumbent government and the 1992 Constitution of the Republic.[1] Was it possible to break the jinx of Ghana's 'praetorian guards'?

Cynicism, apprehension and trepidation were rife; but Ghana's fourth attempt at republican rule, which commenced in May 1992 when the ban on overt political activities was lifted, has endured well beyond a decade and is still ongoing. Some observers and analysts see this effort as having taken root, and therefore speak of it in terms of a 'consolidation' or 'deepening' of democracy in Ghana (Ayee 1998, 2001: 433). One eminent Ghanaian scholar takes the view that 'recent developments, both internal and global, strongly suggest that a successful coup d'état is most unlikely in Ghana in the foreseeable future' (Agyeman-Duah 2002).

Against the above-delineated matrix, the present chapter focuses thematically on Ghana's numerous security agencies, and on national security,

189

from 1992 to 2002, when the fourth republican era of constitutional rule in Ghana took its first tottering steps and first cut its teeth. The constitutional matrix for that fourth attempt is offered by the 1992 Constitution, which is still in force and is firmly cast in the liberal-democratic ideological vein.

Ghana's national security agencies

Security personnel were not only at the centre of coups d'etat and of ruling juntas established prior to Ghana's fourth effort at republican rule, they were also heavily involved in extra-judicial executions and punishments, human rights violations, and in the widespread and prolonged infringement of a wide range of basic civil rights (Oquaye 1980; Jackson 1999; Westwood n.d.).

The 1992 Constitution faced that challenge by making entrenched provisions possibly to forestall, or at worst keep to the barest minimum, a repetition of those infringements by security, or any other, personnel. Thus, fundamental human rights and freedoms are entrenched in the Constitution (Articles 12–33), Directive Principles of State Policy (Articles 34–41), and the Code of Conduct for Public Officers (Articles 284–8). In addition, detailed provisions of the Constitution focused on such traditional security structures of the state as the Police Service (Articles 200–4), the Prisons Service (Articles 205–9), and the Armed Forces of Ghana comprising an army, navy and airforce (Articles 210–15). Indeed, the security terrain in Ghana has grown increasingly complex and sophisticated over the years, as the population grew and the social structure underwent significant changes. From an initial focus on the police and army, the range of security institutions in Ghana by 1992 had widened drastically to include numerous private security agencies, an Immigration Service, a Customs and Exercise Service, various intelligence establishments – the most outstanding of which were the Bureau of National Investigations, the research wing of the Ministry of Foreign Affairs, and the defence intelligence unit of the armed forces – and a short-lived state-funded militia (the 64 Regiment) which owed primary allegiance to the incumbent regime rather than to the state. The national security terrain at the commencement of the fourth republican rule in Ghana, then, was as complex as it was confusing.

The 1992 Constitution sought to establish, among other things, clarity, coherence and order. It made provision for the institution of a National Security Council consisting of the following:

a. The President;
b. The Vice President;

c. The Ministers of State for the time holding the portfolios of Foreign Affairs, Defense, Interior, and Finance; and such other Ministers as the President may determine;

d. The Chief of Defense Staff and two other members of the Armed Forces;

e. The Inspector-General of Police and two other members of the Police Service, one of whom shall be the Commissioner of Police responsible for the Criminal Investigations Department;

f. The Director-General of the Prisons Service;

g. The Director of External Intelligence;

h. The Director of Internal Intelligence;

i. The Director of Military Intelligence;

j. The Commissioner of Customs, Excise and Preventive Services; and

k. Three persons appointed by the President. (Articles 83–5)

The president was to preside at the meetings of the National Security Council. In his absence the vice president was to preside. Functions of the National Security Council included:

a. Considering and taking appropriate measures to safeguard the internal and external security of Ghana;

b. Ensuring the collection of the information relating to the security of Ghana and the integration of the domestic, foreign and security policies relating to it so as to enable the security services and other departments and agencies of the government to co-operate more efficiently in matters relating to national security;

c. Assessing and appraising the objectives, commitments and risks of Ghana in relation to the actual and potential military power in the interest of national security; and

d. Taking appropriate measures regarding the consideration of policies on matters of common interest to the departments and agencies of the Government concerned with national security. (Article 84)

The Constitution explicitly stipulates (in Article 85) that 'No agency, establishment or other organization concerned with national security shall be established except as provided for under this Constitution.'

What, then, are the national security institutions under the fourth republican dispensation? The Security and Intelligence Agencies Act 1996, no. 526, codified and gave flesh to the constitutional provisions stated above. The Act received presidential assent on 30 December 1996, and has since been in force. It makes provision in respect of the National Security Council, it provides for the institution of regional and district security councils, and specifies some of the state agencies responsible for the implementation of government policies regarding state security.

Part 1 of Act 526 establishes regional and district security councils operating as committees of the National Security Council. District security councils are answerable to regional security councils, while the latter, in turn, are answerable to the National Security Council. A regional security council comprises:

a. The Regional Minister, who shall be Chairman;
b. The Deputy Regional Minister or Ministers;
c. The Chief Executive of Metropolitan, Municipal or District Assembly in the regional capital;
d. An officer of the Armed Forces nominated by the Chief of Defense Staff;
e. The Regional Police Commander;
f. The Regional Crime Officer;
g. The Regional Officer of the specified internal intelligence agency;
h. The Customs, Excise and Preventive Service Officer in charge of the region, if any;
i. The Prisons Service Officer in charge of the region;
j. The Immigration Officer in charge of the region;
k. The Fire Officer in charge of the region; and
l. Two other persons nominated by the Regional Minister in consultation with the (National Security) Coordinator.

The functions of a regional security council are as follows: '(a) To perform such functions of the National Security Council as the latter may assign to it; and (b) To provide early warning to Government of the existence or likelihood of any security threat to the region, to the country, or to the Government.'

A district security council, for its part, comprises the following:

a. The District Chief Executive , who shall be the Chairman;
b. The District Police Commander;
c. The Crime Officer;
d. The District Representative of the Internal Intelligence Agency;
e. The Customs, Excise and Preventive Service Officer in charge of the district, if any;
f. The Immigration Officer in charge of the district;
g. The Fire Officer in charge of the district; and
h. Two other persons nominated by the District Chief Executive in consultation with the (National Security) Coordinator.

The functions of a district security council are as follows: '(a) Perform such functions of the Council as the Council may assign to it; (b) Provide early warning to Government of the existence or likelihood of any security threat to the district, to the country, or to the Government.'

The Security and Intelligence Agencies Act 1996 also recognized the existence of Ghana's Bureau of National Investigations and the research department (of the Ministry of Foreign Affairs) as 'the Internal and External Intelligence Agencies of the State, referred to in this Act as "the Intelligence Agencies"'. The wide range of responsibilities assigned to the intelligence agencies under the Act covered the following functions:

a. Collect, analyze, retain and disseminate as appropriate information and intelligence respecting activities that may constitute threats to the security of the State and the government of Ghana;
b. Safeguard the economic well-being of the State against threats posed by the acts of omissions of persons or organizations both inside and outside the country;
c. Protect the State against threats of espionage, sabotage, terrorism, hijacking, piracy, drug trafficking and similar offenses;
d. Protect the State against the activities of persons, both nationals and non-nationals, intended to overthrow the government of Ghana or undermine the constitutional order through illegal political, military, industrial or other means or through any other unconstitutional method; and
e. Perform such other functions as may be directed by the President or the Council. (Republic of Ghana 1996).

The National Security Council is at the centre of national security in Ghana. In meeting its responsibilities, it is aided by the regional and the district security councils. Institutions at the core of national security in Ghana, by virtue of their institutional representation on the National Security Council or on the regional and district security councils, include the Ghana armed forces, the Police Service, the Immigration Service, the Fire Service, the Bureau of National Investigations, the research department of the Ministry of Foreign Affairs, and Ghana's Customs Excise and Preventive Services. Those core institutions apart, the National Disaster and Mobilization Organization and the plethora of private security agencies in Ghana may also be said to be part of the country's security agencies. In practice, however, the armed forces and the police, who bear arms, constitute the essential core of security agencies in Ghana. The private security agencies are debarred from holding arms and operate under severe restrictions; while the Customs, Excise and Preventive Services focus solely on their revenue-generation functions.

Liberalism, constitutionalism and Ghana's national security: review of a decade

A striking feature of the first decade of the Fourth Republic in Ghana has been the success of the security agencies in maintaining the integrity and security of the de jure government, and thus in rolling back, or keeping at bay, Ghana's 'praetorian guards' and its image of being a praetorian polity. Will that success in stemming military intervention in Ghanaian politics (by way of a coup d'etat) become a permanent abandonment of the coup d'etat as a means of entry into national politics?

In the decade under review, the security agencies and forces were brought under civil political control and subjugation. Military intrusion into national politics, through the coup d'etat, has ceased to be a feature of politics in Ghana. Indeed, parliament gingerly exercised its constitutionally stipulated oversight responsibilities of the military and the other security institutions. Thus, parliament, for instance, scrutinized and approved the defence budget, received audit reports covering the Ministry of Defence and security sector institutions, raised questions regarding policy on defence, and asked for relevant statistics regarding the regional and gender composition of recruitment into the armed forces. Regarding parliamentary oversight of the security sector institutions, specifically of the armed forces, there were significant limitations and restrictions, most of which were self-imposed. There was no parliamentary oversight, for example, of the off-budget Armed Forces Peacekeeping Account held in New York. In a similar vein, parliamentary oversight of security sector procurements was limited, if not incomplete. Indeed, parliamentary oversight has resulted in greater transparency with regard to the armed forces in particular. It must be noted, though, that parliament has rather different relations with the various security sector agencies, all of which are nevertheless dependent on parliament for their various budgetary allocations.

Not only were security sector agencies brought under parliamentary control and scrutiny within the decade under review, the notion of national security was redefined, away from a virtually exclusive focus on regime security, to embrace wider notions of security. The events of 11 September 2001 in far-away America, the mysterious serial murder of over thirty Ghanaian women in the couple of years leading to 2001, and the unprecedented famine of 1982–83 in Ghana combined to ensure that security practitioners in Ghana focus on other dimensions of security such as 'human security' and 'food security'. 'Security' was no longer defined in the narrow and old-fashioned sense of maintenance of the incumbent regime in power and the simple protection of Ghana from external aggression. Insurgency, terrorism and such other acts of possible mass violence or activities injurious to human security also fell within the purview of Ghana's security practitioners.

Also during this time, restoration of constitutionalism and the rule of law in Ghana had serious positive implications for the modus operandi and stature of the security agencies. The security agencies restored discipline and hierarchical order within their ranks, both of which had been seriously disrupted, particularly in the armed forces, during the 4 June 1979 mutiny and its revolutionary aftermath. Constitutionalism led to a general withdrawal of the military away from the streets and from general policing duties back to the barracks. The military did indeed offer a supportive role to the police in particular; but it did not supplant nor compete with the latter in the performance of general police duties. The decade of constitutionalism and the rule of law also marked a significant curtailment in the rampant intra-security agency clashes and confrontations that constituted a feature of the era of PNDC rule.

In addition, within that decade, there was a gradual phasing out of the 'politicization' of the security services. Committees for the Defence of the Revolutionary ceased to exist within the security services, and indeed within Ghanaian society as a whole. Not only that, the newly established 64 Regiment was disbanded. Its soldiers were drawn from cadres and other foot soldiers of the 31 December revolutionary processes and movement, and the name was widely believed to derive from 4 June 1979, when the mutiny and revolutionary events commenced.

One of the significant achievements in the security sector following the transition from the Rawlings era to the Kufuor administration, apart from the disbandment of the 64 Regiment, was the retirement of over-aged soldiers in the army. This was carried out peacefully and successfully. In nearby Côte d'Ivoire, a similar exercise had precipitated a coup d'etat, much turmoil and considerable political unrest.

As the years of constitutional rule wore on, the security services in general and the army in particular embarked on major public relations offensives in fairly successful bids to reverse the negative social images they had acquired, especially during the nation's epochs of military rule. A news agency report, entitled 'Ghana Armed Forces Hold Open Day', carries details on how this public relations offensive was carried out in the national capital, Accra (all errors in original):

The Ghana Armed Forces (GAF) on Monday held an 'open day', its fourth, in open-day activities that aims to show-case the armed forces and to enhance civil–military relations.
    The day is designed to create the platform to help civilians understand

195

military life, how it is resourced and the challenges facing the soldier as well as the Service.

As early as 0700 hours, hundreds of people from all walks of life, particularly school children, had thronged to the El Wak Stadium and to the Kotoka International Airport to witness activities scheduled for the day.

The day started at the El Wak Stadium with dog display by the police, where the crowd witnessed how canine species were detecting and arresting criminals.

From there, the crowd was moved in buses to various military facilities at Burma Camp and other locations in Accra to gather first hand information as to how the military operates.

At the Airforce Base, the civilians familiarized themselves with the types of aircrafts at the base but could not be treated to air rides because of the poor weather conditions that were hampering flights of the pilots.

The Armour Reconnaissance Regiment of the GAF also took people on rides in their armoured fighting vehicles, after a series of lectures on some of the armaments used by the regiment.

The Civilians took horse riding lessons as well as watched the equestrian display mounted by the 'Three Mounted Squadron', the home of military equestrian activities.

There was also weapons display by the Five Infantry Battalion and a lecture on some of the weapons used by instructors at the Military Academy and Training Schools of the army.

Other activities the military lined up for the day included a display by the Tema Naval Base, physical training display, amusement at the Teshie shooting range, a photo exhibition, eye and blood tests at the 37 Military Hospitals, and bridge construction by the Engineer Regiment of the GAF.

Patronage to this year's event suppresses previous ones. A military officer the GNA spoke to said the patronage was largely due to continues and enhances civil/military relations pursued by the military. He said those in civil society have shed the negative impressions they had of the armed forces since the day was instituted. The day was observed by all the military garrisons countrywide.[2]

The celebrations were by no means confined to Accra. Other press reports, below, convey how the day was observed in other parts of the country (all errors in original):

The Fourth Battalion of Infantry (4BN) on Monday organized a special Open Day in Kumasi as part of its programme marking the 47th independence anniversary celebrations. The day is designed to bring to the civilian population closer to the military. The battalion displayed some of its basic weapons and ammunitions which included G3, MG3, Carl Gustav, and the 81MM.

In an address, Major Kofi Attah, Officer Commanding the 4BN, said the Open Day programme was started last year to bring the civilian population closer to the military and encourage students to join the army after their schooling.

Another report, entitled 'Students and Adults Visit Military Establishments in the Western Region', tells how a different part of the country marked the open day (all errors in original):

Over a thousand students, pupils and the elderly from all walks of life on Monday paid a familiarization visit to the Air Force, Naval and Apremdo Barracks as part of the 47th Independence anniversary celebrations.

The occasion afforded the populace the opportunity to know at first hand how the various military establishments operate. At the Naval Base in Sekondi, a large number of students from Axim, Takoradi and Cape Coast, undertook guided sea trips in batches and marvelled at the nature of operations of the Ghana Navy.

There were on display live boats and jackets, ceremonial uniforms and other uniforms used by the navy, riffles and colours. The C Company Limited also provided free refreshment for all within the military installations.

Those who went to the Air Force and Apremdo barracks were treated to similar display of military weaponry, uniforms, riffles, and other equipment used by the services.

Master Kweku Boateng-Acheampong of the Tarkwa-Himan Primary and Junior secondary School, expressed his appreciation to government and the military for allowing them to visit the establishment and learning at first hand some of the tools and equipment used by the military.

Other security agencies, and the police in particular, with less tarnished images than that of the military, made their own moves to enhance their public image (CDD-Ghana 2003).

Ironically, the salaries and other conditions of service of security personnel, particularly in the military, witnessed dramatic changes for the better under democratic rule. The Kufuor presidency, in its first term, for example, acquired modern communications gadgets for the Ghana Police Service, procured over five hundred new vehicles for the police, increased police strength from 13,065 to 16,023 and devoted over 10 billion cedis of funds obtained from the highly indebted poor countries (HIPC) initiative to improving sanitation in police cells and in police barracks. The outcome of such investment in the police has been the swift and rapid reaction of

Security agencies

police to deserving situations, constant police patrols in both communities and on highways, increased levels of confidence in the police, and a drastic reduction in Ghana's crime rate (*Daily Guide*, 4 November 2004, p. 3). Similar huge investments have been made in other security agencies, especially the military (*Daily Guide*, 14 October 2004, p. 3; Agyeman-Duah 2002).[3]

Certainly, the security agencies have been very cooperative and have come a long way with their nation in Ghana's march towards consolidation and entrenchment of constitutionalism, democracy and the rule of law. The above indicates in what directions, and to what extent, such progress has been made. But it would be misleading to present this significant and substantial progress as the attainment of a perfectly functioning democracy. The national security agencies in Ghana are not, the efforts indicated above notwithstanding, perfectly at ease and not operating perfectly by the rules all the time. The following press report, titled 'Street Vendors Attacked by Soldiers', illustrates a real, though rare in the current constitutional dispensation, example of the military assuming police duties and, in the process, abusing basic civil rights (all errors in original):

As a follow-up to yesterday's story on the pathetic situation a cross section of street vendors in Accra, Daily Guide herewith furnishes its readers with yet another one, involving certain personnel at Teshie, some two fortnights earlier.

Kennedy Asante (26) is a native of Asante Trede in the Ashanti Region of Ghana. He sells toilet rolls along the Teshie main road, specifically in front of the St. John's Preparatory and JSS, opposite the Police Station.

About four weeks ago, Kennedy had the greatest shock of his life when at about 8.30pm, a group of soldiers, numbering about four, pounced on him unawares, whiles he was standing by the road side displaying his items. The soldiers pummelled him mercilessly.

The Military at Teshie has warned street vendors not to do business in their zone (places that fall under their domain). ... Apparently Kennedy was nowhere near the 'danger zone' when the military men pounced on him. They kicked him in the groin, gave him dirty slaps, and tried to pull him along into their vehicle (pickup). When he refused, one of them run his knife through the lift side of his belly and deserted him, with blood spilling from the wound profusely.

Touched by the plight of their colleague 'hustler', the other street vendors, who witnessed the assault from their hiding places, came to Kennedy's rescue and took him to a near by clinic, where his cuts were stitched. From the clinic, Kennedy was taken to the Teshie Police Station to lodge a complaint. But, to their surprise, the officers on duty told them that they could not assist them since it involved soldiers. So, off they left the station. With no one to plead their cause, they left for their various homes. Meanwhile the soldiers have absconded with Kennedy's money as well the items which he was selling (T-rolls), all valued at about ₵190.000.

Another street vendor, Eric Owusu (28), who was unwittingly baited by a soldier in mufti, toward the KAIPTC, had his share of the ordeal. The soldier bundled this street vendor onto his shoulder and dropped him on the ground. The other soldiers joined and kicked, slapped, squeezed and manhandled Owusu to the extent that his briefs tore. Not satisfied, the soldiers dragged him along the street and in the process destroyed all the items he displayed for sale. It took the intervention of another officer to free Owusu from the grips of the junior soldiers. 'After four weeks of self-medication and some "Good Samaritan" treatment by our colleague street vendors, we have come back to start the business again. We don't have anyone or anywhere to approach for assistance to survive. This is the kind of situation we are facing in our business. Let all Ghanaians know about it', the street vendors told *Daily Guide*. (*Daily Guide*, 14 October 2004, p. 4; *The Heritage*, 10 November 2004).

A similar infringement of democratic norms and practices, this time involving the Ghana police, is offered by the following report entitled 'Man on Trial for Crossing Kufuor's Motorcade – Alleges Assault by Guards' (all errors in original):

A 29-year old motorist who allegedly crossed the President, John Kufuor's guards, has been hauled before the Madina Community tribunal ... he is said to have ignored the presidential siren and crossed the President's guards, according to the Police charge sheet. The police report said the driver did not stop but rather sped off. He was given a chase and arrested on the Spintex Road. The police brief on the case Asmah failed to give any tangible reason for the offence ... According to Asmah there was no presidential convoy in sight on the said day. Asmah rushed to the offices of Public Agenda to narrate his experience: It was about 10.30 p.m and he was driving from Adenta towards the Spintex Road. Before entering the Tetteh Quarshie Roundabout, Asmah recalls hearing distant sirens, but they were nowhere in sight. He went round the Spintex Road for a while, when he noticed bright headlamps flashing from his rear. Initially he thought the driver of the car behind him was just signalling that he was overtaking his Space Wagon.

Asmah said he subsequently gave way for the car to overtake, but the occupants of the car had other ideas. After overtaking his rickety Mitsubishi Space Wagon, the car crossed him. A second one came by his side and a third at the back, sandwiching him between the three cars. The next thing he noticed was a foot flying at his face, sending Asmah's spectacles airborne. 'One of the guards hit me on the ridge of my nose with a gun butt.' He was subsequently slapped across the face several times and pulled onto the ground with the guard still assaulting him. 'They lifted me into one of the cars and drove back towards the roundabout. Sandwiched between two well-built men, they subjected me to both verbal and physical torture from the Spintex Road to the Airport Police Station,' Asmah told *Public Agenda*.

They pounded his thighs with butts of the riffles and taunted him with pronouncements such as 'Who are you to cross the President?' and 'Because of people like you Burger is dead.' Sgt. Owusu, aka Burger, was a member of President Kufuor's dispatch riders. He was killed in September by a motorist in Accra. 'They beat me till I started tasting my sweat in my head', Asmah told *Public Agenda*. After 45 minutes of uninterrupted beatings he was thrown into cells of the Airport Police Station without any charge or writing a statement. The following day at 9 a.m he was taken out of the cells with bloody face and shirt and asked to write his statement. According to a medical report from the Airport Clinic, Nana Asmah suffered multiple tender spots of the inner jaws, contusion of the right ankle joint and multiple facial abrasions as a result of the encounter with the presidential guards. (*Public Agenda*, 19–20 November 2001, pp. 1, 10)

The United States government's 2003 Country Report on Human Rights in Ghana, released on 25 February 2004, while noting that there were no political killings in the year under review, none the less carried allegations and credible complaints of, inter alia, security forces unlawfully killing suspects and innocent bystanders, using excessive force, police brutality, negligence and corruption, and of police resorting to torture and other cruel treatment. It also noted that prison conditions were generally appalling, and occasionally life-threatening.

A serious constitutional and security imbroglio was created by an embarrassing incident on 28 December 1995 when the president of the republic physically attacked his vice president at a cabinet meeting, and the latter went public about the matter (*Free Press*, 30 December 1995; Westwood n.d.: 141–7). The vice president, the victim of the assault, became the running mate of the incumbent president's opponent in the next presidential election. A veteran security professional and intelligence operative in Ghana had strong words about the dilemma posed to national security agencies by the security ramifications of those events:

And so a Vice President, who disagrees with his boss, the President, in that visibly acrimonious way, ought to pack off. But if he does not and then becomes the running mate of the opposition presidential candidate, there surely is no moral or political reason for him to stick to his post. That is subversive of the objectives of democratic practice and good governance. And of course (it constituted) a colossal risk to national security. I have cited this case essentially because of the huge security problems it generated. How do the mangers of national security handle a sitting Vice President who belongs to the inner circle of the opposition party? That indeed was one of the greatest security nightmares I have encountered. As the sitting Veep he had constitutional obligations to attend Cabinet meetings and to participate in the deliberations. As the Vice President he had to attend National Security Council meetings and participate. In the absence of his boss, the President, he presided. As the Vice President, he was the Chairman of the Armed Forces Council and the Police Council. These are two sensitive security institutions, the proceedings of which are classified. How do you expose all that to a disloyal and defected Veep in position?

In my book *Ghana: Peace and Stability*, I observed as follows: 'But I cannot end without re-echoing my disappointment and indeed disgust at the way our academics or intellectuals reacted to that ugly scenario where a serving Vice President turns his back against his President and adamantly clings to office like a stubborn cat.' I still stand by that. (Quantson 2003)

The serial murder of about thirty Ghanaian women, which began in the run-up to the 1999 general election and ended shortly afterwards, and which the police could not satisfactorily explain nor account for, constitutes another dent in the image and performance of the security services in general. The security blunder which led to over a hundred deaths at the Accra sports stadium in the closing minutes of a local football derby is yet another, as is the Yendi regicide affair, which involved the murder of the Ya-Na of Yendi and some forty of his courtiers by a warring and embittered faction of the royal family of Dagbon.

Armed robberies have constituted a serious challenge to the security services who have had some success in dramatically reducing the spate of armed robbery and violence which followed the peaceful transfer of power from the Rawlings regime to the Kufuor regime. Indeed, the police, army and intelligence services have cooperated to check the tide of armed robbery and similar crimes in the country. In those operations, there were initial problems relating to command and operating procedures, but these initial difficulties have been overcome.

The security agencies have also increased the number and scope of their inter-agency joint training and simulation exercises. Since 2002, for example, the security services have organized annual joint security sector agencies training for internal crisis management at the Ghana Armed Forces Command and Staff College, Teshie. There has similarly been an annual three weeks' training in security sector governance and reform for upper echelon personnel drawn from the security services, but there is still a need for more of such joint focused training.

Other problems that confront the security sector in Ghana, even in the era of republican constitutional rule, include the overlapping proliferation of security and quasi-security agencies in the country. For example, the Serious Fraud Office, the Economic Crimes Unit of Ghana Police Service, the Auditor General's Office, the Accountant General's Department, and the Commissioner of Human Rights and Administrative Justice can each raise and investigate issues of corruption.

Act 526, discussed above, states at Article 17(1) that 'the President shall assign ministerial responsibility for the Intelligence Agencies to such Minister as the President shall deem fit'. At 17(ii), 'the Minister assigned responsibility under subsection (i) of the section shall in respect of each year submit a report to Parliament on the Intelligence Agencies'. None of that has been done, so far, and the government has offered no explanation; one is hard put to fathom the reasons or justification for such a failure.

Conclusions

Ghana has no formally issued document setting out its national policy as regards security and related issues. That fact notwithstanding, the Constitution and existing statutes clearly set out the Directive Principles of State Policy which translate into national security goals and objectives as well as regulating the modalities of operation of the security sector. In generic terms, national security and continued survival are set as the bottom-line objectives for the operation of Ghana's security services. National security, in that context, is conceived of not in the narrow sense of mere regime survival or the maintenance and safeguarding of national integrity; these constitute only a part of a minimal core. Security is conceived of in more ambitious terms, to embrace other facets such as 'human security', 'food security', 'personal security' and 'group security'. The procedural restrictions and requirements placed by law on Ghana's security agencies in the performance of their set functions fall squarely within the frame of a liberal-democratic, constitutional order. In that generic framework, there are, for example, civil political control of the security agencies, professionalized and hierarchically structured security agencies subject to democratic civil control, parliamentary oversight of the security agencies, apolitical and non-partisan security agencies, and security agencies with strict respect for the tenets of the rule of law and the constitutional dispensation. The security agencies in Ghana have made impressive and significant progress within the decade under review in complying with the ethos and requirements of civil control and democratic governance. They have abandoned those practices and deeds of the past which do not conform to the ethics and tenets of democracy and constitutionalism.

That having been said, there is still a long way to go before they get anywhere close to establishing freedom and justice under democratic and constitutional governance. The present chapter has sought to identify and to elaborate on what has been achieved so far, a little over a decade since the commencement of such effort. It has also sought to point out outstanding shortcomings and to indicate how such shortcomings can be addressed.

Notes

1 The *Ghanaian Times*, 8 November 2004, carried the news in a front-page article entitled 'Coup Plot Foiled ... 7 Suspects Detained'. The *Daily Guide* of the same date had its version of the report, and also carried on its front page, 'Coup Plotters Arrested. Big Names Involved'. The *Chronicle*, in its front-page report, carried the story under the banner 'Coup Scare ... Seven Arrested and Quizzed'. Other Ghanaian media outlets gave high prominence to the story of a thwarted coup plot. The BBC first broke the news of the arrest of the alleged plotters in its African news broadcasts on 6 November 2004.

2 This and the following two press reports can be found at <www.ghanaweb.com/GhanaHomePage/NewsArchive/artikel.p>, 2004.

3 There has been a major expansion and rehabilitation of both the police and the military hospitals in Accra. In addition, a Kofi Annan International Peace Keeping and Training Centre has been built near the Ghana Armed Forces Command and Staff College to serve the African region as a whole; and numerous other infrastructural and developmental projects have been carried out at the Burma Camp headquarters of the Ghana armed forces. For a discussion of the military since the institution of Ghana's fourth republican order, see Agyeman-Duah (2002).

Sources

Agyeman-Duah, B. (2002) *Civil–Military Relations in Ghana's Fourth Republic*, Critical Perspectives, no. 9 (Accra: Ghana CDD).

Ayee, J. R. A. (ed.) (1998) *The 1996 General Elections and Democratic Consolidation in Ghana* (Accra: Solid Type).

— (2001) 'The Future of Democratic Consolidation in Ghana', in *Deepening Democracy in Ghana: Politics of the 2000 Elections*, Vol. 2 (Accra: Freedom Publications).

CDD-Ghana (2003) *Ghana: Police–Community Relations in an Emerging Democracy, Survey Report*, Research paper no. 12 (Accra: CDD).

Jackson, A. K. (ed.) (1999) *When Gun Rules. A Soldier's Testimony* (Accra: Woeli Publishers).

Ansah-Koi | 8

Ninsin, K. A. (1996) *Ghana's Political Transition 1990–1993. Selected Documents* (Accra: Freedom Publications).

— (1998) *Ghana: Transition to Democracy* (Accra: Freedom Publications).

Ninsin, K. A. and F. K. Drah (eds) (1993) *Political Parties and Democracy in Ghana's Fourth Republic* (Accra: Woeli Publishers).

Oquaye, M. (1980) *Politics in Ghana, 1972–1979* (Accra: Tornado Publications).

Quantson, K. B. (2003) *Ghana: National Security ... The Dilemma* (Accra: NAPASVIL Ventures).

Westwood, J. (n.d.) *The Amazing Dictator and His Men. A Story of Intrigue, Murder, Presidential Zealousness, Mayhem in Ghana* (Accra: NETRESCO).

9 | Organized labour and the liberal state

ABEEKU ESSUMAN-JOHNSON

The relationship between the state and various social groups is largely influenced by the kind of interests that the state at any particular point in time seeks to pursue. The relationship between state and organized labour will be influenced by the policy the state seeks to pursue and the particular social groups it seeks to carry along with it. Where state policy is in harmony with the expectations of particular social groups, relations with the group tend to be harmonious; otherwise, the relations with the group tend to be fractious and tension-packed and the state may use other means to influence or intimidate the group concerned. This chapter looks at the changing relations between organized labour and the Ghanaian state, principally since 7 January 1992 when the country returned to constitutional rule, though it also looks back on how the relationship between the state and organized labour has evolved since the First Republic.

Labour–state relations 1956–82

The relationship between organized labour and the state has a chequered history. The period immediately after independence was to see the Convention People's Party (CPP) government push through parliament the Industrial Relations Act (1958) that set the framework for trade union organization and activity in the country. Under the Act, the state had secured a measure of control over the trade unions through ministerial control over the Trades Union Congress (TUC) and its constituent unions by restrictions imposed on the right of workers to strike. The unions, on the other hand, were strengthened by the recognition given to them by the state and the requirement for employers to bargain with the unions and deduct union dues at source. The CPP exercised considerable administrative control over the TUC through the appointment of the secretary-general and the establishment of party branches in workplaces, which dominated the union in the workplaces especially within the public sector. In a number of state-owned enterprises (SOEs), the manager, local party branch representatives and the local union officials worked together to settle grievances under the hegemony of the party. The TUC was thus described as being in bed with the CPP government during the First Republic (Adu-Amankwah 1990).

The state under Nkrumah adopted the socialist path to development and sought, among other things, to provide jobs for the people. Various SOEs were set up as well as workers' and builders' brigades to provide jobs. That era might as well be described as the golden age of organized labour in Ghana's history, because providing jobs for Ghanaians became state policy. The TUC became more or less the workers' wing of the ruling party, and the leadership of the TUC considered themselves to be members of the CPP. Since the Nkrumah era, the state has been the largest employer in the formal sector of the economy.

Following the overthrow of Nkrumah and the CPP government, the National Liberation Council (NLC) which was then formed did not change the legal framework for trade union organization. Under the NLC the state adopted measures that affected the trade unions. The government appointed a new secretary-general and a number of union leaders were arrested. Growing labour unrest brought the unions into conflict with the state and the latter used harsh measures to deal with the worker agitation. In late 1968, the government supported the dismissal of 2,000 workers at the state-owned Cargo Handling Company in Tema following a one-day strike. Also in 1968, the 'ringleaders' of the Railway Permanent Waymen were arrested following a strike action. In March 1969, the police shot and killed three miners during a strike by over 6,000 workers of Ashanti Goldfields Corporation (AGC) over severance pay, gratuity and entitlements that arose out of the takeover by Lonrho. Thus, under the NLC the state deployed the police against workers and also used mass dismissals to control labour. At the time of the NLC handover to the Progress Party (PP) in October 1969, confrontation between the TUC and the PP government seemed imminent (Adu-Amankwah 1990).

The state under Progress Party rule had a turbulent relationship with the TUC. The government moved to alter the legal regime for the existence of the TUC as the centre of the trade union movement. At the same time the government adopted a hostile attitude to the TUC leadership and its demand for improved wages. The PP government also promoted division within the ranks of the trade union movement and supported the emergence of an alternative national trade union centre: the Ghana Confederation of Labour (GCL). The economic conditions in the country were such that there was sharpened discontent with the minimum wage and incomes policy generally. The government was also dissatisfied with what was seen as the inability of the TUC to control strikes. In the course of 1970 there were purported to have been fifty-five strikes (ibid.).

During 1971, labour conditions continued to deteriorate and a number of major strikes occurred from June to August involving four unions. The government responded to the unrest by direct intervention: the minister of labour ordered the dismissal of 400 dock workers, the dismissal of 150 workers from the public works department (PWD) and issued an ultimatum to the railway enginemen (ibid.). The TUC condemned the government's intervention and accused it of cruelty and arbitrariness. In the wake of the poor industrial relations in the country, the government pushed through parliament, under a certificate of urgency, a new Industrial Relations Law, Act 383, to dissolve the TUC as a legal trade union centre. The PP government sought to give the impression that by dissolving the TUC it offered greater scope to workers for independent trade union organization. However, by dissolving the TUC while already having promoted the emergence of an alternative national trade union centre, the government was simply promoting division within the union movement and seeking to demobilize it. The Act placed heavy restrictions on strike action and vested in the minister power over dispute settlement and the ability to withdraw a certificate from a union. Relations between the state and organized labour under the PP government were at their lowest, due to the government's pursuit of the dissolution of the TUC (ibid.).

NRC–union relations The National Redemption Council (NRC) overthrew the PP government in January 1972 and its first major act in its dealings with organized labour was to repeal Act 383, enacted by the PP government to dissolve the TUC. This was done to court the support of organized labour and it set the tone for relations between them. The NRC sought forms of consultation with trade union leaders and the government encouraged peaceful settlement of labour disputes through negotiation, conciliation and collective bargaining. Furthermore, through the use of price control of 'essential commodities', the intermittent allocation of imported consumer goods to the TUC for distribution to workers and also through increases in wages, the NRC sought to co-opt labour and managed to achieve a measure of cooperation from the TUC leadership. The NRC also transferred formally to the TUC the ownership of the Hall of Trades Unions.

A bone of contention and friction between the state and organized labour was in the promulgation of the Prices and Incomes Board (PIB) Decree NRCD 119 in October 1972. The decree gave the PIB extensive authority and discretion in determining the direction of government policy on income and prices. It was given power to make regulations prescribing guidelines for prices and incomes. The new dimension to the collective bargaining process, which emerged to encumber trade union activity, was a requirement for all signed collective agreements to be lodged with the PIB for their amendment, rejection or acceptance before they could have legal enforceability. The problem was that the PIB could control income rises but was unable to control rises in rents, interests, profits and dividends in the economy. In 1975 the NRC was transformed into the Supreme Military Council (SMC), which consolidated the military establishment and hierarchy within the structure of government. The SMC's relationship with the TUC leadership underwent little change; in fact it was so cosy that, under the leadership of A. M. Issifu, the TUC proclaimed support for the government's political project known as 'union government' which was promoted by the SMC in the face of growing political crisis and popular challenge to its legitimacy (ibid.).

The SMC was overthrown by the Armed Forces Revolutionary Council (AFRC) on 4 June 1979 and was in power for three months. The government was thus unable to develop a clear policy on labour and the trade unions. It was, however, on a national 'house cleaning' exercise to rid the country of corruption. This national policy, together with the government's overall radical pronouncements and support for mass struggles and exhortations to 'insist on your rights' emboldened many workers to challenge managements over obvious malpractices and to insist on the full implementation of their collective agreements. The TUC leadership maintained a low profile during the AFRC period, concentrating rather on the promotion of a political party – the Social Democratic Front (SDF) – to contest the elections following the lifting of the ban on party politics by the SMC in 1979. The SDF as the party of labour failed to win a seat at the elections.

The AFRC handed over power to the People's National Party (PNP) in September 1979 following its victory at the general elections. The twenty-seven-month rule of the PNP saw no significant shift in state attitudes towards the trade unions. The government's handling of the economy lacked firm policy direction. Labour discontent began to express itself and strikes began to take place. In the most manifest expression of workers' militancy against the state and discontent with the TUC leadership, about 5,000 demonstrating workers of the Ghana Industrial Holding Corporation (GIHOC), in mid-1980, invaded parliament in session over the delay in the payment of their wage arrears; they also besieged the Hall of Trades Unions, threatening to assault the TUC leadership. The government ordered the dismissal of 1,000 workers.

Structural adjustment and the restoration of the liberal state

Prior to the PNDC era, Ghana under the Acheampong regime of NRC/SMC I had effectively been through what Akilakpa Sawyer calls the 'African Economic Crisis' of the 1980s in which the economies of the countries of Sub-Saharan Africa (SSA) were characterized by overvalued currencies, poor foreign exchange earnings, famine and so on (World Bank 1981). Sub-Saharan Africa was in economic decline and disaster throughout the 1980s. The international community was moved to provide emergency relief on an unprecedented scale. According to Sawyer, 'this prompted a series of meetings, conferences and seminars around Africa at the UN and other international fora and the adoption of various resolutions and measures for dealing with the crisis' (Sawyer 1990: 1).

Of the various measures that the countries of SSA had to implement, Ghana had to institute programmes of economic reconstruction generally described as 'structural adjustment programmes (SAPs) to remove what were perceived to be the causes of the crisis and to put the economies of the sub-region on a path of development that would prevent any recurrence of such a catastrophe' (Sawyer 1990). This was done under the auspices of or in accordance with the precepts of the Bretton Woods institutions, namely, the International Monetary Fund (IMF) and the World Bank. The African crisis was seen as resulting from failures in economic performance in all the countries of SSA and the initial focus was strictly on economic aspects of the corrective process. The main planks of the SAPs adopted by the countries of SSA were the reduction or removal of direct state intervention in the productive and distributive sectors of the economy and the restriction of the state to the creation (through the manipulation of fiscal and monetary instruments) of an institutional and policy framework conducive to the mobilization of private enterprise and initiative. This, it was believed, would give freer play to both internal and external market forces and provide the appropriate engine for a resumption of economic growth and development (ibid.).

The SAP embarked upon by the PNDC government in April 1983 pursued certain broad policies which included, among others, the following measures:

1. Public Expenditure: The measures sought to reduce public borrowing and budget deficit through expenditure cuts and ceilings and a shift of public investment towards the export sector. Public service emolument expenditure is contained by the retrenchment of public sector staff and a general restraint on salary and wage increases. Reduction and or removal of subsidies for the provision of public services through the generalization of cost-recovery programmes.

2. Rationalization of the State-Owned Sector of the Economy: The object here being to reduce state ownership and control of economic activities to the barest minimum and to make surviving state-owned enterprises (SOEs) more profit oriented and less protected from market conditions. In this

regard profitable SOEs were to be sold or private parties invited to buy in. The unprofitable SOEs are to be liquidated or if of strategic importance, they are to be rationalized by retrenchment of employees. (Sawyer 1990: 21)

According to Eboe Hutchful, adjustment policy went from correcting 'policy distortions' in which there was a stabilization package to reduce inflation and achieve equilibrium and a programme to promote economic growth and export recovery. Then followed a medium-term policy framework to achieve an average annual growth of real GDP by 5 per cent and after 1993 a shift from economic recovery to accelerated growth under which sustainable development and poverty alleviation through private sector development were emphasized (Hutchful 2002: 56–7). Next to correcting 'policy distortions', reforming what was perceived as Ghana's 'runaway' public sector was the most important objective of adjustment (ibid.: 93). The aspect of the public sector reform that affected organized labour directly was the redeployment and retrenchment of workers in the public sector.

The PNDC and organized labour When the Provisional National Defence Council (PNDC) overthrew the PNP on 31 December 1981 it received the support of a mixture of right- and left-wing elements in Ghanaian politics. These forces included soldiers who were associated with Rawlings but had been discharged from the army by the PNP regime, elements in the PNP security network, civilian activists of the June Fourth Movement (JFM) and close associates of Rawlings who in turn had links with critical social groups and interests in the country.

Of these groups, the leftists had greater leverage over the initial political and ideological direction of the PNDC than the 'right'. The country was primed for the left to take advantage and use popular participation and revolution against the status quo. The PNDC fitted the mould of a radical–populist–military regime. The regime claimed to be engaged in a revolution aimed at the socio-economic transformation of the country and at developing grassroots democracy, and it had support from various sectors of Ghanaian society.

Prior to the 31 December 1981 coup there had been some important developments on the labour front, which had sharpened internal contradictions within the trade union movement. The AFRC period had enhanced the conditions for worker militancy within the trade union movement and there had developed strong criticism of the national leadership of the TUC by the branch and local union leaders. In the SMC era, the TUC leadership did not associate itself with the major political struggles then occurring under the leadership of A. M. Issifu. Attempts to challenge the TUC leadership culminated in the formation of the Association of Local Unions (ALU) of Greater Accra. Radical trade union activists who were dissatisfied with the TUC leadership championed the cause of ALU. There was a lot of discontent and disunity within the ranks of the organized labour movement with one faction being supported by sections of the governing PNDC. On 29 April 1982, with the tacit support of the PNDC, the ALU led thousands of workers to besiege the TUC headquarters and declare the suspension of the constitutions of the TUC and the national unions and dissolve the executive board of TUC and the national executive councils of all seventeen national unions. ALU, with the complicity of the PNDC, thus set about taking over the TUC and despite initial resistance from various workers' unions and groups, succeeded.

The PNDC pursued one of the most difficult macroeconomic stabilization packages at the insistence of the IMF/World Bank, which meant that workers had to tighten their belts with the government holding down wages, but prices were allowed to be influenced by market forces. This, naturally, led to clashes between organized labour and the state. The national leadership of the TUC began to demand an independent voice in the determination of the national minimum wage and the formulation of national economic policy. On 5 January 1984, the TUC denied any association with the process of fixing prices in the economy and protested against astronomical government-announced price increases in three basic food items: maize (166 per cent), rice (253 per cent) and sugar (175 per cent) (Adu-Amankwah 1990: 100). The TUC thus drew attention to the erosion in the real wages of workers and put forward a bargaining position asking for an increase in the minimum wage. The state's response to the TUC's concerns about issues of survival was dismissive and hostile. According to the chairman of the PNDC, 'there was a real danger that discussions about a meaningful living wage will be influenced more by blind emotion than by scientific and intelligent analysis' (ibid.). By October 1984, the TUC had come out against the main elements of an IMF-sponsored structural adjustment programme (SAP). The TUC called on the PNDC to 'take steps to wrestle the economy from the grips of the IMF and World Bank and tell the truth about the nation to the working people so that together we can decide the direction of the country' (ibid.).

Labour's lamentation and protestations were largely ignored by the PNDC. The government's response to the TUC was, however, two-fold. On the one hand, ideological attacks were mounted against the TUC leadership and the organization, and on the other hand a show was made of involving the TUC in decision-making. Under the pressure of hostility from govern-

Organized labour

211

ment, tensions began to develop within the trade union movement over the nature of union intervention in the political economy. A militant crop of workers with state support emerged to challenge the TUC leadership's perceived need to avert what appeared to be an imminent crack-down on the organization. At the TUC congress of March 1988 at Cape Coast, the PNDC member in charge of security, Kojo Tsikata, warned the Congress of the risk of electing a militant leadership. The state press continued to malign the TUC, focusing on leaders considered to be too militant by alleging that they were serving interests external to organized labour and also that they were involved in plots of subversion against the regime (ibid.).

The response of the state to the criticism of organized labour seems to have worked because even though economic conditions continued to deteriorate under the PNDC's policies, the TUC, on May Day 1988, presented the PNDC chairman with the 'Best Worker Award'. Later, in a meeting between the PNDC chairman and the executive board of the TUC to thank the chairman for attending the May Day rally, the TUC secretary-general, A. K. Yankey, stated that 'the TUC supports the economic programme' of the PNDC and assured the chairman that 'we will do our best to educate workers on all policies of government so that we can continue to enjoy industrial peace and harmony' (ibid.).

Another issue for which there was united labour militancy within the framework of the TUC against government policy was the violation of collective bargaining rights with regard to the termination of appointments and the payment of terminal awards. The state's response was to resort to the threat of force and political intimidation. In general, the economic recovery programme (ERP) exacted a severe toll on workers as represented by the immense and increasing gap between the minimum wage and the real cost of living. Beyond the general impact of the ERP, the most violent assault of the PNDC's SAP on trade union rights was the attack on the security of employment and the right to work as a result of the massive retrenchment of labour that the programme forcefully carried out.

The restoration of the liberal state

The restoration of the liberal state followed the logical conclusion of the programme of structural adjustment. After nearly a decade of structural adjustment under the PNDC, the need for constitutional rule and return to democratic governance was inevitable, given the fact that the financial support for the SAP came from a western donor community whose political system is a liberal one, and it was paradoxical that they would use their taxpayers' money to support a developing country whose political system was undemocratic and unconstitutional. In early 1990, as Jeffrey Herbst has noted, Ghana began to experience many of the same political pressures for a return to democracy that were affecting other African countries. In August 1991, the PNDC government announced a programme that projected a return to complete civilian rule in the last quarter of 1992 (Herbst 1993: 5). A combination of internal pro-democracy forces and external donor demands led the PNDC government to embark on a managed programme to return the country to constitutional rule. This led to the drafting and promulgation of the 1992 Constitution, the formation of political parties and a general election. The PNDC metamorphosed into the National Democratic Congress (NDC) party, and the NDC became the majority party in parliament. The Ghanaian liberal state was restored after nearly a decade of PNDC rule with the coming into effect of the Fourth Republic on 7 January 1992.

The policy imperatives of the liberal state

The liberal state, however, came into being with the same economic policies prescribed by the IMF/World Bank that had been pursued by the PNDC. This affected organized labour in various ways. Among the policies was the pursuit of the liberal market – a free market in which supply and demand determine the prices of goods and services as well as the allocation of factors of production. This meant the state had to disengage from the determination of prices of goods and services. The liberal state also had to concentrate on governance and get out of doing business. To do this the government had to maintain a leaner workforce that the state could remunerate adequately. The liberal state also had to divest itself of state-owned enterprises (SOEs) and leave the private sector to do business. In allowing the private sector to be the engine of growth, the national economy and organized labour had to learn to work under the new international business doctrine of sticking to their core business and outsourcing non-core business to private contractors.

When the PNDC embarked upon the SAP, it was an unconstitutional government that had seized power from a constitutionally elected government, but the IMF/World Bank had to go along with it to implement one of the most unpopular set of policies the country had seen, using a heavy hand that only a military regime could inflict. The PNDC was ruling by popular acquiescence, as is the case with all military regimes, but it was in the interests of the western donor countries whose bidding was being done by the IMF/World Bank to ensure that the economic policies being pursued could be sustained under a liberal state regime.

A return to constitutional rule, however, did not imply any movement from the economic orthodoxy set out by the IMF/World Bank because the PNDC government, which led the country into the market-led economic orthodoxy of the IMF/World Bank, metamorphosed into the NDC to fight the 1992 general elections. The NDC won the elections and continued its economic policies under the campaign slogan of 'continuity'. As a result of the continuity, the NDC government continued the policy of privatization through the divestiture of SOEs, resulting in the 'downsizing' of the workforce in the public sector and the divested enterprises.

The redeployment programme The policy imperative to rationalize the state-owned sector of the economy was meant to reduce state ownership and control of the economic activities to the barest minimum and make surviving state-owned enterprises (SOEs) more profit-oriented and less protected from market conditions. In this regard, the government announced a redeployment exercise and a divestiture programme for the public sector. The redeployment exercise was meant to reduce what was considered as excess labour in the public sector, and it cost organized labour a sizeable chunk of its membership. Starting in 1987, 235,000 formal sector jobs were lost between 1985 and 1990 (Boateng 2001: 24). The PNDC government set up a labour redeployment management committee to organize the programme (Republic of Ghana 1990: 8). The aim of the exercise was to reduce the rate of growth in public expenditure in order to arrest the sharp decline in real wages and the associated low morale among public servants as well as increasing labour productivity by reducing underemployment and overstaffing in the public sector.

Privatization Privatization has been part of the IMF/World Bank orthodoxy of SAP in many countries in Africa. As an instrument of economic policy, privatization usually involves three main (overlapping) processes, namely divestiture, commercialization of public utilities and services and the nurturing of an atmosphere conducive to private investment. In 1990, public sector employment represented 82.5 per cent of the total formal employment of about 230,000 (Republic of Ghana 1990: 25). Seventeen core public state-owned enterprises (SOEs), in the utilities, transport, petroleum and agricultural sectors, employed about 78,000 workers, representing over 40 per cent of all public sector employment. Most of the SOEs operated at a loss, according to the State Enterprises Commission, amounting to 23 billion cedis in 1989 alone; privatization was inevitable. The privatization of SOEs involved the setting up of the divestiture implementation committee. The divestiture involved selling the SOEs as a way of taking government out of businesses and allowing the private sector to run them. The liberal state essentially makes policy and sets up the regulatory system within which business takes place.

The response of the Civil Servants' Association The response of organized labour to the programme of labour redeployment and privatization reflected the point of view of the TUC and the Civil Servants' Association (CSA) of Ghana. The CSA was engaged in the redeployment mainly of the junior workers. The PNDC government targeted excess labour in the civil and education services, setting up the Labour Redeployment Programme (LRP) whose objectives were: (i) to remove all surplus labour from the civil and education services; (ii) to enable government to pay improved remuneration to workers who remained in these services; (iii) to relocate the redeployed labour force rationally within the private informal sectors of the economy; (iv) to afford the redeployed persons the opportunity to rediscover their potential and develop them to the optimum through training/retraining programmes and mobilization into the agricultural sector ibid.: 8). The CSA, as organized labour, agreed with the rationale behind the programme as set out by the IMF/World Bank and went along with the programme of redeployment. They argued that by doing this they ensured that their members were redeployed as opposed to retrenched, as was the case with workers under the TUC, which disagreed with the rationale behind the programme.

From the point of view of the CSA, redeployment involved a set of guidelines identifying areas of serious overstaffing in the civil service and the Ghana education service (GES). The identified groups included labourers, cleaners and charwomen, drivers, stewards, cooks, porters, sweepers, messengers, security personnel, clerical officers and secretarial personnel, and store officers. To remove the possibility of victimization, the identification of the actual persons to be redeployed was carried out by workplace staff appraisal committees made up of the head of the ministry/department, a middle-level management representative, a workers' representative and a workplace CDR representative.

The criteria set for identifying redeployees was as follows:

i. officers whose work and conduct had persistently been negative and who could be dispensed with
ii. officers whose effectiveness was seriously handicapped because of physical infirmity
iii. officers engaged over and above approved and established schedules
iv. officers who were willing to retire voluntarily and who could be dispensed with

215

v.   officers on secondment outside the civil service/GES and who could be
     dispensed with

vi. officers whose qualifications were proven to be false

vii. last-come-first-to-go – a strategy to be used if the above measures did
     not produce the target figures

The LRP had a compensation package for the affected persons:

(i) a severance payment equivalent to 4 months of gross terminal salary;
(ii) an end of service payment equivalent to 2 months of gross salary for
each year of uninterrupted service; (iii) information, counseling and place-
ment services to facilitate the mobility of the redeployed into productive
jobs; (iv) training opportunities for a manageable number of redeployees
at existing vocational/technical institutions; (v) notwithstanding the enjoyment of the compensation package, the redeployee shall at the due date
of superannuation collect his/her social security contributions or pension;
(vi) assistance to a target group of 9,600 redeployed families in undertaking
agricultural activities through provision of arable farmland, farm inputs,
extension services and transitional food aid. (Republic of Ghana 1990: 10)

The CSA claimed that, by agreeing to the LRP, and therefore serving on
the redeployment management committee, it was able to ensure that its
members were redeployed according to the guidelines set out in the project
document.[1] The TUC, however, did not accept the rationale behind the LRP
and refused to serve on the committee. For this reason, unionized workers
in the GES and the universities, i.e. TEWU members, were retrenched
rather than redeployed. They were given their financial benefits but not
redeployment into other areas of the GES or the universities.

The response of the TUC The Ghana Trades Union Congress (TUC) is made
up of seventeen national unions with the TUC serving as the centre that
coordinates their activities. It has no members except through the national
unions. A TUC survey of 2001 put the number of unionized workers in
the country at 351,487 after years of retrenchment and privatization (TUC
of Ghana 2001). This is about a 50 per cent reduction in a membership
that was estimated at about 750,000 before the redeployment programme
started in 1987.[2] The TUC gets its funds by taking half of the 2 per cent
of the dues that the national unions receive from their paid-up members.
Numbers therefore mean a lot to the TUC. When the PNDC decided to
get rid of excess labour in the civil service and the GES, the TUC felt this
was an IMF/World Bank programme aimed at the working class and were
thus not keen to assist with the redeployment exercise. For this reason the

unionized members of the TUC in the GES and the universities, namely the Teachers' and Education Workers' Union (TEWU) were retrenched and had no access to retraining counselling and replacement in other under-staffed sectors of the GES and the universities. It became clear to the TUC that it had to take steps to help its members as a way of ensuring its own survival. The TUC's response and those of its affiliated unions are discussed below.

ICU INFORMAL The Industrial and Commercial Workers' Union (ICU) was seriously affected by the retrenchment exercise when 28,897 out of a union membership of 74,357 at the Cocoa Board were retrenched.[3] In response, the ICU began to organize various groups of workers in the informal sector, starting with the Ghana Hairdressers' and Beauticians' Association (GHABA) in 1990. This involved reorganizing and restructuring of the association which has about 4,000 members. As a result of the ICU's efforts, they are now affiliated and paid-up members of the ICU.

The ICU has also organized domestic workers, the Batik, Tie and Dye, which also includes Kente and smock weavers (BATMAG), and the basket and leather weavers (GAWAL). Efforts are under way to organize the Ghana Traditional Healers' Association as well as professional and managerial staff. The organization of these informal groups into paid-up affiliates of the ICU has helped the union to survive the retrenchment exercise, given the fact that it is the largest national union of the TUC.

GAWU INFORMAL As a result of the retrenchment, the TUC set up an informal desk at its headquarters to coordinate efforts aimed at organizing the informal sector, efforts undertaken by the GAWU as well as the ICU.

The GAWU has two broad categories of membership, namely, wage-earning rural workers and self-employed rural workers. The former include workers in the cocoa industry, excluding those involved with post-harvest; the plantations producing oil palm, rubber and citrus; commercial farms producing avocado, mangoes and pineapples; commercial poultry and livestock ventures; the agricultural research institutions; and state and para-statal agricultural institutions. From a peak membership of 135,000 in 1982, GAWU membership started to decline as a result of the retrenchment exercise and by 1993 had reached a low of 65,000. The GAWU started to organize the rural self-employed in the mid-1960s when it attempted to organize peasant cocoa farm labourers. Powerful traditional rulers with the aid of the police fiercely resisted this. In October 1979, GAWU decided to create the Rural Workers' Organization Division (RWOD) to cater solely to the rural self-employed. For GAWU the self-employed rural workers include tenants, share croppers, small owner-occupiers and landless peasants who are not in any regular form of employment but may offer their services for payment by the day. Other categories of rural self-employed include potters, basket weavers, artisanal fishermen and others (Hodson 1983).

The SAP affected the rural poor in various ways: through the measures taken to deal with the economic decline Ghana had suffered: namely (i) removing deficits in the fiscal budget and the balance of payments; reallocating domestic resources to more productive areas; reducing the role of the state in commercial and productive activities; and promoting the private sector and the role of market forces (ibid.). Among the range of instruments used to achieve these objectives were liberalization of foreign trade and the provision of incentives for exports, controlling the supply of money, reducing reliance on controlled prices, removal of subsidies and the reform and divestment of public and state-owned enterprises. These measures have affected the agricultural sector and the rural population. They have adversely affected the membership of GAWU due to the link between the smallholding farmers and the wider economy (ibid.). The market and the social economic infrastructure have been the key areas through which the rural self-employed have been affected by the SAPs.

The smallholder farmer disposes of his farm surpluses on the market and purchases food and other goods. A 1986 estimate for Ghana suggested that 20 per cent of producers marketed the bulk of their produce, 54 per cent sold only what was left after family needs had been met, and 24 per cent produced solely for family needs. Most of the producers in the last two categories are GAWU members. The labour market also links the rural poor to the wider economy so as far as it is a source of hiring labour – usually on a seasonal basis – to help meet the demands of the production cycle, and to increase family income through hiring out the labour of household members (ibid.).

Liberalization has affected GAWU membership in other ways. The liberalization of the domestic agricultural markets has been unable to prop up farm produce prices because, prior to the reform, market forces already determined most farm produce prices. As part of the reform programme, the government sought to promote the strategic staples and industrial crops through guaranteed minimum prices for maize, rice, oil palm, cotton and tobacco. Price guarantees have, however, been woefully ineffective for maize and rice, the main crops produced by GAWU members. In a situation where these two crops are not sold in controlled markets like the three industrial crops, and more so in a situation where there is plentiful imported rice, the prices of maize and rice have been severely depressed (ibid.).

The depressed prices of products have even more impact on the income levels of members since they have to pay higher prices for inputs such as fertilizer and agrochemicals, due to the adjustment in the exchange rate and the virtual removal of subsidies. GAWU members have also been affected by the rural labour market. Agricultural production, even for the small rural farmer, is based on the combination of family and hired casual labour. Wages in the informal sector are significantly high. The effect is that for members who do not earn much from their produce and have no significant alternative sources of income, hired casual farm labour is a real strain (ibid.).

Social and economic infrastructure serves as a link between the rural poor and the wider economy. The liberal state, in cutting down on government current expenditure, has brought about the deterioration of facilities such as transport in institutions which are crucial to the small farmer. Thus, it can be said that even though adjustment policy reforms did raise the earnings of a small category of farmers, especially those in cocoa production, the majority of self-employed rural workers have been adversely affected and rendered desperate in their quest for survival. Such rural workers constantly overstretch themselves to find alternative means of income, sometimes through the exploitation of labour. Or they may encroach on forest and game reserves to exploit the trees for marketable and domestic fuel wood and charcoal, or over fish fingerlings, to the detriment of the environment.

THE LABOUR ENTERPRISE TRUST (LET) The boldest response of the TUC to the liberal state's downsizing of labour has been the decision to set up the Labour Enterprise Trust (LET). This is an attempt by organized labour to enter the informal sector to create jobs themselves and create extra income for workers. It is not common for trade unions to be employers, because they are traditionally organizations to protect employees' interests. Following the retrenchment exercise arising out of SAP and the privatization of SOEs, the low capacity utilization by existing private companies and those that emerged from privatization compounded the problem of the unemployed. The LET was one of the TUC's responses to the growing unemployment situation. In 1996, the TUC decided to mobilize resources from its members to establish enterprises in support of job creation in the country, and therefore registered LET. The TUC had projected that if the estimated 500,000 members of the TUC contributed 50,000 cedis each, an amount of 25 billion cedis could be raised as seed money for the new company. The TUC was able to mobilize funds from only 99,000 of its members and thus raised a seed capital of 5.7 billion cedis. It set

219

up the following enterprises using the seed capital: the Unique Insurance Company Ltd, the City Car Park Ltd (in which LET holds 20 per cent of the shares), a water tanker service, a radio taxi service and a workers' property ownership scheme.[4]

These five enterprises have created 186 jobs. Even though this is not a big workforce, it marks a radical shift from the traditional role of trade unions. This is very much in the spirit of the mission of LET which seeks to:

> provide a very efficient, effective, innovative and quality service that would have a positive effect on the lives and well-being of workers and thus promote national development and the well-being of the economy and to create jobs and quality employment through the development and maintenance of sustainable productive and profitable enterprises of all sizes operating in all sectors.[5]

The Labour Act 2003, Act 651 The privatization of the industrial sector has meant that the government has had to bring labour laws into line with the liberalization of the economy. The Labour Act 2003 sought to amend and consolidate the laws relating to labour, employers, trade unions and industrial relations and to establish a National Labour Commission. The Act ensures freedom of association, stating: 'Every worker has the right to form or join a trade union of his or her choice for the promotion and protection of the worker's economic and social interests.' In this regard the Act allows 'Two or more workers employed in the same undertaking to form a trade union'. Similarly, two or more employers in the same industry or trade, each of whom employs no fewer than fifteen workers, may form or join an employers' organization. Each trade union or employers' organization has the right (i) to take part in the formulation, and become a member of, any federation of trade unions or employers' organization and participate in its lawful activities, and (ii) to affiliate to and participate in the activities of, or join, an international workers' or employers' organization.

The new Labour Act thus throws up a challenge for organized labour in relation to the freedom to form and belong to a union. This has had a direct bearing on the decision of the largest national union of the TUC, the ICU, to disaffiliate from the TUC. The problem began when a section of the ICU, the financial workers, tried to break away from the ICU due to internal disagreements. The breakaway group then sought to affiliate itself independently with the TUC. The TUC used its internal mechanisms to manage the conflict but was not successful, so it moved to accept the breakaway ICU group – the Union of Industry Commerce and Finance

(UNICOF). Following the TUC's decision to accept the UNICOF the ICU decided to break away from the TUC. The TUC is faced with a major dilemma. Much as it wants to encourage and promote internal democracy within its affiliated unions, the national unions do not take kindly to their members breaking away. Given the freedom of workers to join or form unions, the unions are going to be under pressure to see to the needs of workers. The TUC may have to face the problem of its unions wanting to break away as ICU has done, and the unions themselves have to face the prospect of blocs of members breaking away.

THE TUC AND INTERNAL CONFLICT MANAGEMENT The disaffiliation of the ICU from the TUC came as a shock to observers of the labour scene, raising questions about how the internal conflict management mechanism of the TUC dealt with the ICU problem. The TUC has no formal structures for dealing with intra-union conflicts. Each union has areas of operation and when there is jurisdictional conflict an ad hoc committee is set up to look at the problem and suggest solutions. Where the conflict is between two unions, a similar ad hoc committee is set up. This created a problem when the ICU–UNICOF split occurred. There had been a similar, earlier conflict and break-up within the ICU in the early 1990s, leading to the formation of TEGLU (Textile and Garments Union). That breakaway had to do with a power struggle during elections between Abraham Koomson and Napoleon Kpoh who were deputy general secretaries. Napoleon Kpoh got the upper hand and Koomson led a group breakaway to form TEGLU. There were attempts to get the TUC executive committee to intervene but their efforts at mediation did not work.

The problem with the ICU–UNICOF split arose over ICU finances in the run-up to the ICU congress. When the issue could not be resolved, some industries decided to break away to form a separate union. The TUC decided to appoint an ad hoc mediation committee to try and resolve the problem and bring back the breakaway group but by the time it started work, the UNICOF had gone ahead with registering itself as a union. The UNICOF had a problem with the TUC committee's terms of reference because it was now a registered union and thus should not be treated as a breakaway union. This meant that the committee was dealing with a conflict between two unions and this created further difficulties for its mediation efforts. The parties, however, indicated their willingness for mediation. The UNICOF's complaint concerned the lack of internal democracy in the ICU and the high-handed approach of the ICU general secretary. When the mediation committee tried to talk to the ICU, it was discovered that the ICU had gone to court to challenge the very existence

221

of the UNICOF. The UNICOF thus found no reason to continue with the mediation and the committee had to report to the TUC that it could not continue. The ICU also accused the TUC leadership of supporting the UNICOF clandestinely.

From the point of view of the TUC leadership, the new Labour Law allowed for pluralism of unions. Furthermore, the TUC leadership felt that despite the UNICOF breaking away there was a need to maintain links with them to avoid a repeat of the breakaway of TEGLU and its recognition by the International Trade Union. That earlier breakaway led to the creation of TEGLU as the second trade union centre in Ghana. The TUC leadership feared that if the UNICOF was not handled carefully, it would set up a third trade union centre in Ghana, adversely affecting the membership of the TUC. Thus, while trying to resolve the problem, efforts were also made to maintain links with UNICOF. On May Day 2004, the ICU argued that if the TUC allowed TEGLU and UNICOF to participate in the workers' parade, it (the ICU) would not participate. The TUC felt there was no point in stopping any group of workers from participating in the parade. The ICU held its parade at TUC headquarters.

The TUC, however, felt that the ICU–UNICOF conflict could still be resolved internally through closed-door meetings with the ICU. As TUC efforts at conflict management and resolution were in progress, a letter was issued from the ICU notifying the TUC of its decision to disaffiliate. The TUC constitution requires a union seeking to disaffiliate to give six months' notice. The problem had a great deal to do with the attitude of the ICU general secretary – Napoleon Kpoh. The other union general secretaries felt the TUC was 'pampering' Kpoh who, on various occasions, had treated the TUC leadership with disdain and had been uncooperative. The TUC pointed to the LET project to which all the unions had agreed to contribute the seed money, except the ICU which had simply refused. The TUC leadership was forced to accept the ICU's note of disaffiliation, arguing that it was better to have a smaller but loyal membership than to have to deal with the disloyal ICU.

The TUC leadership is now turning its attention to conflicts within and between the unions, developing a provision in its constitution that seeks to put in place a mechanism for conflict resolution, starting with conciliatory efforts and arbitration. If after this a breakaway does occur, then the TUC cannot be blamed, as has been the case with the ICU and UNICOF. This would get around the problem the TUC leadership faced when UNICOF applied for affiliation. The TUC also plans to put an arbitration mechanism in place, which will take on board the larger issue of internal democracy within unions. This is, in effect, its policy on organization and internal democracy adopted by the TUC at the 5th Quadrennial Delegates Conference, held at the University of Cape Coast, in 1996 (TUC of Ghana 1996: 17–26).

The policy was developed as a result of the changing socio-economic and political conditions of the last few years. Specifically, it was the result of assaults on trade union rights and dramatic changes in the world of work that threatened the very foundation of unionism. The TUC developed the strategy to enable it to intensify and strengthen the organization as well as to improve the quality of trade union and worker representation (TUC of Ghana 1996: 17). Following the 'downsizing' in the formal sectors of the economy, the TUC now has to face up to the need to organize workers in the informal sector. Furthermore, the organization of the formal sector mainly covered junior staff and excluded senior members of staff and professional and managerial staff from union membership. The challenge for the TUC is to work towards getting professional associations and managerial staff to become fully fledged trade unions.

The policy sets out the following organizational objectives: (a) to sustain the enthusiasm of existing members; (b) to extend systematically the coverage of unions to include senior and professional staff; (c) to lay the foundation for the amalgamation of unions, particularly in the public services and transport sector; (d) to pursue vigorously the organization of workers in the informal sector; (e) to promote internal democracy and greater participation of members, including women in union activities; (f) to begin to develop structures for accommodating union members who lose their jobs; (g) to raise awareness of unionism among young workers, the newly employed and students.

In implementing its policy on internal democracy and membership participation, the TUC believes that monitoring of the implementation has to be instituted within the TUC and its affiliate unions. Steps are to be taken to improve communication between the TUC and its affiliates as well as within the direct structures of the TUC itself; namely, the national and regional secretariats, and the district councils of labour. The TUC sees meetings as the main vehicle by which internal democracy and membership participation can be fostered; higher structures within the union movement must endeavour to attend meetings, as the statutes of the trade union movement require. The higher structures in turn must insist on meetings with the lower structures to ensure that the necessary avenues are created for membership participation. Another means of creating the conditions for greater internal democracy is the promotion of self-education among members. Under this, national unions are to encourage the development of study circles at workplaces, especially among local union executive members. The constitutions and policies of the national unions and the TUC must be widely circulated to reach members at various levels. The TUC would look to making funds available to support the activities of unions at the local, branch and district levels. The national unions are also to see to it that their locals receive their share of union dues. The national unions are to reintroduce union membership cards to promote the spirit of belonging.

Labour–private enterprise relations A number of new enterprises, especially in the mining sector and free zones, have not been very keen on their workers forming or joining unions. Among the mining companies, Resolute Amansie Ltd resisted for five years the efforts of the Mine Workers' Union to organize their workers. Goldfields Ghana Ltd had a tussle with the Mine Workers' Union in 1993 before workers at the Tarkwa mines were allowed to be unionized.[6] This is against the backdrop of the retrenchment exercise, which threw many members of organized labour on to the informal sector as well as introducing new ways of conducting business in the era of globalization. Labour has had to walk a tightrope when dealing with businesses in the private sector that are not keen to maintain a large workforce and that have adopted new ways of doing business, such as the core business, in which non-core business parts of the enterprise are outsourced to private contractors. Those aspects of non-core business mostly outsourced include catering, security and transport. The private contractors are usually not keen to have their workers unionized. The TUC has accepted the challenge and taken the initiative of approaching the private contractors. A number of catering, security services and transport enterprises are now outsourcing jobs that used to be performed by their own human resource departments.[7] For example, many businesses that used to run large fleets of buses for their workforce now have outsourced such transportation to private operators, rendering drivers who drove the company buses redundant. Organized labour recognizes this trend in the employment practices of employers, which is attributed to the impact of globalization. For this reason TUC leaders are now much more understanding of the problems that organized labour faces in the light of this reality, and they are careful about their demands on employers during negotiations.

Labour and political parties The policy of the TUC has been to stay out of politics and desist from openly supporting political parties, given the unpleasant experience of the SDF led by A. M. Issifu when the TUC-sponsored party failed to win any seat, even in Tema where it has one of its most active members dominating the township.[8] At its congress in

1992, the TUC adopted an amendment to its constitution that underlined the independence of the TUC and its neutrality in party politics. The TUC, however, notes that, according to its constitution, the organization:

> Shall work for the strengthening of our national institutions in conformity with our national way of life and aspirations. Our attachment of freedom, justice and democracy. Shall resolutely defend and uphold the democratic foundations on which the future of our Nation must be built. Shall strive to win fully respect for the dignity and rights of the human individual whom we serve. Shall seek the fulfillment of our aspirations and hopes and the achievement of our objectives, through democratic processes and within the framework of constitutional government and concern for the welfare of the country. (TUC of Ghana 1996: 27)

The TUC thus reaffirms its right and duty to intervene in national politics in a manner that safeguards and promotes the interests of its membership, bearing in mind that in doing so it must not necessarily align itself with one political party or the other. The liberal state is a state of political parties that form one of the main pillars of representative democracy.

Conclusion

Organized labour has come a long way from its relations with the state during the Nkrumah regime when it became the workers' wing of the ruling CPP. That was the period when the state set up the largest number of state-owned enterprises, including the builders' and workers' brigades. Since then state–union relations have been influenced by the changes that the state has been through and how organized labour has been able to adapt to changing circumstances. The state has had to reduce its labour force as dictated by the policy imperatives of the economic changes underpinning liberalization. These changes have affected organized labour in various ways, namely in the reduction of labour on the state's payroll which has affected union membership. Similarly, organized labour has had to deal with the changes that globalization has wrought upon private business enterprises by way of outsourcing. Organized labour is now more pragmatic in its relations with both the state and private enterprises while it takes up the more difficult challenge of organizing the informal sector. If the state succeeds in trimming down its payroll and workforce, which is the direction of state policy, and encouraging the private sector to create more jobs, organized labour will have to be much more innovative in the relations it develops with the state and work out the best ways to rise to the challenges posed by organizing the private sector.

225

Notes

1 Interview with Smart Chigahbatia, executive secretary, Civil Servants' Association, 10 October 2004.

2 Estimate given by Kweku Yanney, acting head of industrial relations, Ghana TUC.

3 Data from ICU Greater Accra regional office.

4 LET company profile.

5 Ibid.

6 Interview with general secretary, Mine Workers' Union, 16 September 2004.

7 Ibid.

8 In the 1979 general elections the SDF won three seats.

Sources

Adu-Amankwah, K. (1990) *The State, Trade Unions and Democracy in Ghana, 1982–1990*, unpublished research paper (The Hague: ISS).

Boateng, K. (2001) 'Impact of Structural Adjustment on Employment and Incomes in Ghana', in A. Yaw Baah (ed.), *The Social Dimension of Structural Adjustment in Ghana TUC* (Accra: FES).

Herbst, J. (1993) *The Politics of Reform in Ghana, 1982–1991* (Berkeley: University of California Press).

Hodson, D. F. (1983) *The General Agricultural Workers Union of the TUC (Ghana)* (Geneva: ILO).

Hutchful, E. (2002) *Ghana's Adjustment Experience: The Paradox of Reform* (Geneva: UNRISD).

Republic of Ghana (1990) *Labour Redeployment Programme*, Secretariat of Redeployment Management Committee (Accra).

Sawyer, A. (1990) *The Political Dimension of Structural Adjustment Programmes in Sub-Saharan Africa* (Accra: Ghana Universities Press).

TUC of Ghana (1996) *Policies of the Trades Union Congress*, adopted at the 5th Quadrennial Delegates' Conference, University of Cape Coast, 18–22 August.

World Bank (1981) *Accelerated Development in Sub-Saharan Africa* (Washington, DC: World Bank).

10 | The liberal Ghanaian state and foreign policy: the dynamics of change and continuity

KWAME BOAFO-ARTHUR

January 6 1993 marked the beginning of a serious attempt by Ghana to enthrone the liberal state in all its ramifications. Liberalism in the economic sense stresses a policy mix of a greater role for the market in the allocation of resources, a much-reduced role for the state, and increasing integration into the world economy. In the political realm the modern liberal state is expected to open up the political space to facilitate progressive political contestations for political power by political groupings, uphold the fundamental rights of the people, ensure the rule of law and so on, while at the same time facilitating the necessary institutional changes that will lead to the effective withdrawal of the state from the market. Thus, from January 1993 when the transition to democratic rule was effected, Ghana adopted the apparel of the liberal state and whether or not such a major shift has had any implications for the nation's foreign interactions on the basis of policies formulated to meet the challenges of liberalism is the main burden of this chapter. I argue that the country's quest for economic well-being through the policy of economic diplomacy has equally had profound impact on policy measures taken by the liberal state with regard to either the maintenance of the status quo or a change in foreign policy orientation. Actions taken by the state have been underpinned by the national interest, especially in the area of economic development as exemplified by the strong emphasis on economic diplomacy perceived as a necessary tool for attaining development objectives in a more challenging world. International interactions with a manifest economic bias have clearly overshadowed all other aspects of foreign policy both in terms of importance and the energies that have been exerted in their pursuit. For a dependent nation that currently has no known hegemonic pretensions but is rather bent on enhancing the overall standard of living of its citizens, such an approach cannot be faulted. The interplay between this objective and policy actions in the international system was clearly manifested during the rule of the National Democratic Congress (NDC) led by former President Jerry John Rawlings and has been given even greater attention by the government of the New Patriotic Party (NPP) led by President John Agyekum Kufuor.

Scholarly discourses and their theoretical underpinnings concerning change or continuity in the international system abound and some are discussed in the next section. While some perceive a change in policy orientation as inevitable, others point to continuities in the international system with regard to foreign policy formulation or the orientation of particular regimes.

Debates on change and continuity

According to Macleod (2002), change or continuity in a nation's foreign policy may be influenced, among several other variables, by the following:

1. The general guidelines which characterize a state's relation with the outside world, and which include: the traditional principles which have tended to underlie its foreign policy, often closely identified in realist literature as the 'national interest';
2. the roles it claims to play or aspires to play in the international system and the place it considers that it holds there;
3. its security policy;
4. its alliances;
5. how it grades its relations with its partners and its rivals; and
6. the nature of its relationship with the other members of the system.

Barbara Tuchman, a historian, and Alvin Toffler, a futurologist, perceive change in the international system in general and in the affairs of nations in particular as inevitable and as a natural process. Tuchman argues:

> Events in history do not – I would venture to say cannot – repeat themselves; nor can they be acted out in the same pattern as before because circumstances are never the same as before. They alter as the years pass, and the longer the elapsed time, the more new factors enter the situation. When the pace of change, as in the twentieth century, is rapid, the change can be immense. (Tuchman 1980: 32)

For Tuchman, therefore, comparing the present with the past is not ideal, whether it pertains to international relations or any other phenomena. In other words, the issue of continuity, which implies the constancy of the status quo or elements of the status quo thereof, with regard to policy orientation or commitment, is not appropriate since continuity, by implication, has a link with the past and past events cannot repeat themselves.

It seems to me that in light of international and domestic occurrences it may not be wholly germane to argue that there are no forms of continuities and that changes are inevitable and do occur in all cases and circumstances.

Such a position may amount to ignoring the fact that even though changes occur there are continuities in policy-making. It is contended that one ought to be careful in making categorical assertions that do no justice to existing realities with regard to the pursuit of international policies.

According to Toffler:

> The final, qualitative difference between this and all previous lifetimes is the one most easily overlooked. For we have not merely extended the scope and scale of change, we have radically altered its pace. We have in our time released a totally new social force – a stream of change so accelerated that it influences our sense of time, revolutionizes the tempo of daily life, and affects the very way we 'feel' the world around us. We no longer 'feel' life as men did in the past. And this is the ultimate difference, the distinction that separates the truly contemporary man from all others. For this acceleration lies behind the impermanence ... radically affecting the way we relate to other people, to things, to the entire universe of ideas, art and values. (Toffler 1970: 17)

It cannot be denied that the units of analysis in international politics keep on changing and such changes do affect foreign policy decision-making and, ipso facto, foreign policy orientation. As clearly pointed out by Hoffman, 'there are periods of history when profound changes occur all of a sudden, and the acceleration of events is such that much of what experts write is obsolete before it gets into print. We are now in one of those periods' (Hoffman 1989: 84). I do not think there has been such a magnitude of unexpected transformations in the international system as the tumultuous collapse of the Eastern bloc and the end of the Cold War. Changes that do occur on the international scene and in individual countries often defy prediction. Nevertheless, even in the midst of sudden changes, elements of continuity in policy-making could also be perceived. This is significant because the pursuit of national interests, for instance, has been the major underlying principle of state actions in the international system even though we admit that the means to attain the national interest may vary from government to government on the basis of changing global situations. While certain objectives pursued by states may be sacrosanct over several years, the instruments that may be utilized by states to attain such national objectives may change from time to time. Thus, there may be constant objective interests such as the maintenance of national security and the general well-being of the majority of the people, but the means to bring these about may vary on the basis of changing international situations.

On the other hand, it is also argued that in all circumstances there are changes as well as continuities in the international system. For instance, there has been a remarkable consistency in the pursuit of liberal democratic ideals by the United States of America for a long time. The US has not changed its policy of exporting to other countries the values embedded in liberal democracy, but the policy instruments adopted to propel this policy both internally and externally have undergone changes in the course of time. So if nothing else, elements of continuity move in tandem with the rapid changes and the seeming impermanence in certain areas and policies in the international system. On this, Kenneth Waltz argues:

> International politics is sometimes described as the realm of accident and upheaval, of rapid and unpredictable change. Although changes abound, continuities are as impressive or more so ... The texture of international politics remains highly constant, patterns recur, and events repeat them-selves endlessly. The relations that prevail internationally seldom shift rapidly in type or in quality. (Waltz 1979: 65–6)

Kegley and Wittkopf appear to capture the realities on the ground at all times. Changes in foreign policy do occur but at the same time there are continuities. These may be dictated by the nature of the international system but I believe also that it may be influenced by events in particular polities. As it is at the global level, so it appears to be at the national level. They note:

> If we are adequately to comprehend the present condition of global politics, we must be as sensitive to the magnitude of change as we are to continuities. The global system is dynamic, not static; it is governed by movement as well as constancy. The contemporary world political system is a product of processes that are themselves susceptible to long-term evolu-tionary modification. Hence attention to both change and changelessness in the global forces that structure the world's present existence and future destiny is required if today's global politics are to be understood. (Kegley and Wittkopf 1981: 4)

Kegley and Wittkopf sum up by stating unequivocally that 'world politics consists of interacting continuities and discontinuities' (ibid.: 468).

Indisputably, one can always find some elements of change and continu-ity in the international system whether at the national level or on the global plane. Whereas continuities may not be the exact replica of what is past, it cannot be convincingly argued that the international system is constantly changing without any structure or pattern maintaining its pristine nature. For instance, leadership in particular countries may change but, given the texture of international politics, it could be argued that the policy of a state to be a member of an international organization, especially the United Nations, will never change. It is instructive to note, for instance, that all the past governments of Ghana affirmed their unflinching commitment to the nation's membership of international organizations.

From the beginning of 1993 Ghana endorsed political liberalism to complement the existing economic liberalism that was being pursued by the Provisional National Defence Council (PNDC). Such a change from military dictatorship to a liberal democratic set-up in itself symbolizes a massive transformation in the character of the state. However, this change rarely affected various existing channels of international interactions that the country was engaged in. If anything, the change enhanced and strengthened the nature of other existing relations. Thus, change and continuity tend to characterize the foreign policy orientation of Ghana.

Charles Herman points out that 'changes that mark a reversal or, at least, profound redirection of a country's foreign policy are of special interest because of the demands their adoption poses on the initiating government and its economic constituents and because of their potentially powerful consequences for other countries' (Herman 1990: 4). He goes on to state, however, that 'understanding the conditions for change poses one of the most difficult theoretical problems for scholars and policy makers' and, more especially, 'establishing what constitutes fundamental foreign policy change poses many challenges' (ibid.: 5). There have been instances on the global scene and in individual countries where the same government redirects its original foreign policy orientation for several reasons. A good example is the rapprochement President Anwar Sadat of Egypt reached with Israel leading to the signing of the Camp David Accords and the cessation of hostilities between Egypt and Israel. In Ghana, as in most other countries, many of these unanticipated changes occur when new governments with different perceptions of the political and economic environments and new agendas come to power. For instance, Nkrumah's overthrow in 1966 led to a dramatic change in Ghana's international relations with the expulsion of eastern bloc technical advisers and redirection of foreign policy orientation from the East to the West. The change in the foreign policy character of the state was dramatic and total. An example of the same government redirecting policy orientation basically for economic reasons was the decision of the PNDC to change its Marxist-Leninist ideology and start serious hobnobbing with the West, especially the Bretton Woods institutions, leading to the implementation of the economic recovery and structural adjustment programmes in the 1980s with the support of the Bretton Woods institutions.

Change or continuity is invariably affected by domestic politics. Herman defines three distinct circumstances under which change may occur.

Foreign policy

i. *When issues become a centrepiece in the struggle for political power.* Competing political leaders and their supporters use a foreign policy position to differentiate themselves from opponents. If those out of power are successful at the polls, then the foreign policy of the state may change. In some cases also, an existing regime may change its foreign policy to distinguish itself from political opponents or to prevent defeat. A good example, as noted above, was the PNDC's U-turn from socialist policies to pro-West liberal policies in April 1983. Among other reasons, this was influenced greatly by the realization that political power was likely to slip from their hands if the dire economic conditions, which had been aggravated by chaotic, confusing, debilitating and ambiguous Marxist-Leninist policies, persisted (Ahiakpor 1985: 534–52).

ii. *When the attitudes or beliefs of the dominant domestic constituents undergo a very significant change.* Attitudinal change becomes the underlying source of explanation and some profound stimulus presumably creates realignment in the view of many. A good example in the Ghanaian context, in my view, was the Progress Party government's subdued stance in African politics as opposed to that of the Convention People's Party (CPP) under Nkrumah, and especially its perception on how to deal with the obnoxious apartheid policies of the minority white South African government. While the CPP was supportive of armed struggle by Africans to end apartheid, the leader of the Progress Party government favoured dialogue with South Africa. Given events on the continent at that time, it was not surprising that at an OAU summit the Ghanaian foreign minister voted against dialogue with South Africa and thereby contradicted his prime minister.

iii. *When realignment of the essential constituents of a regime occurs, or a revolution or other forms of transformation of the political system takes place.* For instance, when a military junta seizes political power from civilian political actors, the relevant constituencies change. Several examples abound in Ghana on account of the spate of military coups that have taken place. Even though international friends changed in some instances, in all cases, relationship and membership with international organizations remained the same. It must be emphasized also that restructuring or transforming the economic system also can be a source of foreign policy change (Herman 1990: 7). To be candid, the economic restructuring of the PNDC moved in tandem with realignment of international friends. It is to the credit of the PNDC that they succeeded in having balanced international relations in the teeth of draconian structural adjustment programmes and also at a time when the Cold War had yet to run its full course. As noted elsewhere, 'it was clear that the PNDC had learned objective lessons from the failures of earlier governments that were either overly pro-West or pro-East and thereby foreclosed potential sources of assistance from one or the other. Thus, whereas the regime was doing everything possible, including making the right statements to win Western capital for economic development, it presented another face of dealing evenly with the internationally accepted ideological divide, at least until the collapse of communism. It was a pragmatic approach if not the full essence of political brinkmanship at the international level' (Boafo-Arthur 1999: 85).

On the basis of these theoretical assumptions, one can focus on the domestic and external dynamics that have been influencing the foreign policy actions of the liberal Ghanaian state. The fact, however, that domestic factors have a preponderant influence on a nation's foreign policy behaviour remains incontestable. It is also a truism that at all times a state's international behaviour tends to exhibit changes and continuities depending on both internal and external influences as well as on the history and attributes of the state.

With specific reference to the influence of history on the status and concomitant behaviour of especially African states in the international system, the New Partnership for Africa's Development (NEPAD) document minces no words in pointing to the historical evolution of the current marginalization of Africa and for that matter its constituent states. It further points to the nature and workings of the international economic system as well as the inadequacies of, and shortcomings in, the policies pursued by many countries in post-independence Africa (Organization of African Unity 2001: 5). The net effect of these historical processes 'has been the entrenchment of a vicious cycle, in which economic decline, reduced capacity and poor governance reinforce each other, thereby confirming Africa's peripheral and diminishing role in the world economy. Thus over the centuries, Africa has become the marginalized continent' (ibid.). By implication, historical factors have moved in tandem with other domestic problems of the post-colonial state to perpetuate Africa's, and for that matter Ghana's, subservience in international affairs. Our beef, however, is with the international behaviour of the liberal Ghanaian state. How did the shift from a dictatorial military regime to civilian governance and the unbridled adoption of liberalism in both economic and political terms affect foreign orientation? What accounts for the NDC's obsession with policy continuity both domestically and externally?

The rationale for foreign policy continuity under the NDC

The change in the mode of governance from a military dictatorship to a liberal democratic state, on the surface, would imply a dramatic shift or change in foreign policy orientation. It must be noted, however, that in any nation 'any foreign policy change must overcome normal resistance in political, administrative, and personality structures and processes' (Herman 1990: 8). Common among these opponents to change are bureaucratic inertia and standard operating procedures. It has also been argued that, invariably, 'change in established foreign policy will normally be resisted by various structural elements of government, and the greater the shift the stronger the resistance' (ibid.).

With particular reference to the NDC, the change in policy orientation with regard to issues, mode of international interactions, and the nature of international friends was not dramatic for a number of reasons. First, the PNDC out of which the NDC was born had already committed 'ideological suicide' way back in 1983 when the military regime purged its ranks of ultra-leftist socialist elements and carefully nurtured comprehensive relations with the West, especially the Bretton Woods institutions, with the sole impetus being the need for international economic bail-out. The implication, then, is that even before the formal enthronement of the liberal state in both economic and political terms in 1993, the government of the PNDC had made sure that the economic components of liberalism and liberal economic management practices were being promoted in the country. What was lacking was the political context which also came about in the wake of global transformations in the late 1980s and the purposeful imposition of political conditionalities by external development partners as the yardstick for the granting of external economic assistance to developing countries, especially those in Africa.

Second, there could not have been any dramatic change in foreign policy orientation because the transition to democracy after eleven years of dictatorship did not unleash on the Ghanaian political scene a new breed of political actors. The political elite of the new political dispensation turned out to be the same group of people who for eleven years had ruled the country with the unflinching support of the military. Since there was no political elite turnover and the same old faces paraded the corridors of power, the massive changes that normally characterize the transition of power from military dictatorship to civilian administration were never experienced in Ghana after the metamorphosis of the PNDC to the NDC. As pointed out by Gyimah-Boadi, almost all the key political officials retained their positions after the election of 1992 which was won by the NDC – a political party formed by the chairman of the PNDC. The

NDC was, therefore, the PNDC in civilian garb and 'the most influential portfolios in the first post-PNDC government, went to people affiliated with the PNDC. In fact, many retained the same ministries that they had run under the PNDC regime, while others took positions as top presidential advisers and staffers or as NDC party bosses' (Gyimah-Boadi 1999: 419). The texture of domestic politics was not changed significantly, also because the obnoxious paramilitary institutions that the military dictatorship relied upon to intimidate the populace as well as the reprehensible laws enacted by the PNDC that were an affront to the proper exercise of democratic rights were still operative, even after the transition to democracy in 1993 (Gyimah-Boadi 1990: 323–40; Boafo-Arthur 1998: 1–24). It could be argued, then, that what might have changed immediately was the type or nature of the government in place – civilian as opposed to military – but the mode of governance, to a large extent, did not reflect the freedom the populace clamoured for even though it could be said to be an improvement on what pertained under the military PNDC regime.

Third, in some cases, governments are put under pressure by organized groups such as opposing political parties and active and vibrant civil society organizations to effect changes in policy orientation. This could happen when such essential political constituents have the freedom to operate without fear of political intimidation or harassment. In other words, popular domestic opinion could influence a sensitive government to change certain policies that may be deemed inimical to the long- and short-term interests of a country. This was the case under the NDC because most civil society organizations had been emasculated before the transition to democratic governance and it took them a long time to gather momentum to engage the government with a view to influencing policy measures. For instance, people whose sympathies were with the PNDC, and ipso facto the NDC, had infiltrated the Trades Union Congress (Ninsin 1991). More significantly, the leading opposition party, the New Patriotic Party (NPP), had no solid ground to fault the international behaviour of the NDC because it favoured the neoliberal economic measures of the NDC that incidentally also underpinned the choice of international friends (Boafo-Arthur 1999: 55–8). The NDC's major headache was the reprehensible human rights record of its progenitor, the PNDC. It must be conceded, however, that there was an instance – in the case of the introduction of VAT in 1995 – when the NDC government caved in to popular agitation spearheaded largely by political opposition groups. But this concession was at the cost of the loss of life of four people who were shot in cold blood, allegedly by the paramilitary agents of the supposedly democratic government of the NDC. Thus, by and large, even though there were some changes in domestic policies and laws due to the newly found voice of civil society organizations and the vibrancy of the leading opposition party, the NPP, the international behaviour of the NDC government reflected the pragmatic approach to international interactions bequeathed to it by the PNDC. It was not surprising that the admixture of change and continuity is evident in the foreign policy orientations of the governments of the Fourth Republic, that is, the NDC and the NPP, as the following analyses of their behaviour in the international system portray.

The NDC and the international system

The euphoria that greeted the return to constitutional rule was not because Ghanaians were expecting a dramatic transformation in international interactions but because many felt it would terminate the flagrant disregard for the rights of the people in all aspects of life, political, social and economic. Such disrespect for the basic rights of the people, to a large extent, characterized the rule of the PNDC, and the international community and donor agencies ignored them because the PNDC was implementing to the letter the Bretton Woods-inspired economic management package. Aspects of infractions on the rights of the people were carried over to constitutional rule (Boafo-Arthur 2003: 73–108) and, as pointed out by Hutchful, democratization initially had a minimal effect on the management style of the NDC (Hutchful 2001: 220). Nevertheless, the NDC as the embodiment of the liberal state presented a new face to the international community and was able to make forays into the international arena, and making friends with powerful leaders in the international system such as President Clinton of the United States of America.

As far as foreign policy or international interactions were concerned, continuity rather than change was the guiding principle as noted above. There was no indication whatsoever that the return to constitutional rule and the electoral victory of the NDC in 1992 would signal a redirection of Ghana's foreign policy. As noted by Dr Obed Asamoah, the foreign minister and attorney general, 'despite the return to constitutional rule and victory for the National Democratic Congress (NDC), foreign policy direction of the country will be essentially the same' (Iliasu 1997: 89). Consequently, the NDC, like earlier governments, demonstrated its commitments to international organizations of which Ghana has membership such as the United Nations, the Commonwealth of Nations, the OAU, and sub-regional bodies such as the Economic Community of West African States (ECOWAS). Furthermore, the disintegration of the eastern bloc and the apparent inertia that gripped the Non-Aligned Movement (NAM) did not prevent the government from expressing faith in the NAM. In an address to the diplomatic corps as president-elect on 8 January 1993, Jerry Rawlings noted: 'in spite of the disappearance of bloc politics, it is our conviction that the Non-Aligned Movement is still relevant and has been more so' (ibid.: 91). This may explain why the two-day visit of President Rawlings to the United States in 1996 coincided with the visit of the security chief, Captain Kojo Tsikata, to Libya and then Cuba. In other words, even though Libya and Cuba were not in the good books of the United States, the pragmatic approach to international relations that characterized the PNDC continued under the NDC. Much attention, however, had to be focused on the West African sub-region which was virtually 'boiling' because of the crises in Liberia and the Revolutionary United Front's (RUF) insurgency in Sierra Leone.

Searching for peace in the sub-region

Liberia and Sierra Leone A major problem in the sub-region has been political instability. The main flashpoint was Liberia followed by Sierra Leone. The approach adopted by the NDC was to participate fully in finding solutions to the civil wars in the sub-region, especially in Liberia. This became mandatory on account of the election of President Rawlings as the chairman of ECOWAS in 1994 and his re-election to the post in July 1995. It could be argued also that peace in the sub-region was one of the necessary prerequisites for economic growth and development. Under his chairmanship, several peace talks on Liberia were held. The role in finding peace in Liberia led to the signing of the Akosombo and Accra Accords between the Liberian warring factions on 12 September and 13 December 1994 respectively. In his capacity as chairman of ECOWAS, President Rawlings appealed for international support especially from the United States and the European Union for the ECOWAS Monitoring Group (ECOMOG). It could be argued that through his persistent search for international support for a solution to the Liberian crisis, the United Nations in October 1995 organized a special forum on Liberia at the UN headquarters under the joint chairmanship of the UN Secretary General Boutros Boutros Ghali, Wilton Sankwaulo, chairman of the Liberian National Transitional Government, and President Rawlings. It was at this high-level meeting that the UN appealed for $110 million to cover expenses in Liberia from September 1995 to August 1996. Given the nature of the Liberian crisis, it became necessary for the UN to adjust its operational mandate in Liberia in November 1995 to incorporate the investigation of ceasefire violations, monitoring adherence to other military provisions of the peace agreements and verification of the election process.

Ghana, under President Rawlings, was also instrumental in hammering out the Abuja Accords on 19 August 1995. The positive role Ghana played in the Liberian crisis led to the granting of vehicles worth $900,000 to the Ghana armed forces to facilitate peacekeeping operations in Liberia. The visit of a three-man delegation from the US led by William Twaddel, deputy assistant secretary of state, in April 1996 and the pledge of $30 million for ECOMOG if it kept its neutrality in the Liberian crisis could be attributed, among other things, to the positive role Ghana was playing in finding solutions to that imbroglio (Iliasu 1997: 91–8).

In Sierra Leone, President Rawlings personally interacted with President Ahmed Tijan Kabbah and Foday Sankoh, the leader of the RUF. The two protagonists in the crisis paid a courtesy call on the ECOWAS chairman in April 1996 after a successful meeting between President Kabbah and Sankoh in Yamoussoukro on 23 March 1996.

Because of the government's leading role in the search for peace in Liberia and Sierra Leone, some sort of rapprochement with Togo was reached. Hitherto, the PNDC government's relations with Togo had been turbulent with accusations and counter-accusations of attempts at destabilization of each other's country.

The rest of the world Relations with the rest of the world seemed to have been underpinned by two main reasons. The first was to ensure continued western economic support for the tottering national economy. The traditional diplomacy had been overly political in nature with scant attention paid to the issue of economic interactions that would enhance national development. Importance was, therefore, attached to economic diplomacy. All international interactions appeared to be underpinned by this rationale. In respect of this, newly appointed envoys were given extensive briefings by the relevant ministries of Trade and Tourism, Information, and of course, Foreign Affairs. Working in close collaboration with the Ghana Export Promotion Council (GEPC) and the Ghana Investment Promotion Council (GIPC), foreign service personnel were equipped with the necessary training that would enhance their ability to source funds and sell Ghana abroad so as to woo several investors into the country. The creation of the Trade and Investment Bureau at the Ministry of Foreign Affairs was to facilitate this new form of diplomacy that was basically economic in orientation. Consequently, investment promotion wings were established at some of our missions such as UK, US, Singapore, Japan, South Africa and Malaysia. The government, therefore, made it clear to foreign service personnel the need to be effective agents for trade and investment in the country.

Such a policy called for an aggressive investment drive and this explains the numerous visits by President Rawlings to Japan, UK, US, Denmark, Singapore, Malaysia, etc. The main objective of these visits was to enhance trade between Ghana and such countries in line with the new policy of economic diplomacy.

The second reason was to demonstrate the continued relevance of the non-aligned movement as well as balanced international interactions. For instance, on 1 September 1995, Ghana called on the US to lift the economic blockade against Cuba. Even though the government was highly dependent on western economic support, that did not prevent the NDC government from strengthening ties with Cuba, Libya and North Korea through cooperation agreements in the areas of sports, science, health, culture and information. To some extent, the relationship, especially with acclaimed pariah regimes, was to show independence in the choice of international friends, notwithstanding the economic dependence of the country.

However, the dogged defence of Sanni Abacha's regime by President Rawlings after Nigeria's suspension by the Commonwealth and worldwide condemnation of Abacha's human rights record was contrary to international opinion. Nigeria was suspended for Abacha's gross human rights abuses, especially the execution of Ken Saro Wiwa and eight Ogoni activists in 1995. Perhaps it might have sounded odd to others for Ghana to rush to the defence of Nigeria in such a situation, but such an assertion must be balanced with the fact that Ghana depends on Nigeria for the purchase of petroleum on concessionary terms. It would have been difficult under the circumstances to overturn the apple cart and incur the displeasure of Nigeria. The best approach would have been to maintain some form of stoic silence in public over the issue alongside vigorous secret diplomacy to argue Nigeria's case.

The liberal Ghanaian state's interactions with the international community, as noted, were propelled by the national interest and it is in the area of economic diplomacy that a new approach to foreign interactions was hatched. The trail blazed by the NDC in purposive international relations with economic diplomacy as the focus is currently being followed by the NPP. That notwithstanding, there was a clear shift in approach by the NPP in other areas of international relations apart from the aggressive investment drive it has embarked upon as a ruling party.

The NPP and the international community

For the first time in the history of Ghana, there was a peaceful governmental turnover in 2000 when the NPP defeated the NDC at the polls. With their avowed liberal credentials, the question is whether the NPP is blazing a new trail in foreign policy orientation and a new form of external interactions different from those of the NDC. To what extent are the government's touted liberal-democratic credentials impacting on its external interactions? The new government rode to political power on the slogan of 'positive change', but it is debatable whether in terms of foreign policy orientation and policy formulation there has been any significant departure from the path trodden by the NDC. I am in sync with the view that the changes which have occurred during the administration of the NPP have been differences in emphasis and scope of involvement in international affairs rather than a complete reversal of thrust and objective (*Daily Graphic* 2004: 7). That there has not been any significant departure is not surprising because by the time the NDC was defeated at the polls its political ideology or philosophy was not markedly different from what the NPP espoused. Foreign policy change, as noted above, is influenced by several factors including the ideological orientation of the government. But in a world where ideological differences have diminished due to the collapse of the eastern bloc and the end of the Cold War, ideological symmetry seems to be the order of the day. More importantly, by dining with the Bretton Woods institutions, the NDC, since the U-turn of its progenitor, the PNDC, in April 1983, has been liberal in outlook especially in economic policy. Thus, in ideological terms, there was no change in outlook even though there were changes in the personnel of the state, the enhancement of engagement with the international community and well-defined intercourse with its immediate neigbours. However, the new policy of good neighbourliness espoused by the NPP was a major change from the orientation of the NDC. The nature of this policy and the continuity of relations with others in the international system are discussed below.

The policy of good neighbourliness

Good neighbourliness by words and deeds has become a major plank of NPP policy in the sub-region. This is necessary because peace is required for development and friendly relations with our neighbours, and good neighbourliness is necessary to boost the ECOWAS agenda. However, by the time of the NPP's electoral victory, the country's relations with its neighbours, especially Togo and Burkina Faso, were at an all-time low. Relations with Togo were bad because of accusations and counter-accusations of support for subversive elements being harboured by both countries. Togo had not forgotten the PNDC-sponsored abortive commando attack in 1986 with the objective of ousting Eyadema from power. For Burkina Faso, Blaise Campaore still viewed Rawlings with suspicion because of his close ties with the late Thomas Sankara who was overthrown and assassinated in a counter-coup by Campaore. The need for peace with its neighbours in order to build a vibrant and prosperous Ghana was a major aspect of the inaugural speech of President J. A. Kufuor on 7 January 2001.

It was therefore not surprising that the first foreign visit of President Kufuor was to Togo as guest of President Eyadema for the commemoration of the anniversary of the rise to power of the Togolese government. Despite criticism by the opposition, the government viewed the national interest which was premised on sub-regional peace and stability as paramount. And in any case, President Kufuor was not under any obligation to continue the antagonistic and acrimonious relationship fostered by his predecessor. And the argument that the anniversary was a commemoration of a coup that brought Eyadema into office was porous because the sole determinant here, in my view, was the national interest which calls for harmonious relations with our immediate neighbours. It is instructive to note also that the Togolese leader attended the inauguration of Kufuor.

Since then, there have been several visits to more countries in the sub-region including Nigeria, Côte d'Ivoire and Senegal. Ghana under the NPP has continued with the search for peace in Liberia and Côte d'Ivoire. Peace is regarded as a prerequisite for economic development. The search for peace was deepened when President Kufuor was made the chairman of ECOWAS in 2003 and was re-elected in 2004. More especially, ties with Nigeria have been strengthened and, apart from the presence of the President of Nigeria, General Olusegun Obasanjo, at the inauguration of President Kufuor, there have been several visits between them and close cooperation in the search for peace and stability in West Africa.

Consequently, Nigeria has been a big benefactor to Ghana and provided credit facilities to enable the country to purchase cars to revamp the operations of the Ghana Police Service. Nigeria, again, has provided a soft loan facility of $40 million to enable Ghana to pay for its share capital for the West African gas pipeline (WAGP). The WAGP has drawn Nigeria, Benin, Togo and Ghana into a cooperative agreement to tap gas from the vast reserves of Nigeria for the use of the countries involved in the project.

Visits to Burkina Faso in March and Benin in April 2001 were meant to cement relations between the countries. The visit to Burkina Faso led to the revival of the Permanent Joint Commission for Cooperation which had been in limbo since the death of Captain Thomas Sankara. Even though the visit to Benin was for the inauguration of President Kerekou, the Ghanaian president had fruitful discussions with his counterpart on the need for peace, security and stability in the sub-region in order to enhance regional cooperation and economic development.

The role of the government in finding solutions to the seemingly intractable crisis in Côte d'Ivoire is epitomized by President Kufuor's participation in the Marcoussis Accord signed in France and in several meetings in Accra. The crisis is still simmering not because of dearth of diplomatic attempts

241

by President Kufuor, as chairman of ECOWAS, to resolve it, but, among other reasons, because of the intransigence and entrenched positions that have been taken by President Laurent Gbagbo and the rebels who are now called the New Forces.

To make Ghana's presence strongly felt in the sub-region, new missions were opened. These include a mission in landlocked Mali in order to enhance the utilization of Ghana's ports facilities by Mali. The government has also reopened the country's diplomatic mission in Senegal to facilitate, among other things, the provision of consular services to Ghanaians resident in that country and the Gambia. Similarly, a consulate was opened in Equatorial Guinea where there are migrant Ghanaian workers. Ghana has also entered into bilateral agreement with Equatorial Guinea to make it possible for Ghana to process that country's crude oil.

In sum, the NPP government has successfully charted a vibrant subregional policy that has enhanced the country's reputation both as a peaceful country and a peace-maker in the sub-region. Since the government won a second term in office after the 7 December 2004 elections, the hope is that the positive relations being pursued in the sub-region will be sustained to facilitate economic development.

The rest of Africa The NPP government has continued the positive relations with the rest of Africa with visits by President Kufuor to South Africa, Libya, Morocco and Zambia, among others. Some of the visits were in connection with OAU/African Union meetings which the president capitalized upon to discuss bilateral issues of importance to Ghana's development. The state visit to Morocco from 15 to 18 May 2001 led to the signing of a Joint Commission for Cooperation after exhaustive bilateral discussions in areas including tourism, fisheries, mining and communications. The agreement to reopen embassies in the respective capitals of the two countries crowned the discussions. The president's first visit to South Africa was in connection with the World Economic Forum, 6–8 June 2001. The president had positive bilateral discussions with President Thabo Mbeki which led to the reversal of South Africa's decision to withdraw a credit facility of US $16 million to Ghana. Restoration of this line of credit was important for the procurement of equipment for the Ghana Police Service.

Libya has been a constant factor in Ghana's African relations, especially since 31 December 1981 when the PNDC came to power. The cosy relations were as a result of the alleged support the Libyan head of state, Muammar Gaddafi, gave to Rawlings to stage the 1981 coup. Officially, the relationship had been upbeat because of other forms of assistance the Libyan government gave to the PNDC regime, especially concessionary terms for Libyan crude oil. There was also some level of ideological affinity because of the revolutionary credentials of both Gaddafi and Rawlings.

Of course, Rawlings 'converted' reluctantly to liberal democracy and there appeared to be frostiness in Ghana–Libya relations but the ideological cord between Rawlings and Gaddafi was not completely cut. The self-proclaimed liberal-democratic government headed by President Kufuor was faced with the dilemma of either reinvigorating relations with Libya or abandoning the existing relations, and the government opted for the former. The president, therefore, took his chance at the 5th Extraordinary Session of the OAU, 1–2 March 2001, at Sirte to rekindle and strengthen relations with Libya. This was to ensure that the change of government would not have a negative impact on the existing relations. Ghana obtained the needed good-will for the supply of crude oil from Libya on concessionary terms. Since then, there have been positive relations between the two countries.

Ghana was not party to the origination of the New Partnership for Africa's Development (NEPAD); nevertheless, its strong role in the implementation of this development blueprint has been acknowledged by other African countries and the international community at large. Ghana was the first to accede to the African Peer Review Mechanism (APRM), thus becoming a trail-blazer in the strengthening of good political and corporate governance in Africa. Its strong role in the implementation of NEPAD is underpinned by the economic benefits to be derived from it and by the national quest for rapid economic development. Ghana's role to date explains why President Kufuor, among four others, was invited to participate in the G8 Summit at Sea Island in the US in June 2004.

In sum, relations with the rest of Africa have been very cordial and the NPP government has made a positive impact as the government continues to demonstrate unflinching commitment to good governance in particular and democratic ethos in general. Such commitment was underscored by the country's need to tackle its dire economic problems and this has also defined its relations with the wider international community.

The NPP and the wider international community[1]

It is apparent that the NPP government has paid much attention to international interactions in the West African sub-region because national development depends on peace and stability in the sub-region. However, this has not obscured the importance of relations with the wider international community, especially with the G8, the Bretton Woods institutions, China and other key bilateral partners in Europe and the Arab world.

Foreign policy

243

Incontrovertibly, Ghana needs the support of members of the G8 and the other development partners more than they need Ghana. The dire economic straits of the country underpin the need for the strengthening of relations with the wider international community. The NPP government has therefore gone to great lengths to deepen relations with the members of the Organization for Economic Cooperation and Development (OECD). A good barometer of such close relations was the invitation to the president to attend the Sea Island Summit of the G8.

Relations with Great Britain, US, Germany, Japan, France and Canada, among the G8 members, seem to have reached a higher level than before with official visits by the president to most of these countries. Such visits and reciprocal visits by Prime Minister Tony Blair of Britain and Chancellor Schroeder of Germany culminated in the signing of several bilateral agreements, granting of loans and writing off of debts owed by Ghana to some of the countries. It must be stressed that the mode of relations with the wider international community has been influenced extensively by the government's official adoption of economic diplomacy as a necessary, unavoidable and quintessential diplomatic tool. Even though such commitments to fundamental economic issues in the international system are not novel, the demonstrated dedication to economic diplomacy by the NPP government is unparalleled in the history of the nation.

On 26 June 2001, President Kufuor was invited to the US for a four-day working visit. This coincided with visits by Presidents Abdoulaye Wade of Senegal and Alpha Oumar Konare of Mali. The US dubbed this a 'mini-summit' and discussions centred on strengthening democratic governance, support for NEPAD, the African Growth and Opportunity Act (AGOA), the instability in West Africa and its attendant security implications. President Bush's invitation to President Kufuor highlighted US support for the new NPP administration. There have been other visits in connection with UN activities that were utilized for discussions with high-ranking officials in the US government.

An eight-day state visit to France by the president from 29 November to 6 December 2001 was highly fruitful in that it came in the wake of Ghana's adoption of the highly indebted poor countries (HIPC) initiative and the inclusion of Ghana within the 'Priority Solidarity Zone' by France. The visit culminated in the signing of two agreements. The first was an agreement for a French Development Agency (AFD) concessionary loan of €11.4 million basically for the construction of roads and bridges in rural areas. The second was the HIPC initiative cut-off point and economic issues thereafter. By this agreement, the Paris Club agreed to forgive all credit extended to Ghana between July 1983 and 20 June 1999. The G8 was also expected to implement a 100 per cent write-off of Ghana's debts from the cut-off date of the HIPC initiative.

There have also been state visits by the president to Germany, Canada and Japan at the invitation of the leaders of these countries. In between such visits were other high-level visits by government officials to various western countries with reciprocal visits. A visit to Italy and the Vatican from 8 to 13 June 2002 was in connection with the World Food Summit and the Third Meeting of the NEPAD Heads of State Implementation Committee. These visits also yielded several economic benefits to the nation. For instance, a visit to Bonn at the invitation of Chancellor Gerhard Schroeder in June 2002 led to the conversion of a debt of US $6,745,000 owed by Ghana to the former German Democratic Republic into relief under the HIPC initiative. Similarly, an invitation by the Canadian Prime Minister Jean Chrétien in November 2001 gave President Kufuor an opportunity to highlight Ghana's zeal to garner G8 support for NEPAD and the strengthening of Canada's advocacy role at the G8 for African interests. Significantly, Canada was about to assume the chairmanship of the G8.

Relations with Japan, without doubt, have assumed a very high profile. This is important because of the hullabaloo that characterized the government's adoption of the HIPC initiative. One of the arguments used by government critics was that Japanese aid would be cut off because of the adoption of the HIPC initiative. On the contrary, Japan has improved its assistance to Ghana in diverse ways. The US $80 million grant for the reconstruction of the Mallam–Kasoa–Yamoransa road stands out. This is a key road network that falls within the ECOWAS super-highway project.

In line with the promise of cancelling debts on Ghana's attainment of the HIPC completion point, several western countries, such as Canada, Norway and Germany, have written off parts of Ghana's debts. The Japanese government has cancelled debts totalling US $1.01 billion. And according to Kazuko Asai, the Japanese ambassador to Ghana, this cancellation was possible because through the enhanced HIPC initiative, the government has adopted a disciplined economic management approach with the objective of achieving macroeconomic stability, growth and poverty reduction. Japan was further influenced by the prudent utilization of HIPC funds and the measures adopted by the government to reduce external and domestic debts (*Daily Graphic*: 2001).

In addition to the members of the G8, the NPP government has also strengthened relations with other European countries, especially Spain and the Nordic/Scandinavian countries, as well as China. The president's two visits to Spain were in connection with the annual general meeting of the African Development Fund and the Conference on Democratic Transition and Consolidation held in May and October 2001 respectively. Highly successful discussions between His Majesty King Juan Carlos and Prime Minister Mario Aznar led to the granting of a US $40 million soft loan and a promise of another soft loan of US $120 million on condition that the former loan was applied transparently and successfully. The loan was to be used for the improvement of the cardiothoracic unit at the Korle-Bu Teaching Hospital and the completion of the maternity block at the Okomfo Anokye Teaching Hospital in Kumasi, as well as for the improvement of the water supply system in the Eastern Region. The University of Development Studies and some polytechnics also benefited from the loan facility. The fruitful discussions with the Spanish government were crowned with an agreement to open a diplomatic mission in Madrid to boost economic diplomacy and enhance the government's 'golden age of business' policy.

The government has also stepped up relations with China and there have been several exchanges of high-profile visits by ministers and businessmen on both sides since the NPP took over. This explains the granting of a US $150 million loan facility by Alcatel-Shanghai Bell (ASB) to Ghana Telecom and the expression of interest by Sino Hydro Corporation in Ghana's Bui hydro-electric project. China funded the military and police barracks project which was handed over to Ghana in February 2004.[2]

South–South cooperation has not been ignored by the NPP government. In line with this, the president and high-level entrepreneurs or business executives went to Malaysia on what was termed a 'learning mission' from 1 to 4 August 2002. Apart from cementing South–South cooperation, the government was anxious to clear up a business dispute between Ghana Telecom and Telecom Malaysia to facilitate cordial relations, since Ghana has a lot to learn from Malaysia's rapid development. The visit also afforded the opportunity to President Kufuor and his entourage to participate in the Langkawi Smart Partnership International Dialogue which is an informal platform for world leaders, the private sector, the media, youth, NGOs, labour, etc., to discuss various challenges to Third World development.

The long-standing relationship with India also received a boost from the NPP government after a four-day state visit by the president at the invitation of the Indian prime minister. New areas of cooperation between the two countries were mapped out and this led to the conclusion of four protocols as follows:

- Memorandum of Understanding (MoU) on the establishment of an ICT Centre of Excellence in Accra
- Bilateral Investment Promotion and Protection Agreement

- Cultural Exchange Programme Agreement, 2002–05
- Protocol for consultations between the Ministries of Foreign Affairs of Ghana and India

In sum, the NPP government has ensured continuity in existing relations between Ghana and the international community but the aggressive pursuit of economic diplomacy since its inception into office is a marked departure from its predecessor. In other words, the government elevated economic diplomacy to a higher level than it had had in earlier dispensations. This was unavoidable given the economic and developmental problems the government is contending with.

President Kufuor has often been accused by his political opponents of excessive travelling since he assumed office. This raises the question as to whether such travels were necessary. I believe they were, for a variety of reasons. First, the new government that made history by being the first in Ghana to dislodge a sitting government through democratic elections had to advertise itself in the international system as a result of the long reign of the P/NDC. For nineteen years Rawlings and his team ruled Ghana, first as a dictator for eleven years and as a pseudo-democrat for two terms of four years each. Since the old order had changed, the new rulers had to let the world know their mettle; this could not be achieved simply by sitting in Accra and issuing memoranda. Second, the dire economic state of the country at the time the new administration assumed office necessitated a personal touch to national problems. Visits to the western world and counterparts in the South were aimed to highlight the developmental problems of the nation on a one-to-one basis with the leaders of other countries, especially those countries to whom Ghana is heavily indebted. Direct discussions with such leaders were more meaningful than the dispatches the embassies and high commissions of such countries would send to their home governments. Third, successful diplomacy and especially the stress on economic diplomacy by the NPP government were oftentimes contingent on the cultivation of personal relationships and lasting friendships with other leaders. Throughout history, this mode of cementing relations between countries has yielded more fruitful results than reliance on even high-level diplomats. And, of course, this mode was more imperative because of the long rule of the P/NDC and the severe economic crisis the government inherited.

Conclusion

Several factors account for the international behaviour of nations. Whether there should be a change in the foreign policy orientation of a country or not equally depends on several variables not the least of which is the economic strength of the nation. In the Ghanaian case, the jettisoning of the initial Marxist-Leninists or socialist orientation for a free market economy and the transition from dictatorship to democracy by the PNDC had all been underpinned by the dire economic realities. Since liberal democracy had been embraced, the governmental turnover in 2000 was destined not to witness any significant change in foreign policy orientation. This was because there was only a thin line of demarcation between the worldview of the P/NDC and the NPP.

However, their differences in the perception of the means to national development led to the NPP placing a stronger emphasis on economic diplomacy than had its predecessor government. This necessitated an aggressive approach to international interactions and the direct personal involvement of the president in efforts to woo investors to the country. This diplomatic mode has led to various forms of assistance to the government such as grants, conversion of loans to grants, and the cancellation of foreign debts owed to some major debtors. At the same time, new diplomatic missions such as those in Spain and Morocco were opened and new theatres for international engagements were explored, leading to the signing of various protocols with different countries.

The distinctive commitment to good neighbourliness by the NPP government in contra-distinction to the P/NDC is a clear departure or change in policy orientation in the sub-region. Nevertheless, both demonstrated vigour and commitment to the sustenance of peace in the sub-region. This is underlined by the fact that both ex-President Rawlings and President Kufuor had two terms as chairman of ECOWAS at periods of high tensions and manifest instability in the sub-region.

It stands to reason to state that elements of change and continuity in foreign policy orientation are intertwined. And with the end of the ideological polarization between the East and the West, a total change in policy orientation occasioned by the different ideology of an incoming regime may not be explicit. Nevertheless, a different emphasis will continue to be placed on international issues at any point in time, depending on the needs of the nation.

Notes

1 Most of the information in this section, especially on issues concerning the visits of the President of the Republic of Ghana, H.E. John Agyekum Kufuor, were distilled from an undated write-up titled 'Visits Abroad Undertaken by the President' obtained from the Ministry of Foreign Affairs, Accra.

2 See Review of Bilateral Relations between Ghana and China, Ministry of Foreign Affairs (no date).

Sources

Ahiakpor, J. C. W. (1985) 'The Success and Failure of Dependency Theory: The Experience of Ghana', *International Organisation*, Vol. 39, no. 3 (Summer): 534–52.

Boafo-Arthur, K. (1998) 'Structural Adjustment Programs (SAPS) in Ghana: Interrogating PNDC's Implementation', *Journal of African Policy Studies*, Vol. 4, nos 2 and 3: 1–24.

— (1999a) 'Ghana: Structural Adjustment, Democratization, and the Politics of Continuity', *African Studies Review*, Vol. 42, no. 2 (September): 41–72.

— (1999b) 'Ghana's Politics of International Economic Relations Under the PNDC, 1982–1992', *African Studies Monographs*, Vol. 20, no. 2 (Kyoto University).

— (2003) 'Emerging Democracies and Their Impact on Human Rights', in B. Sam (ed.), *Contemporary Human Rights Issues in Commonwealth West Africa* (Accra: Commonwealth Human Rights Initiative/Commonwealth Foundation of UK).

Daily Graphic (2001) 8 November.

— (2004) 24 August.

Gyimah-Boadi, E. (1990) 'Economic Recovery and Politics in PNDC's Ghana', *Journal of Commonwealth and Comparative Politics*, Vol. 28, no. 3: 323–40.

— (1999) 'Ghana: The Challenges of Consolidating Democracy', in R. Joseph (ed.), *State, Conflict, and Democracy in Africa* (Boulder, CO and London: Lynne Rienner).

Herman, C. F. (1990) 'Changing Course: When Governments Choose to Redirect Foreign Policy', *International Studies Quarterly*, Vol. 34, no. 1 (March).

Hoffman, S. (1989) 'What Should We Do in the World?', *Atlantic Monthly* (October).

Hutchful, E. (2001) *Ghana's Adjustment Experience: The Paradox of Reform* (Geneva: UNRISD).

Iliasu, A. M. (1997) *The Behaviour of States: Continuity and Change in Ghana's Foreign Policy, 1982–1996*, Unpublished MA dissertation, Legon Centre for International Affairs.

Kegley, C. W. Jr and E. R. Wittkopf (1981) *World Politics: Trend and Transformation* (New York: St Martin's Press).

Macleod, A. (2002) *Civil Society and Foreign Policy Making in Liberal Democracies*, Paper prepared for the 43rd Annual Convention of the International Studies Association, New Orleans, Louisiana: 'Dissolving Boundaries: The Nexus Between Comparative Politics and International Relations', 24–27 March; see <www.isanet.org/noarchive/macleod.html>, accessed 21 December 2003.

Ninsin, K. A. (1991) 'The Impact of the PNDC's Economic Reform Policies on Ghanaian Society and Politics, 1983–1988', *Legon Journal of Humanities*, Vol. 5.

Foreign policy

Organization of African Unity (2001) *The New Partnership for African Development* (NEPAD) (October).

Sullivan, M. (1976) *International Relations: Theories and Evidence* (Englefield Cliffs, NJ: Prentice Hall).

Toffler, A. (1970) *Future Shock* (New York: Bantam Books).

Tuchman, B. W. (1980) 'Is This the Summer of 1914?', *Washington Post*, 11 May.

Waltz, K. N. (1979) *Theory of International Politics* (Reading, MA: Addison-Wesley).

11 | Women and politics in Ghana, 1993–2003

BEATRIX ALLAH-MENSAH

Political behaviour includes people's participation in electoral politics, running for office and lobbying. This has propelled some political analysts to advocate strategies to transform politics in general and democracy in particular to ensure more equity in the processes and outcomes if democracy is to exhibit its liberal character and bring about more inclusiveness. It is perhaps for this reason that the general secretary of the Commonwealth remarked that 'issues of peace, governance and democracy, and socio-economic development cannot be divorced from those of gender equality'.[1] Reiterating this stance on equality, the executive secretary of the Economic Commission for Africa identified six challenges facing citizens' participation. These included the nurturing of democracy and the challenge of mainstreaming women in politics and public administration.

These explain why women's participation in the front line of democracy, peace and reconstruction efforts continues to gain recognition, leading to efforts by governments, political institutions, multilateral institutions, complemented by civil society organizations (CSOs), and individuals to realize these potentials.

There is no gainsaying the fact that such efforts have, to some extent, positively changed the perception, acceptance and role of women in politics. The truth, however, is that the number of women in politics is still below expectation. Consequently, there is much to be done to ensure that women contribute to the political, social and economic enhancement of their nations and communities.

This chapter looks at the role of women in the political arena and their impact, if any, over the past decade of democratization. It focuses on four key issues. First, it addresses the historical and current trends that have influenced women's participation in Ghanaian politics. Second, it looks at the contribution of women to the evolving democratic process that set the democratic ball rolling in 1993. Third, attention is given to women in local government politics. Fourth, the study focuses on political parties and their impact through their manifestoes and activities, if any, on women's participation in the democratic and political process. In the fifth segment, the chapter discusses the outcome of Election 2000 results in terms of the performance of women by political parties and how the number of women in parliament is actually reflected at committee level where many of the key political and socio-economic issues are debated; it also reflects on the role of civil society organizations.

The low representation of women in both numbers and substance in politics exerts pressure in two directions. First, it places significant stress on the few women in such positions who must carry a huge burden of making an impact with widespread positive implications for the majority; and, second, such situations contribute to lengthening the time taken for authorities to act, since the few women in such positions need to reiterate their points and claims more forcefully than their male counterparts. In other words, it takes longer for authorities to listen to and act effectively on the demands of women in politically powerful positions.

Women and politics, 1956–66

Women made significant contributions to politics in the pre- and post-independence era. The role of women was evident in their support of the Convention People's Party (CPP); it is on record that women traders were keen supporters of the CPP government, which in turn offered financial assistance and supportive services. The women's section of the party, according to Tsikata (1989), was largely responsible for the development of the women's wing of the party and also for the youth organization. The party leadership therefore institutionalized this initiative by making constitutional provisions for a women's league at branch and ward levels as the main organizing framework for women in the party. It was therefore not surprising that the party gave credit to women for the internal solidarity, cohesion and success of the CPP. Manu records that women were efficient organizers who could bring thousands of people together for a rally at very short notice (Manu 1991: 110).

These skills went beyond the confines of the party and spread to other political organizations involving women: viz, the formation of women's groups, inter alia, the Ghana Women's League (GWL), the Ghana Federation of Women (GFW) and later the National Council of Ghana Women (NCGW) in 1960 (Tsikata 1989: 77). Indeed, it is noted that the NCGW and other groups were systematically and strategically co-opted into the CPP and given party membership cards as the only valid membership cards. Even though there was a very high level of politicization in the formation and subsequent co-optation of the women's groups, it was nevertheless a good beginning.

The prelude to independence, however, saw some slight but significant changes. Traditionally, Ghanaian women have a long history of organization. Tsikata traces the involvement of women in economic activities and their fight for equality on the economic front as well as their involvement in the political affairs of the nation, particularly between 1951 and 1966 (ibid.: 79). Thus, with the attainment of independence, many keen social observers expected some changes in the role of women in the political economy, particularly because of their dogged contribution to the process of decolonization through the CPP.

Upon the attainment of self-government in 1957, the party rewarded women for their hard work, resilience and contribution to the independence struggle. According to Tamale: 'an assessment of the CPP government's policies towards women has noted that it consciously encouraged the participation of women in politics and public life with the result that a few women held high political offices as members of parliament, deputy ministers and district commissioners, and that these were not acts of tokenism, but a recognition of their abilities' (Tamale 1999: 23). In consonance with this, Ghana is noted for being one of the first African countries to introduce a quota system for women – in 1960 the CPP passed a law allowing for the nomination and election of ten women to the National Assembly.

While this was a marked departure from the existing status quo, there was still much more to be done to ensure an effective representation of women in politics and other equally important sectors. There was an expectation that an increase in the number of women would run in tandem with the progress towards the consolidation of independence and the nurturing of democracy within a liberal environment. Any progress, however, suffered a setback with the onslaught of democratic disruptions and subsequent successive and intermittent coups d'etat. Such a hopeful beginning was not given the needed nurturing, as deterioration in the political climate did not augur well for the systematic and sustained development of women's participation in national politics. This corroborates Zakaria's stance that while constitutional liberalism could lead to democracy, it was not always the case that democracy brings about constitutional liberalism (Fareed 1997).

The period of democratic disengagement

Ghana experienced political and economic hiccups with the first military coup that overthrew the CPP government in 1966. From 1966 until the elections in 1992, Ghana's political economy experienced what might be described as uncomfortable and non-progressive political exchanges between the military and civilian governments. This unstable political and economic climate affected not only the political economy but also social integration and the building up of social capital, the basis for social group formation.

In addition, by its very nature and formation, the military system was not very gender-sensitive and hence had very few women in the ranks. In fact, there is no record of any woman taking up or being offered a political position in any of the military regimes except the Provisional National Defence Council (PNDC) regime. This is indicative of the fact that military regimes in Ghana were not only averse to women's political participation but also largely inhibited women's full contribution to the development of politics and administration. The only regime that tried to change this perception of the military and women's participation was the PNDC government, which ruled the country between 1981 and 1992.

The Provisional National Defence Council and women in Ghana, 1982–92 The Provisional National Defence Council (PNDC) government is so far the longest ruling government in the history of Ghana. Under this government a prototype of Nkrumah's co-optation strategy took place through the formation of the 31 December Women's Movement (31 DWM). While members of the movement vouch for its political neutrality and independence from the ruling PNDC government, it was evidently clear that such an image was only a public relations showpiece.

The 31 DWM engaged in a number of mobilization efforts that gave some women a level of respite from economic challenges by creating an environment in which they could engage in certain economic activities, albeit minimal. Gari processing machines were provided to some women's groups to enhance their economic status. Although these activities have been lauded in some circles for (arguably) opening up the economic and the political space for women, they have equally been challenged as exhibiting all the negative tendencies of politicization, which does not augur well for Ghanaian women who would have taken advantage of the offered opportunity.

Nevertheless, there is ample evidence supporting the fact that many of the women who contested and won the district-level elections held in 1988, and subsequently the 1992 general elections, were all politically connected to the movement. It was therefore not surprising that the majority of the women parliamentarians in the first parliament of the Fourth Republic were National Democratic Congress (NDC) members with strong links to the 31 DWM. In other words, the 31 DWM created some political opportunities for women's participation in politics at the local and national level; albeit in an undemocratic and politically restrictive environment.

Consequently, it is not far from the truth to state that successive coups d'etat since 1966, which overthrew legitimately elected governments, dragged down with them this rare opportunity for women to participate in politics. Military regimes and women's political participation are certainly incompatible. Put differently, intermittent and politically disruptive military interventions were the final straw against women's efforts and attempts at meaningful participation in politics. These unpleasant political exchanges between military and civil administrations, which started in 1966, came to a somewhat hopeful end after the longest military regime responded to internal and external pressures for a return to democratic governance in early 1990.

Women and the constitution-making process, 1991–92 In Ghana, the commencement of a new era of democratization in the early 1980s is connected with the establishment and work of the National Commission for Democracy (NCD). The NCD was set up by PNDC Law 42 in 1982. Section 32 of the law requires the NCD to perform the functions of an electoral commission (EC) and to help in developing a programme for a more effective realization of democracy in Ghana. In addition, it educated Ghanaians on the objectives of revolutionary transformation and on the need to assess and identify those limitations to the achievement of democracy that might be due to existing inequalities, thus enabling the government to address them (Ninsin 1996: 98; Bluwey 1998: 103-4).

After series of regional fora, the NCD presented its report on the uncompromising demand of Ghanaians for a return to constitutional rule, leading to the promulgation of the PNDC Law 252 and the setting up of the Committee of Experts. The Committee of Experts was to draft a constitution for the Fourth Republic. Section 4 of the Law provided that the committee 'shall in its deliberations' take into account the following:

1. The Report of the National Commission for Democracy of 25 March 1991, on 'Evolving a True Democracy'.
2. The abrogated constitutions of Ghana of 1957, 1960, 1969 and 1979 and any other constitutions.
3. Such other matters relating to proposals for a draft constitution as the Council may refer to it.
4. Any other matter, which in the opinion of the Committee is 'reasonably related to the foregoing'.

The membership of the Committee of Experts appointed by the PNDC attracted little criticism from the general public, although some suggested that the term 'experts' did not really reflect the composition of the membership. Out of nine committee members, only two were women. This affected issues of particular relevance to women, even when the two women were assertive and some of the male members were liberal gender advocates.

In spite of this, there were references to issues that had to consider gender as a factor. For instance, the committee recommended that a council of ministers be appointed on the basis of special expertise, experience and equitable regional and gender representation. In a rather comprehensive exposition, the committee laid emphasis on women's rights to cover issues such as debilitating customary practices, female circumcision, maternity issues, property rights, guaranteed equal conditions of work and equal representation and participation of women and men on boards and in appointments to public positions. It should be noted that these comprehensive expositions of the rights of women were watered down in the 1992 Constitution, which was debated by a consultative assembly which had more women members than the Committee of Experts.

However, in its proposed criteria for the composition of a Council of State, the committee did not exhibit the same gender awareness, recommending a council that would be national and non-partisan in character, consisting of eminent personalities selected on the basis of experience, expertise, competence and sensitivity to national unity. The Council of State was expected to help in ensuring responsible and democratic governance and fidelity to the basic tenets of constitutionalism, effective government, stability and national harmony. One can infer that, by not recognizing gender as an important factor in the composition of the membership of the proposed Council of State, the committee implied that it was not essential to the achievement of effective, democratic government, stability and national harmony; an implication which is problematic for the running of democracy.

Women and the Consultative Assembly The Consultative Assembly (CA) was established under PNDC Law 253, 1991, and inaugurated on 26 August 1991, to formulate the final constitutional document using the report of the Committee of Experts as the basis for its deliberations. During its inauguration, the then chairman of the PNDC government, Flight Lieutenant Jerry John Rawlings, was emphatic that the responsibility of the CA was not to the government of the PNDC, but first and foremost to the generality of both current and future citizens of the country. More significantly, he made reference both to the contribution of women to the socio-economic development and dynamics of Ghanaian society and to the importance the Committee of Experts had given to the status of women, urging the CA to consider measures that would enhance equality of opportunity and participation in social and political decision-making processes (Ninsin, 1996: 119, 123–4).

The membership of the CA was an interesting one from a gender perspective. Prior to its establishment (according to Ninsin), when rural support proved inadequate, the PNDC government turned to urban informal sector agents. As a result, in 1990 it sponsored the formation and registration of over thirty informal organizations. From this, the only exclusively women's organizations, by inference, were the Hairdressers' Association of Ghana and the Chop Bar Keepers' and Cooked Food Sellers' Association. On the other hand, the only groups that did not have women as members, also by inference, were the National Garage Owners' Association, Refrigeration and Air Conditioning Workshop Owners' Association, the Ghana Gold and Silver Smiths' Association, the Radio and Television Repairers' Association, the Butchers' Association and the Video Operations Association.

Most notably, the CA had 121 members drawn from sixty-two identifiable groups, including those mentioned above, previously regarded as non-political. Other women's groups represented included the National Council on Women and Development (NCWD) then controlled by the 31 DWM Women's Movement which alone had ten seats (Bluwey 1998).

The number of seats allocated to the NCWD and the 31 DWM was both politically and culturally significant. From a political standpoint, the latter was the undeclared wing of the PNDC government and so its presence and that of other identifiable groups indicated a bias in favour of the government. Much more significantly, the inclusion of women's groups, from the hairdressers and dressmakers to the chop bar operators and the NCWD, was an important landmark for women in Ghanaian politics, especially under a military regime. This statement is more significant when it is considered against the backdrop of representatives of more 'intellectual' groups like the Ghana Bar Association (GBA), the National Union of Ghana Students (NUGS), the Christian Council (CC), the Catholic Bishops Conference (CBC) and the University Teachers' Association of Ghana (UTAG), which were allocated only one seat each (ibid.).

If numbers are anything to go by, then women were better represented in comparison with the other groups mentioned above. Nevertheless, the participation of women in the Consultative Assembly deliberations was not commensurate with their numerical strength. A member of the CA recalls that though there were some women who were very vocal and made significant contributions to discussions, the majority did not perform to expectations. This, indeed, has implications for the content and outcome of the Constitution with regard to women's issues and concerns.

Women and local-level politics in Ghana, 1988–2002

The local government system in Ghana is central to government's efforts at developing the country and balancing the administrative machinery. In 1988, the then ruling government of the Provisional National Defence Council (PNDC) embarked on an ambitious overhaul of the existing local government system. These changes were far-reaching and affected not only the conceptual basis but also the practice of decentralization in the country. For women, these changes were critical because of the element of flexibility embedded in the new system, its non-partisan nature and the argument that local government administra tion offers better opportunities for women to participate in politics.

The decentralization policy and the legal framework make the 110 district assemblies (DAs) the highest political, administrative, legislative and deliberative organs at the district level, and they are therefore charged with the onerous duty of ensuring development in an atmosphere of peace in their respective jurisdictions. The system is made up of four-tier metropolitan and three-tier municipal DAs. Each of these is constituted by 70 per cent elected and 30 per cent nominated members, with a presiding member (PM) and an overall administrative metropolitan, municipal or district chief executive (MCE or DCE). These are supported by the work of sub-committees.

The elected positions are keenly contested, though without the party political furore characteristic of general elections because the system is (controversially) non-partisan. It was within the elected positions that women's performance would subsequently be analysed. As part of the efforts to establish institutions, some DAs created Women in Development sub-committees. Where assemblies could not elect an adequate number of women, the government nominated women as government appointees shore up their number (Brown et al. 1996).

Since 1988, the performance of women in politics at the local level has recorded some steady but slow progress in the number of women contestants and the number of those who actually win. Although these numbers are not significant, they do offer some modicum of hope for women's political participation at the local level and a foretaste of what will happen at the national level as more women are elected and gain the necessary experience.

Brown et al. placed the position of women in the local government system in the public domain through their examination of the subject. Their study also sought to analyse the factors affecting the extent of women's participation and to design appropriate strategies for the enhancement of women's political rights. Since then, there have been integrated studies

TABLE 11.1 Readiness to vote for a woman generally considered capable

Would you vote for a woman generally considered capable to represent you in the DA?

		Frequency	(%)	Valid (%)	Cumulative (%)
Valid	Yes	1,518	85.4	86.2	86.2
	No	243	13.7	13.8	100.0
	Total	1,761	99.1	100.0	
Missing	System	16	0.9		
	Total	16	0.9		
Total		1,777	100.0		

Source: Department of Political Science, 2002 District Level Elections Survey Data in Allah-Mensah 2003.

on women in public life generally, including the performance of women in local government administration.

Brown et al. reiterated that women's political participation has a link with the effectiveness of their political activities and their ability to make an impact on local political establishments and communities, and to give direction through their involvement in policy- and decision-making (ibid.: 21). The study reported opinions about women's participation in politics. Some of the respondents believed that women were ineffective in politics, that they should not rub shoulders with men politically and should remain home-makers. They supported this by arguing that women were not firm in making decisions and implementing policies. On the other hand, another set of respondents opined that women could function as a unifying force in local politics, and a third group confirmed the need for the empowerment of women in spite of the traditional setting and cultural demands (ibid.: 22).

Interestingly, the outcome of surveys conducted by the Department of Political Science of the University of Ghana, Legon, for the 2002 district-level elections showed a strong indication towards a positive shift in the perception of women's participation in politics, not only as a unifying force but also as part of the nurturing culture needed to humanize democracy and subsequently consolidate it.

The 2002 district-level elections offer some interesting results on these issues. Asked whether they would readily vote for a woman generally considered as capable, 86 per cent of 1,761 respondents were more ready to vote for a woman who is adjudged capable of performing (see Table 11.1).

The dilemma here is that many of those who expressed the desire to vote

TABLE 11.2 Society's perception of the capacity of men and women in the political arena

Do you think that women are as capable as men in political leadership roles?

		Frequency	(%)	Valid (%)	Cumulative (%)
Valid	Yes	1,222	68.8	69.5	69.5
	No	356	20.0	20.3	87.7
	Don't know	181	10.2	10.3	100.0
	Total	1,759	99.0	100.0	
Missing	System	18	1.0		
	Total	18	1.0		
Total		1,777	100.0		

Source: Department of Political Science, 2002 District Level Elections Survey Data in Allah-Mensah 2003.

for a woman candidate did not have the chance to prove their commitment because in most of the electoral areas there were no women candidates. This was closely followed by a question on how the public perceived the capacity and capabilities of men and women (see Table 11.2).

The above data testify to respondents' (69.5 per cent) certainty that women are as capable of taking leadership roles or positions as men. In a similar vein, respondents believed that women had an equal chance of being elected as assemblywomen (see Table 11.3): over 54 per cent of respondents expressed this view while 34.6 per cent disagreed.

Those who felt that women had an equal chance with men said that provided a woman could do the job, they would give her the needed support. These sentiments have been translated into some level of action but not to an appreciable level. Since 1994, the number of women candidates at the district level has witnessed a modest increase (See Table 11.3).

TABLE 11.3 Number of women contestants and elected at the district level, 1994–2002

Year	1994	1998	2002
No. of women contestants	348	580	981
No. of winners	94	199	368
% of total	27	34	38

Source: Adapted from Allah-Mensah 2003, p. 149.

As much as one may want to be sceptical about the very small increases in the actual numbers of women, it is important to note that, because of the chequered history of democratic politics in Ghana, there are reasons to be hopeful since the number of women who expressed an interest in politics at both the national and local levels increases after each election. With education, commitment, determination and the support of those women already occupying key positions in the political set-up, there would be a corresponding increase in the number of women in politics. This is also linked to, and partly dependent on, the strength of women in public institutions, including parliament, responsible for policy formulation and implementation.

Women and political participation at the national level, 1993–2003

Women's political roles in Ghana have grown and expanded steadily since the drafting and launching of the 1992 Constitution; but whether this is effective in terms of a meaningful participation in Ghanaian politics is a matter that needs to be analysed.

Promoting women in political life requires attention to facilitate links and dialogue between women inside and outside political structures in order to build accountability, especially during periods of legislative change (Baden 1999). It has been observed that the presence of significant numbers of women in parliament can help improve the quality of debate and policy-making. Since 1993, Ghanaian women have shown consistent enthusiasm for contributing to the democratic process in different ways and at different levels. Although the challenge is enormous, consistent progress is being made.

In 1992, Ghana had its first experiment with multi-party elections after more than a decade of military governance under the PNDC. From the presidential candidacy perspective, no women contested even at the primaries. The available statistics indicate that, in terms of real figures, the

TABLE 11.4 Numbers of women in parliament, 1960–2000

Year	1960	1965	1969	1979	1992	1996	2000
Seats	104	104	140	140	200	200	200
Women	10	19	1	5	16	18	19
% of total	9.6	18.2	0.7	3.5	8	9	9.5

Source: Compiled from different sources by the author.

261

TABLE 11.5 Number of women contestants and elected to parliament, 1996 and 2000

Year	1996	2000
Contestants	53	95
Winners	18	19
% of total	31	20

Source: Compiled from different sources by the author.

number of women in the legislature has not increased in any significant way, although the number of women candidates has witnessed a steady increase (see Table 11.4).

The percentages are dismal, although there is an insignificant increment in the figures. It is notable, though, that the number of women who show an interest in contesting parliamentary positions has risen steadily since 1992 (see Table 11.5).

Between 1996 and 2000, the number of interested women increased by almost 100 per cent, but there was only an insignificant increase in the number of women elected to parliament. Though it may be true that numbers in themselves do not necessarily indicate a corresponding increase in the quality of debate, there is equally no guarantee that men are necessarily better at representing women's issues and concerns. On moral grounds and for the sanctity and meaning of democracy to come alive, women have a duty to represent not only women but also to contribute their unique perspective to democratic development and efforts at consolidation. Besides, one major institution that has the potential to enhance the role of women in politics is the political party, to which we now turn.

Political parties and women's political roles

Mainwaring makes a challenging statement that, in spite of citizens' dissatisfaction with political parties in many countries, parties continue to be the main agents of representation and are virtually the only actors with access to elected positions in democratic politics (Mainwaring 1999: 11). As institutions, political parties have greater access to state power if they win elections. They therefore have the tendency to influence policy processes and, more significantly, to contribute to the process when their legitimacy is assured. Consolidation of democracy has important implications for all aspects of governance including the formulation, implementation and evaluation of policies needed to effect change. A party can make these changes through the translation of its manifesto into a policy document

(Allah-Mensah 2001: 122–3). It is important, then, to examine the 2000 manifestoes of some of the contesting political parties.

The National Democratic Congress (NDC) and women In the 2000 manifesto of the NDC, reference is made to the NDC government's adoption of a programme of affirmative action for women, which, inter alia, makes a commitment to women's representation in 40 per cent of executive positions and at all governmental levels. A women's desk was also established for the presidency. Statements in the manifesto made reference to the party's commitment to implementing the Beijing Plan of Action, the African Plan for Action and the National Affirmative Action Policy, including the proposal for a 40 per cent representation of women at conferences and congresses of the party and in government and public service. The party is committed to continuing to implement policies aimed at including women in national affairs, as well as promoting increased female access to education, healthcare, nutrition, employment and other socio-economic infrastructure and services and to improving the institutional capacities of key women-oriented organizations.

The manifesto further stated that the party as government would intensify public education against negative socio-cultural practices that discriminate against women and enact legislation to safeguard the dignity of women and create conditions to facilitate their advancement. Moreover, the party affirmed its belief in women's rights as natural rights and pledged to ensure that 'men and women stand side by side as equal partners in progress'.

It may not be fair to judge the party on what it intended to do if it won the 2000 elections. Nevertheless, political parties have ways of influencing policies in favour of certain constituencies, like that of women, especially within the party hierarchy. The level and nature of women's involvement in internal party organization can give an indication about the commitment of a political party to the inclusion of women. The content of the manifesto concering women's issues did not seem to be reflected in the party's leadership structure. This is not to say that the NDC party did not have any affirmative action programmes. Indeed, the election for offices within the party attracted women contestants, though mainly for positions such as treasurer, vice treasurer and secretaries, a phenomenon which is widespread in organizational formation in Ghana from educational institutions (formal) to home town clubs (informal). The manifesto commitment to women is not reflected in their positions and roles in the party structure. One regional women's organizer attributed this to the lingering colonial legacy.

It is therefore not surprising that women receive very little support from men, who sometimes ridicule them when they endeavour to state their (women's) position or views on an issue of national or party significance and interest. All of this is connected to the erroneously negative perception some men have about women in politics. Regrettably, some women also have this perception. For them, the struggle to rise to the top of the party hierarchy is so challenging that it is not possible to be successful without being promiscuous.

The New Patriotic Party (NPP) In the 2000 manifesto of the NPP party there were four paragraphs dedicated to 'opportunities for women'. It began with an acknowledgement of the contribution of women to the family and the economy, but stated that the voice of women is not sufficiently heard in government and the legislature. It welcomed the new international agenda of empowerment of women, and promised that an NPP government would move beyond merely talking about it to ensuring that it is effected in Ghana.

Furthermore, the manifesto stated that an NPP government would repeal laws interfering with the attainment of full equitable treatment for women, and would enact laws ensuring the attainment and reinforcement of equal rights. The manifesto also promised to strengthen women's groups, especially the National Council on Women and Development (NCWD), to ensure that the Ghanaian woman's voice was heard at the highest levels. Moreover, women would be encouraged to become part of the policy-making process, through sensitization on their civic responsibilities. It also promised that women's participation in the economic, political and social life of the nation would be properly acknowledged and enhanced. Under the party's industry revival programme, female-owned and female-headed enterprises would have greater access to credit on favoured terms. Such a programme would also support female entrepreneurial activities and initiatives and assist women venturing into business or self-employment. In a final statement, the manifesto mentioned that in order to ensure implementation of the policies on women's affairs, an NPP government would establish a women's ministry with the minister being a cabinet member.

Perhaps the most visible adherence to these statements is the establishment of the Ministry of Women's and Children's Affairs (MOWAC) with the NCWD as a department of the ministry. According to the national vice chairperson of the party, the creation of MOWAC was one of the major successes of the government in its bid to protect the interests and rights of women. She noted that 'the creation of MOWAC is a holistic national response to the varying challenges of empowering women and children, ensuring and protecting their rights and advocating for changing traditional and cultural practices and attitudes which denies them equality' (*Ghanaian Times*, 17 April 2004, p. 10).

Contrary to all this, women's representation in the party hierarchy sends a different signal. In an eighteen-member national executive body, only two members (11 per cent) are women: the second national vice chairperson and the national women's organizer. Of the nineteen-member support staff, five (26 per cent) are women. Within the NPP, support from male colleagues has been mixed. Some of the men offer different forms of support to encourage and enhance the performance of the women, and acknowledge the difficulties and multiple challenges women face; others, like their counterparts in the NDC, are subtly antagonistic towards women who express their views and who maintain an independent stance on issues concerning the party and the nation.

The reasons are not so different from the 'common knowledge' that states that women who are in politics have 'transcended' their boundaries and 'strayed' into uncharted territories. In other words, they have crossed their 'traditionally allocated' space as far as political issues are concerned.

Another challenge that NPP women executives, and all those women in the party aspiring to higher political office, encounter is financial constraints. This is crucial because of the economic status of many women in Ghana and the fact that poverty in Ghana is more widespread among women than among men.

Arguments advanced by some gender advocates and activists that parties should consider giving 'safe seats' to women parliamentary candidates as a step towards increasing the number of women in parliament, have not received favourable attention from the party leadership. Expatiating on these, an administrator of the NPP noted that the implementation of the party's affirmative action is easier with appointive positions than with elective ones because the latter are competitive and quite difficult to influence without sounding undemocratic – this, in spite of the fact that women are strongly encouraged to stand. Nevertheless, he was quick to add that the selection of candidates is strategic and dependent on a number of factors, including the strength of the party and its opponent's choice of candidate for a particular constituency. Put differently, the party is directed more by strategic steps than by what has been controversially described as 'gender gimmicks'.

The People's National Convention (PNC) The People's National Convention (PNC) had a rather modest six-page manifesto according to which a PNC-led government would uphold UN and all other conventions on women, and create a ministry for women to increase the awareness of the vital role females play. It would also help to enhance the role of women in the nation, that is at cabinet level and in ministries. It would institute a national day for women, as well as supporting and encouraging the formation of academic institutions and a system for integrating women in national development.

The party can be considered to have an agenda for women as portrayed in its women's wings. Beyond that, the PNC manifesto states that pregnant women and mothers on maternity leave would receive free medical care and 20 per cent salary allowances respectively. In addition, with its firm support of the Domestic Violence bill, a PNC-led government would ensure that the rights of women and children were safeguarded, using education as the channel. In addition, it would work with stakeholders to develop a women's manifesto that would be the mobilization machinery for integrating gender issues into Ghana's political processes.

At the party level, out of the thirteen positions within the party hierarchy, there is only one held by a woman. However, to get more women into positions in the party and in politics generally requires some financial strength, which is a problem encountered by most women political aspirants; other problems include the balance between married life and a political career.

The Great Consolidated People's Party (GCPP) The GCPP did not have a known manifesto in the 2000 general elections. Interestingly, according to the national women's organizer (NWO) that does not make it less gender-sensitive than other parties. Advancing the party's popular stance, or perhaps slogan, of 'domestication', the NWO interestingly stated that the slogan is attractive to women and accounts for many of them joining the ranks of the party; she claims that women find the 'domestication' notion appealing because they believe they can rely on themselves, something they have always had to do, fending for themselves and their families. For the NWO, this coincides with the party's affirmative action position and its plans to pay monthly allowances to all single mothers.

For the GCPP also, the challenges many women political aspirants encounter are mainly financial. In addition, the party notes that most husbands would not allow their wives (as part of the general traditional trappings) into what they consider to be 'dirty' politics. Furthermore, Ghana's chequered democratic history does not make politics an attractive option for women, some of whom are still sceptical about the future of democracy in Ghana.

The Convention People's Party (CPP) The CPP is credited with creating opportunities for women to participate in politics. This, though, has not grown since Ghana embraced Samuel Huntington's 'third wave' democracy. In other words, there has not been any significant improvement in the gender composition of party positions since 1992. According to the national women's deputy organizer, however, there is some light at the end of the tunnel because of unfolding events. For instance, a woman contested and won the position of the first vice chairperson and more women continue to exhibit a keen interest in parliamentary positions and other hitherto 'male reserved positions' like the vice chairmanship.

The national women's deputy organizer stated that, politically, women are often used as tools to achieve targeted aims since it appears easier to engage women. The CPP's institutional mechanism is a committee, charged with the responsibility of visiting tertiary institutions to sensitize and educate young women on the need to become involved in politics and have a positive impact on the process.

Due to their powerful positions, parties can give a voice to some interests and mute others that might have a negative impact on the political atmosphere within which they operate. Political affiliation influences a woman's chances of winning an election. It has been argued that women candidates from ruling parties are usually better positioned, equipped and placed than those in the opposition and far better placed than those who run without any party affiliation as independent candidates (Allah-Mensah 2001: 124). This may be supported by the results of the 1996 and 2000 general elections and what they imply for women's role in politics.

In 1996, there were fifty-three women contesting parliamentary positions, mainly on the National Democratic Congress (NDC) Party and the New Patriotic Party (NPP) tickets. Those who won (eighteen) were only about 32 per cent of the total number of candidates, with fourteen being NDC members and the remaining four being NPP members. There was one independent candidate (see Table 11.6 for women candidates by region and by party).

Women candidates did comparatively well in only two regions, the Central and the Northern regions with 50 per cent and 67 per cent success rate respectively. The percentages can be deceptive because the Northern region had only three contestants, two of whom were elected.

The NDC's success with women candidates was not surprising, looking at the background of the contestants and the role of the 31 DWM in enhancing women's position in the country. The NPP was at a disadvantage because it had already boycotted the 1992 parliamentary elections due to accusations of manipulation and vote-rigging after the presidential

TABLE 11.6 Women parliamentary candidates by region in the 1996 election

Region	No. of contestants	No. of winners	Party: NDC	Party: NPP	% of winners
Ashanti	9	2	1	1	22
Brong Ahafo	5	3	3	–	60
Central	8	4	3	1	50
Eastern	7	1	1	–	14
Greater Accra	8	4	3	1	38
Northern	3	2	2	–	67
Upper West	0	–	–	–	0
Upper East	3	1	1	–	33
Volta	3	0	–	–	0
Western	7	1	–	1	14
Total	53	18	14	4	32

Source: Extracted from parliamentary results, 1996.

elections. This political decision, which has been described variously by political commentators as 'strategic' and 'flawed', did not allow the NPP to develop its political platform well enough. There were, however, some positive changes with respect to women's political interests and ambitions in the 2000 general elections.

Women and the 2000 general elections

The seven registered political parties keenly contested the 2000 general elections (see Table 11.7). There were many interesting factors in the 2000 general elections, including the formation of the National Reform Party (NRP), an offshoot of the NDC, the robust role of the media and the crossing of the floor by key political functionaries from one party to another, but notably from the main opposition to the NDC party. The enthusiasm that characterized the election was also reflected in the number of women who showed an interest in participating. Table 11.7 gives a breakdown of female parliamentary candidates by party and region.

At the close of nominations on 13 September 2000, the NDC had fielded the highest number of female candidates (approximately 23.2 per cent of the total) followed by the NRP with 21 per cent, the NPP 17.9 per cent, and the CPP 16.8 per cent. The United Ghana Movement (UGM) fielded the lowest number of female candidates: 4.2 per cent. Not surprisingly, the GCPP did not field any candidates. From this we may argue that the NDC, the NRP, the NPP and the CPP were the most gender-sensitive parties. From

268

TABLE 11.7 Female parliamentary candidates by party and region

Region	NDC	NPP	NRP	PNC	UGM	GCPP	CPP	IND	Total
Ashanti	5	2	4	2	–	–	4	–	17
Brong Ahafo	1	1	1	–	–	–	1	1	5
Central	4	3	–	–	–	–	1	–	8
Eastern	3	–	2	2	–	–	–	2	9
Greater Accra	3	2	6	4	2	–	3	–	20
Northern	2	2	1	–	–	–	1	–	6
Upper East	1	3	1	1	2	–	2	–	10
Upper West	1	1	1	–	–	–	1	–	4
Volta	1	–	1	2	–	–	3	1	8
Western	1	3	3	1	–	–	–	–	8
Total	22	17	20	12	4	0	16	4	95

Source: Summary of Parliamentary Nominations, Research and Monitoring Department, Electoral Commission, adapted from Allah-Mensah (2001: 135).

fifty-three women contestants in 1996, there was an appreciable increase to ninety-five (a 56 per cent increase).

This increase could perhaps be attributed to the commitment of all contesting political parties to ensure that women were given the chance to participate effectively in the political process. This was in support of the 40 per cent of women parliamentarians recommended by the 'Cabinet of the Republic of Ghana's Statement of Policy on the Implementation of Proposals and Recommendations for Affirmative Action Towards Equality of Rights and Opportunities for Women in Ghana' (*Daily Graphic*, 16 July 2000). On this note, each of the parties made commitments that confirmed their support for women in politics. For instance, the Great Consolidated Popular Party (GCPP) highlighted the need for capacity building for women and for education to make them aware of political issues and processes. The 31 December Women's Movement's efforts in this direction did not escape the notice of the National Democratic Congress (NDC) which asserted that groups and networks affiliated to the party were being given appropriate education and sensitization for proper action and follow-ups.

For their part, the Convention People's Party (CPP) reiterated the challenges facing women aspiring to political offices and encouraged political parties to demonstrate their commitment through nominations and appointments. The New Patriotic Party affirmed its position on a democracy based on equality and proposed that where a man and a woman were equally qualified for a seat they were both contesting, the woman should be

TABLE 11.8 Women elected as MPs by region and party, 2000

Party	Region										Total
	C	W	V	E	A	N	UW	UE	GA	BA	
NDC	3	1	1	–	1	1	1	–	1	–	9
NPP	1	3	–	–	2	–	–	1	1	2	10
Total	4	4	1	–	3	1	1	1	2	2	19

Key: C=Central, W=Western, V=Volta, E=Eastern, A=Ashanti, N=Northern, UW= Upper West, UE= Upper East, GA= Greater Accra, BA= Brong Ahafo.

Source: Public Affairs Department, Electoral Commission, extracted from Allah-Mensah (2001: 136).

selected. The National Reform Party (NRP) was more radical in its approach; it proposed that a revolution or remodelling of politics to include party activities at the grassroots level where women are most active and visible in politics would afford them the opportunity to change the status quo. In addition, the NRP recommended long-term training for younger women to groom them for the rigours of political life. The People's National Convention (PNC) expressed the view that women who qualified under party requirements should be encouraged to stand for office.

These declared positions were consolidated in a resolution in which political parties affirmed their recognition of the challenges encountered by women interested in politics. The Electoral Commission also encouraged political parties to 'adopt, publicize and implement clear measures and positive actions to increase the number of women parliamentary aspirants' (Allah-Mensah 2001: 133–4).

In spite of all these commitments and the good-will shown by the parties and the Electoral Commission (EC), the actual number of women who won was far below expectations (see Table 11.8). This implies that, while political parties, either willingly or by legislative requirement, may field women parliamentary candidates, there is no guarantee for their success. Consequently, the parties need to go beyond this and do extensive sensitization of the electorate to understand the necessity to vote for qualified women. This is a challenge that needs the support of all stakeholders.

After the election it became clear that only the two relatively well organized parties had women candidates who won seats. In fact, only about 18.9 per cent of women candidates were successful. This seems to give credence to the suggestion that the choice of political party is a key determinant in a woman's political success. This is not to say that all women should join the same party; it does imply, though, that political parties have a duty to ensure that they are well organized and funded. When this happens, it is expected that women's issues will permeate all political traditions and circles.

Political party structures and women in politics

To avoid accusations of not being gender-sensitive or of not encouraging women into the party fold, almost all political parties have women's wings as part of their structural organization. Chigudu and Tchigwa (1995) note that these are created as a way of legitimizing the existence of political parties and serve as the leadership's acknowledgement of the need to secure electoral victories by capturing women's votes. In addition, some political parties perceive the creation of women's wings as part of the call for women's empowerment, therefore making them appear gender-sensitive in the eyes of the general public. However, I would argue that the creation of women's wings does not necessarily make political parties gender-sensitive or gender-friendly. Their existence should be exploited to enhance the ideals of equal representation and push the genuine concerns confronting women in general, and especially those who have political ambitions, further up the party's policy agenda. This is one means by which the existence of these sub-structures can effectively be utilized for the mutual benefit of the party and women, on one hand, and the nation and democracy, on the other.

The implication is that the relatively well-organized and consolidated political parties have a major responsibility to ensure that gender issues in general and women's concerns in particular both within and outside the party are recognized and worked at as an equally important component of the party system and structure. We argue here that political parties that do not have comprehensive gender or affirmative action policies cannot be considered to be democratic institutions. This is premised on the fact made clear by Galoy (1998: 19), and Nelson and Chowdhury (1994: 18) that women's participation in politics creates the congenial atmosphere needed to humanize gender relations in politics and that democracy without a reasonable number of women is not democracy.

For her part, Karam opines that the challenge goes beyond achieving the election of large numbers of women into the legislature to ensure that they will correspondingly increase the pressure they bring to bear on parliamentary decision-making, especially on policies that affect women and children, in order to eliminate discriminatory policies at all levels (Karam 1998: 11).

In the light of this, we now focus on the inclusion of women in the

TABLE 11.9 Membership of select committee by gender

Committee	1993–96		1997–2000		2001–04		Grand total 1993–2004	
	W	T	W	T	W	T	W	T
Lands and Forestry	1	18	2	18	1	18	4	58
Agriculture, Food and Cocoa	N/A	N/A	1	19	5	20	6	45
Local Government and Rural Development	2	20	3	19	3	20	8	67
Works and Housing	1	18	1	18	1	18	3	57
Constitutional Legal and Parliamentary	0	18	1	17	0	18	1	54
Health	3	20	3	19	3	20	6	65
Communication*	2	18	2	18	3	20	7	63
Roads and Transport*	2	18	-	-	1	18	3	39
Defence and Interior	1	18	0	17	1	18	2	55
Foreign Affairs	4	20	2	18	3	20	9	67
Youth, Sports and Culture	N/A	N/A	0	16	1	18	1	35
Education	2	20	2	20	1	19	5	64
Mines and Energy	2	18	3	18	2	18	7	61
Environment, Science, Technology	1	18	2	17	1	18	4	57
Employment, Social Welfare and State Enterprises	1	20	2	19	2	20	5	64
Trade, Industry and Tourism	2	20	3	20	1	20	6	66

Key: W= Women, T= Total, N/A= Not Applicable (committee not created).
* Between 1993 and 2000, the names of these select committees changed from Communication to Transport and Communication.

Source: Adapted from the First Meeting of the Second Session of the Third Parliament of the Fourth Republic of Ghana, February 2002. Compiled by the research department of parliament.

different parliamentary standing and select committees and in the leadership structure of the legislature for 2001–04 (see Tables 11.9 and 11.10 respectively), which constitutes the basis for decision-making and legislative formulations.

Select and standing committees in parliament

A number of factors are taken into account in the composition of select and standing committees. These include members' preferences, background, expertise and experience of members and constitutional provision. Article 103(5) of the 1992 Constitution requires that the composition of the committees shall as much as possible reflect the different shades of opinion in the house. In this regard, the composition of committees is largely based on proportional representation of political parties in the house.

It must, however, be noted that many MPs tend to avoid certain committees, especially those considered to be very technical such as Constitutional, Legal and Parliamentary Affairs, Environment, Science and Technology and Defence and Interior. The Subsidiary Legislation Standing Committee has also suffered a similar fate over the years.

The composition of the select committees as depicted in Table 11.9 gives ample support to the need for an increase in the number of women, who appear to be only a drop in the ocean. On a more serious note, men occupy the chairmanship and vice chairmanship positions in all the committees. During the 1993–96 session, the highest leadership position of a woman was held by the Hon. (Mrs) Ama Benyiwa Doe in Employment, Social Welfare and State Enterprises. Between 1997 and 2000, there were two women vice chairpersons for the Local Government and Rural Development and Lands and Forestry committees, which was an improvement on the 1993–96 period when there was only one woman in a leadership position as a ranking member.

The situation is no different with the fourteen standing committees. There is only one leadership position occupied by a woman, and not surprisingly it is on the Gender and Children Committee.

While some of the committees, such as Standing Orders and Subsidiary Legislation (2001–04) did not have any women members, the Gender and Children's Committee had 25 per cent women membership, the highest percentage of female membership in 2002. By 2003, the Gender and Children's Committee had ten women members out of a total of twenty-five. Indeed, it is the only committee where the chairperson, vice chairperson, ranking member and deputy ranking members are all women. Tables 11.9 and 11.10 indicate the almost invisible presence of women in the legislature. It should be noted that the number of women in parliament from 2001

TABLE 11.10 Membership of standing committee by gender

Committee	1993–96 W	1993–96 T	1997–2000 W	1997–2000 T	2001–04 W	2001–04 T	Grand total 1993–2004 W	Grand total 1993–2004 T
Government Assurances	1	23	3	25	2	25	6	73
Business	2	20	2	20	3	20	7	60
Appointments	1	24	1	26	2	26	4	76
Finance	4	25	2	25	2	25	8	75
Public Accounts	3	25	0	25	1	25	4	75
Selection	3	20	2	17	2	20	7	57
Subsidiary Legislation	1	25	1	25	0	23	2	73
House	3	25	3	26	4	26	10	77
Members Holding Offices of Profit	0	20	1	26	3	25	4	71
Privileges	1	25	2	31	1	31	4	87
Gender/Children	N/A	N/A	N/A	N/A	10	21	10	21
Judiciary	N/A	N/A	N/A	N/A	3	21	3	21
Special Budget	N/A	N/A	N/A	N/A	0	23	0	23
Standing Orders	3	23	1	22	3	21	7	66

Key: W=women, T=total, N/A=not applicable (committees had not been created)

Source: Adapted from First Meeting of the Second Session of the Third Parliament of the Fourth Republic of Ghana, February 2002, research department of parliament.

to 2004 was greater than the number in 1993–96 (sixteen) and 1997–2000 (eighteen). It follows logically, therefore, that women's representation in the standing and select committees was smaller in those years than in the 2001–04 session.

The above gender consideration puts an onerous duty on political parties to ensure that more women are elected as MPs in order to change the socio-politically unacceptable disparities of the gender structure of the parliamentary committees. There is no way this can change unless political parties act with consistency, commitment and with sustained advocacy to champion the cause of gender mainstreaming and equality. This leads us to the role of one such civil society organization – Ibis.

Ibis and women's political empowerment Ibis is a Danish solidarity and development organization working in Africa, Latin America and Europe. Since 1999, it has been working in Ghana as the headquarters for the Africa region. Ibis works to promote the democratization of political structures, social justice and the equitable distribution of economic resources. It operates on the premise that poor people and communities must have a greater influence over their lives.

A major focus is public participation in local government. In connection with this, the programme's development objective aims at empowering and enabling 'poor rural and urban districts, and marginalized women and men, households and organizations, to play an active and responsible role in the governance of their communities and to participate in the management of their development, thereby actively contributing to the reduction of poverty and the alleviation of its social impact' (Ibis 2002: 2). This is linked to the broad national interest with respect to public participation in local governance.

Ibis has been supporting a number of local non-governmental organizations (NGOs) and community-based organizations (CBOs) in a variety of focused areas. One that is of interest to this chapter is its support for the political empowerment of women at the local and national levels. In connection with this, Ibis reported that greater motivation and self-confidence has been identified among women who contested for the district assemblies with an upward trend in participatory levels of women as contestants and as winners (Ibis 2002: 11). In those regions where Ibis had its project (Volta, Northern, Upper East and Upper West) there was a significantly stronger trend. For instance, the number of women who contested increased by 231 per cent against 54 per cent in the rest of the country. The women who won from these regions also rose by 181 per cent as against 63 per cent nationwide (ibid.). Particularly in the Upper

West, the number of elected women increased from three to sixteen in the last elections. Ibis reckons that there is a need for affirmative action for women who were competing with powerful and more experienced men and encountered discrimination and unfair treatment. As part of its gender sensitization programmes, Ibis held workshops at the district and regional levels for policy-makers, traditional rulers and other opinion leaders on affirmative action.

Beyond the elections, Ibis continues to engage women at all political levels to ensure that they acquire or sharpen the requisite skills for optimum performance. One such was held for women in unit committees in the Ashiaman constituency in November 2003 at Dodowa in the Greater Accra Region and in the Upper West Region. In two area councils in the Sisala district of the Upper West Region, Zini and Sakai, no women attended the seminars because none was represented in the unit committees (ibid.: 23). Along these lines, Ibis has also been engaging the media to project the need for women to become involved in general policy-making. This, for some women contestants, boosted their image and created opportunities to articulate their vision for the electorate. These took place in English, Dagaari and Sisala (ibid.: 18). This, for Ibis, requires a more bottom-up approach to educate women throughout the year on the need to become involved in politics all the time and at all levels (ibid.: 16–17).

As a forward-looking strategy, Ibis also supported the Women's Commission of the National Union of Ghana Students (NUGS) for coordination of the work of women commissioners in tertiary institutions (ibid.: 24). This is crucial because advocacy is needed to ensure that young women become involved in politics and build the skills needed for leadership positions in the future.

Conclusion

The chapter has illustrated the state of women in politics from the party level through to national politics in a historical context. It is undisputed that women have made significant progress in some areas, and this must be commended. For instance, the number of women in local government has seen a consistent increase over the last two elections as compared to women in politics at the national level. Yet the blurred picture created of numbers and subsequently impact on policy as the basis for furthering the cause of women in Ghana needs to be clarified. It was observed that the majority of efforts depend on active, realistic and committed support by political parties and governments. Policy-making is the road map for a nation's development agenda and programme. For this reason, every member of the policy community has the power to determine how policy decisions affect different social groups, redirect individual and group life and enforce social, political and economic values necessary for sustained development.

If Ghana is to achieve the sustained development needed for an established democracy, then extra attention needs to be paid to the issue of women in political positions, where they can contribute effectively and meaningfully to decisions and policy formulation. Limited scenarios with respect to women's roles not only lead to stunted democracy but also affect developmental efforts and interrogate the very basis of democracy.

Note

1 Building on Achievements, Report of the Secretary-General on the Implementation of the 1995 Commonwealth Plan of Action on Gender and Development and its update (2000–05), Commonwealth Secretariat, United Kingdom, November 2003.

Sources

Allah-Mensah, B. (2001) 'Political Parties, Gender and Representation: The Case of Ghana's Election 2000', in J. R. A. Ayee (ed.), *Deepening Democracy in Ghana: Politics of the 2000 Elections*, Vol. 1 (Accra: Freedom Publications).

— (2003) 'Gender and Local Governance in Ghana: The Case of the 2002 District Level Elections', in N. Amponsah and K. Boafo-Arthur (eds), *Local Govenment in Ghana: Grassroots Participation in the 2002 Local Government Elections* (Accra: Uniflow Publishing), pp. 137–65.

— (2004) 'The Role of Women in Constitution Making in Ghana', paper presented at a Workshop on Constitutions and Constitutionalism in Commonwealth West Africa, Palm Grove Hotel, Banjul, The Gambia, 26–27 January, by Commonwealth Human Rights Initiative (CHRI) in collaboration with Ford Foundation.

Ayee, J. R. A. (2000), 'Participation', paper presented at a two-day workshop on Democracy, Poverty and Social Exclusion: Is Democracy the Missing Link organized by DPMF and the International IDEA, Addis Ababa, 15–16 May 2000.

Baden, S. (1999) 'Gender, Governance and the Feminization of Poverty', background paper no. 2, Meeting on Women and Political Participation: 21st Century Challenges, United Nations Development Programme, New Delhi 24–26 March.

Bauzon, K. E. (1992) 'Introduction: Democratization in the Third World – Myth or Reality?', in K. E. Bauzon (ed.), *Development and Democratization in the Third World, Myths, Hopes and Realities* (Washington, DC: Crane Russak).

Bluwey, G. K. (1998) 'State Organizations in the Transition to Constitutional Democracy', in K. A. Ninsin (ed.), *Ghana: Transition to Democracy* (Accra: Freedom Publications).

Brown, C. K., N. K. T. Ghartey and E. K. Ekuma (1996), *Women in Local Govern-*

ment in Ghana – a Case Study of Central Region (Accra: Friedrich Ebert Foundation).

Chigudu, H. and W. Tchigwa (1995) 'Participation of Women in Party Politics', Zimbabwe Women's Resource Centre and Network, Discussion Paper (February).

Cornwell, L. (2000) 'Gender, Development and Democracy', in H. Solomon and I. Liebenberg (eds), *Consolidation of Democracy in Africa: A View from the South* (Aldershot: Ashgate).

Fareed, Z. (1997) 'The Rise of Illiberal Democracy', *Foreign Affairs* (November).

Galoy, M. R. (1998) 'The Electoral Process and Women Contestants: Identifying the Obstacles in the Congolese Experiment', in P. McFadden (ed.), *Reflections on Gender Issues in Africa* (South Africa Regional Institute for Policy Studies).

Ibis Regional Office Ghana/West Africa (2002) *Annual Activity Report.*

ISSER (Institute of Statistical, Social and Economic Research) (1998) University of Ghana Legon and Development and Project Planning Centre (DPPC), University of Bradford, *Women in Public Life*, Research Report submitted to the Department for International Development (February).

Karam, A. (1998) *Women in Parliament: Beyond Numbers* (Stockholm: International Institute for Democracy and Electoral Assistance, IDEA).

Konde, E. (1992) 'Reconstructing the Political Roles of African Women: A Post-Revisionist Paradigm', *Working Paper in African Studies*, no. 161 (Boston, MA: African Studies Center, Boston University).

Mainwaring, S. P. (1999) *Rethinking Party Systems in the Third Wave of Democratization: The Case of Brazil* (Stanford, CA: Stanford University Press).

Manu, T. (1991) 'Women and Their Organization During the CPP Period', in K. Arhin (ed.), *The Life and Works of Kwame Nkrumah* (Accra: Sedco Publishing).

Meintjes, S. (1995) 'Gender, Citizenship and Democracy in Post-Apartheid South Africa', unpublished paper presented to the Institute for Advanced Social Research, University of the Witwatersrand, Johannesburg, 24 April.

Nelson, B. J. and N. Chowdhury (eds) (1994) *Women and Politics Worldwide* (New Haven, CT and London: Yale University Press).

Ninsin, K. A. (1996), *Ghana's Political Transition, 1990–1993: Selected Documents* (Accra: Freedom Publications).

O'Barr, J. and K. Firmin-Sellers (1995) 'African Women in Politics', in M. J. Hay and S. Stichter (eds), *African Women South of the Sahara* (New York: Longman Scientific and Technical and John Wiley).

Ofei-Aboagye, E. (2000) 'Promoting Women's Participation in National Politics', Workshop Report (Accra: Electoral Commission and Friedrich Ebert Foundation).

Pietila, H. and J. Vickers (1994) *Making Women Matter: The Role of the United Nations* (London and New Jersey: Zed Books).

Rahnema, M. (1993) 'Participation', in W. Sachs (ed.), *The Development Dictionary: A Guide to Knowledge as Power* (London: Zed Books).

Rai, S. M. (1994) 'Gender and Democratization: Or What Does Democracy Mean for Women in the Third World?', *Democratization*, Vol. 1, no. 2.

Randall, V. (1992) *Women and Politics* (London and Basingstoke: Macmillan).

Rowland, J. (1997) *Questioning Empowerment: Working with Women in Honduras* (Oxford: Oxfam).

Tamale, S. (1999) *When Hens Begin to Grow: Gender and Parliamentary Politics in Uganda* (Boulder, CO: Westview Press).

Tsikata, D. (1989) 'Women's Political Organisation, 1951–1987', in E. Hansen and K. A. Ninsin (eds), *The State Development and Politics in Ghana* (London: CODESRIA).

— (2001) 'Gender Equality and Development in Ghana: Some Issues which Should Concern a Political Party', in D. Tsikata (ed.), *Gender Training in Ghana: Politics, Issues and Tools* (Accra: Woeli Publishing).

UNDP (1997) 'Gender Balance and Good Governance: African European Dialogue on Women in Decision-making', Conference Report, Helsinki, 25–28 September.

Waylen, G. (1996) *Gender in Third World Politics* (Boulder, CO: Lynne Rienner).

General bibliography

Addae-Mensah, I. (2000) *Education in Ghana (A Tool for Social Mobility or Social Stratification)* (Accra: Ghana Academy of Arts and Sciences).

Addo, M. K. (1988) 'The Justiciability of Economic, Social and Cultural Rights', *Commonwealth Law Bulletin* (October).

Adu-Amankwah, K. (1990) *The State, Trade Unions and Democracy in Ghana, 1982–1990*, unpublished research paper (The Hague: ISS).

Afari-Gyan, K. (1995) *The Making of the Fourth Republican Constitution of Ghana* (Accra: Friedrich Ebert Foundation).

Aguire, L. P. P. (1993) 'The Consequences of Impunity in Society', in ICJ (eds), *Justice Not Impunity* (Geneva: International Commission of Jurists).

Agyeman-Duah, B. (2000) *Elections in Emerging Democracies: Ghana, Liberia and Nigeria*, Ghana Critical Perspectives, no. 4 (Accra: Ghana Centre for Democratic Development [CDD]).

— (2002) *Civil–Military Relations in Ghana's Fourth Republic*, Ghana Critical Perspectives, no. 9 (Accra: Ghana CDD).

— (2003) *Between Faith and History: A Biography of J. A. Kufuor* (Trenton, NJ and Asmara: Africa World Press).

Ahiakpor, J. C. W. (1985) 'The Success and Failure of Dependency Theory: The Experience of Ghana', *International Organisation*, Vol. 39, no. 3 (Summer): 534–52.

Ajayi, S. I. (2000) 'Globalisation and Africa', *Journal of African Economies*, Vol. 12 (Supplement) (Oxford University Press).

Ake, C. (2000) *The Feasibility of Democracy in Africa* (Dakar: CODESRIA).

Allah-Mensah, B. (2001) 'Political Parties, Gender and Representation: The Case of Ghana's Election 2000', in J. R. A. Ayee (ed.), *Deepening Democracy in Ghana: Politics of the 2000 Elections*, Vol. 1 (Accra: Freedom Publications).

— (2004) 'The Role of Women in Constitution-making in Ghana', paper presented at a Workshop on Constitutions and Constitutionalism in Commonwealth West Africa, Palm Grove Hotel, Banjul, The Gambia, 26–27 January 2004, by Commonwealth Human Rights Initiative (CHRI) in collaboration with Ford Foundation.

Alston, P. and K. Tomasevski (eds) (1984) *The Right to Food* (Dordrecht: Martinus Nijhoff).

Amoakohene, M. (2004) 'Assessment of Advertising and Sponsorship Trends in the Ghanaian Electronic Media', *Ghana Social Science Journal*, Vol. 3, no. 1 (June).

Amponsah, N. (2000) 'Ghana's Mixed Structural Adjustment Results: Explaining the Poor Private Sector Response', *Africa Today*, Vol. 47, no. 2 (Spring): 8–34.

Anebo, F. G. K. (2001) 'The Ghana 2000 Elections: Voter Choice and Electoral Decisions', *African Journal of Political Science*, Vol. 6, no. 1 (June).

Aryeetey, E. (1994) 'Private Investment Under Uncertainty in Ghana', *World Development*, Vol. 22, no. 8.

Aryeetey, E., J. Harrigan and M. Nissanke (eds) (2000) *Economic Reforms in Ghana: The Miracle and the Mirage* (Oxford: James Currey and Woeli Publishers).

Aryeetey E., A. Baah-Nuako, T. Duggleby, H. Hettige and W. F. Steel (eds) (1994) *Supply and Demand for Finance of Small Enterprises in Ghana* (Washington, DC: World Bank).

Aubynn, A. K. (1997) *Beyond the Transparent Box: The Significance of the 1996 Elections in Ghana*, Working Paper, no. 5 (Helsinki: Institute of Development Studies).

Ayee, J. R. A. (1997) *Ghana's 1996 General Elections: A Post-mortem*, Occasional Paper Series, Vol. 1, no. 1 (Harare: AAPS).

— (ed.) (1998) *The 1996 General Elections and Democratic Consolidation in Ghana* (Accra: Gold Type).

— (1999) 'Ghana', in L. Adamolekun (ed.), *Public Administration in Africa: Main Issues and Selected Country Studies* (Boulder, CO: Westview Press).

— (2001) 'Leadership in Contemporary Africa: An Exploratory Study', *United Nations University Leadership Academy Occasional Papers*, no. 3: 1–140.

— (ed.) (2001) *Deepening Democracy in Ghana: Politics of the 2000 Elections*, Vol. 2 (Accra: Freedom Publications).

— (2004) 'Leading Large States', in C. Clapham, J. Herbst and G. Mills (eds), *Africa's Big Dysfunctional States* (Cape Town: SAIIA).

Baden, S. (1999) 'Gender, Governance and the Feminization of Poverty', background paper no. 2, Meeting on Women and Political Participation: 21st Century Challenges, United Nations Development Programme, New Delhi, 24–26 March.

Badu, K. A. and J. Larvie (1997) *Elections 96 in Ghana*, Part 2 (Accra: Gold Type).

Bartolome, F. (1989) 'Nobody Trusts the Boss Completely – Now What?', *Harvard Business Review* (March–April): 135–42.

Bates, R. H. (1999) 'The Economic Bases of Democratization', in R. Joseph (ed.), *State, Conflict and Democracy in Africa* (Boulder, CO: Lynne Rienner).

Bauzon, K. E. (ed.) (1992) *Development and Democratization in the Third World: Myths, Hopes and Realities* (Washington, DC: Crane Russak).

Berlin, I. (1969) 'Two Concepts of Liberty', in I. Berlin, *Four Essays on Liberty* (Oxford: Oxford University Press).

Bimpong-Buta, S. Y. (1995) *The Law of Interpretation in Ghana* (Accra: Advanced Legal Publications).

Biro, L. P. (2002) 'Some Thoughts About a Liberal Legal Culture', mimeo (Toronto).

Bluwey, G. K. (1998) 'State Organisations in the Transition Constitutional Democracy', in K. A. Ninsin (ed.), *Ghana: Transition to Democracy* (Accra: Freedom Publications).

Boafo-Arthur, K. (1995) 'Managing Inter-party Conflict in Ghanaian Politics: Lessons from the NDC and NPP Dialogue', in M. Oquaye (ed.), *Democracy and Conflict Resolution in Ghana* (Accra: Gold Type).

— (1998) 'Structural Adjustment Programs (SAPs) in Ghana: Interrogating PNDC's Implementation', *Journal of African Policy Studies*, Vol. 4, nos 2 and 3: 1–24.

— (1999) 'Ghana: Structural Adjustment, Democratization, and the Politics of Continuity', *African Studies Review*, Vol. 42, no. 2 (September): 41–72.

— (1999) 'Ghana's Politics of International Economic Relations Under the PNDC, 1982–1992', *African Studies Monographs*, Vol. 20, no. 2 (Kyoto University, Japan).

— (2003) 'Emerging Democracies and Their Impact on Human Rights', in B. Sam (ed.), *Contemporary Human Rights Issues in Commonwealth West Africa* (Accra: Commonwealth Human Rights Initiative and Commonwealth Foundation of UK).

— (2004) 'Election Monitoring in Ghana: The Case for Domestic Monitors and Observers', in S. E. Quainoo (ed.), *Africa Through Ghanaian Lenses* (Binghamton, NY: Vestal International Press).

Boateng, K. (2001) 'Impact of Structural Adjustment on Employment and Incomes in Ghana', in A. Yaw Baah (ed.), *The Social Dimension of Structural Adjustment in Ghana* (Accra: FES).

Borner, S., B. Aymo and B. Weder (1995) 'Policy Reform and Institutional Uncertainty: The Case of Nicaragua', *KYKLOS*, Vol. 48, no. 1.

Bratton, M. and N. van de Walle (1997) *Democratic Experiments in Africa: Regime Transitions in Comparative Perspective* (Cambridge: Cambridge University Press).

Bratton, M., R. Mattes and E. Gyimah-Boadi (eds) (2005) *Public Opinion, Democracy, and Market Reform in Africa* (Cambridge: Cambridge University Press).

Brown, C. K., N. K. T. Ghartey and E. K. Ekuma (1996) *Women in Local Government in Ghana – A Case Study of Central Region* (Accra: Friedrich Ebert Foundation).

Burns, J. (1978) *Leadership* (New York: Harper and Row).

Burton, M. and J. Higley (1987) 'Elite Settlements', *American Sociological Review* (June).

— (1989) 'The Elite Variable in Democratic Transitions and Breakdowns', *American Sociological Review* (February).

Callinicos, A. (2003) *An Anti-Capitalist Manifesto* (Cambridge: Polity Press).

Campos, J. E. and H. L. Root (1996) *The Key to the Asian Miracle: Making Shared Growth Credible* (Washington, DC: Brookings Institution).

CDD (Center for Democracy and Development) (2002) *Democracy Watch,* Quarterly Newsletter of Ghana CDD (September).

— (2003) *Police–Community Relations in an Emerging Democracy. Survey Report*, Research Paper no. 12, Accra (August).

Centre for Policy Analyses (1996) *Macroeconomic Review and Outlook* (Accra: CEPA).

Chazan, N. (1983) *An Anatomy of Ghanaian Politics: Managing Political Recession, 1969–1982* (Boulder, CO: Westview Press).

— (1987) 'Anomalies and Continuity: Perspectives on Ghanaian Elections Since Independence', in F. M. Hayward (ed.), *Elections in Independent Africa* (Boulder, CO: Westview Press).

Chigudu, H. and W. Tchigwa (1995) 'Participation of Women in Party Politics', Zimbabwe Women's Resource Centre and Network, Discussion Paper (February).

Clift, J. (2003) 'Beyond the Washington Consensus', *Finance and Development* (September).

Cobbe, J. (1991) 'The Political Economy of Educational Reform in Ghana', in D. Rothchild (ed.) *Ghana: The Political Economy of Recovery* (Boulder, CO and London: Lynne Rienner).

Commission for Africa (2005) *Our Common Interest*, Report.

Conger, J. A. (1989) 'Leadership: The Art of Empowering Others', *Academy of Management Executive*, Vol. 3, no. 1.

Conteh-Morgan, E. (1997) *Democratization in Africa: The Theory and Dynamics of Political Transitions* (Westport, CT and London: Praeger).

Cornwell, L. (2000) 'Gender, Development and Democracy' in H. Solomon and I. Liebenberg (eds), *Consolidation of Democracy in Africa: A View from the South* (Aldershot: Ashgate).

Courier, The (1994) 'Country Report, Ghana: Striving to Keep Up the Momentum', *Journal of the African-Caribbean-Pacific and European Union*, Vol. 44 (March–April).

Desewu, E. E. (2004) 'Private Sector Proposals for Trouble-free Land for Investments', *Ghana Business Week*, no. 069, 21–27 June.

De Villiers, B. (1996) 'The Socio-economic Consequences of Directive Principles of State Policy: Limitations on Fundamental Rights', *South African Journal of Human Rights*, Vol. 8: 188–98.

Diamond, L. and M. Plattner (1999) *Democratization in Africa* (Baltimore, MD: Johns Hopkins University Press).

Diamond, L., J. Linz and S. Lipset (1995) *Politics in Developing Countries: Comparing Experiences with Democracy* (Boulder, CO: Lynne Rienner).

Dicey, A.V. (1959) *The Law of the Constitution*, 10th edn (London: Macmillan).

Dogbevi, E. (2002) 'Land Management in Ghana: Some Knotty Issues', *FOELINE*, Vol. 15 (January–March), Friends of the Earth magazine (Accra).

Dunn, J. (1975) 'Politics in Asunafo', in D. Austin and R. Luckham (eds), *Politicians and Soldiers in Ghana 1969–1972* (London: Frank Cass).

— (ed.) (1992) *Democracy: the Unfinished Journey, 508 BC to 1993* (Oxford: Oxford University Press).

Ephson, B. (2003) *Countdown to 2004 Elections* (Accra: Allied News).

Evans, P. (1995) *Embedded Autonomy: States and Industrial Transformation* (Princeton, NJ: Princeton University Press).

Fareed, Z. (1997) 'The Rise of Illiberal Democracy', *Foreign Affairs* (November).

Fosu, A. K. (1992) 'Political Instability and Economic Growth: Evidence from Sub-Saharan Africa', *Economic Development and Cultural Change*, Vol. 40, no. 4: 829–41.

Frempong, A. K. D. (2001) 'Ghana's Election 2000: The Ethnic Undercurrents', in J. R. A. Ayee (ed.), *Deepening Democracy in Ghana: Politics of the 2000 Elections*, Vol. 1 (Accra: Freedom Publications).

Friedman, M. (1982) *Capitalism and Freedom* (Chicago and London: UCP).

Fukuyama, F. (1992) *The End of History and the Last Man* (New York: Avon Books).

Galoy, M. R. (1998) 'The Electoral Process and Women Contestants: Identifying the Obstacles in the Congolese Experiences', in P. McFadden (ed.), *Reflections on Gender Issues in Africa* (South Africa Regional Institute for Policy Studies).

Gould, J. and S. Szomolanyi (1997) 'Elite Fragmentation in Industry and the Prospect for Democracy', *Intermarium*, Vol. 1, no. 2.

Greven, M. T. and L. W. Pauly (eds) (2000) *Democracy Beyond the State?* (Toronto: University of Toronto Press).

Grindle, M. (ed.) *Politics and Policy Implementation in the Third World* (Princeton, NJ: Princeton University Press).

Gyandoh, S. O. (1969) 'The Constitutional Protection of Human Rights in Developing Nations', Bangkok World Conference on World Peace Through Law.

Gyimah-Boadi, E. (1990) 'Economic Recovery and Politics in PNDC's Ghana', *Journal of Commonwealth and Comparative Politics*, Vol. 28, no. 3: 323–40.

— (1991) 'Tensions in Ghana's Transition to Constitutional Rule', in K. A. Ninsin and F. K. Drah (eds), *Ghana's Transition to Constitutional Rule* (Accra: Ghana Universities Press).

— (1998) 'Representative Institutions', in *Democratic Consolidation in Africa: Progress and Pitfalls*, conference report (Johannesburg: Center for Policy Studies).

— (1999) 'Ghana: The Challenges of Consolidating Democracy', in R. Joseph (ed.), *State, Conflict, and Democracy in Africa* (Boulder, CO and London: Lynne Rienner).

— (2000) 'Six Years of Constitutional Rule in Ghana: An Assessment and Prospects of the Executive and the Legislature', in Friedrich Ebert Foundation (ed.), *Six Years of Constitutional Rule in Ghana: 1993–1999* (Accra: Gold Type).

— (2001) 'A Peaceful Turnover in Ghana', *Journal of Democracy*, Vol. 12, no. 2 (April).

Hagan, G. P. (1995) 'Democracy as a Conflictual System – the Needed Cultural Premise', in M. Oquaye (ed.), *Democracy and Conflict Resolution in Ghana* (Accra: Gold Type).

Handy, C. (1989) *The Age of Unreason* (London: Hutchinson).

Herbst, J. (1993) *The Politics of Reform in Ghana, 1982–1991* (Berkeley: University of California Press).

Herman, C. F. (1990) 'Changing Course: When Governments Choose to Re-direct Foreign Policy', *International Studies Quarterly*, Vol. 34, no. 1 (March).

Higley, J. and M. Burton (1988) 'Elite Settlement and Taming Politics', *Government and Opposition* (MTF).

Hirschman, A. O. (1958) *The Strategy of Economic Development* (New Haven, CT: Yale University Press).

Hodson, D. F. (1983) *The General Agricultural Workers Union of the TUC (Ghana)* (Geneva: ILO).

Hoffman, S. (1989) 'What Should We Do in the World?', *Atlantic Monthly* (October).

— (1995) 'The Crisis of Liberal Internationalism', *Foreign Policy* (Spring), <www.ub.edu.ar/facultades/feg/crisis.htm>.

Hermann, C. F. (1990) 'Changing Course: When Governments Choose to Redirect Foreign Policy', *International Studies Quarterly*, Vol. 34, no. 1 (March): 3–21.

Holecek, B, G. (1993) 'Paying the Piper: Conversations with Jerry Rawlings', *Transition*, Vol. 62.

Hope, K. R. Sr and B. C. Chikulo (eds) (2000) *Corruption and Development in Africa: Lessons from Country Studies* (New York: St Martin's Press).

Hutchful, E. (1995) 'Why Regimes Adjust: The World Bank Ponders Its "Star Pupil"', *Canadian Journal of African Studies*, Vol. 29, no. 2: 303–17.

— (2002) *Ghana's Adjustment Experience: The Paradox of Reform* (Geneva: UNRISD).

Ikenberry, G. J. and M. W. Doyle (eds) (1997) *New Thinking in International Relations Theory* (Boulder, CO: Westview Press).

Iliasu, A. M. (1997) *The Behaviour of States: Continuity and Change in Ghana's Foreign Policy, 1982–1996*, unpublished MA dissertation, Legon Centre for International Affairs.

ISSER (Institute of Social Statistical and Economic Research) (1994) *The State of the Ghanaian Economy in 1993* (Legon: ISSER, University of Ghana).

— (1998) and Development and Project Planning Centre (DPPC), University of Bradford, *Women in Public Life*, Research Report submitted to the Department for International Development (February).

— (2004) *The State of the Ghanaian Economy in 2003* (Legon: ISSER, University of Ghana).

Jackson, A. K. (ed.) (1999) *When Gun Rules. A Soldier's Testimony* (Accra: Woeli Publishers).

Jefferies, R. (1980) 'The Ghanaian Elections of 1979', *African Affairs*, Vol. 79, no. 316 (July).

Jennings, I. (1953) *Some Characteristics of the Indian Constitution* (Madras and New York: Oxford University Press).

Johnston, B. F. and J. W. Mellor (1961) 'The Role of Agriculture in Economic Development', *American Economic Review*, Vol. 51: 566–93.

Jonah, K. (1998) 'Political Parties and the Transition to Multi-party Politics in Ghana', in K. A. Ninsin (ed.), *Ghana: Transition to Democracy* (Accra: Freedom Publications).

Kane-Berman, J. (2004) 'Empowerment: The Need for a Liberal Strategy', <www.fnf.org.za/New/empower.htm>.

Karam, A. (1998) *Women in Parliament: Beyond Numbers* (Stockholm: IDEA).

Karikari, K. (1998) 'The Press and the Transition to Multi-party Democracy in Ghana', in K. A. Ninsin (ed.), *Ghana: Transition to Democracy* (Accra: CODESRIA).

Keefer, P. and S. Knack (1997) 'Why Don't Poor Countries Catch Up? A Cross-national Test of an Institutional Explanation', *Economic Inquiry*, Vol. 25 (July): 590–602.

Kegley, C. W. Jr and E. R. Wittkopf (1981) *World Politics: Trend and Transformation* (New York: St Martin's Press).

Kelsen, H. (1979) *Pure Theory of Law* (Berkeley: University of California Press).

Kilby, P. (1969) *Industrialization in an Open Economy, Nigeria 1945–1966* (Oxford: Oxford University Press).

Killick, T. (2000) 'Fragile Still: The Structure of Ghana's Economy (1960–94)', in E. Aryeetey, J. Harrigan and M. Nissante (eds), *Economic Reforms in Ghana: The Miracle and the Mirage* (Oxford: James Currey and Woeli Publishers).

Konde, E. (1992) 'Reconstructing the Political Roles of African Women: A Post-revisionist Paradigm', *Working Paper in African Studies*, no. 161 (Boston, MA: African Studies Center).

Kotey, E. N. A. (1995) 'The Supreme Court and Conflict Resolution in Ghana's Fourth Republic', in M. Oquaye (ed.), *Democracy and Conflict Resolution in Ghana* (Accra: Gold Type).

Kotter, J. P. (1988) *The Leadership Factor* (New York: Free Press).

Kraus, J. (1991) 'The Political Economy of Stabilization and Structural Adjustment in Ghana', in D. Rothchild (ed.), *Ghana: The Political Economy of Recovery* (Boulder, CO: Lynne Rienner).

Kumado, K. (1995) 'Forgive Us Our Trespasses: An Examination of the Indemnity Clause in the 1992 Constitution of Ghana', *University of Ghana Law Journal*, Vol. 19.

Kuznets, S. (1966) *Modern Economic Growth* (New Haven, CT: Yale University Press).

Leach, S. and D. Wilson (2002) 'Rethinking Local Political Leadership', *Public Administration*, Vol. 80, no. 4: 665–89.

Leith, J. C. (1996) *Ghana: The Structural Adjustment Process* (San Francisco, CA: International Center for Economic Growth).

Lindley, R. (1986) *Autonomy* (London: Macmillan).

Lowry, C. (2000) 'A Defense of Individual Autonomy in a Multination Liberal State', *Prolegomena* (Winter), <www.philosophy.ubc.ca/prolegom/papers/Lowry.htm>.

Macpherson, C. B. (1977) *The Life and Times of Liberal Democracy* (Oxford: Oxford University Press).

Mainwaring, S. P. (1999) *Rethinking Party Systems in the Third Wave of Democratization: The Case of Brazil* (Stanford, CA: Stanford University Press).

Manu, T. (1991) 'Women and Their Organization During the CPP Period', in K. Arhin (ed.), *The Life and Works of Kwame Nkrumah* (Accra: Sedco Publishing).

Meier, G. M. (1976) *Leading Issues in Economic Development* (New York: Oxford University Press).

Meintjes, S. (1995) 'Gender, Citizenship and Democracy in Post-apartheid South Africa', unpublished paper presented to the Institute for Advanced Social Research, University of the Witwatersrand, Johannesburg, 24 April.

Midlarsky, M. I. (ed.) (1997) *Inequality, Democracy, and Economic Development* (Cambridge: Cambridge University Press).

Muczyk, J. P. and B. C. Reinmann (1987) 'The Case for Directive Leadership', *Academy of Management Executive*, Vol. 1, no. 4: 301–11.

Nelson, B. J. and N. Chowdhury (eds) (1994) *Women and Politics Worldwide* (New Haven, CT and London: Yale University Press).

Nelson, J. M. and S. J. Eglinton (1992) *Encouraging Democracy: What Role for Conditioned Aid?* Policy Essay, no. 4 (Washington, DC: Overseas Development Council).

Ninsin, K. A. (1991) 'The Impact of the PNDC's Economic Reform Policies on Ghanaian Society and Politics, 1983–1988', *Legon Journal of Humanities*, Vol. 5.

— (1991) *The Informal Sector in Ghana's Political Economy* (Accra: Freedom Publications).

— (1995) 'Conflict as Pursuit of Liberty', in M. Oquaye (ed.), *Democracy and Conflict Resolution in Ghana* (Accra: Gold Type).

— (1996) *Ghana's Political Transition, 1990–1993: Selected Documents* (Accra: Freedom Publications).

— (ed.) (1998) *Ghana: Transition to Democracy* (Dakar and Accra: CODESRIA and Freedom Publications).

— (2003) 'Formalization and Ghanaian Politics', in H. Lauer (ed.), *Ghana: Changing Values/ Changing Technologies*, Ghana Philosophical Studies II, Cultural Heritage and Contemporary Change Series II, Vol. 5.

Ninsin, K. A. and F. K. Drah (eds) (1993) *Political Parties and Democracy in Ghana's Fourth Republic* (Accra: Woeli Publishers).

Nugent, P. (1995) *Big Men, Small Boys and Politics in Ghana* (Accra: Asempa Publishers).

Nyanteng, V. and A. W. Seini (2000) 'Agricultural Policy and the Impact on Growth and Productivity: 1970–95', in E. Aryeetey, J. Harrigan and M. Nissanke (eds), *Economic Reforms in Ghana: The Miracle and the Mirage* (Oxford: James Currey and Woeli Publishers).

OAU (Organization of African Unity) (2001) *The New Partnership for Africa's Development (NEPAD)* (October).

O'Barr, J. and K. Firmin-Sellers (1995) 'African Women in Politics', in M. J. Hay and S. Stichter (eds), *African Women South of the Sahara* (New York: Longman Scientific and Technical and John Wiley).

O'Connell, S. and B. Ndulu (2000) 'Africa's Growth Experience: A Focus on the Sources of Growth', mimeo (Nairobi: AERC).

O'Donnell, G. and P. Schmitter (1986) *Transitions from Authoritarian Rule: Tentative Conclusions About Uncertain Democracies* (Baltimore, MD: Johns Hopkins University Press).

Ofei-Aboagye, E. (2000) 'Promoting Women's Participation in National Politics', Workshop Report, Electoral Commission and Friedrich Ebert Foundation, 2000.

Olukoshi, A. (1992) 'The World Bank, Structural Adjustment and Governance in Africa: Some Reflections', mimeo (Dakar: CODESRIA).

Oquaye, M. (1980) *Politics in Ghana, 1972–1979* (Accra: Tornado Publications).

— (2001) *Government and Politics in Contemporary Ghana (1992–1990) – A Study*, Governance Series, Vol. 1, no. 1 (Accra: African Governance Institute).

Osei, P. D. (2000) 'Political Liberalisation and the Implementation of Value-Added Tax in Ghana', *Journal of Modern African Studies*, Vol. 32, no. 2: 255–78.

Pellow, D. and N. Chazan (1986) *Ghana: Coping with Uncertainty* (Boulder, CO: Westview Press).

Pietila, H. and J. Vickers (1994) *Making Women Matter: The Role of the United Nations* (London and New Jersey: Zed Books).

Prempeh, K. H. (2002) 'Rule of Law, Constitutionalism and Human Rights', Ghana CDD Briefing Paper, Vol. 4, no. 4.

Pressman, J. L. and A. Wildavsky (1973) *Implementation: How Great Expectations in Washington are Dashed in Oakland* (Berkeley: University of California Press).

Przeworski, A. (1991) *Democracy and the Market* (Cambridge: Cambridge University Press).

— (1995) *Sustainable Democracy* (Cambridge: Cambridge University Press).

Przeworski, A., M. Alvarez, J. A. Chebub and F. Limongi (1996) 'What Makes Democracies Endure?' *Journal of Democracy*, Vol. 7, no. 1.

Putnam, R. D. (1993) *Making Democracy Work: Civic Traditions in Modern Italy* (Princeton, NJ: Princeton University Press).

Quantson, K. B. (2003) *Ghana: National Security ... The Dilemma* (Accra: NAPASVIL Ventures).

Quashigah, E. K. and O. C. Obiora (eds) (1999) *Legitimate Governance in Africa: International and Domestic Legal Perspectives* (The Hague, London and Boston: Kluwer Law International).

Quinn, J. B., H. Mintzberg and R. M. James (1989) *The Strategy Process* (Englewood Cliffs, NJ: Prentice-Hall).

Rahnema, M. (1993) 'Participation', in W. Sachs (ed.), *The Development Dictionary: A Guide to Knowledge as Power* (London: Zed Books).

Rai, S. M. (1994) 'Gender and Democratization: Or What Does Democracy Mean for Women in the Third World?', *Democratization*, Vol. 1, no. 2.

Randall, V. (1982) *Women and Politics* (London and Basingstoke: Macmillan).

Republic of Ghana (1990) *Labour Redeployment Programme* (Accra: Secretariat of Redeployment Management Committee).

— (1992) *The Constitution of the Republic of Ghana, 1992* (Accra: Ghana Publishing Corporation).

— (1995) *Ghana – Vision 2020 (The First Step: 1996–2000)*, Presidential Report to Parliament on Coordinated Programme of Economic and Social Development Policies, 6 January (Accra: National Development Planning Commission).

— (1997) *Ghana – Vision 2020: The First Medium-Term Development Plan (1997–2000)* (Accra: National Development Planning Commission).

— (1999) *A Draft Comprehensive Development Framework Towards Ghana Vision 2020*, Tenth Consultative Group Meeting, 23–24 November, Accra.

— (2000) *Ghana Living Standards Survey (Report of the Fourth Round (GLSS 4)* (Accra: Ghana Statistical Service).

— (2002) *Ghana Poverty Reduction Strategy, 2002—2004: An Agenda for Growth and Prosperity: Analysis and Policy Statement* (Accra: National Development Planning Commission).

— (2002) *The Coordinated Programme for Economic and Social Development of Ghana* (Accra: National Development Planning Commission).

— (2003) *Ghana Poverty Reduction Strategy (2003-2005)* (Accra: Ghana Statistical Service).

Robinson, M. (1996) 'Economic Reform and the Transition to Democracy', in R. Luckham and G. White (eds), *Democratization in the South: The Jagged Wave* (Manchester and New York: Manchester University Press).

Roht-Arriaza, N. and L. Gibson (1998) 'The Developing Jurisprudence on Amnesty', *Human Rights Quarterly*, Vol. 20: 843–85.

Rothchild, D. (ed.) (1991) *Ghana: The Political Economy of Recovery* (Boulder, CO and London: Lynne Rienner).

Rowland, J. (1997) *Questioning Empowerment: Working with Women in Honduras* (Oxford: Oxfam).

Saffu, Y. (2004) 'Deepening Our Democracy: The Functioning of Our Democratic Institutions', *Governance Newsletter* (Accra: Institute of Economic Affairs).

Sandbrook, R. (1992) 'Patrons, Clients and Factions: New Dimensions of Conflict Analysis in Africa', *Canadian Journal of African Studies*, Vol. V, no. 1.

— (2000) *Closing the Circle: Democratization and Development in Africa* (London: Zed Books).

Sandbrook, R. and J. Oelbaum (1997) 'Reforming Dysfunctional Institutions Through Democratization? Reflections on Ghana', *Journal of Modern African Studies*, Vol. 35, no. 4.

Sarpong, K. (1996) 'Institutional Framework and Policies for Private-sector-led Development', in *Agenda '96: Preparing Ghana for the 21st Century; Some Economic and Social Issues* (Accra: Friedrich-Naumann-Stiftung).

Sawyer, A. (1990) *The Political Dimension of Structural Adjustment Programmes in Sub-Saharan Africa* (Accra: Ghana Universities Press).

Schumpeter, J. A. (1950) *Capitalism, Socialism and Democracy*, 3rd edn (New York: Harper and Brothers).

Shillington, K. (1992) *Ghana and the Rawlings Factor* (London: Macmillan).

Smith, D. A. and J. Temin (2001) 'The Media and Ghana's 2000 Elections', in J. R. A. Ayee (ed.), *Deepening Democracy in Ghana: Politics of the 2000 Elections*, Vol. 1 (Accra: Freedom Publications).

Solow, R. (1956) 'A Contribution to the Theory of Economic Growth', *Quarterly Journal of Economics*, Vol. 70, no. 1: 65–94.

Songsore, J., P. W. K. Yankson and G. K. Tsikata (1994) *Mining and the Environment: Towards a Win-Win Strategy*, Report for the Ministry of Environment, Science and Technology and the World Bank (Accra).

Spiegel, S. L. (1995) *World Politics in a New Era* (New York: Harcourt Brace).

Stein, H. (1994) 'Theories of Institutions and Economic Reform in Africa', *World Development*, Vol. 22, no. 12.

Steiner, H. J. and P. Alston (eds) *International Human Rights in Context* (Oxford: Clarendon Press).

Stiglitz, J. E. (1998) *Post Washington Consensus, Initiative for Policy Dialogue*, mimeo, Columbia University.

Stoker, G. (1998) 'Governance as Theory: Five Propositions', *International Social Science Journal*, no. 155 (March).

Szerezewski, R. (1965) *Structural Changes in the Economy of Ghana: 1891–1911* (London: Weidenfeld and Nicolson).

Tamale, S. (1999) *When Hens Begin to Grow: Gender and Parliamentary Politics in Uganda* (Boulder, CO: Westview Press).

Tangri, R. (1992) 'The Politics of Government–Business Relations in Ghana', *Journal of Modern African Studies*, Vol. 30: 97–111.

Toffler, A. (1970) *Future Shock* (New York: Bantam Books).

Tsikata, D. (1989) 'Women's Political Organisation, 1951–1987', in E. Hansen and K. A. Ninsin (eds), *The State, Development and Politics in Ghana* (London: CODESRIA).

— (ed.) (2001) *Gender Training in Ghana: Politics, Issues and Tools* (Accra: Woeli Publishers).

Tsikata, G. K. (1995) *The Gold Sub-Sector and Economic Growth and Development in Ghana*, Report for the Minerals Commission and the World Bank.

— (1996) *Economic Growth in Ghana: Some Stylized Facts*, Legon Economic Series (Legon: Department of Economics, University of Ghana).

Tsikata, G. K., Y. Asante and E. M. Gyasi (2000) *Determinants of Foreign Direct Investment in Ghana* (London: Overseas Development Institute).

Tuchman, B. W. (1980) 'Is This the Summer of 1914?', *Washington Post*, 11 May.

UNDP (1997) 'Gender Balance and Good Governance: African–European Dialogue on Women in Decision-making', Conference Report, Helsinki, 25–28 September.

van de Walle, N. (1996) 'Crisis and Opportunity in Africa', *Journal of Democracy*, Vol. 6, no. 2.

Van Hoof, G. J. H. (1984) 'The Legal Nature of Economic, Social and Cultural Rights: A Rebuttal of Some Traditional Views', in P. Alston and K. Tomasevski (eds), *The Right to Food* (Dordrecht: Martinus Nijhoff).

Waltz, K. N. (1979) *Theory of International Politics* (Reading, MA: Addison-Wesley).

Waylen, G. (1996) *Gender in Third World Politics* (Boulder, CO: Lynne Rienner).

Westwood, J. (n.d.) *The Amazing Dictator and His Men. A Story of Intrigue, Murder, Presidential Zealousness, Mayhem in Ghana* (Accra: NETRESCO).

Williamson, J. (ed.) (1990) *Latin American Adjustment: How Much Has Happened?* (Washington, DC: Institute for International Economics).

— (2000) 'What Should the World Bank Think About the Washington Consensus?', *World Bank Research Observer*, Vol. 15, no. 2 (August).

World Bank (1981) *Accelerated Development in Sub-Saharan Africa* (Washington, DC: World Bank).

— (1988) *Adjustment Lending: An Evaluation of Ten Years of Experience*, Policy and Research Series (Washington, DC: World Bank).

— (1989) *Sub-Saharan Africa: From Crisis to Sustainable Growth* (Washington, DC: World Bank).

— (1992) *Ghana 2000 and Beyond: Setting the Stage for Accelerated Growth and Poverty Reduction* (Washington, DC: World Bank, West Africa Department).

— (1999) *Country Assistance Strategy for Ghana 2000–2003* (Accra: World Bank, Ghana Office).

— (2000) *The Quality of Growth* (Oxford: Oxford University Press).

— (2001) *World Development Report: Attacking Poverty* (New York: Oxford University Press).

— (2001) *Ghana, International Competitiveness: Opportunities and Challenges Facing Non-Traditional Exports*, Country Report, no. 22421 – Africa Region (Washington, DC: World Bank).

— (2003) *Africa Development Indicators* (Washington, DC: World Bank).

Yeebo, Z. (1991) *Ghana: The Struggle for Popular Power* (London: New Beacon Books).

Bibliography

List of contributors

Beatrix Allah-Mensah Lecturer, Department of Political Science, University of Ghana, Legon.

Nicholas Amponsah Lecturer, Department of Political Science, University of Ghana, Legon.

Kumi Ansah-Koi Senior Lecturer, Department of Political Science, University of Ghana, Legon.

Joseph R. A. Ayee Professor, Department of Political Science; Dean of the Faculty of Social Studies, University of Ghana, Legon.

Kwame Boafo-Arthur Professor and Barrister-at-Law, Department of Political Science, University of Ghana, Legon.

Abeeku Essuman-Johnson Senior Lecturer, Department of Political Science, University of Ghana, Legon.

Alexander K. D. Frempong Lecturer, Department of Political Science, University of Ghana, Legon.

Kwame A. Ninsin Professor, Department of Political Science, University of Ghana, Legon.

Kofi Quashigah Associate Professor of Law, Faculty of Law, University of Ghana, Legon.

G. Kwaku Tsikata Senior Lecturer, Department of Economics, University of Ghana, Legon.

Index

Index

Index

Breinigsville, PA USA
19 May 2010
238325BV00001B/26/P